Home divisions

MANCHESTER
UNIVERSITY PRESS

Politics, culture and society in early modern Britain

General Editors

PROFESSOR ANN HUGHES
DR ANTHONY MILTON
PROFESSOR PETER LAKE

This important new series publishes monographs that take a fresh and challenging look at the interactions between politics, culture and society in Britain between 1500 and the mid-eighteenth century. It seeks to counteract the fragmentation of current historiography through encouraging a variety of approaches which attempt to redefine the political, social and cultural worlds, and to explore their interconnection in a flexible and creative fashion.

All the volumes in the series will question and transcend traditional interdisciplinary boundaries, such as those between political history and literary studies, social history and divinity, urban history and anthropology. They will thus contribute to a broader understanding of crucial developments in early modern Britain.

Already published in the series

Forthcoming

Home divisions

Aristocracy, the state
and
provincial conflict

THOMAS COGSWELL

Manchester
University Press

Published by Manchester University Press
Oxford Road, Manchester M13 9NR, UK

British Library Cataloguing-in-Publication Data
A catalogue record is available from the British Library

ISBN 0 7190 5360 9 *hardback*

First published 1998

05 04 03 02 01 00 99 98   10 9 8 7 6 5 4 3 2 1

Typeset in Scala with Pastonchi display
by Koinonia Ltd, Manchester

Printed in Great Britain
by Redwood Books, Trowbridge

Contents

Contents

Contents

List of figures, tables and plates

FIGURES

TABLES

PLATES

TO TERESA GAHN COGSWELL
AND
IN MEMORY OF DAVID GAGE COGSWELL

Acknowledgements

In July 1990, while perusing the lists of deeds and rental agreements contained in the catalogue of the Hastings manorial documents at the Huntington Library, I spotted amid HAM 53 an item rather vaguely described as a book of warrants, 1614–27. Although I was then largely interested in charting the impact of the Thirty Years War on the provinces and in Parliament, I had nothing better to do that afternoon, having already worked through the more likely areas in the Earl of Huntingdon's personal papers. A quick inspection revealed that this document was in fact Huntingdon's lieutenancy book for Leicestershire and Rutland, and my amazement increased as I appreciated that the earl's secretary had, with remarkable thoroughness, chronicled not simply the county's militia business, but many of its internal feuds. Celebrated among contemporaries as a 'cockpit', Leicestershire has long interested scholars, but even the most diligent of them has been able to find only tantalising echoes of these local furores among the surviving records in the county record office. Careful reading of HAM 53, however, soon revealed that the answer to many of the puzzles about this county was to be found neither in Leicester nor in London but rather in a suburb of Los Angeles. Fascination with the new insight into the old conundrums about Leicestershire led me back to the archives across the Atlantic and eventually to write this study.

With rising costs increasingly making detailed archival research on two continents an expensive luxury, the project would have foundered without considerable financial assistance, which I would now like to acknowledge. Generous help from the National Endowment for the Humanities allowed me to begin composing the book at the Folger Shakespeare Library and to finish it, rather fittingly, at the Huntington Library. In addition, the Research Committee of the University of Kentucky and Dean Richard Edwards of the College of Arts and Sciences have regularly provided timely financial support. Above all, I am indebted to the Huntington Library which provided me fellowships in 1990, 1993 and 1995–96. There I am much obliged to Roy Ritchie, the Research Director, for his continued support and good humour, and to Mary Robertson, the Curator of Manuscripts, who not only guided me through the darker corners of the Hastings Collection but even managed to smile on the notion of establishing an East Midlands Research Center at the foot of Mt Wilson.

Acknowledgements

In friends, as in patrons, I have been fortunate indeed. Aspects of the book have figured prominently and regularly in my conversations with Christopher Brooks, Martin Butler, Barbara Donegan, Tim Harris, Cynthia Herrup, Mark Kishlansky, Karen Kuppermann, and Steve Pincus; their interest has done much to speed its completion. Even more helpful were Cathy Patterson, Victor Stater, Mark Summers, Christopher Thompson, and David Underdown, as well as Ann Hughes, Peter Lake, and Anthony Milton, who all read various drafts; the end result owes much to their careful reading and thoughtful queries. Allison Gill greatly advanced my work by sharing her exhaustive work on Ship Money. For invaluable technical assistance I am indebted to Shirley and Rich Philobosian in Pasadena and to Diana and Nigel Woods in Birmingham. For their unfailing efficiency and kindness, I would like to record my thanks to the staff of the Public Record Office and the Bodleian Library; and in particular, to the Librarian of Queen's College, Oxford, who allowed me to consult some documents at short notice, and to the Archivist and staff of the Leicestershire Record Office, who always managed to find room for me, even in their old cramped quarters in New Walk. The obligation which I owe to Richard Cust is particularly great. In an effort to broaden my perspective beyond Whitehall and Westminster, he has patiently guided me, sometimes literally, to local record offices and through their collections. Quite simply, this study would have been impossible had he not placed his unrivalled knowledge of the early seventeenth-century provinces at my disposal. Finally, Carole Davis Cogswell cheerfully put up with an unexpected detour into provincial history, and, more important, she applied her customarily felicitous touch to my often unruly prose.

These obligations, while profound, nevertheless pale in the end before the debt which I owe to my parents. The dedication of this book therefore records a wayward son's belated thanks for their steady support and bemused tolerance.

T.C.

Abbreviations

AJLH	*American Journal of Legal History*
APC	*Acts of the Privy Council*
BIHR	*Bulletin of the Institute of Historical Research*
CD	*Commons Debates 1621*, ed. by W. Notestein *et al.* (New Haven, 1935)
CJ	*The Journals of the House of Commons*
CPCC	*Calendar of the Proceedings of the Committee for Compounding*
CSPD	*Calendar of State Papers Domestic*
D'Ewes (Coates)	*The Journals of Sir Simonds D'Ewes*, ed. by W. H. Coates (New Haven, 1942)
EcHR	*Economic History Review*
EHR	*English Historical Review*
FSL	Folger Shakespeare Library
Hastings Letters	*The Letters of Francis Hastings*, ed. by Claire Cross (Taunton, 1969)
HEH	Henry E. Huntington Library, San Marino, California
HJ	*Historical Journal*
HLQ	*Huntington Library Journal*
Holles Letters	*The Letters of John Holles*, ed. by P. R. Seddon (Nottingham, 1975)
JBS	*Journal of British Studies*
LJ	*Journal of the House of Lords*
LRLB	Leicestershire and Rutland Lieutenancy Book, Huntington Library, Hastings Manorial, Box 53, item
Nichols	John Nicols, *The History and Antiquities of the County of Leicester* (London, 1795)
PP 1628	*Proceedings in Parliament 1628*, ed. by R. C. Johnson *et al.* (New Haven, 1977)
Private J	*The Private Journals of the Long Parliament*, ed. by W. H. Coates *et al.* (New Haven, 1982)
Rushworth	John Rushworth, *Historical Collections* (London, 1659)
THSLC	*Transactions of the Historical Society of Lancashire and Cheshire*
TLAHS	*Transactions of the Leicestershire Archeological and Historical Society*
TRHS	*Transactions of the Royal Historical Society*
TT	Thomason Tracts

A note on sources

The riches of the Hastings family archives present two distinct problems, which could easily double, if not triple, the length of the notes. To correct this tendency, the present study has adopted the following conventions. Because so many of the citations deal with material from the Earl of Huntingdon and his relations, the notes will refer to them by the following initials:

H   Henry Hastings, fifth Earl of Huntingdon
ECH   Elizabeth Stanley Hastings, the Countess of Huntingdon
FEH   Ferdinando Hastings, later sixth Earl of Huntingdon
HLL   Henry Hastings, later Lord Loughborough
GEH   George Hastings, fourth Earl of Huntingdon

In addition, the full citations from the Huntington Library are often lengthy. Therefore, this study will use a more abbreviated system in which, for example, the reference to Box 1, Item 2, will be expressed as 1/2. Further, it will employ the library's shorthand references to major classes. Thus:

HA Corr.   Huntington Library, Hastings Correspondence
HAP   Huntington Library, Hastings Personal
HAF   Huntington Library, Hastings Financial
HA Legal   Huntington Library, Hastings Legal
HAM   Huntington Library, Hastings Manorial
HA Misc.   Huntington Library, Hastings Miscellaneous
HA Military   Huntington Library, Hastings Military
HA Parliament Huntington Library, Hastings Parliament

Finally, one of the key texts, the Leicestershire and Rutland Lieutenancy Book [Huntington Library, Hastings Manorial (Leicestershire), Box 53, item 6], has been abbreviated as *LRLB*.

Leicestershire

Two thousand pounds and upwards that [have] beene drawne out of the Country within this twentie years by tenn shillings and nyne shillings and seaven shillings at several tymes and the proiect hath alwaie beene to furnish the countrey with Power, Match and bullet and is it soe unfurnished nowe, nothing being spent that there is need of two thousand pounds at one slap in a tyme of peace.

[Sir William Fawnt to Sir Wolston Dixie, 16 November 1626]

And if wee take into consideration the present braverie of the anemies abroad, and our home-divisions, our great boughs beating one with the other, no man that is not extreamely stupid but will easily finds that God is angry with his people and that our sinnes deserve the hastening of the last judgement.

[Thomas Pestell, *Gods Visitation in a Sermon Preached at Leicester*, 1630]

If such gentlemen as you shalbe suffered to sharke the Country of their money, it wilbe a very pretty thing.

[Sir Arthur Hesilrige speaking to Sir John Skeffington, 28 November 1632]

... so sad have been the sufferings of that County, and Rutland, by the reason of the disharmony there. Poore Leicestershire! not a County more right for the Parliament, and yet no County so tottered and torn as it hath been, can it be imagined?

[Parliament Scout, 15 August 1644]

Introduction

I n the summer of 1620, the county elite pressed into the Leicester Town Hall to hear a major address from the Lord Lieutenant. Although few contemporaries fortunate enough to have received an invitation skipped this event, modern historians have not found it as alluring. After all, the speaker was Henry Hastings, the fifth Earl of Huntingdon, hardly a name with which to conjure. In the canonical sources, from Clarendon and Chamberlain to Rushworth and Wilson, he scarcely rated a fleeting reference. *The Dictionary of National Biography* does not even accord him that much, passing over his life in silence. Fortunately *The Complete Peerage* has saved him from oblivion, but its notes on the fifth earl could also serve as the archetype of the routine entry.

The justice of such scant coverage is hard to deny. When Huntingdon attended the House of Lords, and he frequently did not, he never cut an impressive figure. At Whitehall, his family visited the court so infrequently that his wife was astonished during a rare royal audience when the king still recognised her. Not only was Huntingdon at best a second-rate figure on the early Stuart stage, but his parts initially seem perfunctory, if not hackneyed. Alan Everitt was merely presenting the standard interpretation of early seventeenth-century Leicestershire when he ascribed the county's recurrent conflicts to the extended aristocratic feuds between the Greys and the Hastings. By the 1640s,

> the division between the two families went back to personal feuds of far longer standing than the Civil War, in fact to their rivalry for the control of the county since the mid-sixteenth century. For the two families the Rebellion was, at one level, simply a further stage in the long-drawn out battle for local domination.[1]

Anything that a protagonist in this quarrel like Huntingdon might say was likely predictable and certainly desultory. Hence with contemporaries rapidly filling up the Town Hall, good manners might well tempt the polite modern scholar to give up a seat to those who really wanted to listen to Huntingdon; with more significant personalities looming elsewhere, it could hardly be reckoned a great loss.

The present study emphasises the wisdom of hanging on to a seat and of paying careful attention. What is so astonishing about this obscure local governor is that he has so much to say. Notwithstanding several notable efforts, scholars by and large have not found early Stuart Leicestershire particularly fertile ground. Anthony Fletcher rated it with Berkshire as those unfortunate shires whose history is hobbled by the disappearance of any quarter sessions records. Further complicating this fundamental 'archival problem' is the paucity of the county's surviving gentry collections, which now render a classic 'county study' a thoroughly maddening, if not utterly impossible, project. Presumably these problems helped to thwart Everitt's projected book on *Leicestershire and the Great Rebellion*.[2] Nevertheless the county possesses remarkable, and often neglected, veins of evidence. The Corporation of Leicester carefully preserved a full set of financial records as well as the copies, if not the originals, of practically every scrap of paper which it ever received or produced. Furthermore, the survival of several constables' accounts allows the experience of several isolated villages to be set against that of the county town. Even more unique are Huntingdon's own papers.

Thirty years ago, in a biography of the third Earl of Huntingdon, Claire Cross revealed the lavish possibilities of the Hastings MSS in the Huntington Library. While scholars have made little of her find, no less than the Privy Councilors themselves marvelled over the richness of the collection. When they insisted on a full accounting in 1627, the earl's agent confidently announced that his master could present 'such an account as I thought all the Lords of England could not make the like'. After surveying the documents, the Lord President of the Council 'reiouced'; so too should modern scholars.[3] The Hastings MSS contain a remarkably full set of a Lord Lieutenant's papers, both personal and official. In fact the sheer volume of the collection has effectively buried an extraordinarily detailed lieutenancy book for 1614–27. Furthermore, the earl's legal papers contain hundreds of folios chronicling extended court battles with local antagonists. Consequently, many of Huntingdon's contemporaries, who can claim greater historical importance, remain two-dimensional figures, and their outlines only become more shadowy when set beside the brilliant light which the Hastings MSS cast on this local governor.

When turned on a local landscape, long dismissed as thoroughly mundane, this archival floodlight reveals some startling features. Even contemporaries, who accepted a certain level of local bickering as only natural, found the shire's general enthusiasm for disputes to be exceptional. Indeed, one startled observer dubbed the shire 'a cockpit, one spurring against another'.[4] Yet when the new information illuminates the aristocratic feuds, the customary explanation of the county's turmoil, the results are unsettling. Admittedly the Greys and the Hastings revived their old feud in the very early seventeenth century and did so again during the Civil War. In the intervening period, however, the two families behaved so amicably towards one another that they shared the county as a political condominium. If these aristocratic rivalries were not constant, as scholars have assumed, then the shire's recurrent 'home divisions' certainly were quite real. This fact raises the compelling question of who and what was causing all the trouble.

The answer, this book will argue, falls into three sections, the first of which can be simply stated: more than squabbling peers, and at least as much as religion, what disturbed the shire's tranquillity was the growth of the state. Compared with what stirred to life after 1642, the administrative Leviathan of the early Stuart monarchs appears puny and scarcely worthy of notice. Such broad perspective, however, was unavailable to early seventeenth-century residents of Leicestershire. All that they could see was that after 1618 the central government abruptly developed a rapacious appetite for their young men and their purses. Granted, such statements sit ill with the received notions of early Stuart England. Since 'the system the Stuarts inherited was, in essentials, that of the fourteenth century', contemporaries, Conrad Russell noted, were simply witnessing 'the painful death of that system'.[5] This much is beyond question. But, as this book will show, what is equally indisputable is that the early Stuart state did not go quietly, and by expanding the customary focus on parliamentary supply and a few successful extraparliamentary schemes to include local rates and especially militia levies, we can appreciate the ratepayers' awe and irritation at the regime's persistent efforts to tap the county's resources.

The rough outline of this argument is not entirely novel. In a pioneering 1974 study of 'the interaction of local and central affairs' Hassell Smith found that the recurrent rows in Elizabethan Norfolk were linked with the central government's rapidly mounting demands, and in this volatile situation, the fundamental question dividing local gentlemen was simply 'who paid for what'. Compelling evidence of 'the weight and incidence of county taxation' led Smith to wonder about a general correlation between 'county constitutional opposition and the incidence of county taxation'. Although tantalising, his suggestions have had only a modest impact. Admittedly his conclusions did not readily fit the dominant 'localist' thesis. More important, the overall utility of his findings, he conceded, was dependent on the discovery of similar results elsewhere. Unfortunately, subsequent local studies failed to replicate his conclusions; indeed, Dairmaid MacCulloch's splendid work on Elizabethan Suffolk, easily the most influential local study of Tudor England, found that the same pressure, which had polarised Norfolk, tended to foster a sense of unity among the local elite in the neighbouring county. These developments, Penry Williams argued, left only one conclusion: Norfolk was uncharacteristic of other counties 'in the sharpness of its divisions', and its 'pattern of lieutenancy versus JPs' was not repeated elsewhere.[6] The past quarter of a century, therefore, has witnessed the transformation of what was initially regarded as a promising line of research into something of a historiographical anomaly.

In recent years, with the dawning realisation that early modern England was not a collection of autonomous cantons, the field has become more interested in the early modern state's impact on the provinces. Anthony Fletcher has called for closer attention to 'the impact of the whole range of early Stuart policies from Arminianism in the church to fiscal expedients and the exact militia', and in particular, he lamented the absence of work on 'the subject of taxation, which is central to the relationship between the centre and localities and which cries out for research'. Others have echoed Fletcher's call for a shift to 'centre–local relations rather than local administration and society'.[7] In a pioneering effort to map the growth of the early modern 'fiscal state', Patrick O'Brien and Philip Hunt have conceded that their efforts have been hobbled by the manifest uncertainties surrounding the ability of the pre-Restoration state to extract money. More recently, Michael Braddick's work has done much to clarify the issues surrounding national taxation, but in the process, it has also exposed the vagaries of local levies. The fact that 'national armies were partly financed from local rates like coat and conduct money', he noted, only increases 'the difficulties of quantifying a total burden of taxation'. Yet with his hands full sorting out national taxation, Braddick wisely avoided this thorny question, noting simply that 'the importance of local rates should not, therefore, be underestimated'.[8] Meanwhile suspicions about the possible size of local rates has led Conrad Russell to speculate that 'Nationally England was a lightly taxed country but locally it may have been another story.' Consequently the validity of the query which O'Brien and Hunt posed still stands: 'it would be useful to discover the national share of expenditures for the defence of the Tudor and Stuart realms which emanated from "local" taxes.' All of these queries have become more insistent with John Brewer's depiction of the dramatic growth of the British state after 1688, a study which begs the question of the state's earlier nature.[9] In essence, the present study proposes a belated return to Hassell Smith's suggestion and an exploration of the complex relationship of Whitehall and Leicestershire before the Civil War. By exploiting the extraordinarily rich seam of financial information, *Home Divisions* seeks to establish, at times down to the shilling and pence, the precise burden of both 'national' and 'local' taxation on the shire.

This exploration of early modern accounting allows us to link the state's mounting financial demands with the county's political conflicts, and this linkage in turn will restore a significant element to the spectrum of early Stuart England, which has hitherto been almost invisible. In Diarmaid MacCulloch's study of sixteenth-century Suffolk, the local gentlemen increasingly assumed the responsibility for local government which the magnates had abandoned. By the end of Elizabeth's reign, the result was 'an increasingly self-contained county whose day to day running was in the hands of an oligarchy of Puritan-minded gentry', a development which Hassell Smith also found in Elizabethan Norfolk.[10] The only difficulty with these books is the temptation to assume that the same progression took place elsewhere, a temptation which a spate of brilliant local studies has made even more irresistible. Lords Lieutenant, while not absent from these works, certainly do not occupy centre stage in any of them. On closer examination, it becomes clear that a common thread linked the Herbert brothers, successive Earls of Pembroke and Lieutenants of Somerset, with the Earls of Dorset, their counterparts in Sussex, and the Earls of Northampton in Warwickshire: they were all absentee administrators. Even the most energetic non-resident Lieutenant produced a distinct style of local government, one in which his Deputy Lieutenants and JPs exercised an autonomy verging on independence. Because these three shires, which have received the most detailed attention, all shared this administrative structure, there is the natural tendency to assume that the same pattern applies elsewhere. Indeed, the careful examination of one of these shires and its non-resident Lord Lieutenant has recently prompted Thomas Barnes to suggest that the 1620s witnessed a general 'institutional failure of the lieutenancy'.[11]

Such an argument would be more persuasive, and local history much easier to synthesise, if all counties conformed to the same pattern. Yet if Leicestershire is any guide, they did not. 'Lieutenancy,' Barnes rightly observed, 'was the sole responsibility of the lord lieutenant, and only he could have performed for that institution the function performed by judges in magistracy,' and the turmoil surrounding the Somerset militia ineluctably followed from the fact that this officer 'had withdrawn from any active part in the institution committed to his care'. In Leicestershire, however, the Lord Lieutenant had not withdrawn, and this fact alone is of considerable historiographical importance. A lieutenancy, Brian Quintrell has observed, 'was very much what the individual holder chose to make of it'. Either the Lieutenant could 'regard the appointment as more for form than substance', or he 'could use it to emphasize and extend his existing sway over the county or counties under his command'. Most resident Lieutenants followed the latter style of government; Huntingdon certainly did. A quasi-feudal paternalism may have expired elsewhere, but not in Leicestershire. With Huntingdon scrutinising every action, the Deputy Lieutenants, to say nothing of the JPs, would have been amazed at the leeway given to their opposite numbers in other counties. In fact, Huntingdon's position in Leicestershire had much more in common with that of the Duke of Norfolk in East Anglia a century earlier. The startling novelty of this situation is best captured in John Morrill's recent remark:

> [after reading] Hassell Smith on Elizabethan Norfolk and Diarmaid MacCulloch on Tudor Suffolk, I am struck again by the slow decline of local power structures built around the noble household, the liberty and the manor, and the gradual rise of the institutions of the shire – lieutenancy, commission of the peace, revival of the

shrievalty.[12]

Yet in Leicestershire, right up to the Civil War, the decline of aristocratic power, if it occurred, was so gradual as to be imperceptible. Consequently, when the 'institutions of the shire' developed, the local magnate dominated them.

This style of local government, which at first glance might seem an anomalous holdover from the Wars of the Roses, was surprisingly common. Recently Victor Stater has noted that of the sixty-four early Stuart Lords Lieutenant, only half held court office; the other half were 'mere' magnates. To name only a few obvious examples, the Earl of Derby in Cheshire and Lancashire, the Earl of Warwick in Essex and the Earl of Newcastle in Nottingham and Derbyshire shared Huntingdon's passion for administration. No JP could have casually dismissed the political importance of this fact. With an active Lord Lieutenant 'casting a very long shadow over virtually the whole of the remainder of his functions, the local magistrate', Robert Ashton shrewdly noted, 'may be excused a certain apprehensiveness that, as in the case of patents, he was being reduced to the status of a mere administrative assistant at the beck and call of a higher, centrally oriented authority'.[13] Leicestershire in short represents a significant as well as a common administrative style, which historians have not fully appreciated. On sober reflection, this conclusion should not be too astonishing. Although the vigour with which some historians have recently argued for the continuing importance, if not primacy, of the early Stuart peerage has verged on the excessive, the general point is well taken; and since the peers often exercised considerable influence over events at court and in the Parliament House, then it only stands to reason that their power should have been felt at least as keenly in their provincial strongholds. *Home Divisions* therefore will emphasise the importance of peers in general and Lords Lieutenant in particular.

While political dinosaurs like aristocratic magnates still roamed the early seventeenth-century landscape, the species had nonetheless subtly adapted to the new political environment. Unlike their early Tudor ancestors, the nobility laboured heroically, if ineffectively, to counteract 'the generally downward trend of aristocratic finances'. Hence, in Lawrence Stone's celebrated judgement, 'a landed aristocracy has rarely had it so bad'. Although there were exceptions to Stone's law, Huntingdon was not among them. Consequently his critics in the shire suggested that something other than *noblesse oblige* was behind the earl's obsession with dominating all aspects of local government, especially those dealing with taxation. In late sixteenth-century Norfolk, contemporaries were baffled by neighbours who 'were willing, indeed eager', to execute royal decrees 'efficiently, if not ruthlessly ... no matter what additional financial burdens they imposed upon the county in the process'. Either these men were 'forward-looking men, who considered the local administrators should implement policies formulated in "national" terms by the central government', or they were 'selfish men who aimed at enhancing their prestige and increasing their income through acting as agents of the Crown'.[14] A few decades later, the same questions were still being asked in Leicestershire.

Since these questions played a critical role in fuelling the county's recurrent turmoil, this study will consider the extent to which public administrators were also private men eager to advance their own interests. Underneath the administrative minutiae, this study is also effectively a biography of the fifth earl. Thanks to the thoroughness with which the early Stuart aristocracy has been examined, the peers cannot claim neglect. Nevertheless individual peers who are not parvenu courtiers have received little more than fleeting scholarly attention.[15] The wholesale abandonment of aristocratic biography either to family hagiographers or to popular historians is lamentable to behold. In Leicestershire, contemporaries found the personality of Whitehall's local agent at least as important as the central government's decrees. Therefore, *Home Divisions* will examine Huntingdon's strengths and weaknesses as well as his fluctuations over the quarter-century before the Civil War.

On their own, any of these factors – the state's increasing demands, the Lord Lieutenant's broad powers, or a magnate's schemes – would have been volatile enough. But when mixed together in the correct amount and sequence, they were explosive, and the results of these reactions regularly punctuated the calm of early Stuart Leicestershire.

The ensuing political pyrotechnics, this book will argue, deserve an attentive scholarly audience. Some thirty years ago, after having long been consigned to the cranky and the overly enthusiastic, local history suddenly burgeoned into one of the major scholarly growth industries as scholars debated the central tenets and corollaries of the 'localist thesis', which Alan Everitt first advanced and which John Morrill popularised.[16] The only thing more astonishing than the meteoric rise of localism was its equally precipitous decline. Dark clouds began gathering over this halcyon world in the 1980s as localism, having spawned a series of distinguished studies, received a critical barrage from Ann Hughes and Clive Holmes.[17] In the classic pattern of scholarly debates, a tantalising thesis would eventually generate a reaction, but the result of this criticism was startling; rather than defend or modify their position, the 'localists' simply abandoned it altogether. In the wake of their decision, local history has plunged into a near total eclipse from which it has yet to emerge, while postgraduate students and publishers alike, alarmed at the sudden onset of darkness, have given the entire subject a wide berth. Admittedly a few scholars have braved the gathering gloom. In 1985, David Underdown proposed a connection between cultural and political diversity, and although this provocative study generated a spirited debate with Morrill and eventually produced Mark Stoyle's study of Devon, it cannot be said to have filled the intellectual void left by the hasty evacuation of the 'localist'

7

camp.[18]

The briefest reflection reveals the potentially devastating implications of the sudden collapse of local history for the entire field. Only by testing larger concepts on a limited basis can we best assess their overall validity, and there is no clearer illustration of the utility of local history than the recent furore over revisionism. With Olympian condescension, the doyens of the field initially ignored the early findings of the 'localist' school, but younger scholars, eager to challenge the Whiggish paradigm, did not. Consequently, the 'revisionist' willingness to take on board the novel 'localist' conclusions lent considerable force to the 'revisionist' assault. Admittedly the field eventually moderated revisionism as well as localism, but this sober wisdom came only after a decade of general historiographical confusion and dismay. To return to a professional state of cheerful indifference to all things provincial, therefore, is to accord the next paradigm shift much more impact than it might otherwise merit.

Anxious to forestall this perilous state of affairs, this book consciously seeks to return the prominence and lustre to local studies. Its research agenda, of course, is not the only means of ensuring such a revival. Provincial towns are now the subject of careful attention, which they have long deserved and only fitfully received.[19] Likewise some of the scrupulous care normally accorded to metropolitan divines is being lavished on provincial clerics.[20] Finally disputes among the gentry are being analysed to uncover contemporary notions of honour and community.[21] While these topics all represent fruitful avenues of inquiry, this book will pursue another one – the growth of the state.

The prospect of employing provincial history to chart the emergence of the early modern state has the additional benefit of closing the fissure which currently divides early modern English and French historiography. With only a few exceptions, English historians have been largely uninterested in joining the collective effort of French scholars, eager for 'a major re-evaluation of the nature of the early modern state'. Had they been less averse, they might have found a surprisingly close fit between French research topics and English sources. The stunning prospect can be glimpsed in William Beik's thorough study of state power and provincial aristocracy in Languedoc. He began by wondering whether the royal agents in the hinterlands were 'making the state bourgeois or feudalising it?' To arrive at an answer, Beik examined how the 'attitudes, allegiances and interests' of the royal agents 'fitted into the fabric of local political life'. This exercise led him first to appreciate that even in distant Languedoc, the Thirty Years War represented 'a fiscal turning point which altered the relationship between state and society'. This allowed the dangers of the scholarly obsession with 'the rise of the bourgeoisie and the rise of capitalism' to emerge. These developments, although undeniable, should not obscure an equally dramatic transformation in which 'the aristocracy consistently renewed itself'. Thus the development of the early modern French state did not involve the subjugation of the aristocracy so much as 'a restructured feudal society' in which 'both the king and his landed aristocracy were exploring ways of defending their interests in a changing world without, at the same time, undermining them'.[22]

Since many of these same themes loom large in the present work, the result, it is hoped, will underscore the wisdom of setting early modern English history in a European as well as a British context. 'The control of the militia,' Robert Ashton has generally observed, 'was to be a crucial issue over which the final break between the king and his opponents came in 1642,' but it 'had, though in a different form, already been an issue for decades'. Consequently, 'the apparently outrageous claims of Pym and his colleagues in 1642 may have evoked a more sympathetic response than might normally be expected from traditionalist country gentlemen'.[23] The study of early seventeenth-century Leicestershire illustrates the perceptiveness of both Ashton and Beik. The turmoil, which Hassell Smith vividly captured in Elizabethan Norfolk, returned with the outbreak of the Thirty Years War and remained a near constant source of tension for over two decades. At the centre of the controversy was not the militia regiment, but its commander. Local gentlemen would have gladly testified that it was not the quickening pace of Whitehall's demands after 1618 which troubled them. There was also the baffling phenomenon in which the regime's new demands also strengthened the county's traditional magnate. Had contemporaries known of the concept, they might well have described the growth of the early Stuart state as feudalising local government. Hence, when Pym began to challenge the king for control of the militia, Leicestershire provided much more than an attentive audience. The county produced some of Pym's most prominent deputies, and it generated much of the telling evidence of abuses with which he galvanised support in the Commons.

At the centre of the firestorm in 1642 were the policies and practices of his Lord Lieutenant in Leicestershire, the fifth Earl of Huntingdon, the same man who had summoned the county elite before him nearly a quarter century earlier. Admittedly the speaker has almost vanished from the pages of history. Nevertheless, given the astonishing amount of information about Huntingdon which relates to vital historiographical questions, it is high time to summon him out of scholarly oblivion.

NOTES

1 ECH to H, 18 January [1627], HA Corr. 12/4839; and Alan Everitt, *The Local Community and the Great Rebellion* (London, 1969), p. 15.

2 Anthony Fletcher, *Reform in the Provinces* (New Haven, 1986), p. 358; and Alan Everitt, *The Community of Kent and the Great Rebellion* (Leicester, 1966), p. 34, n. 1.

3 Claire Cross, *The Puritan Earl* (London, 1966); and Rudinge to H, 6 June [1627], *LRLB*, fol. 210.

4 *Terrible News from Leicester*, TT, E.108(16).

5 Conrad Russell, *The Causes of the English Civil War* (London, 1990), p. 166.

6 A. Hassell Smith, *County and Court* (Oxford, 1974), [vii] and pp. 334 and 337–8; Diarmaid MacCulloch, *Suffolk and the Tudors* (Oxford, 1986), pp. 258–84 and 346–7; and Penry Williams, 'The Crown and the Counties', *The Reign of Elizabeth I*, ed. by C. Haigh (London, 1984), pp. 138–9.

7 Fletcher, *Reform*, p. 360; and 'National and Local Awareness in the County Communities', *Before the Civil War* (London, 1983), p. 154.

8 P. O'Brien and P. Hunt, 'The Rise of a Fiscal State in England, 1485–1815', *BIHR* LXI (1993), pp. 135–6; and Michael Braddick, *The Nerves of State* (Manchester, 1996), p. 196; and Michael Braddick, *Parliamentary Taxation in Seventeenth Century England* (London, 1994), p. 3.

9 Russell, *The Causes of the Civil War*, p. 175. See also John Brewer, *The Sinews of Power* (London, 1989).

10 MacCulloch, *Suffolk and the Tudors*, p. 338; and Smith, *County and Court*.

11 Thomas Barnes, 'Deputies not Principals, Lieutenants not Captains: the institutional failure of the lieutenancy in the 1620s', *War and Government in Britain, 1598–1650*, ed. by M. C. Fissel (Manchester, 1991), pp. 58–86; and Barnes, *Somerset 1625–1640: a County's Government during the 'Personal Rule'* (Cambridge, Mass., 1961); Anthony Fletcher, *A County Community in Peace and War: Sussex 1600–1660* (London, 1975); and Ann Hughes, *Politics, Society and Civil War in Warwickshire, 1620–1660* (Cambridge, 1987).

12 Barnes, *Somerset*, p. 279; B. W. Quintrell, Introduction, *The Maynard Lieutenancy Book 1608–1639* (Chelmsford, 1993), xlix; and John Morrill, 'County Communities and the Problem of Allegiance in the English Civil War', *The Nature of the English Revolution* (London, 1993), p. 186.

13 Victor Stater, *Noble Government: the Stuart Lieutenancy and the Transformation of English Politics* (Athens, Ga., 1994), p. 14–5; and Robert Ashton, *The English Civil War* (London, 1978), p. 50.

14 Lawrence Stone, *The Crisis of the Aristocracy* (Oxford, 1965), p. 197; and Smith, *County and Court*, p. 333.

15 For one of the few honorable exceptions, see Esther Cope, *The Life of a Public Man: Edward, first Baron Montagu* (Philadelphia, 1981).

16 For the pioneering works of this movement, see Everitt, *The Community of Kent*, and John Morrill, *The Revolt of the Provinces* (London, 1976).

17 Clive Holmes, 'The County Community in Stuart Historiography', *JBS* XIX (1980), pp. 54–73; and *Seventeenth Century Lincolnshire* (Lincoln, 1980); and Ann Hughes, 'Militancy and Localism: Warwickshire Politics and Westminster Politics, 1643–1647', *TRHS* 5th series, XXXI (1981), pp. 51–68; 'Local History and the Origins of the Civil War', *Conflict in Early Stuart England*, ed. by R. Cust and A. Hughes, (London, 1989), pp. 224–53; and *Politics, Society and Civil War in Warwickshire*.

18 David Underdown, *Riot, Revel and Rebellion: Popular Politics and Popular Culture in England, 1603–1660* (Oxford, 1985); Mark Stoyle, *Loyalty and Locality: Popular Allegiance in Devon during the English Civil War* (Exeter, 1994); and J. S. Morrill, 'The Ecology of Allegiance in the English Civil War', *JBS* XXVI (1987), pp. 451–67.

19 See, for example, David Underdown, *Fire from Heaven* (New Haven, 1992); David Harris Sacks, *The Widening Gate* (Berkeley, 1991); Catherine Patterson, 'Leicester and Lord Huntingdon: Urban Patronage in Early Modern England', *Midland History* XVII (1990), pp. 45–61; and Richard Cust, 'Parliamentary Elections in the 1620s: the case of Great Yarmouth', *Parliamentary History*, X, pp. 171–91.

20 See, for example, John Fielding, 'Opposition to the Personal Rule of Charles I: the Diary of Robert Woodford, 1637–1641', *HJ* XXXI (1988), pp. 769–88; Tom Webster, *A Peculiar People* (Cambridge, 1997); Ann Hughes, *Godly Reformation and its Opponents in Warwickshire* (Stratford, 1995); and 'Thomas Dugard and his Circle in the 1630s: a "Parliamentary–Puritan Connection?"' *HJ* XXIX (1986), pp. 779–93; Richard Cust, 'Anti-puritanism and Urban Politics: Charles I and Great Yarmouth', *HJ* XXXV (1992), pp. 1–26; and Peter Lake, 'Serving God and the Times: the Calvinist Conformity of Robert Saunderson', *JBS* XXVII (1988), pp. 81–116.

21 See, for example, Richard Cust, 'Honour, Rhetoric and Political Culture: the Earl of Huntingdon and his Enemies', *Political Culture and Cultural Politics*, pp. 84–111; Richard Cust, 'Honour and Politics in Early Stuart England: the Case of Beaumont *v.* Hastings', *PP* no. 149 (1995), pp. 57–94; and Steve Hindle, 'The Shaming of Margaret Knowsley: Gossip, Slander, Gender, and the Experience of Authority in Early Modern England', *Continuity and Change* IX (1994), pp. 391–419.

22 William Beik, *Absolutism and Society in Seventeenth Century France* (Cambridge, 1985), pp. 14–16 and 21.

23 Ashton, *English Civil War*, p. 54.

Prologue

Everyone under
their own fig tree

In the search for an appropriate rhetorical motif, James I, the self-styled Rex Pacificus, naturally enough adopted the classic formulation of prosperity and contentment in the Old Testament. Micah arguably said it best when he prophesied that after mankind had hammered their swords into ploughshares and spears into pruning hooks, 'they shall sit every man under his vine and under fig tree: and none shall make them afraid'. Hence whenever anxious to highlight the achievements of his reign, James's speeches often were simply variations on Micah. After years of 'bloodshed, oppressions, complaints and outcries', he told Parliament in 1607 that he had transformed the land, and thanks to his wise rule, his subjects

> now live every man peaceably under his owne figgetree, and all their former cries and complaints turned onely into prayers to God for their King, under whom they enjoy such ease and happy quietnesse.

Lest anyone might have missed this fundamental point, James was fond of reiterating it.[1]

Aside from their self-congratulatory tone, the most notable aspect of these speeches was their apparent dissonance with the common perception of James's reign. Indeed, between the astonishing displays of conspicuous consumption and the apparently unending scandals at court, some contemporaries and many later scholars have had difficulty even noticing the 'ease and happy quietnesse' of Jacobean England. James, however, had ample grounds for self-satisfaction. Peace and prosperity characteristically never receive their due, and so it was for much of James's reign. More important, the moral ambiguity of James's reign obscures an even more astonishing fact than an extended peace. Simply put, the English state under Elizabeth had swollen to an unprecedented size and developed a formidable rapacity, and under James it shrank. Armies were paid off, fleets mothballed and the various fiscal

devices by which the central government had supported these measures weak-
ened their grip on the local ratepayers. Indeed, for the decade before 1618, the
state's demands on Leicestershire dwindled to the point where they verged on
the non-existent. To be sure, the Exchequer's total receipts actually grew under
James I, but much of the increase came from the repayment of Elizabethan
loans to Henri IV and to the Dutch Republic or from new loans from the
Corporation of London. Meanwhile less and less came from ordinary taxpayers. Consequently gentlemen in Leicestershire could have acknowledged
that, for much of James's reign, they had indeed sat at comparative ease in the
shade of their vines and fig trees. Even more remarkable, although their plants
regularly produced bumper harvests, James himself scarcely shared in their
prosperity at all.

Admittedly James I had not willingly sought this role. While he abhorred
war, and quickly ended the foreign conflicts which he had inherited from his
Tudor cousin, he had no objections to parliamentary supply. His Parliament
men on the other hand had trouble comprehending the need for extraordinary
supply in the midst of peace. It took three years of badgering before the House
finally voted a supply. The 1606 grant certainly was a handsome one, ultimately netting the Exchequer nearly £400,000. It was also the only one
passed in his first eighteen years in England. So neglected did he feel that in
1621 James complained that Elizabeth had received more in one year than he
had in all of his reign.[2] The irritation with this development, needless to say,
was confined to residents of Whitehall. For almost everyone else in the 1610s,
the failure of the Great Contract in 1610 and the hasty dissolution of the
Addled Parliament in 1614 literally made the decade a golden one, as local
gentlemen never had subsidy commissioners disturb their financial calculations.

The parliamentary impasse forced James's ministers to exercise their
inventiveness, and their success in articulating and implementing 'fiscal
feudalism' would later make some Parliament men question the wisdom of
the Commons' early frugality. Yet the fact of the matter was that for the first
fifteen years of his reign, the attention of royal financial officers was fixed on
the profits of the metropolitan business elite. Hence as Exchequer tellers cut
tallies for hundreds of thousands of pounds in loans from the City and in new
impositions on foreign merchants, they effectively forgot the more modest
incomes of county farmers and Leicester merchants.[3]

Periodically the memory returned as Whitehall launched schemes to tap
provincial wealth. At various times, the central government appealed for
assistance on Prince Henry's knighting or Princess Elizabeth's marriage, and
it sporadically attempted to collect benevolences. Yet because the central
government's gaze became decidedly myopic outside of the Home Counties,
comparatively remote shires like Leicestershire yielded the Exchequer such
disappointing results that the trifling amounts did nothing to encourage

repeat performances. Take for instance the shire's response to the 1614 bene-volence. Although the local gentlemen had promised approximately £1,000, the county's collector eventually turned up at the Council table with only £400, a sum 'so base and meane' that the councillors dubbed it 'very unwor-thy his [James's] acceptance'. What followed was a stern chastisement of the local bench and an end of the affair. Leicestershire's experience only under-scores the validity of Brian Quintrell's general observation that the Council 'took its decisions singly and generally separately; it seldom cross-referenced them, and very rarely tried even to co-ordinate them'.[4] Through the resulting gaps in the Council's awareness entire counties regularly slipped.

Leicestershire was equally fortunate in Whitehall's general lack of interest in all things military. In 1621 James sought to encourage parliamentary gener-osity with the recollection that 'Ye are not troubled with pressing of men these eighteen years past'. Technically his statement stretched the truth; five years earlier he had ordered Leicestershire to gather men to reinforce the Irish garrisons. Yet he did not stretch it far, since he had requested only twenty-five men. After the hundreds of conscripts whom the state had summoned to fight Elizabeth's wars, the county's Parliament men were understandably unwilling to gainsay the monarch over such a trifling error.[5]

The state's requirements were scarcely more demanding with the shire's militia regiment of 1,100 men, about whom the councillors often seemed utterly indifferent. With the Peace of London in 1604, the Leicestershire regiment rapidly degenerated from a reasonably impressive military unit to a glorified social club. The musters themselves, on the rare occasions when they occurred, were rambunctious affairs in which ill-trained officers attempted, and sometimes failed, to maintain order over hundreds of men in varying stages of intoxication. With such officers and men, actual military exercises were as potentially dangerous as they were ultimately futile. The equipment itself ranged from the antique to items borrowed from a neighbouring militia man. The latter practice was so ordinary that a local preacher ridiculed it from the pulpit: 'if the Armour see the Sunne above once a year, it is when out of a charitable mind, it is lent out to be shewed some ten myles at another Mustring'.[6] Consequently in these years, the infrequent musters were chiefly occasions when a group of men more interested in enjoying themselves than undergoing the rigours of military discipline presented a wildly varying array of weapons in various states of repair.

To their credit, the local officials appreciated the need to check, if not reverse, the militia's precipitous decline. Whitehall, however, generally did not. Even after the local regiment narrowly proved the equal of some rioting peasants in 1607, the Council quashed local pleas for more regular musters, Lord Treasurer Salisbury himself arguing it was 'as yet no convenient time'. Instead the Council dismissed all the realm's militiamen on their celebrated 'long vacation', which was to last from 1608 to 1612. A worsening crisis in Cleves and Julich eventually forced the Council to abandon its benign neglect, and the more attentive attitude inspired the Lord Lieutenant and his deputies to embark on an ambitious plan to retain a cadre of paid professionals led by an experienced Muster Master. These veterans were to supervise an intensive three-day drill, and at the end of the training, the bandsmen were to display their new prowess at a public spectacle in which half of the regiment would storm entrenchments defended by the rest of their colleagues.[7]

Such splendid designs quickly became entangled in political reality. A decade of near total somnolence had left the county unprepared for activity on such a scale. Consequently the new military professionals soon found themselves confronted with widespread resistance from truculent bandsmen and defiant ratepayers. More important, since the councillors meanwhile proved unwilling to intervene in this local dispute, the problem of defaulters proved intractable. The regiment's arrearages soared, internal disputes escalated, and a number of officers, including the Muster Master himself, resigned in disgust. Two years of this administrative chaos eventually brought the experiment to an ignominious end. By 1616 the deputy lieutenants had glumly concluded that any serious attempt to improve the regiment was doomed since 'we fear the country will much distaste the payment'. Needless to say, with such ill-trained soldiers, the militia officers regretfully judged even a mock battle beyond their men's ability. Therefore lest the men hurt themselves, they cancelled the public skirmish.[8] This bitter experience left the Deputy Lieutenants so frustrated that when the councillors in the following year failed to order a muster, they were in no mood to prod their memory. The one positive aspect of this administrative debacle was that it left Leicester's forty trained men free to concentrate on the one task which they could perform with any skill – escorting processions of the Corporation.

It must be conceded that Leicestershire's ability to evade the state's demands, while impressive, was never absolute. After all, the local taxpayers never found an effective means of dodging the demands of purveyance. By the early seventeenth century, a medieval monarch's right to purchase foodstuff at reduced prices had evolved into a rigid system obliging the shire to provide the royal household with forty oxen, 600 mutton, 400 lambs, twenty capons, thirty hens, forty pullets, twenty chickens and 800 lb of beeswax. The Crown purchased these items at roughly 30 per cent of their market value, leaving the county to make up the difference. The officials of the Green Cloth were quite willing to send up agents to select the county's annual contribution. Yet since local residents equated purveyors with locusts, they were understandably willing to do almost anything to forestall such a disruptive action. To forestall this dire visitation, the county bench late in Elizabeth's reign agreed to an annual composition of £983 17s. 4d., and there the county's contribution remained for the next fifty years. Periodically the county sought more favourable terms, but the Green Cloth invariably won the day by threatening to purchase the county's contributions in the more expensive London markets, which, as the officials explained to the JPs, 'will occasion a greater chardge and offense to the Countie, then is like to growe by your ordinarie courses'. If the county balked at paying this bill, then a purveyor would then come down to distrain cattle. With the Green Cloth officials holding all the high cards, any local protests quickly folded.[9]

The situation was particularly annoying on several accounts. First of all, in a county where a parliamentary subsidy netted only £750, this composition was far from notional. Furthermore local residents could scarcely be pleased with the inequities of a system which called for nearly £1,000 from them and a mere £207 from their neighbours in Nottinghamshire. Not surprisingly a prominent JP attempted to have the county's composition cut almost by half.[10] Yet counterbalancing the aggravation of the compositions was the plain fact that for much of James's reign these payments represented the Jacobean state's largest and certainly most consistent intrusion into the purses of local residents. Other than that, the state largely left them alone. Therefore aggrieved ratepayers may have found some consolation in the realisation that they had the better end of the bargain; in return for the shire sending down reasonably regular purveyance payments, Whitehall effectively forgot the way to Leicestershire.

The shire's experience with the Jacobean state forces us to think again about the warmth with which many contemporaries were to recall James's reign. To be sure, much of the posthumous praise of James's rule was a backhanded criticism of his son's less adroit administration. But what contemporaries remembered with fondness was much more than James's ecclesiastical tolerance. Plainly he had encouraged the development of the notion of 'the divine right of kings', but notwithstanding all the controversies over absolutism in his reign, the fact of the matter was that he was much more interested in establishing his prerogative rights than he was in exercising them. New impositions of custom duties were of course the major exception to this rule. No one denounced the new rates with more vigour than Leicestershire's Knight of the Shire, Sir Thomas Beaumont, did in 1610, and there is no reason to doubt his insistence that his constituents were eager to see their abolition. Nevertheless for Beaumont and his neighbours who had little direct relation to foreign trade, the mere idea of impositions pained them more than their actual fiscal burden. Few in Leicestershire therefore would have objected when at James's funeral in 1625 Bishop Williams sought to establish the dead king's claim to being 'Great Britain's Solomon'. 'Every man liu'd in peace under his vine, and his Figge-Tree in the daies of Salomon,' Williams observed, 'And so they did in the blessed daies of King James.'[11]

What ensured that the memory of such balmy days remained well burnished was the sudden end of the county's autonomy. Indeed, the halcyon world in which Whitehall kept a safe distance from the local residents did not even outlast James himself. In late April 1618, a messenger left the Council Table to hasten to Leicester with the first of a series of orders, which ensured that the local residents were no longer alone in the shade under their vines and fig trees.

NOTES

1 Micah, iv–4; and 'A Speach to ... Parliament,' 31 March 1607, *King James VI and I: Political Writings*, ed. by J. P. Sommerville, (Cambridge, 1994), p. 169. See also I Kings, iv–25; II Kings, xviii–31; Isaiah xxxvi–16; and Zechariah iii–10; and 30 January, *CD 1621*, II, p. 7.

2 30 January, *CD 1621* II, p. 7–8. On Jacobean finances, see also Frederick C. Dietz, *English Public Finance, 1558–1641* (New York, 1964), pp. 100–43; and 'The Receipts and Issues of the Exchequer during the Reigns of James I and Charles I', *Smith College Studies in History* XIII (1928), pp. 136–41.

3 Robert Ashton, *The Crown and the Money Market, 1603–1640* (London, 1960), pp. 113–31; and Julian Martin, *Francis Bacon, the State, and the Reform of Natural Philosophy* (Cambridge, 1992), pp. 105–40.

4 Council to Sheriff and Justices of Leicester, 5 February 1615, *APC* 34, pp. 42–3; and Quintrell, 'Lancashire and the Privy Council', *THSLC* CXXXI (1981), p. 40.

5 30 January, *CD 1621* II, p. 7. On the Irish levy, see PC to Huntingdon, 31 July 1616, *APC* 34, 697–9; and Huntingdon to Head Constables, 31 August 1616; and 'The accompt of 25 footemen', *LRLB*, fols. 26v–27v.

6 Samuel Buggs, *Miles Mediterraneus: the Midland Souldier* (London, 1622), p. 25. On the problems in this period, see Huntingdon to DLs, 19 October 1614, *LRLB*, fols 6–7; and L. Boynton, *The Elizabethan Militia* (London, 1967), pp. 209–12.

7 Bodley to Huntingdon, 4 July 1607, HA Corr. 6/5424; and Huntingdon to DLs, 24 September and 2, 5 and 19 October 1614, *LRLB*, fols. 5, 5v–6 and 6–7. See also *The Earl of Hertford's Lieutenancy Papers, 1603–1610*, ed. by W. P. D. Murphy (Devizes, 1969), p. 198; and Boynton, *Elizabethan Militia*, pp. 212–36.

8 DLs to Huntingdon, 28 May 1616, *LRLB*, fols. 21–1v. On the difficulties of implementing the design, see Huntingdon to the Constables, July 1615; Hastings to Huntingdon, 29 June 1616; and Beaumont to Huntingdon, 11 June [1616], *LRLB*, 14v, 22, 23v–24.

9 Green Cloth to H, 15 May 1617 and 1 October 1621, HA Corr. 7/4126 and 8/4132; and 'The perticulars of all the Compositions', PRO LS 13/279, fol. 73v.

10 Richard Cust, 'Purveyance and Politics in Jacobean Leicestershire', in *Regionalism and Revision: English Provincial Society, 1250–1650*, ed. by P. Fleming and A. J. Gross, (London, forthcoming). See also A. Woodworth, *Purveyance for the Royal Household* (Philadelphia, 1945); G. E. Aylmer, 'The Last Years of Purveyance, 1610–1660', *EcHR*, second series, X (1957–58), pp. 81–93; and Eric Lindquist, 'The King, the People and the House of Commons: the Problems of early Jacobean Purveyance', *HJ* XXXI (1988), pp. 549–70.

11 John Williams, *Great Britains Solomon* (London, 1625), p. 39. See Beaumont's speech, 7 November 1610, *Proceedings in Parliament 1610*, ed. by E. R. Foster (New Haven, 1966) II, pp. 317–9.

Part I

<hr/>

'An Example for other Counties to follow'

·

Leicestershire at war, 1618–26

<hr/>

Wee have been made acquainted ... touching the Exacte and good accompt you have given ... and wee doe hartyly wish that your Lordshipp mought bee made an Example for other Counties to followe and cannot but take notice unto you and give you many thanks for the exquisite performance of this Service.

[Privy Council to Huntingdon, December 1625]

The Council's message reached a short, slight man in his early thirties. Henry Hastings, the fifth Earl of Huntingdon, then had to implement this directive without unnecessarily aggravating the county. This administrative challenge was to become all too common for the earl. After 1618, similar requests came thick and fast from Whitehall. Indirectly, if not directly, he was intimately involved in the execution of all these commands. Given the formidable number of administrative balls which the councillors had to keep in the air after 1618, their attention to developments in a single shire was understandably fleeting. Nevertheless even the harried bureaucrats at Whitehall came to appreciate that Huntingdon was achieving marvels in Leicestershire. Local governors were more likely to receive censure than commendation, and this fact only underscores the extraordinary nature of the praise which the councillors began to lavish on Huntingdon. His 'exquisite performance', their most fulsome testimonial ran, had transformed Leicestershire into 'an Example for other Counties to followe'.

Their praise was richly deserved. Part I will analyse how the county and the earl managed to earn such remarkable encomiums. After introducing Huntingdon and his associates, it will examine Leicestershire's involvement in the war effort and the perfection of its trained band. It will conclude with a discussion of the sole campaign which its militiamen ever conducted.

Chapter 1

'Careful to do my dewtie'

The portrait of a local governor

When the messenger finally delivered the Council's order to Huntingdon, he found the earl ready for action. Indeed, he had been ready for at least a decade. His household staff had long laboured under strict regulations governing their behaviour. These were necessary, he explained to them, because the efficient administration of his retinue 'doth nearest resemble the government in publicke offices which men of my rancke are verie often called unto and do most commonly happen to them'. Hence he would not tolerate their misconduct jeopardising his future career. Years earlier he had cautioned his infant son to govern himself in the knowledge that 'by thy birth thou art a publique person'; consequently it was 'likely thou shalt be called to publique place and imployment, either at home in the Cuntry wher thou resides or some place of iudicatyes or abrode'.[1] By 1618, he had at least gained a public place at home as Lord Lieutenant of Leicestershire and Rutland. Yet, as the militia debacle of 1614–16 illustrated, the Privy Council was uninterested in Huntingdon performing anything other than honorific duties. The rapidly spreading war on the continent therefore forced the central government to abandon its wonted lethargy and allowed him to display his aptitude for public affairs. Unfortunately, this opportunity also threw into sharp relief a potentially crippling limitation of any Lord Lieutenant.

The new orders flowing out of Whitehall allowed Huntingdon to make extraordinary demands on the local community, which naturally enough generated some complaints. In the first instance, anyone bold enough to question his authority would likely be presented with the Lord Lieutenant's commission. Bearing a massive seal and the royal signature, the document itself looked impressive, and the text itself conferred equally remarkable powers. Huntingdon alone was authorized to 'levy, geather and call togeather' the militiamen to ensure their readiness to 'resiste, represse and subdue, slay, kill, and put to execution of death' all 'enemyes, traytors, and rebells'. To the royal Lieutenant all other local officials had to defer, for the monarch expressly gave him power over 'our justices of peace, mayors, sheriffes, bayliffes, constables, hedboroughes, and all other our officers, ministers, and subjects'. In addition, if the Lord Lieutenant ever ran into any opposition, the Privy Council stood ready to back up his authority.[2]

Such wide powers masked the fact that a Lord Lieutenant's position was far from impregnable. When analysing the lieutenancy, it is easy to assume that it was simply a matter of bureaucrats in Whitehall writing orders to their man in the county. In practice the mechanics were much trickier. First of all, the notion of Lords Lieutenant as nascent intendants, intimately connected with the central government, falls far wide of the mark. While some Lieutenants were court grandees, others were not. The latter usually resided in the county which they administered and generally had only formal relations with Whitehall. Most communications from the councillors were form letters sent to the entire lieutenancy, and even these were infrequent. In peacetime, the annual volume of letter traffic could easily be only *a* letter, and some years passed without any communication at all. A direct letter to a Lord Lieutenant about specific problems was rarer still, much to the frustration of the local governors. In three decades of service, Huntingdon was to receive roughly a dozen private letters from the Council, and given their rarity, he understandably prized them. Communication with Whitehall was often as peculiar as it was erratic. Although the Council actually administered the realm for the monarch, a host of fundamental bureaucratic problems generally thwarted the smooth execution of this goal. Brian Quintrell has neatly summarised the difficulties; the Council, he noted,

> had developed little or no notion of 'policy' in any modern sense, and had difficulty enough in keeping its various lines of action untangled and not actively working against each other ... Its correspondence with a county on any subject tended to reveal a lack of continuous attention, as though with each letter the Councillor were coming to the matter for the first time.[3]

Consequently, the intellectual distance between Lieutenants and councillor often exceeded their actual physical separation.

Isolation from the centre only exacerbated a more fundamental problem. When Huntingdon issued orders, he did so with questionable legality. His warrants sounded as if they were in accordance with the 1558 Militia Act, which, as late as 1639, Huntingdon was still solemnly invoking. Unfortunately, in 1604 Parliament had repealed that measure, only to fail to pass an alternative, and later sessions regularly attempted to remedy the problem, all to no avail.[4] Consequently, the success of a county militia depended in no small part on the Lieutenant's prestige and reputation.

Fortunately for Henry Hastings, anxiety over his pedigree never troubled his sleep. By any reckoning, the fifth Earl of Huntingdon, the tenth Lord Botreux, the ninth Lord Hungerford, the seventh Lord Hastings and Moleyns, the Lieutenant of the Forest of Leicester, the Steward and Receiver of the Honour of Leicester in the Duchy of Lancaster, the Custos Rotulorum of Leicestershire and Lord Lieutenant of Leicestershire and Rutland had prestige to spare. Not only did his earldom date from 1529, but one of his baronies stretched back to 1368 when Edward III ennobled one of Huntingdon's ancestors. If anything, his immediate family was still more distinguished. His brother-in-law was the Earl of Chesterfield, and the roll of his first cousins included the Earls of Lincoln, Manchester and Northampton as well as Lucy, the Countess of Bedford. For uncles he had to make do with the Earl of Worcester and Lord Harington. Meanwhile after his father's premature death, his mother had quickly remarried a succession of courtiers, first Lord Zouche and finally Sir Thomas Edmondes. Huntingdon's wife, Elizabeth Stanley, added further lustre along with brothers-in-law, the Earl of Bridgewater and Lord Chandos, and with uncles, the Earl of Derby and Lord Spencer. With ample reason, Huntingdon advised his son not to worry about a potential bride's pedigree, since he was 'descended from noble and honorable parents and allied to most of the nobilitie either by me or thy mother'.[5]

The advantages of such an immediate family were obvious. The early Stuart literary world had no better guide than the Countess of Bedford, who presided over an entourage of poets and playwrights, among them Ben Jonson, John Donne and Michael Drayton.[6] Financial shortfalls were nothing more than temporary embarrassments with the assistance of Lord Spencer, one of the wealthiest men on the island. Inside legal advice flowed readily from no less than the Lord Chancellor himself; Huntingdon's mother-in-law remarried Lord Ellesmere, and she was not above slipping her son-in-law confidential information from the king's chief legal officer. In any dealings with the central government, Huntingdon was admirably well connected. Worcester was Lord Privy Seal, Zouche Lord Warden of the Cinque Ports, Edmondes Treasurer of the Household, while Chandos and Northampton were successive Presidents of the Council of Wales. On the Privy Council itself, his relatives almost singlehanded formed a quorum; Bridgewater, Edmondes, Harington, Worcester and Zouche were members, while Manchester presided over it as Lord President. Well might Huntingdon habitually hail his kin with the observation that 'that howse hath the greatest assurance of continuance that hath most branches'.[7]

The family's blood line also had more than a touch of royalty. Huntingdon could choose whether he fancied claiming descent from the Plantagenets or the Tudors. Four of Edward III's sons produced heirs, and from each of them Huntingdon could claim direct descent. Consequently, during the Tudors' succession problems, contemporaries looked to the Hastings as possible heirs. Royal kinship of course was dangerous as well as flattering; it took the third earl several years of vigorously denying any claim to the throne before Elizabeth decided to employ him. The fifth earl's marriage succeeded only in tightening the royal affinity, for Elizabeth Stanley's grandfather had married the granddaughter of Mary Tudor, Queen of France and Duchess of Suffolk.[8]

Friendship as much as blood lines tied Huntingdon to the ruling dynasty. The first Lord Harington served as the governor of James I's daughter, and Huntingdon's intimacy with his great-uncle can be seen in the fact that the future earl was born at the Harington country house at Exton Park. This relationship also afforded Huntingdon unparalleled opportunities to meet the young Princess Elizabeth. The passage of time did little to dim the memory of this early relationship, for the Countess of Bedford remained her close friend, and another Harington cousin long served as one of her ladies-in-waiting.[9] The Harington connection also brought the young earl into contact with Prince Henry, whose intimate friend was another cousin, the second Lord Harington. This friendship blossomed, until by 1610 it was only natural for the young fifth earl to have held Henry's train during his investiture as Prince of Wales.[10] In short, when the peerage seemed almost overwhelmed with 'court mushrooms', there was little danger of mistaking Huntingdon for a parvenu.

In addition to a distinguished pedigree, the earl's political stance reduced the likelihood of a challenge even further. At the beginning of the Thirty Years War, Huntingdon was one of those sympathetic to 'the Protestant cause', committed to the defence of the godly abroad, 'the ancient constitution' at home and colonial expansion overseas. Intimately involved with the Virginia Company, his labours to recruit skilled settlers, among them military engineers, earned him the thanks of the Company and a place on the Council for Virginia.[11] Given this interest, it only followed that he should have been involved with the Guinea expedition in 1617–18; the earl lent Raleigh some cannon from Ashby Castle as well as his younger brother, Edward Hastings, who captained a vessel and died on the voyage.[12]

These activities were hardly surprising, since devotion to the 'Protestant cause' practically defined the earl's friends. Admittedly thorny problems at Whitehall sometimes made Huntingdon work through his Catholic uncle, the Earl of Worcester, 'a good courtier and a suer solicitor'. A more likely intermediary was the third Earl of Pembroke, to whom Huntingdon turned when he lobbied for the lieutenancy of Rutland or when he wished to be excused for a parliamentary session. When the Lord Chamberlain politely replied that 'I think my self very happy' that Huntingdon 'is pleased to commanded me to doe you any service', it is more likely that the happiness was entirely that of Pembroke's provincial cousin.[13] Huntingdon was equally close to the third Earl of Southampton. A frequent stop on the earl's journeys to London was Titchfield

House, the Wriothesleys' country house, where Huntingdon left behind almost £30 after a particularly long card game in 1619. The legacy of these visits
can be seen in the joking familiarity of the letters which Huntingdon received
from Southampton and his protégé, Sir Edwin Sandys.[14] Naturally enough,
when Huntingdon had to leave his proxy in the Lords, it went either to
Southampton or to Pembroke.[15] Among his fellow peers, the Earls of Warwick
and Essex and Viscount Saye and Sele were frequent guests at his table.
Friendship and common interests even brought Huntingdon and Essex on
the stage together when local gentlemen and their ladies performed a masque
mocking upstarts at court and celebrating the homely virtues of 'honest Harrie
of Ashbie' and 'Bonny Bob of Lichfield'.[16] Binding all of these men together
was Huntingdon's cousin, the Countess of Bedford, who entertained him at
her London town house.[17] Such public friendships made it easy for contemporaries to place Huntingdon among the pro-war 'patriots' of the 1620s.

Huntingdon's exemplary piety and morals only bolstered his standing in
an age where dissolute peers were all too common. In his youth, a capacity for
self-control was already so apparent that his elder cousin, Sir John Holles,
later the Earl of Clare, reckoned that the young man ran no risk of acquiring
the 'multitudes of villanies' which often came from the grand tour. Indeed,
such worldly temptations would do the young man good, since 'he hath
already too much water in his wine and needs rather the sunshine than the
shade'.[18] In the event, continental influences were never allowed to soften his
dignified and reserved manner. Yet a personality which a courtier might well
have found tedious was ideally suited to a local governor. A bout of youthful
extravagance in the royal entourage left him profoundly dubious about cosmo-
politan sophistication. He urged his son 'to spend the major parte of thy life in
the Country where thou shall receive more pleasure better contentment, be
respected and doe greater good then to live in this glittering miserie' at court.
To be sure, he cultivated his contacts at Whitehall; as he explained to his son,
'the most parte of the world' will 'esteeme thee as thou hast power to doe them
good or hurt', and that power 'must grow cheifely from the kinges favoure
towards thee'. Yet this necessity did not mean he liked these visits, and he
certainly never lingered there. In later years, the battle against the allure of
Whitehall, which he himself won early on, was one which he had to wage all
over again with his eldest son. Here, too, he was implacable, all of his arguments being variations of the line: 'I should bee sory that you should like a
Courte life'.[19]

Instead, he revelled in the life of a local magnate whose house was open to a
steady stream of visitors. His hospitality attracted eminent guests; in 1603,
Huntingdon entertained Queen Anne and Prince Henry, and in 1612, 1614
and 1617 the king himself. Yet the majority of his guests were the local
gentlemen, whose well-being the earl made his *raison d'être*. These gatherings

rarely got out of control, thanks to his insistence on nothing more than a glass of wine with dinner. So too did a willingness to endure squires who often could

> talke of nothinge but subsidies, the provision of pettie penal Statutes for the punishing of Roagues, feedinge of Oxen or Sheepe, manuringe of land or the changes of the seasons that thinges are deare or cheape.

Painful though such conversations were, Huntingdon always sought to turn them to more important matters; thus

> he to whom thou hast spoke unto may see thou diddest discend unto his discourse in respect of his Affections and yet thou have abilitie to talke of better will make him more careful to educate their own children.[20]

What further increased the desire for education was the fact that the Muses had taken up residence at Donnington Park. Local poets like Thomas Pestell, William Sampson and Thomas Bancroft found the earl and countess generous patrons.[21] So did more celebrated authors like John Marston, John Fletcher, and John Donne, who each hymned the idyllic existence in the Charnwood. The warm reception which they had received made Sir Thomas Roe, while on his Indian embassy, long to return to Donnington Park, where he promised to arrive well 'stored with discourse for two Christmases, to talk out candles and fires and all patience'.[22]

This grave exterior was only an extension of Huntingdon's religious beliefs. At first glance, shameless flattery apparently overwhelmed any trace of reality in Edward Vaughan's fulsome praise of Huntingdon as 'an example unto others for the diligent hering of Gods holy word preched and for the sincere receiving of the Sacrament'.[23] In this case, however, abundant evidence confirms Vaughan's assessment.

The best means of establishing Huntingdon's religious beliefs is to chart his attitudes towards Rome and Geneva. In sharp contrast with some courtiers, Huntingdon did not regard recusancy as an idle theological eccentricity. He refused to call them Catholics, since 'that Title' he insisted 'iustly belonges unto us'. When other more ecumenical souls argued for tacit, if not outright, toleration, the earl found comfort in 'a iust and Honorable lawe which doth make it high Treason for theise unnaturall Vipers to live in the Bowells of their Country'. Given his attitude to the penal laws, James's decision to suspend the operation of that 'iust and Honorable lawe' in 1622 naturally prompted the dejected peer to compose 'A short mediation uppon the ill newes of a Tolleration'. The king's action left him in 'a labathinth [sic] of feares'; since these indicated that 'thy Image is departinge from us', Huntingdon could interpret them only as a sure sign of 'thy displeasure and our destruction'.[24] Easily the most salient aspect of his religion, therefore, was his aversion to the old faith.

Such intolerance did not extend to puritans. Quite carefully he cautioned his son about the use of the name 'puritan'; it was, he warned,

> a reprocheful name given them ether by the Papists that doe hate all ministers exceptinge their owne and seeing the Kinge doth dislike them would under this ... [*page torn*] bringe religion into contempt, or [by] Atheistes or men extreamely vitious that think everie man that will not be drunke, sweare, lye, whore, is a Puritan.

The clearest evidence of these beliefs in practice comes from St Helen's, Ashby de la Zouch, where the earl's ancestors rested. There the long-time incumbent was Arthur Hildesham, the sometime Nonconformist preacher who had attracted James's personal disfavour. Huntingdon, who held the presentation of Hildesham's living, declined to support efforts to turn him out. Admittedly Hildesham was the earl's distant relation, but the political costs of sustaining him were considerable, as Archbishop Abbot himself warned the earl. Huntingdon's support, however, never wavered, and in Hildesham's last book, the aged minister offered 'public testimony unto the world of my duty and thankfulness unto your honour, and unto your noble house'. Others anxious for the earl's patronage could think of no better recommendation of their godly credentials than Hildesham's support. Given Huntingdon's attitude, it is no wonder that the godly community in Leicestershire flourished. Hence later in the 1620s when Laudian critics of Bishop Williams sought evidence of his loose administration of the far-flung diocese of Lincoln, they knew where to find it; one report concluded that 'if there were not such disorderly preaching in Lincolnshire, yet ther was in Leicestershire'.[25]

A leniency towards puritans did nothing to erode his fundamental devotion to the Church of England. A good deal of his wife's meditations, for example, involved pleas for enough divine grace to ensure that 'I may be acknowledged for one of thy elect when I shall appeare before thy iudgment Seat'. This much Huntingdon was willing to share with more extreme members of the godly, he refused to argue over what he regarded as non-essential aspects of theology. 'As for the dissention amongst ourselves,' he explained to his son, 'it is not about the fundamentall and materiall pointes, but thinges of indifferencie and ceremonie which would to God they had never bene broched.' In the category of 'indifferent things in the power of the kinge either to comand or to prohibite as he pleases' the earl placed 'the Cappe and Surplusse, ... The Croasse in Baptisme, Ringes in matrimonie, kneelinge at the receivinge of the Sacramentt' as well as the episcopacy itself. All of these were 'indifferent thinges in them selves, yet being commanded it is a sinne not to conforme unto them'.[26] These attitudes placed the earl among those contemporaries who were moderate Calvinist conformists.

His personal manners and piety clearly reflected his piety. For alcohol he had no use, aside from a glass or two of wine with meals; servants who required more were brusquely dismissed. Clothes for him were simply useful, and even when visiting court, his son was advised to wear only 'neate though not costly' apparel. Meanwhile his conversation, although gracious and polite, verged on the taciturn: as he told lord Hastings, 'let thy words be vera, rara et ponderosa'. If such an austere lifestyle failed to restrain his son's emotions, then the earl suggested 'macking walkes and water courses' as well as indulging in bowls and riding.[27] With this carefully controlled existence went decidedly Calvinist interests. Huntingdon's detailed parliamentary diaries make it clear that the topics most likely to persuade this reserved man to speak were generally religious. While an increasing number of his fellow peers were bored with the traditional godly legislative agenda, Huntingdon was not. In 1614, he carefully prepared reports on non-resident ministers; after the 1624 session, his list of pressing Bills gave pride of place to one to augment clerical salaries and to another to protect the Sabbath; and in 1628 when the Lords discussed the appropriate punishment for Dr Montague, the idea of burning his books came from Huntingdon. Not surprisingly, the only text of a proposed Bill in the extensive Hastings MSS was one against pluralities.[28] While all of these issues deeply concerned him, Sabbatarianism obsessed him. After returning one Sunday morning from an all-night card game, a brush with death on a wild horse left him firmly opposed to any 'Bodily Exercise' except those 'which necessitie compells and holines commaunds'. 'Necessitie' did not even include an order from the Privy Council. In their panic over a possible invasion in 1626, the councillors mandated intensive militia drills on all holidays and 'holy days'. In relaying the order to his captains, Huntingdon unilaterally amended the command to read: on all holidays and 'holy days (except Sundaies)'.[29]

Secular manifestations of his faith, which were all too easy to find, help account for the county's deference to him. No improving landlord enamoured of rack rents, Huntingdon dealt with his tenants fairly; indeed, his grandson in the 1670s was still complaining about his preference for a grateful tenantry over his own prosperity. For the earl, peace among the county elite was equally important; hence he was quick to intervene in local quarrels to arrange reconciliations. Likewise after the revival of the Grey–Hastings feud, Huntingdon strove to ensure that the old enmity would not return. Consequently, when Lord Grey, later the Earl of Stamford, came of age in the mid-1620s, the fresh memory of 'hart burning, disgraces, crossings and old factions' led Huntingdon to co-opt rather than to isolate him. In 1625, in his eagerness for reconciliation, he appointed his potential rival to the politically sensitive post of Deputy Lieutenant.[30] The result was a golden age of harmony between the two families.

His zeal for tranquillity and harmony also extended to the lower orders. Poor families overwhelmed by tragic accidents regularly found Huntingdon quick to organise a contribution for their relief.[31] His concern readily embraced old cottagers involved in law suits in London; in one case, the earl asked the judges to transfer a suit to Leicester, since the defendants 'are soe very aged that they cannot possibly travel thither without danger of their lives'. The same kindness can be found in his Christmas presents: along with the great and the powerful were entries for 'a poore old man, a cake and some apples and peares' and for a 'poore man, some oringes, lemans and one pomegrant'. Benevolent paternalism also guided him at the quarter sessions. 'Althoughe the Common people be very tedious in their speech', he cautioned his son that 'thou must indure it'; otherwise glib country lawyers would always carry the day. The expeditious resolution of cases was equally important, lest delays make 'a Poore mans heart bleede ... being unable by reason of theire poore estate to lye at siege with their adversaries'. Even when delivering a severe sentence, Huntingdon advocated acting 'to be afflected and trobled, for that will make the partie delinquent beare a miserablenes of fortune the better though he smarte for it'.[32] Plainly, the earl must have encouraged obedience as much as he demanded it.

Equally important was his attitude to Whitehall. Unlike those courtier Lieutenants whose responsibilities were more an honour than a duty, Huntingdon took his seriously. He presided over the county not from Whitehall, but from his seat at Donnington Park, and his travels rarely took him outside of the east Midlands, where personal and family memories surrounded him. Paramount among these was that of his grand-uncle and namesake, the third earl, Elizabeth's long-time Lord President of the North. The celebrated 'Puritan' earl had taken his grand-nephew into his household at York to instil notions of piety and duty, which were to guide his later life. Yet even if he had sought to flee from this spiritual inheritance, he would have found it hard to avoid the third earl. Admirers of the Lord Lieutenant regularly compared him with 'your Renowned Unkle', and with equal regularity, in his dealings with Whitehall, Huntingdon cited his predecessor's labours on the Crown's behalf. In fact, literally dominating the Leicester Town Hall, the stage for much of the political drama of Huntingdon's life, was a large portrait of the third earl and a fulsome statement of the town's gratitude.[33]

Thoroughly local roots and a worthy role-model led ineluctably to an admirable stance as Lord Lieutenant. In his efforts to equal his great-uncle's achievements, Huntingdon was eager to earn distinction as one of the monarch's most efficient Lieutenants. As he reminded Charles I in 1627, 'I have ever been carefull to doe my dewtie'. Thus when the Council in 1625 praised his administration as 'an Example for other Counties to followe', he prized the citation as a talisman. At the same time, he was not willing to earn distinction at Whitehall at the expense of his neighbours and tenants. His administrative credo therefore was that 'the world shall see that I make every mans burden as light as may be so as I preserve the king's service'.[34] Those anxious about the central government overburdening the shire can only have found comfort in such an equitable local governor at the helm.

The war years represented the greatest challenge to Huntingdon's balancing act. War allowed a local governor to rise in central government's opinion. At the same time, it could also diminish his standing with the local gentlemen, whose highest goal was for the government, whether national or provincial, to leave them and their revenues alone. At times, the earl was not above bullying the county into line. Defaulters often learned not so much of the Council's displeasure as of Huntingdon's wrath; on Huntingdon's express command, the Deputies frequently informed the wayward 'how ill I shall take it of them that are deficient herein which cannot but make me conceive that they doe litle valewe me'. Benevolent co-option, however, was generally more apparent than ruthless coercion. In the county elections, for example, he always strove to name one, if not both, of the MPs, but his selection was far from arbitrary. 'I wilbe very careful,' he assured the electors in 1625, 'to nominate such a one unto them as shalbe fitting ... both for his religion, wisdom and estate and such a one as may best be accommodated to doe the Cuntrie service.'[35]

Huntingdon, in short, represented almost the archetype of the ideal local magnate. On this contemporary poets concurred, from the lamentable efforts of Mary Fage, praising the earl as a star 'Neere to our radiant Sol', to the polished rhymes of Robert Herrick, who observed that it was enough to say that 'He was an Hastings, and that one Name has/In it all Good that is, and ever was.' Such a venerable worthy understandably left behind a potent memory as 'a person of Greate honor or vertue and Temperance, and that conscientiously on a true sense of religion'. Years later it was still recalled how he had chosen as his motto 'Honorantes mee honorabo, intimating that those only should bee esteemed by him who did faithfully Honor God'.[36] With such a local governor as 'honest Harrie of Ashby', it was likely to be unnecessary as well as dangerous to challenge his authority.

NOTES

1 [Instructions to his staff], HAP 14/18; and 'Certaine Directions', HAP 15/8, [fol. 13].

2 H's lieutenancy commission, *LRLB*, fols. 1–2v. For the following chapter, I am indebted to Victor Stater, *Noble Government*, pp. 8–31.

3 Brian Quintrell, 'Government in Perspective: Lancashire and the Privy Council, 1570–1640', *THSLC* CXXXI (1981), pp. 40–1. See also Derek Hirst, 'The Privy Council and the Problem òf Enforcement in the 1620s', *JBS* XVIII (1978), pp. 46–66.

4 A. Hassell Smith, 'Militia Rates and Militia Statutes, 1558–1663', *The English Commonwealth*, ed. by Peter Clarke *et al.*, (New York, 1979), pp. 93–110. On the late use of the

statute, see H's charge to the session, 8 January 1639, HAM 26/6.

5 'Certaine Directions', HAP 15/8, fol. [5Av]. On the family tree, see *The Complete Peerage* under Derby, Worcester, Harington, Lincoln, Bridgewater, Chandos, Spencer and Huntingdon; and Barry Coward, *The Stanleys, Lords Stanley and Earls of Derby* (Manchester, 1983), pp. 41–55.

6 On the visits, see 'The Booke of my Lordes expences', 1619, HAF 8/4 [unfoliated]. See also Barbara Lewalski, 'Lucy, Countess of Bedford: Images of a Jacobean Countess and Patroness', *Politics of Discourse*, ed. by K. Sharpe and S. Zwicker (Berkeley, 1987), pp. 52–77.

7 'A note of such money', 1614, HAF 11/7 [unfoliated]; Countess of Derby to Huntingdon, 18 February 1614, HA Corr. 7/2513; and 'Certaine Directions', HAP 15/8, fol. [18Av]. See also L. Knafla, *Law and Politics in Jacobean England* (Cambridge, 1977), pp. 32–4.

8 For the Hastings claim to the throne, a late sixteenth-century genealogy, HA Genealogy 2/12; and Cross, *Puritan Earl*, pp. 142–7.

9 M. A. Everrett-Green (with revisions by S. C. Loomis), *Elizabeth Queen of Bohemia* (London, 1909), pp. 4–120; and Harington to H, 1 January and 2 February 1636, HA Corr. 15/13,875 and 13,876.

10 Roy Strong, *Henry, Prince of Wales* (London, 1986), pp. 42–4; and 'Relation of the Formalities', 10 June 1610, *HMC Downshire*, II, p. 316.

11 See, for example, the Company's resolution at the General Court, 28 June 1620, *The Records of the Virginia Company of London* (Washington, 1906), I, pp. 383; 'the names of some of the adventurers', [1610–11]; and H's letter of attorney to Nicolas Martiau, 5 April 1620, HA Americana 1/1 and 1/5; and H to Martiau, 8 July 1624; Martiau to H, [1626?], and 12 December 1628, HA 10/5486, 12/9169 and 13/9170. See also J. B. Stoudt, *Nicolas Martiau* (Norristown, Pa., 1932), pp. 5–22.

12 V. T. Harlow, *Raleigh's Last Voyage* (London, 1932), pp. 148, 151–2, 156, 159 and 161; and Council to Carew, 23 May 1619, 21 February 1620, 20 December 1621, *APC XXXVI*, p. 457; XXXVII, p. 137; and XXXVIII, p. 105.

13 Montague to H, 28 January 1613; and Pembroke to ECH, 22 August [?1616–30], HA Corr. 7/9343 and 6732. See H to Pembroke, 2 March 1614, 4 August 1634; and Pembroke to H, 6 October 1616, HA Corr. 7/5445; 14/5536; and 7/6731.

14 Entries at Titchfield, 'The Booke of my Lordes expences', 1619, HAF 8/4 [unfoliated]; and Southampton to ECH, n.d.; and Sandys to H, 11 January 1620, HA Corr. 11/13,684 and 8/10,673. On their relationship, see C. C. Stopes, *The Life of Henry, Earl of Southampton* (Cambridge, 1922), p. 428.

15 H to Southampton, 18 February 1624, HA Parliament 2/1; and same to Pembroke, 28 June 1625 and 15 February 1626, HA Corr. 11/5501 and 12/5510.

16 'Mr. Robies Accompts' [the earl's table], April–July 1628, HAF 8/36, see entries for 3 May, 9 and 18 June; and the Coleorton masque, cited in Rudolf Brotanek, *Die Englischen Maskenpiele* (Vienna, 1902), p. 330. See also Gordon McMullan, *The Politics of Uneuse* (Amherst, 1994), p. 30.

17 See, for example, ECH to H, 18 January [1627], HA Corr. 12/4839; and Bedford to Cornwallis, 9 September [1914], *The Private Letters of Jane Lady Cornwallis* (London, 1842), p. 24. On their relation with Bedford, see S. L. Adams, 'Foreign Policy and the Parliaments of 1621 and 1624', in *Faction and Parliament*, ed. by K. Sharpe (Oxford, 1978), pp. 143–4.

18 Holles to GEH, February 1603, *HMC Portland* IX, p. 79.

19 'Certaine Directions', HAP 15/8, fol. 7v–7A; and H to FEH, 23 January 1627, HA Corr. 12/5515.

20 'Certaine Directions', HAP 15/8, fol. 17v. See also J. Nichols, *The Progresses of James I*, I, p. 170; II, pp. 22, 421 and 458*; and 'Remembrances ... to my Lorde's officers and servantes', printed in Nichols, *History and Antiquities*, III, p. 597.

21 Thomas Bancroft, *Epigrammes and Epitaphs* (London, 1640); *The Poems of Thomas Pestell*, ed. by Hannah Buchan, (Oxford, 1940); and William Sampson, *Virtus Post Funera Vivit* (London, 1636).

22 Roe to ECH, 30 October 1616, HA 7/10561. See also John Marston, 'The Entertainment of the Dowager Countess of Derby', *The Poems of John Marston* (Liverpool, 1961), pp. 189–207; John Donne, 'To the Countess of Huntingdon' (Man to Gods Image), and 'To the Countess of Huntingdon' (That unripe side of earth), *The Complete English Poems* (London, 1983), pp. 236–41; and John Fletcher's poem to the countess, [early 1620s], HA Corr. 12/13,333; McMullan, *The Politics of Unease*, pp. 1–36; and James Knowles's forthcoming work on Huntingdon's literary circle.

23 Edward Vaughan, *A Divine Discoverie of Death* (London, 1612), sig. [A2v].

24 'Certaine Directions', HAP 15/8, fol. 1v; [Treatise on Recusancy], HA Religious 3/2, [fol. 1]; and 'A short mediation', HA Religious 1/14.

25 Arthur Hildersham, *CVIII Lectures on the Fourth of John* (London, 1629), dedication; and 'For the Lord Keeper and the Lord President', November 1627, SP 16/84/27. See also Cross, *The Puritan Earl*, pp. 141–2; and C. E. Welch, 'Early Nonconformity in Leicestershire', *TLAHS*, XXXVII (1961–62), pp. 29–43.

26 'Certaine Collections of the ... Countess of Huntingdon', HEH Bridgewater MSS, El 6871, fols. 2v and 10v; and 'Certaine Directions', HAP 15/8, fols. 1v–2.

27 'Certaine Directions', HAP 15/8, fols. 4v, [8Av] and 18.

28 'The names of those that have pluralities', 14 April 1640; and 'A Bill ... against Nonresidents', HA Religious 1/12 and 1/4; 13 June, *PP 1628* V, p. 637; and 'Remembrances against the Parliament', 13 October 1624, Bodleian Library, Carte 77, fol. 272.

29 'Certaine Directions', HAP 15/8, fol. 3; and PC to H; and H to PC, 24 June 1626, *LRLB*, fols. 162 and 162v.

30 'Observations concerning T[heophilus] H[astings] undigested', Bodleian Library, Carte 78, fol. 411; and Spencer to H, 10 January 1624, HA Corr. 10/12541. See, for example, his handling of the Herrick–Danvers quarrel, 'My lord Huntingdon's order', 12 September [1622], Bodleian Library, MS Eng. Hist. C.476, [Herrick MSS], fol. 46–50.

31 See, for example, H's letters on behalf of Robert Beccles of Bagworth and of Masson Packington, 28 December 1618 and December 1623, HAM 53/10.

32 H to [the Judges], 5 March 1619, HAM 25/10; under Loughborough, 'New Yeres guifts sent', 1629, HAF 9/8 [unfoliated]; and 'Certaine Directions', HAP 15/8, fol. 13–[13av].

33 Francis Markham, *The Booke of Honour* (London, 1625), p. 85; and Cross, *The Puritan Earl*, p. 129. See also H to Middlesex, 18 September 1623, Bodleian Library, Carte 77, fol. 286; Davies to H, 22 July 1624, HA Corr. 10/1929; and Hildersham, *CVIII Lectures*, dedication.

34 H to PC, 14 June 1627, SP 16/67/2; and H to Staresmore, 6 July 1625, *LRLB*, fol. 127–7v.

35 H to DLs, 9 March 1619, *LRLB*, fols. 43v–44; and H to Wright, 1 April 1625, HA Corr. 11/5499.

36 Mary Fage, *Fame Roule* (London, 1637), p. 19; *Lachrymae Musarum* (London, 1649), p. 38; [William Dugdale], 'Observations', Bodleian Library, Carte 78, fol. 411.

Chapter 2

'More trouble than heretofore'
The county and
the demands of war

The anxiety overcame the Mayor and aldermen of Leicester early in 1619. Since their Recorder, Francis Harvey, was in London on business, they urgently requested his advice about Huntingdon's recent order 'for Mustering and trayning'. The gravity of the situation soon overcame their customary parsimony, and they resolved that they would rather listen to Harvey's counsel than to read it; hence, notwithstanding the expense, they requested his immediate presence. On the way, he was to ponder such questions as 'what nomber of Trayned Souldyars and howe many monie the Leifetenants hadd of them and howe many they trayned' as well as the comparative size of the Northamptonshire regiment. Subsequent consultations with Harvey eventually emboldened the Corporation to risk a confrontation with the earl. A delegation duly rode out to Ashby de la Zouch well armed with legal precedents, handsome gifts, and the Mayor's lamentations: 'there is like to bee more trouble ... then heretofore hath bene'.[1]

The Corporation's agitation illustrates the visceral impact of the central government's new demands after 1618, and if the rest of the county ratepayers did not yet share the dismay of the Mayor and his brethren, they soon would. Nevertheless, in this end, Huntingdon eventually soothed rattled nerves and cajoled his neighbours into shouldering most, if not all, of the state's new burdens. In order to understand this process, the present chapter will analyse Whitehall's requirements as well as the earl's powers of persuasion.

BENEVOLENCES AND SUBSIDIES

The most noticeable change which the continental war brought on Leicestershire was that schemes to collect large amounts of money became an almost ubiquitous feature of life. The best means of appreciating how the county reacted to these new demands is to follow the county elite as they pressed into the Leicester Town Hall to hear an important address in July 1620. For a person as reserved as Huntingdon, public speaking did not come easily, and in the preceding years he had had little incentive to correct this deficiency. Yet in 1620 he found his voice. What had stiffened his resolve was the voluntary benevolence, which James I in April 1620 had authorised Baron von Dohna, the Bohemian ambassador, to collect across the realm. Hitherto, historians have scarcely noticed this appeal. S. R. Gardiner simply noted that the initial expectations of raising £100,000 had by May proven wildly optimistic, and given the lamentations of Dohna's treasurer that 'wee want money', later scholars have felt content with Gardiner's fleeting coverage of the levy. But there was far more to the story. Only at the end of May did Dohna's appeal even begin in the counties outside London.[2] Admittedly, the money came in slowly, but it did come in, and the amounts were far from notional. If it had been otherwise, then James I would not have consciously modelled his own Bohemian benevolence later in the year on that of Dohna. Unfortunately the reason for the comparative success of the campaign also explains the historiographical lacuna: the money entirely bypassed the Exchequer and its record-keeping personnel. Enough has survived elsewhere, however, to reveal that the reaction of the Lord Lieutenant largely determined the size of the county's yield. Some like the Marquis of Buckingham in Buckinghamshire or the aged Lord Chandos in Gloucestershire merely went through the motions.[3] Others, like the Earl of Southampton in Hampshire and Lord Zouche in the Cinque Ports, placed their full weight behind the appeal.[4] The best example of a sedulous Lord Lieutenant, however, can be found in Leicestershire.

The news of the Princess Elizabeth's involvement in the widening conti-nental war produced an almost Pavlovian response in Huntingdon, who prized a gift from her as a quasi-sacred relic. Dohna's letter on her behalf led him to construct a careful campaign across the two shires in his charge. First, he instructed the constables to ensure the attendance of all worth more than £40 a year at one of three meetings in Leicester, Ashby and Rutland. Nor was he in any mood to humour slackers, whom local officials were to report. To encourage local co-operation, he relayed the late-breaking news of 'what Darbyshire hath done'. There, some gentlemen had offered £50 outright, and others volunteered £100 over five years. Their generosity had prompted equal liberality from the common sort, down to 'the lowest Condition', who offered 10s. To second the impact of such propaganda, he and his deputies conspired with some leading gentlemen so that 'those that will express themselves in the bountifullest manner doe make offer first whose example the rest may be the better encouraged'.[5] Nothing in short was left to chance.

Huntingdon's address was worthy of such elaborate preparation. Although he had spoken to the county on other occasions, he assured his audience that Dohna's appeal was 'a business of a higher nature and of far greater moment'.

Then after reading the envoy's letter and asking for a generous donation, the earl pressed on. Since 'by many hands else the matter is brought to you', he thought it better to refute 'certayne Cimericall obiections spunne by ill affections' than to outline the situation in the Palatinate. The request for funds did not have parliamentary approval, but he begged his hearers to consider that 'the celerity of a warr canot stay the formality that soe greate a Councill as a Parliament will require'. Lest fear of potential illegality check their generosity, Huntingdon stressed that not only had all the Lords Lieutenant endorsed this action, but 'the right Reverend Judges have brooke the ice ... by their bountyes'. Moreover, the money would not disappear into James's coffers, but would proceed direct to Dohna. Nor would this levy intensify the crippling shortage of coin: 'this money is not to goe out of the kingdom but to supply such thinges as the Marchants shall have order to doe'. Reasoning then gave way to exhortation; 'you have examples in all the four corners of the earth and of all conditions above you equall with you and beneath you Noble men Bishops Judges knights gentlemen and Minors soe as you cannot be sadde for want of Company'. But in their gifts, he warned them to have an eye on the contributions from other shires; since equalling their levels would 'make noe greate report', he exhorted them to 'excell and goe beyonde them' and so 'adde to the greatnes of your fame'. Finally, for those who had written off Frederick's cause as hopeless, he reminded them of the recent rain which had just averted a drought. 'The glorious carpet of the earth as it were wrought with many collors' should make them aware of the fact that 'then is his mercy nearest us when with the eyes of our understandinge wee apprehend the least hopes'.[6]

In the extensive material on Huntingdon, there is no finer example of such logic and lyricism. His performance so moved the Mayor and aldermen that this normally tight-fisted group seconded their personal contributions with a gift from the Corporation. Such early success led to no relaxation of effort as the earl scrutinised the pledges to spot meagre contributions. Those who objected to an increase found themselves confronted with their subsidy assessments, a manoeuvre which persuaded some, like Sir Maurice Berkeley, to add another £20.[7] Notwithstanding such methods, the total disappointed Huntingdon, who apologised for it in his final report to Dohna. Yet in fact Huntingdon had achieved wonders, for with some prodding, Leicestershire and Rutland paid in £1,578. By comparison, the two subsidies voted in 1621 barely produced £1,510. Hence, in little more than a year in 1620-21, the shire paid the equivalent of four subsidies on behalf of the Palatine cause.[8] On a national level, Leicestershire's payments were more striking; Hampshire and Surrey, both more populous and wealthy, contributed £2,717 and £1,166 respectively. All things considered, the gentlemen of the shire had offered up an impressive gift for 'a great branch of the Imperiall Crowne', while the earl had fulfilled 'my obliged duty and religion which hath taught me alwayes to recommend their Majesties prosperous estates in my best prayers'.[9]

The requirements of duty and religion did have distinct limits. For Huntingdon and many others, Dohna's levy was acceptable because, after this emergency measure, Parliament was responsible for later funding. The earl's devotion to this principle was not pious rhetoric. When faced with demands for extraparliamentary taxation, other local governors followed a handy maxim: 'be not hastie to pay: let yours come last in of anie other'. Huntingdon had developed a similar approach. First, he always dragged his feet until he learned 'what they doe in other counties nere us'. Then, it was simply a matter of discovering 'the lowest some that he [the king] desires'. Occasionally Huntingdon erred on the side of caution as he had in 1614 when the county's contribution of £400 had offended the councillors. Yet in the 1620s, these twin principles of procrastination and parsimony guided the shire through these awkward appeals with a minimum of aggravation.[10]

When James first launched his own Bohemian benevolence late in 1620, Leicestershire did nothing, and the opening of the 1621 Parliament soon excused the administrative sloth. But when the parliamentary dissolution revived the campaign, Huntingdon this time remained on the sidelines, allowing his Deputies to go through the motions. Months of desultory appeals produced some pledges; a few towns promised as much as a full subsidy, and Leicester almost £100. Yet even these modest results brought forth, not any payment, but rather the bench's plea for more time.[11] Only in 1623 did any money reached the Exchequer and then only in the trifling amount of £181, the bulk of which came from Sir William Cockaine, the London financier who owned land in Leicestershire.[12] Huntingdon ran true to form in the Privy Seal loans of 1625–27. After stalling for months, he eventually submitted the schedule of proposed 1614 contributions, which the councillors found so low that they unilaterally doubled them.[13] Even this arbitrary action failed to produce results. Only in May 1626 did William Ive, a Leicester merchant, receive a reward of £8 18s. 9d. for acting as 'collector of loane upon privy Seale'. The Exchequer records are erratic for the preceding period, but since other collectors routinely were given 6d. out of every £1 collected, Mr Ive apparently prodded the county into paying approximately £360.[14]

Both levies together paid in about £500. In their attempt to explain such meagre yields in 1622, the JPs frankly confessed that 'wee finde it by experience that whatsoever cometh from them in any sorte by waie of guyfte is procured with extreame difficultie'. Their assessment was of course only partially correct, for in 1620 the county gave Frederick and Elizabeth three times as much as the county paid in for both of these extraparliamentary levies. The difference in the yields cannot justly be ascribed to the county's faltering interest in the war. As will be seen shortly, the returns from parliamentary taxation in the same period remained almost constant. Rather the county plainly discriminated between the various levies, and it generally greeted extraparliamentary ones with indifference. In this, Leicestershire was not unique. Neither the royal Bohemian benevolence nor the Privy Seal campaign was a success elsewhere; in fact, Lord Saye and Sele, another stalwart of the war party, went to prison rather than pay the Bohemian benevolence.[15] In short, for Huntingdon and the bulk of the local elite, their commitment to the war effort did not extend to subverting the 'ancient constitution'. On the other hand, when the state requested financial aid in the customary, parliamentary manner, money effortlessly flowed out of the shire.

The two successive Lords Keeper, Williams and Coventry, shared an axiomatic belief in the fact that 'the summe of their aydes was growne lesse neare by half then it was in former tymes'. The decline in the subsidy, while a grave problem, was not a consistent one. When, for example, Sir Benjamin Rudyerd in 1628 took the steady decline as an administrative fact of life, Sir Edward Giles immediately protested that 'my country holds up the subsidies well enough'. Leicestershire's members could easily have seconded Giles.[16] The second of the two subsidies voted in 1621 eventually brought in £755 9s. 2d. Fragmentary records prevent similar precision with the first subsidy, but Huntingdon's later statement that both totalled £1,500 suggests that the first one was not more than a few pounds off the second.[17] Returns for the next parliamentary grant are even more problematic; the extraordinary provisions of the 1624 Subsidy Bill were so successful that the independent parliamentary treasurers left no trace of the money in the Exchequer. Fortunately, the size of the 1624 grant can be deduced from the precise figures for the two subsidies in 1625, the first of which produced £744 13s. 4d., and the second £752 13s.[18] Given that the 1621 and 1625 subsidies each netted within a few pounds of £750 and given the contemporary understanding that a fifteenth was worth about half of a subsidy, the three subsidies and three-fifteenths of 1624 most likely brought the Exchequer a total of £3,400. The same steady returns can be seen in the five subsidies which Parliament approved in 1628. The first two netted £1,497 5s. 2d., or approximately £742 13s. 4d. each.[19] For the third the county paid in £718 15s. 2d.; for the fourth, £736 3s. 6d.[20] The only departure from this otherwise constant pattern occurred with the last of the five subsidies, which produced only £687 17s. 6d. But the anomaly is not hard to explain, given the turmoil that followed the dramatic conclusion of the 1629 session.[21]

From these figures, two clear points emerge. First, none of the extensive information on financial disputes relates to these numbers. To be sure, the Corporation of Leicester, ever zealous to defend its rights, sometimes lobbied for sympathetic subsidy commissioners. Beyond that, the most striking aspect about the parliamentary taxation in the 1620s is the almost complete silence surrounding its collection. The entire operation proceeded with an ease and regularity that is astonishing. Not only were the collections easy, but the amounts collected were also surprisingly uniform. By contrast, in other counties like Sussex, the decline in the value of a parliamentary subsidy was so dramatic as to be dubbed a 'fiscal catastrophe'.[22] Several factors accounted for this phenomenon; among them was that the Lord Lieutenant and many of the inhabitants were committed to the war effort. To argue otherwise is to remain baffled by a local community whose parliamentary collections were stable and whose extraparliamentary offerings came to another £2,100.

THE PRESSED MEN

The local gentlemen were no more willing to part with their young men than with their money. Since Leicestershire dispatched over 700 men overseas in the 1620s, impressment represented a major challenge for the Lord Lieutenant, particularly since the shire had not been seriously troubled with such a request in over two decades.

The first recruiting drum to beat in the county did not present significant problems, for it only summoned volunteers. In the summer of 1624, Sir John Radcliff came to fill a company of troops for service in Lord Willoughby's regiment, one of four which James dispatched to assist the Dutch Republic. Huntingdon eased Radcliffe's task by organising a recruiting sweep. The captain arrived at each of six sites to find that the local constables had already given potential recruits Huntingdon's assurance that all would go well. 'Theis noble personages' in charge of the expedition, whose number included his friends, the Earls of Southampton and Essex, 'I have bene long acquainted with', and the Captain 'I assure you wilbe very carefull of the men'.[23] With such an endorsement, the recruitment proceeded without incident.

The situation became much less casual when the earl had to press men. Scarcely had Radcliff and his company left than Huntingdon had to select another 150 men to accompany Count Mansfelt's multinational expedition against the House of Habsburg. In this task, Huntingdon could have followed the convention enshrined in a Hampshire JP's book of precedents, which cross-listed 'Warres' with 'Idle persons to be taken up'. The councillors themselves did not offer much guidance: all they required were 150 men 'of able bodies and yeares' who were not in the militia.[24] Huntingdon characteristically developed his own procedure. While he ordered each parish to present two to four men, from whom he would select the ablest, the net was not cast randomly over the population. If at all possible, the constables were to pass over married men, agricultural labourers and, above all, vagrants. Cloth workers idled in a trade slump, however, were fair game. Huntingdon's hallmark was little touches, and in this case, his personal attention was clear for all to see as the Leicestershire levy marched past, each bedecked with several feet of ribbon. Such thoughtfulness notwithstanding, some of the new soldiers remained unhappy with their fate. John Goodwyn, for example, responded to the news of his selection by assaulting a local official, vowing 'he would be revenged upon him', and by denouncing the Mayor of Leicester with 'verie unprochfull speeches'. Promptly hauled before the Mayor's court, Goodwyn received a predictable punishment: he was 'sent awaye for a souldyer'.[25]

Aside from Mr Goodwyn's outburst, the rest of the first impressment proceeded smoothly until, on the march to Dover, almost fifty men took advantage of lax supervision to slip away. The only thing for it was to ignore local grumbling and to call a second levy of another fifty recruits.[26] The necessity of punishing the deserters was not lost on the earl; otherwise, 'it wilbe impossible for any conductor to bring them to any port'. The assize court eventually convicted six of the deserters, imprisoning them indefinitely as 'examples to deterr others'.[27] To compound the confusion, the Earl of Lincoln hastily attempted to raise a horse troop of volunteers at the same time as the constables were rounding up the deserters and their substitutes. Although Huntingdon urged his Deputies and constables to assist his cousin, the distracted officials had neither time nor patience for Lincoln's request.[28]

Mansfelt's expedition taught local governors across the realm the painful lesson that 'there goes more to the furnishing and setting out of an army then bare penn and yncke'. Yet there was a silver lining to the otherwise sobering experience. For many of the better sort, Huntingdon's guidelines for impressment, arbitrary though they might seem, were splendid means of relieving overpopulation, a problem which constantly vexed the authorities. In particular, they could scarcely keep their eyes off the sturdy beggars who, as Lord Keeper Williams reminded the Corporation in 1622, 'swarme with whole troupe of Rogues Beggars Egiptians and idle persons'. Therefore Thomas Barnes, a godly preacher, was not being particularly heartless when he argued that for such idlers

> it is a great deale fitter for themselves and better for our kingdome that they be working in garrison, exercising armes, and fighting in the field … than ranging our streets, haunting our tavernes, tipling in our tap-houses … and lying like burthens upon the shoulders of our State.

Since this scheme offered the poor an honourable life and, possibly, a glorious death, things they could not expect at home, Barnes concluded that war 'may be a meanes to make men better'.[29]

This logic remained persuasive as long as estimates of the 'surplus' unmarried males remained high. Leicestershire first learned of the error of this miscalculation in the spring of 1625 with orders for another 150 men to assist Wimbledon's invasion of Spain. The Council again left the earl to his own devices, suggesting only that the 'able bodies' should come out of the 'most populous areas', and he simply revived the same procedure which had proven so effective in the Mansfelt levy. Unfortunately this time, these guidelines produced a host of problems and protests. Sir Alexander Cave wanted a household servant released, while Sir Henry Skipwith, Sir Matthew Saunders and Lady Herrick each lobbied on behalf of only sons of elderly retainers. One argued for 'the staffe of his father life'; another insisted the aged parent's 'grey haires would with greife be brought to the grave'; and a third pointed out more likely candidates who avoided the constable 'by the voluntary absentinge and withdrawinge'.[30] Then there was the phenomenon of the village without un- married men; Coatts for example protested that Mansfelt had got their last one. Nor were many of the weavers still unemployed; those who had not found work in local collieries were by May fully occupied in seasonal farming, and as Huntingdon's servant reminded him, his own estates desperately required labourers for 'your Lorships harvest'. The awkward became even more awk- ward when potential recruits showed up at the selection with their landlords.[31]

The Wimbledon levy thus represented an early challenge to Huntingdon's guiding principle 'to charge the Countrey as little as may stand with the well performance of the Council's orders'. In response, he seems to have quietly approved all petitions, for none of the men in question was ultimately shipped out. Yet such kindness left unresolved the question of locating 150 fit men. Huntingdon's first impulse was to clear the county prison, especially of Mansfelt's six deserters, only to have Judge Bromley convince him that 'this business was of greater consequence then to send gaole birds'.[32] Meanwhile, the same pressures which had caused him to excuse some men with connec- tions were also working on the constables, and the result at the selection was an alarming number of men scarcely fit for life, much less military service, whom Huntingdon had to excuse. To sweeten the pill for those who remained, Huntingdon again sought to make the service as attractive as humanly possi- ble. Innkeepers in and around the selection site were duly warned of the recruits' arrival and cautioned against mistreating them.[33] The troops them- selves marched out in new blue coats, over whose design and production Huntingdon had fussed. In addition, the Lord Lieutenant provided 'extras' over and above the royal provision ranging from flags and drums on the long march to Plymouth to an extra penny a day for beer for the thirsty men.[34]

For all of his diligence, Huntingdon had failed to consider that the conduc- tors might quietly exchange the pressed men with those whom he had earlier rejected, confident that the unfit men would soon be released. So it was that the Leicestershire contingent marched into Plymouth with a collection of misfits remarkable even by contemporary standards. The official report on the twenty-six men discharged only deepens the mystery about how they even survived eleven days on the road. Many were lame in either an arm or a leg, and several had ruptures, one of whom was 'troubled with a bloody issue', and another insisted that recently 'his gutts fell out of his belly with a hurte with a sithe'. However pitiable these men were, they could at least feel sorry for the poor man with a mysterious ailment which produced 'issues in both his brests'. For Huntingdon, the sting of this incident became even sharper after the Council demanded a thorough investigation. Fortunately since the blame eventually settled on the conductors, the episode did not discredit his otherwise energetic administration.[35]

These periodic requests from Whitehall produced brief, albeit intense, pressures on the Lord Lieutenant and the county. All involved were able to endure the pressures, although not always with the best of grace. A more constant burden was not supplying men and money for another grandee's army; rather it was gathering them for his own regiment.

ALL ACCORDING TO THE MODERN FASHION

The Jacobean regime had never consistently paid attention to the militia until 1618 when 'the leavying of forces ... almost thoroughout all the partes of Christendome' made even James apprehensive about 'the safety of his owne domynions and people'. The result was a flood of orders to correct 'the manie defects that by this lounge time of peace and securitie were grownen'. Powder stocks had to be increased; calivers, which were 'unserviceable' in 'the moderne use', had to be replaced with muskets; and 'it is high tyme at length after so many admonitions ... that the troopes of horse in the county be filled up and made compleate with all provisions and furniture appertayning'. These commands were not merely advisory; the councillors also demanded a 'strict accompt' of their execution and insisted on compliance. In the circumstances, Lieutenants and militiamen all across the realm had little choice but to take their responsibilities much more seriously. In the Midlands, Samuel Buggs noted how the new orders set 'some scouring of their pieces, others shaking their pikes, some harnessing of their horses, others whetting of their swords and bending of their bowes'.[36]

Huntingdon, as befitted a devotee of the Protestant cause, embraced the new orders, and his enthusiasm was an inestimable advantage, for the task before him was formidable indeed. The county financed a trained band of 500 infantrymen under the command of three captains as well as a troop of 100 horse under another captain. In addition another 500 'private' men, who provided their own arms and supplies, operated under the same command and discipline as the trained bands themselves. The origin of these 'private' men was wrapped up in the popular mythology of the Armada year, but by the 1620s their mere existence was surprising. Technically, all militia units were supposed to blend private and trained men. But constant complaints about the expense of maintaining private men had persuaded other Lieutenants to let the practice fade to the point where most county units were comprised entirely of trained men.[37] While the regiment could be used against either Catholic fifth columnists or rioting peasants, its main function was dictated by geography: 'beinge one of the confyninge Counties upon Lyncoln which lies upon the Sea Coast', Leicestershire's primary responsibility was the relief of its neighbour when a system of warning beacons summoned them.[38]

By 1618, the near total ruin of the beacons was the least of Huntingdon's problems. The men themselves had only rarely mustered and had never trained; and it was hard to disregard this hiatus in meetings, given their tendency to disorder. To tackle the problem, the earl converted Donnington Park into a military academy where he and his Deputies discussed the militia's deficiencies and possible remedies. In 1618 they numbered his cousin, Sir Henry Hastings of the Abbey, Sir Thomas Hesilrige and Sir Thomas Compton. By 1625, death and superannuation had brought on an entirely new team: Lord Grey, Sir Wolstan Dixie, Sir Henry Skipwith and Francis Staresmore. With the latter's death in 1626, Sir John Skeffington rounded out the number.[39] It would have been hard to find a more distinguished lot: a peer of the realm, a brother and a cousin of a peer, three baronets and three knights. All were veteran militia officers, and in a county with only four parliamentary seats, five of the Deputies – Hastings, Hesilrige, Morison, Skeffington and Staresmore – served as Parliament men. Huntingdon's Deputies, in short, were all senior members of the interlocking directorate of families who dominated the shire.

For all their diligence, the Lord Lieutenant and his Deputies were in fact mere amateurs; Sir Richard Morison, however, was not. Normally the Lieutenant General of the Ordnance would be out of any Lieutenant's reach, but Morison had married into the Haringtons, the earl's kin, and held land in the shire. Hence, with the new insistence on a professional militia, Huntingdon promptly appointed Morison in 1618 to a deputy lieutenancy, since there was 'noe man within the Countrey more able and sufficient in those businesses then your self'. Although Morison's duties often kept him in Whitehall, the earl regularly consulted him by letter and, more importantly, employed the royal munition experts as the county's agent in recurrent arms deals.[40] More readily available was Captain Edward Savile, a veteran of extended 'service done in the late Q. Elizabeths tyme' and more recently in the Dutch army. Advanced age prevented him from serving as Muster Master; after all, Huntingdon's father had pressed the Earl of Essex to take Savile with him to Ireland in the 1590s. His skills, however, were indispensable; hence Huntingdon named this 'olde souldier' Assistant Muster Master, and after the Privy Council had created the new county office of Provost Marshal in 1626, Savile was the obvious candidate.[41] Almost as useful was Thomas Gerard, who had also served in Ireland before returning to serve on the bench. Conversations with these 'iudicious Soldiers' and careful reading of several military primers made Huntingdon a devotee of the 'modern style' of warfare.[42]

These discussions and readings only magnified the task before him. 'Defects in Armour and other things,' he acknowledged, 'are many.' The musketeers were full of petronels and calivers, and generally missing their 'Bandaliers and Restes'. The situation was no better among the pikemen, most of whom wielded 'exceedinge longe and heavie' antiques rather than the 'new Spanish Pykes'.[43] Sudden changes in this establishment would inevitably cause confusion. To ensure that it did not cause turmoil, Huntingdon carefully explained the situation to the petty constables, who would have to collect the money for the rearmament. Although he had long known of the questionable arms, 'the care and desire I have had to put the Countrey to as little charge as might be hath caused me hitherto to forbeare to performe this necessary duty'. But recent orders altered the situation; 'the old and unserviceable' weapons and armour 'which hath too longe bene tollerated at former Musters may nowe be at last changed'. Given the worsening situation on the continent, 'I cannot leave it to a sudden Alarum when thinges by the straightnes of tyme cannot possibly be supplied'.[44]

The resolution to rearm the entire regiment only brought on the baffling question of where to find the arms. Local businessmen, while eager for the custom, proved a dubious source; an early purchase came at 'excessive rates' and yielded 'rotten Pikes and Patcht and peiced Armes neither sightly nor serviceable'. London armourers meanwhile were 'soe extreame deare' that the search for 'the cheapest course' led the increasingly frustrated Lord Lieutenant as far afield as Amsterdam before Morison uncovered more reasonable metropolitan dealers. Yet even a Lieutenant General could not overcome all problems; in spite of paying London armourers to bring their wares to a muster – an arrangement that Huntingdon felt was generous in the extreme – they were 'clamorous against mee' for immediate payment.[45] Nevertheless by 1623 he could report with a straight face that the armour and weapons of the foot companies 'are very compleat and fitt for present service'. After a muster two years later, Francis Staresmore reported that the only problems were 'very fewe and smale defects ... which are not scarce noting'. Therefore 'for sufficiency of Armes they are very Compleat', so complete that 'noe county of England can compare with them'.[46]

This transformation had been far from painless. Defects which were clear to Huntingdon's officers were not so apparent to the men who had purchased them, albeit decades ago. Years later, William Earle, a yeoman presenting a lance for his landlord, still remembered the day when he arrived at the muster to find the ominous presence of a London armourer's cart. His worst suspicions were confirmed when John Everard, the Muster Master, 'disliked and disallowed' the outfit which 'had been formerly allowed of' by Everard himself;

he then ordered Earle to take up new arms at his master's expense. Earle refused, protesting 'his owne armes were sufficient and that hee conceaved his Master for that cause would not paye for newe Armes'. At this point Everard had Earle's breastplate removed. A last appeal to the Lord Lieutenant brought only the answer that 'hee must take newe Armes'. To soothe Earle, Everard demonstrated the need for a replacement by firing a pistol at the breastplate. The bullet came through, but the result, Earle objected, was scarcely surprising since Everard had stood 'very neare'. This extended scene prompted Mr Yates, one of the Leicester bandsmen, to observe that 'better Armes were then shott throughe then any Armour which the saide Armourer had then in place to bee sould'. Confirmation of this remark came when Earle asked the waiting armourer if he could test the new plate as Everard had his old one. The merchant rejected the idea out of hand; since 'hee had not shott att his ... Armour, neither should hee [Earle] ... shoote att his'. The final indignity for Earle's master came when the old armour, once repaired, went on to have an unobjectionable career on a Northamptonshire militiaman.[47]

As Earle's case illustrates, rearming 1,000 foot soldiers was child's play compared with getting 100 horsemen to pass muster; 'the greatest difficulty', Huntingdon reported to the Council, 'is in making of the horse Compleat'. His assessment was an understatement. In the ill-fated 1614 campaign, the troop had filled Huntingdon with anxiety: 'I feare the greatest want wilbe in the horse.' The situation had scarcely improved, and in 1619 'such defalts and defects' in the horse troop shamed the normally punctual Lord Lieutenant into missing the Council's deadline for a full report; he could not bring himself to confess that 30 per cent of the men were either defective or absent altogether.[48] Several years of constant badgering only brought on embarrassing scenes in 1623 when a third of the horses were 'very meanely furnished' and 'could neither Gallop nor trot, much lesse make ready turnes and stopps'.[49] The worst offenders came from the more prosperous clergymen, who sent men 'nether personable nor well apparrelled soe as my Deputie Lieutenants were ashamed to exercise them amonst the Trayned Bands'. But at least they showed up; absenteeism, while practically non-existent in the foot companies, regularly claimed between 25 per cent and 40 per cent of the horse troop. Still Huntingdon persevered, stubbornly vowing not to 'leave of untill I have brought this worke of the band of the Horse to perfection'.[50]

Part of the problem was the cost. Galloping around the county in a cuirass, while undeniably gallant, was also expensive. The regulation equipment for a light horseman called for 'a good Hargobus or Dragon', a belt to carry the weapon as well as 'a Flaske, Priming Box, Key, and Bullet bag, an open Headpeece with cheekes, a good Buffe coat with deepe skirts, Sword, Gridle and Hangers, a Saddle, Birdle, Bitt, Petrell, Crooper with Strappes for his sack of necessaries'. The accoutrements alone came to £5 19s., while a cuirassier required almost twice that amount.[51] Nor do these figures include the costs of the mount itself. While horses were plentiful in Leicestershire, the 'great horse' necessary for the militia was not. In fact, the shortage became so desperate that the earl authorised the substitution of large geldings. The irony of his solution was not lost on one local gentleman upset with his assessment in the horse troop; he facetiously congratulated Huntingdon for not being 'soe ill an husband as to keepe greate horse'.[52]

This quip aptly reveals another part of the problem; while most foot soldiers dared not challenge the earl, the cavalrymen could and did. The result was a running battle over the horse troop. Some, especially absentee land-lords, objected to any contribution. In more tranquil times, a certificate stating that the gentleman in question contributed to another militia would have been excuse enough, but at the Council's insistence, a stricter attitude replaced such courtesy. Thus Huntingdon pestered, and ultimately presented, promi-nent men ranging from Sir William Cockaine, the London financier, to Sir Nicholas Tufton, the wealthy Kentish gentleman soon to become the Earl of Thanet, while remaining deaf to personal appeals from the Earls of Exeter and Essex on behalf of relations.[53] Equally aggrieved were the richer clergymen, hitherto exempt from contributions, and this question brought the Lord Lieu-tenant head-to-head with their diocesan, the Bishop of Lincoln. George Montaigne begged Huntingdon as 'a Patron of learning and religious men' to appreciate that 'there are many' of his Leicestershire clergy 'that greviously complaine'. Huntingdon's rigidity eventually drove the bishop to exclaim that he 'marveled he should be more troubled with the busines of Armes in the Countie of Leicester then in all other places in his dioces'. Clerical complaints abruptly ceased with the elevation of Lord Keeper Williams to the bishopric. All it took was a list of clerical defaulters and a delicately phrased message from Huntingdon; the certainty of their correction 'shall make me out of the respect I beare to my lord Keeper forbeare to acquaint the Lords of the council therwith'.[54] Thereafter, the clergy became more biddable.

Local gentlemen upset with their assessments were less tractable. Sir George Manners, the Earl of Rutland's brother, objected to an assessment higher than that of anyone under the rank of baronet, and Sir William Fawnt asked how he had offended Huntingdon 'so farre that I am now charged with two horses which heretofore have allwayes escaped with one'.[55] Individual protests became more explosive once they were linked with charges of favour-itism. Before the entire 1625 muster, Huntingdon's cousin, Sir Henry Hast-ings of Braunston, announced 'others of farr greater estate being not deepelier charged and some not at all, for which disproportion he would complaine to the lords of the Council'. Consequently, the horse troop presented a ticklish situation: while the earl needed local goodwill, he could not unilaterally dis-band the horse troop. Hence he clung to his guiding principle that 'the world shall see that I make every mans burden as light as may be so as I preserve the kings service'. For aggrieved gentlemen, this meant that the earl was willing to reduce assessments, provided he achieved some degree of compliance.[56]

Genial accommodation, however, had distinct limits, and if it failed, the earl had to resort to his ultimate sanction, the Privy Council. Initially, Huntingdon sought to avoid such a drastic remedy by casting non-compliance as a personal insult. In 1619, he cautioned defaulters that 'I will take such a course with them as is fitt for such persons to receive that thus contemne his Majesties pleasure signified to me.' Constables were to tell the recalcitrant 'how ill I shall take it of them' whose defiance 'make me conceive that they doe litle valewe me'. While such threats might intimidate lesser gentlemen, they scarcely daunted the county elite. Consequently, by 1622 he shifted to ominous brevity: defaulters could expect that 'I will send them ymmediately up to the Lords of the Councell'. Behind this confident assurance was a good deal of uncertainty; after all, the Council's order in 1620 to send up the defaulters had not been repeated in subsequent instructions. Thus, when he sent up the list of defaulters in 1623, he begged the councillors to 'make the others doe their duties', while Sir Richard Morison personally told them that if they did not 'take a severe course with theis gentlemen', then 'others wilbe more encouraged in the neglect of their duties' and Huntingdon 'shall not otherwise be able to make up the troope Compleat'.[57] In the event, the councillors understood the gravity of the situation. First, they lavishly praised 'the care you have had of his Maiestie's service in which wee can not but commend your good indeavours and do pray your Lordship to continue the same'. As for those gentlemen 'so backward in shewing of the horse', the councillors ordered the earl to bind them over for appearance at the Council table, where they would 'answeare their Contempt', and a messenger soon arrived to escort the defaulters to Westminster. Confident in such firm support, the earl promised the obstinate 'a more speedy and Sharpe Course'; his best advice was 'fayle you not at your perills'.[58]

The 'Sharpe Course' itself speaks more about the contemporary notions of honour than about the repressive apparatus of the early Stuart regime. After noting defects, the earl gave defaulters ample time, usually up to a year, to make amends. Only continued non-compliance brought defaulters before the Privy Council, and while awaiting the councillors' leisure, defaulters could meditate on their errors, either in the Fleet or in Marshalsea prison. Release from confinement lay in a scene of private humiliation. On their knees before the councillors, penitents had to recite a set statement; after announcing that they were 'hartily sorry for having shewed such remisnes in that his Majesties soe important service', the offenders then begged that 'the punishment I have nowe undergone may blott out the remembrance theirof'. On any Foucaultian table of signal punishments this scarcely ranks at all, but the prospect of such shameful humiliation was enough to make even a repeat offender like Sir Henry Hastings of Braunston vow to 'be more carefull in sending serviceable and sufficient horses'. Certainly Sir William Noel found the experience degrading enough that he refused to speak to one of Huntingdon's Deputies after an unscheduled visit to Westminster.[59]

Persuading 1,100 men to equip themselves in the 'moderne fashion' was ultimately pointless without enough powder and match. Since Buckingham had considerable difficulty finding munitions, it is not surprising that Huntingdon found it an awkward task in the east Midlands. In 1619, the Council had suddenly doubled the county's usual stock of 1,000 lb of powder and 300 lb of match.[60] To reach the new goal, the earl suspended all private sales until the county's stocks reached the new levels. When such draconian measures failed to achieve the desired goal fast enough, Huntingdon borrowed from the Corporation of Leicester's reserves.[61] The experience made Huntingdon readily concur with Lord Treasurer Middlesex's impeachment in 1624; after all, wilful neglect of the realm's powder stocks might have 'emboaldened the kings enemies to have made a sodaine invasion which had been unresistable'. Success in gathering over a ton of explosives only brought on the problem of storing it. The answer was the erection of a county magazine in Leicester, which successive improvements transformed into a place of considerable strength.[62] An extended struggle to improve the county's powder supply had left Huntingdon with a keen appreciation of the vital importance of munitions and of the difficulty of securing them.

Success in Huntingdon's campaign against obstinate local gentlemen unfortunately was not repeated in awkward skirmishes with the Corporation of Leicester. Although the town presented only forty out of the 1,100 soldiers, this platoon nevertheless represented the Lord Lieutenant's greatest administrative headache. Driven by the town's long cherished desire for increased autonomy, the Corporation interpreted the earl's efforts to revitalise the county militia as simply another attempt to erode its independence.[63]

In 1618, the town opened the battle by refusing to present private as well as trained men, and rather than stir up a hornet's nest, Huntingdon quietly dropped the request.[64] A far more serious row erupted in 1625 when Huntingdon ordered a muster at Lutterworth, ten miles away. Although Leicester's trained band mustered outside of the city, legal counsel in 1625 advised the Mayor and his brethren that 'by the lawes of the Realme wee needed not to have done' so. Therefore, they stood on their rights, declined to attend the Lutterworth muster, and rallied support at Whitehall. Since the city was a principal town of the Duchy of Lancaster, the Corporation insisted on gaining the support of the duchy's attorney and chancellor, even though the latter was in bed with a serious bout of nausea. Both duly expressed amazement at Huntingdon's cavalier attack on 'the anycent Towne and Corporation

... which hath ever beene patronised by your self and your noble Auncesters'.[65] In addition, the city fathers gave a passing Deputy such an earful of complaints that he begged the earl to 'cast your eye upon the statute of musters of the 4 & 5 Philip and Mary'. Huntingdon's first impulse was a compromise which would summon all subsequent musters to Leicester, if the trained band attended the one at Lutterworth. But as the storm broke over him, he abandoned even that position, excusing Leicester's men altogether.[66] These forty men were simply not worth the trouble, especially when the quarrel might jeopardise Huntingdon's struggle to revive a phenomenon last seen in the Elizabethan wars – actual training.

Thomas Goddard, a long-serving constable, well remembered what had usually happened at musters in the 1610s; 'they have nott been trayned but onely have shewed their Armes paide their money and been discharged'. The difference with what happened after 1618 lay at the heart of the 1625 dispute over the site of the county muster. Huntingdon never questioned the town's exemption from musters outside Leicester, but he noted that 'there is noe mention in that Statute of Trayning'. The distinction, he argued, was a very real one. 'To muster' was simply 'to viewe the men and Armes'; this had been the norm during the Jacobean peace. 'Trayning' on the other hand 'is to teach them their postures and to bee exercised and disciplined to inable and fitt them in the true use of their Armes'.[67] This determination to show the soldiers the 'true use of their Armes' raises the question of what they had been doing with them before. In peacetime, the arms themselves were the important thing, and busy militiamen dispatched sons or tenants to 'show' their arms. Attending musters, however, was something the 500 trained men rarely missed since the local authorities paid their expenses without placing a cap on the daily tab. This blank cheque naturally led to 'a great abuse'; after spending 'very largely of the Townes purse' on food and drink, the troops turned up in varying states of inebriation and 'carry themselves unrulilye'.[68] With men in such a state, 'connivance' was the wisest order of the day for the officers. Hence, safe in the knowledge that their captain would look away, some bandsmen pawned or even sold their arms and armour; at the rare inspection, they would simply borrow a friend's equipment from another unit.[69] Truly, the Jacobean militia often proved more of a threat to itself and to the county treasury than to any enemy.

Since any hope of perfecting the regiment was futile until these abuses were corrected, the earl began jailing unruly militiamen, and to encourage a clean and sober attitude, he paid local ministers to attend the musters. The officers' casual attitude went next; they found themselves enjoined to hold 'a strict and precise course' towards the men 'without connivance to be shewed to any'.[70] Likewise, the practice of shuffling arms between companies ended after Huntingdon had the militia's weapons stamped and numbered; those who continued selling their arms were allowed to justify themselves at the quarter sessions. Eventually, he prohibited altogether the practice of random substitution.[71]

Having restored some discipline, Everard, Gerard and Savile showed the men and their officers the complicated evolutions of pikes and musketeers. Memories of how things had been done in the Irish and Dutch service were useful, and any remaining confusion ended in 1623 once the government had issued its own *Instructions for Musters and Arms*. Eventually, at the earl's insistence, the county provided each captain with a copy, which was to guide the regiment for years.[72] As the realm came closer to open war, so too the pace of training increased. Musters, which had been irregular events in the 1610s, quickly became annual, and after 1625 semi-annual, affairs. Between 1618 and 1630, the only exception came in 1621, when Parliament called Huntingdon out of the shire, but in subsequent years, not even the plague disrupted this pattern. When it first broke out, Huntingdon had the men trained in their hundreds; after it abated, he called a county-wide muster, while excusing those from towns where 'the disease is extreame hot'.[73]

In February 1626, the pace of training dramatically increased when the councillors dispatched Sergeants Cave and Smith from the English regiments in Dutch service to train the Leicestershire militia. The lack of uniform commands and the possibilities of chaos if the units ever had to operate together had long alarmed military experts. The 1623 *Instructions* and subsequent manuals did much to correct this problem, but by sending two sergeants to each county the Council went one better. Subsequently, the officers received individual daily instruction, while their companies drilled every fortnight from 9.00 a.m. to 4.00 p.m.[74] Then the three companies, each with over 300 men, unwieldy units even by contemporary standards, were broken up into five more manageable companies. These for the first time developed NCOs – 'leaders', 'bringers up', and 'middlemen' – who were essential to mastering early modern drill. Likewise, target practice for the musketeers became marksmanship competitions which, the government hoped, would encourage the men to practise 'on those daies and in those times' which 'would bee worse spent in an Alehouse'. Huntingdon adopted this suggestion, and soon the contest winners brought home either cash rewards ranging from 3s. 4d. to 10s. or prizes of hats with feathers, pairs of gloves or 'silver litle things'. Quite rightly the county treasurer dubbed this period as 'the tyme of the drilling'.[75]

'The oftener exercisinge', far from wearying the Lord Lieutenant, appears to have exhilarated him, and his delight in his work was readily apparent in the frills that the troops began to acquire. In order to enhance the regiment's logistical reach, Huntingdon ordered a few 'cartes with geares', and the Lord Lieutenant himself put the unit through its paces atop an ornate new saddle.

But the most telling illustration of his infatuation with all things military was a large tent. Haunted by the fact that Northamptonshire had long had one, he spent years fussing over the proper design, interviewing potential suppliers and haggling over a just price. Ever wary of fraud, he insisted on as 'good Canvas as anie is usually made of', and finally, in 1625, the county could sport a comfortable pavilion with the royal coat of arms prominently displayed. There, the officers could relax with 'wine and tobacco', and local dignitaries could watch as Huntingdon took the salute from his regiment passing in review.[76]

Procurement was simply the more glamorous side of the constant battle to hold down expenses. At first glance the earl's badgering a Deputy Lieutenant over a missing £1 3s. 8d. might sound excessive, but the same eye for financial detail allowed him to spot a larger discrepancy in accounts worth £43 3s. 8d.[77] Likewise the practice of deferring non-essentials became a constant policy, as the county's tent illustrates. Although he had repeatedly budgeted for its purchase, he received one only in 1625 and then only after haggling a Clerkenwell tentmaker down from a 'very great' price.[78] Significantly when protests over his cheeseparing first arose, they came, not from aggrieved taxpayers, but from militiamen. In 1623, the councillors, concerned that the musketeers might 'blow away their powder in vaine', suggested that they practise only with the more economical 'false fires', and Huntingdon, never one to waste money, immediately adopted the suggestion. This 'Sparing allowance' unfortunately only produced 'discontent' soldiers who demanded 'a more liberall proportion'. Their protest brought only a temporary restoration of their old rights before the new economy measure held sway.[79] Economisation, the militiamen were beginning to discover, had become Huntingdon's obsession. Hence first in 1622 he capped the *per diem* expenses of the trained men at 8d., and then in 1626 cut it to 6d.[80] If nothing else, the earl subscribed to the time-honoured notion that if he looked after the shillings and pence, the pounds would look after themselves.

By 1625, the earl's efforts were paying admirable dividends. Since 1618, even though Whitehall's new demands had come thick and fast, Huntingdon had successfully weathered them all. He had co-opted the only other potential aristocratic rival in the shire, forced his will on successive Bishops of Lincoln, and convinced local deadbeats that they could not escape his reach. His crowning achievement was plain to see several times a year for all who cared to join him in the county's tent. At the beginning of the campaign, the earl's goal had been to get the militia to the point where 'the iudgements of Martiall men cannot take exceptions'. Even before Sergeants Cave and Smith arrived, the offical 1625 report on the regiment maintained that 'noe county of England can compare with them'. The horse admittedly remained less than distinguished, but they were 'better then at anie tyme synce I have had the honor to be Lieutenant'. In its magazines, the county had a ton of powder and 1,200 lb of match. Its musketeers shouldered weapons 'all of one bore according to the Tower gage', and the pikemen wielded pikes 'all of one length with Spanish heades'. All indeed was 'according to the moderne forme'.[81]

AN EXQUISITE PERFORMANCE

Early in 1628, fed up with the local commanders assessing their own performance, the councillors ordered a series of regional musters where royal officers and in some places the king himself would inspect all the realm's horse troops. Not surprisingly the local officers, long accustomed to their own autonomy, were unenthusiastic about the plan, and their protests began to stream into the Council. Some, like those of Devonshire and Yorkshire, objected to the heavy expense and begged for a postponement, if not a cancellation.[82] Others warned royal officials not to expect too much. Even Secretary Coke's brother could promise only 'reasonably good satisfaction' from the Derbyshire troop, given the lack of 'fatt horses' and the dearth of weapons. Opposition to the idea was almost universal – except in Leicestershire where the Lord Lieutenant warmly endorsed the scheme as an answer to fervent prayers. 'On my parte,' Huntingdon vowed, an outside inspection 'hath binne a longe desired occasion by which I have ever sought to expresse my care and fidelity in my place.'[83] His enthusiasm was quite sincere. By 1628, he had spent a decade perfecting his regiment, and while his troops did not universally share his zeal, their periodic grumbling could not obscure the magnitude of his achievement. The Lord Lieutenant's greatest frustration therefore was the lack of a fitting occasion to parade his regiment before outsiders. Unfortunately for him, the Council soon countermanded the order, and so a decade of fussing over the regiment ended without Huntingdon ever finding the 'longe desired occasion' for an impartial review of his troops.[84]

The earl, however, could console himself with the one campaign ribbon which his unit had won, and that had been earned in an offensive against the local Catholic population. Huntingdon's religious views made him anxious about the potential threat which the recusants posed in a conflict with the House of Austria. As early as 1619 he queried the councillors about

> what course is to be taken upon information given of divers Armes secretly kept in the hands of such as (though not Recusant convict) yet have neither received the communion not heard divin service ... for divers yeares last past.

At a time when James I was intensely involved with negotiations with the Most Catholic King, the earl's fervour was lost on the councillors, who blandly replied that 'it is fitt that this be carefully looked into' and then thought no more about it.[85] Yet six years later, Huntingdon's anxieties were much more appropriate as Wimbledon and 150 pressed men from Leicestershire were about to invade Spain.

With hostilities imminent, disturbing rumours ran through Leicestershire. A late-night discussion of the news led a Leicester recusant to confess his admiration for Spinola, the great Habsburg general, and his hatred of the term, 'papist'. More provocatively, he vowed that within a year English 'hereticks', who currently lorded it over the recusants, 'may be glad to creepe'. His outburst became even more unsettling with reports of the local Catholics stockpiling arms, tales of midnight musters in Charnwood Forest, and whispers of a larger Catholic plot across the entire Midlands. Nor were these reports limited to Leicestershire; in neighbouring Derbyshire, the only certainty for Sir Francis Coke was that the recusants were moving about 'in great troopes' and becoming 'very insolent ... as scorning us'.[86] These same rumours alarmed Lord Grey enough for him to urge that the upcoming militia muster be turned into a general pre-emptive strike led by 'some choyse muskiteers'; otherwise, Huntingdon's newest Deputy Lieutenant was afraid that 'wee shall not have soe fitt an opportunitie hereafter'. Grey was of course preaching to the converted, but until more information came to light, a quiet investigation, the earl replied, was the best policy; after all, in times of crisis, 'many tymes a man may gather Magnum ex parvo'. Nevertheless he set a watch on the county's powder magazines, while loudly proclaiming it part of a broader scheme to intercept plague-ridden Londoners in order not to tip off the Catholic conspirators. By that time, Grey's apprehensions had spread to his fellow Deputies; Staresmore and Dixie insisted on strengthening the county magazine, begged for more munitions, and in the meantime, set about interrogating suspects. In the end, even the discovery of reports 'soe darke and obscure that they seeme to be of smale moment' did not curb their excitement; legal action, they conceded, would be impossible on this slender information, but they forwarded the reports nonetheless, certain that 'by theise clowdy glimpses, a scantling may be taken of their trayterous intentions and disaffection to the state' and 'fearefull symtomes of ensuing dangere'.[87]

By mid-October Huntingdon and his deputies no longer had to search for legal grounds. The Privy Council, unable 'to distinguishe betweene the well and worse affected' among the recusants, authorised searches for arms caches in all Catholic residences, avowed or suspected. Rather than tip off the recusants with a badly planned operation, Huntingdon quietly conferred with his officers. The result was a plan which divided them into a half-dozen posses so that they could 'with secrecie and expedition' cover the entire county in one day without their actions being 'noysed abroad' to warn their quarry.[88] The swoop came off like clockwork, and in less than twenty-four hours, the earl and his men discovered the full extent of their paranoia. Of the several dozen houses searched, only two contained any arms; both of these produced trifling amounts and one of them belonged to Huntingdon's cousin, Sir Henry Hastings of Braunston. Further investigation revealed that the stories of midnight military preparations had come from a passing Lancashire pedler.[89] Nonetheless, nothing, not even these pitiful results, could take away the fact that it had been a brilliantly orchestrated campaign.

This assessment was not merely that of an overly fond Lord Lieutenant; the councillors also shared it. 'Wee doe well approve,' they wrote the earl, of his smooth campaign, and their praise for a job well done then broadened into a general paean for Huntingdon's reformation of the militia. No less a personage than Secretary Conway, the veteran of many Dutch campaigns, made an 'exact and good account' of the recent Leicestershire musters, and he spoke warmly 'of the care you have had and the diligence you have used as well in the viewe and exercise of the foote forces as of the horse'. All of which led the councillors to declare that 'wee doe hartelie wish that your Lordshipp mought be an example for other counties to followe'. Hence they could do nothing other than 'give you many thanks for the exquisite performance of this service'. Such was their extraordinary regard for Huntingdon's achievement that they vowed to tell Charles himself of it. For themselves they assured the Lord Lieutenant that they took 'speciall knowledge of it as you shall have occasion to expect the encouragement or make use of the favour of the Board'.[90]

This lavish commendation, far exceeding anything he had ever received, represented the pinnacle of the earl's administrative career. A decade earlier Huntingdon himself had observed that exemplary service in the militia was the surest way to 'credit and honour' with Whitehall. Little wonder then that when he finally received fulsome praise from the Council he kept the letter as a talisman, which he wheeled out in later years whenever trouble threatened. After such a thorough triumph, it only stands to reason that Huntingdon's opinion of himself and his achievement should have become a little inflated. When problems arose in Rutland, for example, he had no doubt about the most fitting example for the beleaguered deputies there; in their efforts to perfect the tiny militia, 'you shall have this Cuntry [Leicestershire] for your precedent'. As far as he was concerned, if the councillors found Leicestershire good enough to serve 'as an example for other counties to followe', then it was good enough for Rutland. Likewise even a year after the Council's kudos, Huntingdon warned the Leicester Corporation against challenging his authority; after all, he pointed out to them, he had proven himself to be 'a master of Artes in the execution of this office'.[91]

NOTES

1 Remembrances to Mr Recorder, 25 February 1619 and [March 1619], Leics. RO, BR II/18/13, fols. 361 and 386; and Chamberlain's Accounts, Michaelmas, 1618–19, Leics. RO, BR III/2/77, fol. 160.

2 S. R. Gardiner, *Prince Charles*, I, pp. 322–3; and Williams to Tremble, 18 August 1620, BL Tremble MSS, XVI/122. See for example Dohna to the Leicester Gentlemen, 13 and 26 May 1620, HA Corr. 8/20 and 21.

3 Buckingham to Buckinghamshire DLs, 25 June 1624, HEH, Temple MSS, STT 702; and Chandos to JPs, 10 September 1620, Gloucestershire Lieutenancy Book, Badminton House MSS, 504/M14/31, no. 3.

4 Southampton to [Oglander], 7 July 1620, Isle of Wight RO, Oglander MSS, OG 17/12; and Zouche to the Cinque Ports, [June 1620], SP 14/116/97.

5 H to DLs, 19 June 1620, *LRLB*, fol. 60v; and same to Corporation, 19 June 1620, Leics. RO, BR II/18/13, fol. 486. For Elizabeth's gift, see FEH to LCH, [late 1620s], HA Corr. 11/5499; and for the Derbyshire example, see H's copy of Cavendish to the Derbyshire JPs, 16 May 1620, Bodleian Library, Carte 77, fol. 176.

6 'The effect of my speech in Leycester shire', 13 July 1620, HAM 53/8.

7 Chamberlain's accounts, Leics. RO, BR III/2/78, p. 65; Berkeley to H, 22 July 1620; and Bulstrode to same, 30 August 1620, HA Corr. 8/706 and 1120.

8 H to Dohna, 1 June and 30 October 1620, *LRLB*, fols. 60 and 60v–61. On the 1621 subsidy yields, see entries for 28 April, 7 and 14 May and 16 June 1621, PRO E401/1906; and PC to Leicestershire Subsidymen, 28 February 1626, HA Corr. 12/4221.

9 Dohna's Receipt to Surrey, 18 October 1620, Loseley Park MSS, 3/15; same for Hampshire, 26 November 1620, Hampshire RO, Wriothesley MSS, 5m53/971; and H to Dohna, 30 October 1620, *LRLB*, fol. 61.

10 Owen Wynn to Sir John Wynn, 8 March 1626, NLW, Wynn of Gwydir MSS, 9061E/1395; and H to DLs, 28 September 1625, *LRLB*, fols. 133v. On the 1614 campaign, see above, pp. 15–16.

11 H to PC, 9 May 1622; Corporation to same, 14 May 1622; and Bulstrode to H, 13 May 1622, HA Corr. 9/1121.

12 Entries in Heyricke's accounts for 23 February and 30 March, and Egioke's for 5 February 1623, PRO E401/2435.

13 H to DLs, 28 September 1625; same to PC, 11 October 1625; and 'The names of those that had privie seales', *LRLB*, fols. 133v, 135v–7, and 145–5v.

14 'Mutuum ... de private Sigill', PRO E401/2323, unfoliated; and the entry under Rewards, 8 June 1627, 'The Book of Certificates', PRO E405/226.

15 JPs to PC, [July 1622], SP 14/133/44; Fletcher, *Sussex*, pp. 361; and Marc Schwarz, 'Lord Saye and Sele's Objections to the Palatinate of 1622', *Albion* IV (1972), pp. 12–22.

16 [Coventry] to Corporation, [1629?], Leics. RO, BR II/18/16, fol. 327; *Proceedings in Parliament 1628*, II, p. 303. See also Williams to Corporation, 31 August 1625, Leics. RO, BR II/18/15, fol. 634; and Anthony Fletcher, 'Honour, Reputation and Local Officeholding', in Anthony Fletcher and John Stevenson, eds., *Order and Disorder in Early Modern England* (Cambridge, 1985), p. 105.

17 Entries for 31 October, 5, 6, 8 and 26 November, 22 December 1621 and 15 February 1622, PRO E401/1907; Entries for 28 April, 7 and 14 May and 16 June 1621, PRO E401/1906; and PC to H, 28 February 1626, HA Corr. 12/4221.

18 Entries in Pitt's accounts for 7, 10 and 24 November 1625, 1, 11 and 18 February 1626, PRO E401/2441; and for 20 April, 8, 20, 27 and 28 June 1626, PRO E401/2442. On the 1624 Bill, see Michael Young, 'Revisionism and the Council of War, 1624–1626', *Parliamentary History* 8 (1989), pp. 1–27.

19 Entries in Pitt's accounts, 9 and 19 September 1628; and for 9 October, 23, 27 and 29 November 1628, and 25 February 1629, PRO E401/2444 and 2445.

20 Entries in Pitt's accounts, 21 October, 14, 19 and 27 November 1628, 17 January, 3, 13 and 20 February, 16 and 18 April 1629, PRO E401/2445 and 2446.

21 Entries in Pitt's accounts, 19 May, 19, 20 and 26 June and 7 November 1629, PRO E401/2446 and 2447; L. J. Reeve, *Charles I and the Road to Personal Rule* (Cambridge, 1989), pp. 58–117.

22 [Corporation] to Hericke, [1621]; and Mayor to May, [May 1625], Leics. RO, BR II/18/14, fols. 42 and 345; and Fletcher, *Sussex*, p. 205.

23 PC to H, 23 June 1624, *APC* 39/249–51; and H to DLs and JPs; and same to Constables, 7 July 1624, *LRLB*, fols. 88 and 89.

24 Sir Henry Whitehead's book of precedents, Hampshire RO, Southwick MSS, 4M53/140; James to H, 29 October, *LRLB*, fols. 95-6; and PC to the same, 31 October 1624, *APC* 39/351–2.

25 H to Constables, November 1624, *LRLB*, fol. 97; and Mayor's Court, 31 November 1625, Leics. RO, BR II/18/15, fol. 477. See also S. J. Stearns, 'Conscription and English Society in the 1620s', *JBS* XI (1972), pp. 1–23.

26 Rudinge's Accompts, SP 16/70/70; James to H, 30 November 1624, *LRLB*, fol. 99; and Mayor to same, 23 November 1624, Leics. RO, BR II/18/15, fol. 494.

27 Skipwith to H, 28 December 1624, HA Corr. 10/10886; and H to Hobert and Bromley, 15 March 1625, *LRLB*, fol. 109.

28 PC to H, 30 November 1624, *APC* 39/387; Lincoln to H, 3 December 1624; and H to DLs, 6 December 1624, *LRLB*, fols. 102 and 103v; and DLs to H, 22 December 1624, HA Corr. 10/10613.

29 Chamberlain to Carleton, 8 January 1625, *Letters*, II, p. 596; Williams to Corporation, 21 September 1622. Leics. RO, BR, II/18/14, fol. 88; and Thomas Barnes, *Vox Belli* (London, 1626), pp. 14–15. See also *Reform in the Provinces*, pp. 183–228.

30 PC to H, 5 May 1625, *APC* 40/42-4; Cave to H, 14 May 1625; Skipwith to same, [May 1625]; Heyricke to same, 15 May 1625; and Skipwith to Tomson, [May 1625]; and Rustat to same, 15 May 1625, HA Corr. 11/1282, 10880, 10881, 6752 and 10611.

31 Gerard to H, 14 May 1625; and Skipwith to same, 16 May 1625, HA Corr. 11/2884 and 10885; and H to Noel, 19 May 1625, *LRLB*, fol. 119.

32 Indentures of pressment, 18 May 1625; H to Noel, 19 May 1625; and H to Hobert, 11 May 1625, *LRLB*, fols. 117v-8, 119 and 112.

33 'A note of Souldiers returned', *Records of the Borough of Leicester*, IV, pp. 222–3; and H to Mayor, 12 May 1625, *LRLB*, fol. 117v.

34 Legge to H, 12 May 1625; H to Legge, 12 May 1625; same to Noel, 14 May 1625; and 'Disburst about ... the 150 souldiers', *LRLB*, fols. 114, 115 and 116v–117.

35 'A note of Souldiers returned', Leics. RO, BR II/18/15, fol. 595; PC to JPs, 31 August 1625, *APC* 40/153; and [the investigation's report], [late 1625], SP 16/22/5. See also H to the [JPs?], 1 November 1625, HA Corr. 11/5503; H to Noel, 21 July 1625; Noel to H, 6 October 1625, *LRLB*, fols. 128 and 134v.

36 PC to H, 25 April 1618, 11 February 1619, and 31 May 1620, *APC* 36/118–20 and 363–5; and 37/215–17; and Buggs, *Miles Mediterraneus*, p. 7.

37 'A note of the particulars', 10 May 1627, HA Military 1/12; the 1614 certificate; and H to PC, 28 July 1626, *LRLB*, fols. 12 and 174v. See also Fletcher, *Reform*, pp. 310–13; and Boynton, *Elizabethan Militia*, pp. 161–2.

38 H to DLs, 28 July 1626, *LRLB*, fol. 174; and Fletcher, *Reform*, p. 283.

39 Nichols, *History and Antiquities*, II, p. 756; III, p. 278, 368 and 449; and IV, pp. 187 and 506; and *Complete Peerage* under 'Stamford'.

40 H to Morison, 9 October 1618, *LRLB*, fol. 37v; and 'The Quarter Book of the Ordinance', March 1619, SP 14/11/112. On the Harington connection, see G. Aylmer, *The King's Servants* (London, 1961), pp. 286–7.

41 Depositions in H *v*. Fawnt, [1637], HA Legal 6/2, p. 12; H to W. Hastings, 31 October 1614, *LRLB*, fol. 8v; and Sir Edward and Sir Francis Hastings to Essex, [January 1599], *Hastings Letters*, p. 71. See also Nichols, IV, p. 51.

42 'Gerard's answer', 26 April 1631, HA Legal 5/3; and H to PC, 25 February 1618, SP 16/105/133.

43 H to DLs, 12 May 1618; same to Constables, 14 September 1618; same to PC, 15 April 1619, *LRLB*, fols. 32, 34v–5 and 55v.

44 H to Constables, September 1619; and same to DLs, 12 October 1619, *LRLB*, fols. 54–4v and 55.

45 Hesilrige to H, 20 October 1623, HA Corr. 9/6746; and H to DLs, 9 March and 14 October 1619; and same to Morison, 4 June 1622, *LRLB*, fols. 43v–4, 56 and 67.

46 H to PC, 20 May 1623, SP 14/145/11; and Staresmore to H, 26 June 1625, *LRLB*, fol. 126v.

47 Earle's Deposition in H *v*. Fawnt, 19 March 1638, HA Legal 7/3, pp. 20–8.

48 H to DLs, 19 October 1614, *LRLB*, fol. 7; and same to Edmondes, 15 February 1619; and same to PC, 15 April 1619, SP 14/105/106, and 14/108/45.

49 H to [PC], 20 May 1623, *LRLB*, fol. 70; and Hesilrige to H, 20 October 1623, HA Corr. 9/6746.

50 H to Lambe, 12 November 1623, *LRLB*, fol. 79; Dixie's Deposition in H *v*. Fawnt, [1637], HA Legal 6/2, pp. 23; and H to Hesilrige, 4 September 1623, *LRLB*, fol. 74.

51 *Instructions for Musters and Armes* (London, 1623), sig. [B2v]; and Sir John Haydon, 'Cuirassier, etc'. [citing the 1628 prices], 15 June 1635, HEH, Bridgewater MSS, El 7617.

52 Hesilrige to H, 18 June 1625, *LRLB*, fol. 127; and H to PC, 25 February 1618, SP 16/105/133. See also Peter Edwards, *The Horse Trade in Tudor and Stuart England* (Cambridge, 1988), pp. 38-46.

53 PC to H, 31 May 1620, *APC* 37/ 215–17; 'A note [of defaulters]', 30 November 1625, *LRLB*, fol. 148v.; Exeter to H, 25 May 1619, HA Corr. 7/1301; and Essex to same, [1619?], SP 14/111/118.

54 Montaigne to H, 20 February 1619; and Hesilrige to H, 15 November 1619, HA Corr. 8/ 9346 and 6745; and H to Lambe, 12 November 1623, *LRLB* fol. 79.

55 Manners to H, 30 March 1619; and Fawnt to same, 25 June 1624, HA Corr. 8/4137 and 10/3147. See also Harpur to same, 9 October 1619, HA Corr. 8/4588.

56 Staresmore to H, 26 June 1625; H to Staresmore, 6 July 1625, *LRLB*, fols. 126v and 127–7v; and Rudinge's accounts, SP 16/70/70.

57 H to Constables, 9 March 1619; same to Morrison, 19 May 1623, *LRLB*, fols. 71 and 43v–44; PC to H, 30 June 1620, *APC* 38/274-5; and H to PC, 20 May 1623, SP 14/145/11.

58 PC to H, 20 June 1623; and Warrant to Daniell Bucocke, 30 June 1623, *APC* 39/21 and 41; and H to Constables, 14 October 1623, *LRLB*, fol. 78.

59 'The forme of a submission'; PC to H, 20 June 1623, *LRLB*, fols. 64 and 71v; and Hesilrige to same, 20 May 1620, HA Corr. 8/6743.

60 Leicestershire certificate, 1614; and H to DLs, *LRLB*, fols. 12 and 39v; and PC to H, 11 February 1619, *APC* 36/363-5.

61 H to DLs, 25 February 1619, *LRLB*, fol. 41v; and Chamberlain's Accounts, Michaelmas 1619–20, Leics. RO, BR III/2/77, fol. 149.

62 H to Davies, 15 April 1625, HA Corr. 10/5483. On the magazine, see H to Hastings, 10 September 1624; same to Staresmore, 14 October 1625; and same to Conway, 30 November 1625, *LRLB*, fols. 90v, 139–9v and 148.

63 On the Corporation's desire for more autonomy, see 'Remembrances in renewing the Charter', 1629, Leics. RO, BR I/2/45; and Patterson, 'Leicester and Lord Huntingdon'.

64 Gillot to Harvey, 31 May 1619, Leics. RO, BR II/18/13, fol. 397. See also 'Remembrances to Mr Recorder', *ibid.*, fol. 386.

65 Corporation to H, 5 June 1625, *LRLB*, fol. 123; and May and Moseley to same, 18 June 1625, Leics. RO, BR II/18/15, fol. 581. See also Wadland to Corporation, 19 June 1625, Leics. RO, BR II/18/15, fol. 588.

66 Staresmore to H, 18 June 1625; and H to Corporation, 14 June 1625, *LRLB*, fols. 125 and 123–3v; and Corporation to H. May, 22 June 1625, Leics. RO, BR II/18/15, fol. 582.

67 Goddard's testimony in H *v.* Fawnt, 19 March 1638, HA Legal 7/3, p. 53; Mayor to H, 5 June 1625; H to Mayor, 14 June 1625; and same to same, 14 March 1627, *LRLB*, fols. 123, 123–3v, and 197v–8.

68 H to [Palmes], 2 June 1626; H to Constables, 6 June 1622 and 4 September 1623, *LRLB*, fols. 16v, 67v–68 and 73–74v. See also H to Head Constables, 26 September 1615, *LRLB*, fol. 16v.

69 H to DLs, 30 August 1622, *LRLB*; and 'Instructions for my Lords deputie Lieutenants', 2 October 1623, *LRLB*, fols. 69–9v and 76–6v.

70 'Instructions for my Lords deputie Lieutenants'; and H to DLs, 9 March 1619, *LRLB*, fols. 76–6v and 43v; and Rudinge's accounts, SP 16/70/70.

71 Warrant against William Pickering, 20 June 1624, HA Manorial 53/14; H to DLs, 30 August 1622; and H to [Palmes], 2 June 1626, *LRLB*, fols. 69–9v and 16v.

72 *Instructions for Musters and Arms* (London, 1623); Rudinge's accounts, SP 16/70/70; and Thomas Meautys to H, [1625], HA Military 1/17. See also Boynton, *Elizabethan Militia*, p. 240.

73 H to Constables, [late May 1625] and 24 September 1625; Rudinge's note, [late 1620], *LRLB*, fols. 122, 131–1v and 65; and H to Constables, 27 July 1626, HA Military 1/21.

74 H to Constables, 3 February 1626; and 'A note how the Captaines companies are devided', *LRLB*, 153–4. See also Charles to PC, 14 January 1626, SP 16/18/55; and PC to H, 24 January 1626, APC 40/321–2.

75 H to B. Hesilrige, 14 September 1625; 'My Lords desires', [February 1626], *LRLB*, fols. 130 and 157; Rudinge's accounts, SP 16/70/70; and *Instructions for Musters*, [B4].

76 H to Hastings, 10 September 1624; and same to Mansell, 31 May 1624, *LRLB*, fols. 84v and 90v; and Rudinge's accounts, SP 16/70/70. See also *The Montagu Musters Book*, ed. by J. Wake (Northampton, 1926), pp. 147, 192 and 194.

77 H to Hastings, 16 June 1620 and 12 November 1623, *LRLB*, fols. 54 and 78v.

78 H to Mansell, 31 May 1624; and 'A note what money was received', June 1624, *LRLB*, fols. 84v and 92; and Rudinge's accounts, SP 16/70/70.

79 *Instructions for Musters*, sig. [B3v–b4]; DLs to H, 2 October 1623; and H to DLs, 2 October 1623, *LRLB*, fol. 77v.

80 H to DLs, 30 August 1622; and same to Mayors, 6 February 1626, *LRLB*, fols. 69–9v and 156v.

81 H to Constables, September 1619; Staresmore to H, 26 June 1625; and H to Conway, 30 November 1625, *LRLB*, fols. 54–4v, 126v and 148.

82 PC to H, 10 January 1628, APC 43/227–8; Clifford to PC, 2 February 1628; and the Devonshire DLs to PC, 15 February 1628, SP 16/92/10 and 16/93/41. See also North-ampton to Conway, 24 February 1628, SP 16/94/36.

83 F. Coke to J. Coke, 5 March 1628, BL Add. MS 64,895, fol. 58; and H to PC, 1 February 1628, SP 16/92/1.

84 PC to Huntingdon, 31 May 1628, APC 43/470–2.

85 'A particular of the Queres', [April 1619], *LRLB*, fol. 52.

86 Testimony of Hugh Watts, 3 December 1624, Leics. RO, BR II/18/15, fols. 485 and 487; and F. Coke to J. Coke, 17 November 1625, BL Add. MS 64,885, fol. 64.

87 Grey to H, 5 October 1625; H to Grey, 6 October 1625; same to Staresmore and Dixie, 14 October 1625; Dixie and Staresmore to H, 18 October 1625, *LRLB*, fols. 134–4v and 139–40.

88 PC to H, 4 October 1625, APC 40/188–90; H to DLs, 27 October 1625; and same to Noel, 27 October 1625, *LRLB*, fols. 141v and 142. See also B. W. Quintrell, 'The Practice and Problems of Recusant Disarming, 1585–1641', *Recusant History* XII (1984), pp. 216.

89 'The Presentment of the Grand Jury of Constables', [late 1625]; and Ashbe to H, 23 November 1625, *LRLB*, fols. 142v–144 and 144v.

90 PC to H, 12 December 1625, APC 40/268.

91 H to DLs, 19 October 1614 and 27 June 1626; H to [Corporation], 14 March 1627, *LRLB*, fols. 6, 165v–6 and 197v–8. For the later use of PC's commendation, see H to PC, 28 May 1627, *ibid.*, fol. 208.

Analysis

Passing in review

G iven Huntingdon's triumphant reformation of the militia, the regi-ment deserves a final opportunity to pass in review, for the ceremonial flour-ishes provide the appropriate atmosphere to consider the magnitude of Huntingdon's achievement. Simply put, his performance casts a profound scepticism over blanket indictments of the regime's failure to perfect the militia, and this in turn compels scholars to think again about the structure of local administration.

First of all, it is impossible not to note the sheer novelty of seeing much of anything on the militia before 1626. To be sure, Lindsay Boynton has pre-sented a perceptive portrait of the Elizabethan militia, but understandably eager to press on to the later campaign for a 'perfect' militia, Boynton largely skated over James I's attempts to improve the militia. Nothing else exists on Whitehall's goals in this campaign, and the results of attempting to follow the story in local studies are only marginally better – and often with good reason. In Sussex, a voluminous lieutenancy book began only in 1624, leaving Fletcher uncertain about what to make of the earlier years. His frustration is nothing compared with that of Hughes, stymied by the near complete absence of information on the Warwickshire militia.[1] Barnes was dealt a much stronger archival hand, and he fully exploited the wealth of information on the Somerset militia. Unfortunately Barnes's decision to begin with Charles I's accession necessarily meant that his study cast a blind eye on the bustle of activity in the last years of Rex Pacificus. Likewise a focus on Charles's reign limits the utility of D. P. Carter's otherwise excellent article analysing the Lancashire militia.[2] Patchy though this coverage is, it is even more fleeting in other local histories where the lack of either sources or interest thwarted a thorough analysis of the militia in this period.[3]

The importance of the wealth of Leicestershire information becomes abun-dantly clear after considering the situation elsewhere. In Somerset, the Deputy

Lieutenants had by 1625 scarcely begun to stir the local militia, an institution then suffering from 'premature aging through inactivity'. Consequently, their attentions focused simply on bringing some order to men attired in 'aged, rusty and seldom complete' armour, and armed with 'a queerly assorted' array of pikes 'resembling agricultural implements more than weapons'. Not surprisingly, 'very low' morale and a 'lax' attitude infected the Deputies and constables as well as the officers and men, and since 'no one had been trained for war', these 'flaccid amateurs' found it nearly impossible even to go through the motions, enthusiasm having 'seeped out of every militiaman from the lord lieutenant to the humblest pikeman'. The situation in Sussex was scarcely any better. As late as 1625, fully half of the militia remained in an 'unselected' state, barely armed and in no position to do anything other than routine policing. Nearly overwhelmed by the task of bringing these men up to the minimal standards of the trained band, the Deputy Lieutenants had little energy left to do much with the trained men. Hence in 1624, they confessed to the Council that not only were the majority of the trained band's weapons 'olde fashion', but 'we feare we shall hardly reforme' the situation in the foreseeable future. A year later, far from correcting the situation, the Deputies instead denounced the Council's insistence on 'the moderne fashion' for 'all the armes through the county' as unrealistic.[4]

The contrast could not have been starker with the situation in Leicestershire where the militia regiment in 1625, long fully manned and fully equipped, had already achieved a remarkable air of efficiency. Indeed, it had earned a glowing commendation from the Privy Council itself. Years of subsequent pressure from the Council were not able to do much to close the gap between these county militias. The government's plans for regional cavalry musters in 1628 'raised the ire of even the best affected deputy lieutenants' in Somerset, and had Whitehall not cancelled the scheme, the county's response, Barnes predicted, 'would have been unsatisfactory if not unprintable'.[5] Conversely, in Leicestershire, what caused consternation was not the original order for the rendez-vous, but its eventual cancellation.

The discovery of wildly varying levels of preparedness and efficiency, while initially startling, can be taken as further validity of the most fundamental rule of local history: every county is different. Yet before insisting on the reduction of early modern history to some three dozen provincial molecules, we would do well to consider the possibility that there may be a general pattern in these varying reports, which might spare us a good deal of trouble. After examining Sussex, Fletcher pronounced the exact militia 'an impracticable programme'; since the Lords Lieutenant declined to summon defaulters before the Council, the central government had to rely on 'independently-minded gentry to enforce its will'. Equally uncompromising was Barnes's verdict on Somerset. The lieutenancy as an institution was 'foredoomed to perpetual weakness' in the wake of 'the lord lieutenant's virtual withdrawal from direct activity in local government'. Given that the Lieutenant had 'lost contact with the [local] administration' so much 'that he had ceased to be a county officer at all', Barnes pronounced his withdrawal 'the basic cause of the failure to perfect the militia'.[6] These harsh judgements are richly merited. All of these court grandees attended musters in their counties, at very best, at the rate of once in their lieutenancy. After years of threats, the third Earl of Dorset finally turned up in 1619 to inspect the Sussex regiments, and his record, however pathetic, remained unequalled by either his colleague, Arundel, his brother, the fourth earl, or the third Earl of Pembroke in Somerset.[7] In Leicestershire, the situation was wholly otherwise. Far from having withdrawn, the Lord Lieutenant was so inextricably bound up with the most minute aspect of the militia that it was almost impossible to imagine one without the other. In this environment those independent-minded gentlemen who dared to default on their militia obligations, much less to think of challenging Huntingdon's control, quickly found themselves with the extended leisure to contemplate the error of their ways in a Whitehall anteroom as they waited to receive a dressing-down from the Privy Councillors.

The sharp contrast in administrative styles between resident and non-resident Lords Lieutenant does much to explain the varying standards among county militias. 'Obviously a crucial factor affecting the county's response' to the Whitehall's insistence on a 'perfect' militia, Anthony Fletcher observed, was 'the attitude of the lieutenant to his responsibilities'. Some of the Lords Lieutenant were 'idle, tactless or remote': Pembroke, Arundel and Dorset easily fall into that category. In 1624, the fourth Earl of Dorset abruptly broke an engagement to preside over a muster; and as an excuse, he cited an apprehension that he might 'receave but little content in the present view'. In point of fact, if he was serious about finding contentment, his best course would have been to attend and as frequently as possible. 'Even an occasional appearance at musters,' Fletcher has rightly observed, 'would have been a useful stimulus to those inclined to shirk their obligations.' In Leicestershire, shirkers never managed to elude the psychological, if not the physical, presence of Huntingdon for very long. Such careful attention from the local magnate in turn gave particular force to his warning to recusants about 'how ill I shall take it of them'.[8] Quite simply, from non-resident Lieutenants similar threats failed to sound particularly ominous.

Huntingdon's success with the militia thus throws into sharp relief the fact that Leicestershire represents a different political system from those in other shires with which scholars are more familiar. In Sussex and Somerset, the physical and mental distance between the magnates and their counties was so vast that it permitted the emergence of a self-confident and largely autonomous local elite. Yet in Leicestershire, both the Justices and the Deputy

Lieutenants were under Huntingdon's thumb. Consequently once scholars are able to appreciate the significance of a resident Lieutenant, they too can join contemporaries from counties with non-resident peers in their amazement over a thousand well equipped and well trained soldiers marching past the Earl of Huntingdon.

NOTES

1 Boynton, *Elizabethan Militia*, pp. 237–43; Fletcher, *Sussex*, p. 180; and Hughes, *Politics*, pp. 22 and 60.

2 Barnes, *Somerset*, p. vii; and D. P. Carter, 'The Exact Militia in Lancashire, 1625–1640', *Northern History* XI (1975), pp. 87–106.

3 See for example, Holmes, *Lincolnshire*, pp. 96 and 104; Peter Clarke, *English Provincial Society from the Reformation to the Revolution* (London, 1977). p. 328; and S. J. Watts, *From Border to Middle Shire: Northumberland, 1586–1625* (Leicester, 1975).

4 Barnes, *Somerset*, pp. 123 and 113–14; and Fletcher, *Sussex*, pp. 182–3.

5 Barnes, *Somerset*, p. 253.

6 Fletcher, *Sussex*, pp. 184–5 and 200; and Barnes, *Somerset*, pp. 98, 102 and 279.

7 Fletcher, *Sussex*, pp. 178–88; and Barnes, *Somerset*, pp. 99–103.

8 Fletcher, *Sussex*, pp. 180 and 184.

Part II

'The uncertaine
state of man'

The pressures on
the local community
1618–26

And hence have learn't th'uncertaine state of man,
And that no height of glitt'ring honour can
Secure his quiet: for Almighty God,
Who rules the high, can with His powr'full rod
Represse the greatest, and in his mercy daignes
With dang'rous ioyes to mingle wholsome paines.
[Sir John Beaumont, 'To my Lord Viscount Purbeck']

At first glance, John Beaumont's career was that of a successful poet. Brother of Francis Beaumont the playwright and friend of Ben Jonson and Michael Drayton, Beaumont was a habitué of celebrated 'wit-combats' at the Mermaid Tavern. From there it was an easy step to Whitehall, where Beaumont spent a decade producing a steady stream of courtly panegyrics. When death prematurely claimed him in 1627, his career was at its height, for only a few months earlier Charles I had awarded him a baronetcy. His contemporary prominence easily ensured him an honoured resting place in Westminster Abbey.

In this otherwise stereotypic profile of a canny metropolitan litterateur, two unexpected facts about Sir John stand out. The first is his devotion to Leicestershire, where he resided deep in the Charnwood only a few miles from Donnington Park. Rather surprisingly, the muse of this successful court poet was 'a plaine and countrey' one, whom Beaumont generally encountered when 'I to solitary hills retire' near his country house. Admittedly he made periodic trips to Westminster, but Beaumont was someone who 'from dust of worldly tumults flies'.[1] Along with a refusal to sever his provincial roots, the other surprise about Beaumont is the darker side to his normally bubbly panegyrics. Along with fulsome verses hymning assorted grandees, he produced a steady stream of poems brooding on the dangers of striving for success, either in the arts or in politics. One cautioned against abandoning 'Vertue' for the fatal allure of 'Pleasure, Riches, Fame'; another proclaimed that the only way to gain 'Great honour, perfect pleasure, peace and wealth' lay through spiritual devotion, not court preferment; and a third warns about the folly of pursuing 'Vaine honour', since 'We cannot in these outward things be blest;/ For we are sure to lose them.'[2] This consistent theme strikes a sombre counterpoint to Beaumont's more public verse lavishing praise on the virtues, real or imagined, of court worthies.

Sir John's two characteristics can best be seen in a poem congratulating Viscount Purbeck, another native son of Leicestershire, on his return to health. Even here, amid couplets rejoicing over the happy news, Beaumont cannot resist an opportunity to weave in a homily on 'th' uncertain state of man'. The most fortunate who had reached 'the height of honour' could not be certain of

> quiet: for Almighty God
> Who rules the high, can with His pow'rfull rod
> Represse the greatest ...[3]

Such melancholy appears out of place in a study of a resourceful, dedicated local governor whom the councillors had praised for his 'exquisite performance'. Nevertheless, Huntingdon should have taken Beaumont's warning to heart.

Everything in the preceding section is quite accurate. The earl had faced a series of daunting challenges, and aside from bad luck with the county's conductors in 1625, he had triumphed over them all. The Council's lavish praise of his performance was equally real. Nevertheless these extraordinary accomplishments were only part of the story. Along with his admirable qualities, Huntingdon also had more troubling, not to say alarming, characteristics, and those contemporaries who earlier politely overlooked these flaws found that his actions in the 1620s made it increasingly difficult to do so. For Huntingdon, as for all other early Stuart local officials, what was administratively brilliant was often politically dangerous, for by marshalling the county's resources for the war effort, he had incited a local political conflict. Resentment over the state's intrusion into the local community played a large part in fuelling the growing crisis; so too did Huntingdon himself. Whitehall's demands after 1618 had allowed the earl to fashion his own regime in the county, effectively representing a 'local state' in which he exercised unparalleled authority. At the same time, many outside of this charmed administrative circle found Huntingdon's tightening grip on the shire an appalling development. Given the mounting irritation with his rule, Huntingdon might well have listened when Beaumont cautioned those who stood at the 'height of glitt'ring honour' that a 'pow'rfull rod' stood poised to 'represse the greatest'.[1]

Part II will discuss the flip side of Huntingdon's 'exquisite performance'. First, it will examine the earl's personal problems before anatomising the groups within the local elite whom the earl had irritated. Then it will carefully calibrate the precise weight of the burdens which the state imposed in the 1620s. Only then is it possible to understand how a single Council order in the summer of 1626 ignited a conflagration which set the local community ablaze and which nearly consumed 'the House of Ashby'.[2] Huntingdon should have paid more attention to Beaumont, if only because this courtly poet helped spark the blaze in 1626.[3]

NOTES

1 *The Poems of Sir John Beaumont*, ed. by A. B. Grosart (n.p., 1869), pp. 165 and 97. Beaumont badly deserves a serious reappraisal; for the interim, see Florence Skillington, 'Sir John Beaumont of Gracedieu', *TLAHS* XLVII (1971–72), pp. 43–50.

2 *Ibid.*, pp. 78, 86 and 93.

3 *Ibid.*, p. 170.

Chapter 3

───◆───

A declining torn and miserable estate

E arlier in 1626, as Huntingdon coped with his new fame, assessments of the earl might well shade into the superhuman. Regrettably the Lord Lieutenant was all too mortal, and the problems which surrounded him were almost crippling. When petitioning for royal bounty, contemporary convention required the supplicant to exaggerate his plight. Yet in one of the fourth earl's pleas to James I, there was more than a little ring of truth when he lamented his own 'declyninge torne and miserable estate'.[1] If anything, the situation had only become more desperate for his grandson. The sombre details of the family's problems are well worth careful analysis, because they make his devotion to duty markedly less altruistic and his apparently invulnerable position disintegrates altogether.

THE HOUSE OF ASHBY

Huntingdon's obsession with his illustrious great-uncle was part of a larger sense of family obligation, which required the fifth earl to protect and advance 'the House of Ashby', the numerous Hastings offspring. A remarkable number were laudable individuals, like his uncle, Henry Hastings of the Woodland; his brother, Sir George Hastings; or his cousin, Sir Henry Hastings of the Abbey. With his own children, he and his wife also had the good fortune to produce dutiful offspring. Yet such a large clan inevitably included more dubious members. Within the family, as within England, the Reformation had initiated a bitter struggle. Not for nothing had Cardinal Pole in Queen Mary's reign taken such pains with the education of his Hastings grand-nephews. Thanks to his attention, only two of the third earl's four brothers were committed Protestants; his long-lived mother and the two other brothers, one of whom was his heir, remained crypto-Catholics. Pole therefore institutionalised an uneasy division within the family.

Although Rome was anathema to the fifth earl, his Catholic relatives did not have to face his wrath alone; they had only to appeal to their Catholic relative, the Earl of Worcester, James I's Lord Privy Seal. And he had Hastingses to protect. Along with a large dowry, Dorothy Port, the fourth earl's wife, also brought her Catholicism and her nephew, the formidable Father Gerard. Likewise Walter Hastings, another of the third earl's younger brothers, had married a sister of the recusant Lord Vaux. While doubts flourished about Walter's devotion to the Established Church, there were none about his wife, who refused to hide her Catholicism. Given these religious irregularities, Walter Hastings's failure to receive a knighthood becomes more comprehensible. Logically the fifth earl should have given a wide berth to this awkward great-uncle, depending instead, as the third earl had, on Walter's staunchly Protestant elder brother, Sir Francis Hastings. Huntingdon, however, did the reverse, relying heavily on Walter's advice, insisting on his advancement in spite of local opposition, and loaning him thousands of pounds. Meanwhile Sir Francis remained almost unknown to his grand-nephew. 'It griveth me,' Sir Francis wrote, 'to become a stranger to the lords of Ashby, or that of Ashby shoulde be made a stranger to me.' Such lamentations failed to improve the relationship of the two relatives.[2]

The earl's fondness for 'unkle Walter' did not extend to his son, Sir Henry Hastings of Braunston, who a local pot-poet rudely described as someone who 'looks as he would shite/ pufft up in his owne pride'. Hauteur was the least of his problems. Disgusted with his father's timely displays of conformity, Sir Henry followed his mother's practice of open Catholicism. Thus in the 1614 Parliament Huntingdon had to endure public denunciations of Sir Henry, 'a great son of Leicestershire', for his enthusiastic support of the Catholic seminary at Saint-Omer. Such was his zeal that Sir Henry asked Father Gerard to guide him through the Spiritual Exercises, an intense round of prayers and meditation.[3] Gerard also guided Sir Henry to another county resident, Sir Everard Digby, and to near involvement in the Gunpowder Plot. 'When I come to Tryall,' Hastings was confident that 'I shall prove no dishonest man neither to my soveraigne nor to my cuntry.'[4] The opportunity never came, leaving Sir Henry's relationship with his noble cousin badly strained. In later years, the earl willingly denounced Sir Henry as a militia defaulter, turned him in as a poacher, awarded him the highest assessment in the 1611 Privy Seal loan, and subjected him to the indignity of having his house searched late in 1625.[5] Given their relationship, it understandably took two years and the Privy Council's intervention to retrieve £86 14s. 7d. of public funds which had inadvertently fallen into Sir Henry's hands. This public obligation was much more tractable than the substantial private debt which Walter Hastings owed the earl on his death and his heir never settled. Their difficulties became so well known that the Earl of Manchester could only acknowledge them: 'I knowe your Lordship is not well pleased with him.'[6]

Huntingdon's fondest hope was that Gerard's influence would lead Sir Henry and his wife into celibacy; then the manor of Kirby Muxloe, which the third earl had generously leased to Walter Hastings and his male heirs for £20 a year, would revert to the earl. Unfortunately, Lady Hastings brought this happy prospect to an end by producing a son. Sir Henry's children proved no less awkward. Consider the surprising answer which the authorities received when they asked where Christopher Dorman had acquired a rosary and a crucifix: these gifts, he freely confessed, had come from Sir Henry's daughters. The influence from Kirby Muxloe was morally as well as ecclesiastically dubious. In 1620, when local officials intervened to stop a disturbance in an inn, they found a Mr Thistlewaite, and Walter Hastings, Sir Henry's son, at the centre of it. Problems had arisen when Hastings had greeted Thistlewaite's attempt to relieve himself in a chamberpot with a drunken toast: 'You that are pissing there I will drinke to you.' Thistlewaite's request for a few moments' delay led first to a blow from Hastings, and then to a general fracas. At this point, the landlady, who was several months pregnant, came between the two men, 'telling him [Hastings] shee was with Childe and prayed him not to fright her'. This earned her a barrage of cups and plates from the tipsy Hastings.[7]

In these awkward incidents, Sir Henry consistently played his trump card with his cousin, concluding his letters to the earl with the salutation, 'your lordshipps unfortunate kinsman'. For Huntingdon, the misfortune was entirely his own. And yet, for all that, Sir Henry and his family remained the earl's close relatives, and in such matters the third earl's example was unambiguous. 'All the world can witnes it,' his brother Francis recalled, 'howe honorablie hee did deale with all of us that were his brethren.' This was especially true 'for suche as were farther of to him in kindred, his care not wantinge to doe them anie good'. The fifth earl may well have grumbled that charity came more easily to his great-uncle, who spent much of his adult life in the comparative safety of York. Nevertheless, even Catholicism was not enough to make Huntingdon abandon his relatives. In his advice to his son, he warned that with wayward relatives, 'though thou seest and knowes many weaknesses in them connive at it and let not their misfortunes make thee disavow them'.[8] Misgivings notwithstanding, the fifth earl did what he could for Sir Henry and his family.

The problem with the pronounced strain of Catholicism in the family was that it inevitably compromised the purity of Huntingdon's motives. No matter how strenuously the earl attacked the old faith, doubts naturally arose about his sincerity with Sir Henry Hastings of Braunston in the wings. Unfortunately for Huntingdon, contemporaries were not simply wondering about the Catholics within the family.

A TOTTERING HOUSE

Late in 1623, the Lord Treasurer ordered a survey of the earl's estates, and Huntingdon's reaction deftly illustrates his most notable failing. He immediately dispatched his brother to argue that the great 'Puritan' earl had ruined the family estates. For their part, Huntingdon's grandfather, the fourth earl, and Huntingdon himself had diligently labored to pay off their family's obligations; although the sale of 'fourescore and fourteene manners' had still left a massive debt to the Crown, it allowed Huntingdon to say with some pride that his family had paid 'a greater yerely revenue' into the Exchequer 'then out of any one subjects estate in the kingdome though some other mens debts have beene greater then his'. These contributions let the earl beg that 'out of the dismembered estats my auncestors left I may have some small meanes to subsist'. On the heels of this pathetic letter came another. Eager to give the Crown as much satisfaction 'as the smalenes of my fortune will beare', he proposed to raise his annual rent from £80 to £100. Although the increase was not much, 'I beseech your lordship out of your noble favours to mee be pleased to accept therof in regard my meanes are soe smale in respect of the honor it hath pleased God to cast upon me.' Fortunately for Huntingdon, Middlesex's fall soon halted the re-examinaton of the Hastings debt, and these pleas eventually prompted James to drop the matter, since he was 'not willing to take the extremity of advantage' which he held over Huntingdon.[9]

While this episode makes Huntingdon's satisfaction with Middlesex's impeachment appear less than disinterested, its greatest utility is to hammer out the *Leitmotiv* of Huntingdon's career. Family pride and religious affinity did not alone fix the earl's attention on his Elizabethan ancestor. The most sombre volume in the fifth earl's collection was a full account of the third earl's land sales, a long work recording painfully large sums of money, possibly as much as £90,000. Even more depressing, the spate of land sales had not ceased with the third earl's death. His brother struggled to rein in spending, only to have two long-lived widows undercut his best efforts by annually drawing over £1,700 out of the estate. Meanwhile the fourth earl had sold off land which yearly produced £2,549 2s. 1d. in order to bring his brother's debts down to £13,700. So bleak was the situation that, one year, he found himself with exactly £37 14s. to live on.[10]

In this impasse, he sought the traditional route to solvency, a wealthy bride for his grandson, and found Elizabeth Stanley, one of the co-heiresses of the Earl of Derby. With this brilliant match, the family seemed to have belatedly climbed into the black. Hence William Dugdale later praised the fourth earl's achievement; after inheriting an estate 'almost quite torn in pieces and ruin'd, ... he did exceedingly repaire it; and at last left it such though not comparable to what it had been formerly; yet not unsutable to his dignitie and degree'. Yet in spite of the Stanley dowry of £4,000, serious financial problems remained, as his successor learned even before the fourth earl was in his grave. Although he left behind £3,733 3s. 11d. in ready cash, the cost of the fourth earl's funeral and the repayment of urgent debts exceeded this bequest. Thus, for his inheritance, the fifth earl glumly concluded that 'theire remayneth in this Accomptants handes nil, for hee is and shalbee in surplusage more than he hath or shall receive the some of £276 19s. 9d'.[11] In short, even a timely windfall like the Stanley dowry ultimately did not stop the family's financial haemorraghing.

The sensation of struggling to run in place while sliding inexorably backwards became all too common for the fifth earl. In 1612, he found himself almost equal to his great-uncle, at least in one category; having run up debts totalling £57,470, he too launched extensive land sales in order to keep his creditors at bay. His need for ready cash even drove him to place his wife's jointure lands on the block. To justify such extreme action, he had agreed to compensate her with other estates once the financial emergency had passed, but as that happy day increasingly never seemed imminent, the earl's embarrassment reached new heights when 'his friends' had to insist that he provide for the countess. Long negotiations ensued as Huntingdon repeatedly attempted to scrape together enough fragments of land to satisfy his relatives, only succeeding in 1617.[12]

In this appalling situation, Huntingdon was nothing if not inventive. Efforts to increase the productivity of his estates were quite promising until a corrupt steward bled some £20,000 out of the earl. Meanwhile, the notion of literally striking it rich mesmerised the earl. The fact that his great-uncle's investments in the Canford mines had done 'greate hurte of himselfe and mayme to his howse and posteritie' did not dissuade Huntingdon from his own mining speculations, but he pursued coal pits close to home rather than precious metals in distant shires. Neighboring gentlemen became used to the earl's requests for exploratory digs on their land, a few of which developed into viable operations. Yet even in the best years, the profits accounted for only a very small percentage of his total income.[13] His interest in exploiting timber resources was more successful. As the Lieutenant of the Forest of Leicester, the earl required no coaching on the potential profit in trees, and wholesale deforestations of manors produced substantial, if irregular, amounts of cash. One clearance in 1628 for instance yielded almost £200. Indeed, his reliance on this practice was so well known that his critics complained of his overly enthusiastic culling of the royal forests.[14]

All of these efforts were for comparatively small stakes, but larger gains were possible by speculating on undervalued property. Wealthy relatives like Lord Spencer, who expected only the repayment of the principal, were quite handy. Unfortunately with large purchases, accommodating kinsmen could not save Huntingdon from moneylenders; hence his periodic forays into the land market succeeded only in binding him more tightly into the inexorable demands of interest rates around 10 per cent, which in 1620 consumed 30 per cent of his income. The most chilling illustration of the burden of high interest rates came in 1621 with the fifth earl's scheme to retire a debt of £8,743. If in the following decade he sold off lands in Chellison and Loughborough, leased property in Melbourne, Oakthorpe, Woodlawn, Kirby Muxloe and Measham, and sold a reversion on the Diseworth parsonage, his total indebtedness would still stand at £12,483 10s.[15] Painful memories lay behind his advice about loans. Be 'watchful', he warned his son, 'least thou come in debt for believe me thou shalt have Hercules labours before thoust get out'. 'Many occasions and unexpected accidents' would sabotage the fondest plans of easy repayment, and in the meantime, the interest mounted:

> I have felte it by deare bought experience that ten in a hundred will eate out the goodnes of any purchase and where thou thinkes to add a supply to thy Howse thou wilt finde it will not only drawe awaye it selfe, which thou hast bought but a greate deale of the land thou haddest.

Grim reminders of this adage littered the Hastings rent rolls as the hollow shells of manors. High hopes of making a shrewd land purchase, Dugdale noted, invariably proved 'little to the advantage of himselfe or his descendants'; the pressure of debt servicing forced Huntingdon 'not long after' to sell it again 'by parcells, receiving only the Royaltie and some chief Rents, which scarcely were sufficient to satisfie the fee-farme Rent to his maiestie'.[16]

Consistent failures in land speculation only intensified efforts at retrenchment, for the earl eventually appreciated the importance of controlling personal expenditure. 'Sparingnes,' he told his son, 'thou shalt finde a great Revenue,' and the rigorous application of this motto was one of the few financial things Huntingdon did well. His family was placed on a strict budget, carefully enumerating items down to shillings and pence. In such plans the customary displays of aristocratic glory had no place. While a large retinue was 'a brave thing', the expense, he concluded, will always 'make this pleasure cease in a shorte tyme'. Hence the Countess of Derby's entertainment of 1607 was the last Hastings masque; Huntingdon's company of actors soon had to find another patron; and Donne's poems to the countess soon stopped. Likewise, the earl's architectural ambitions for Donnington Park eventually yielded to financial reality. His obsession with the bottom line even extended to interior design; a list of expensive temptations highlighted 'Delicat furniture', which, unlike sensible, if doughty, pieces, 'in ordinary use will weare soe fast'.[17]

Such unaristocratic economies eventually had a reward of sorts; by 1620 Huntingdon had reduced his debts, once in excess of £60,000, to a more manageable £10,000. This remarkable achievement had come only with a frightening wave of land sales. His income in 1620 came to £2,032 8s. 2d., of which some 55 per cent came from the two manors of Ashby and Loughborough; the rest derived from a host of smaller fees and rents, the pathetic legacy of the Hastings' once awesome rent roll. Even this total was deceptive, for another £400 immediately went back out in rents and a staggering £500 to the moneylenders. Finally, although the estate had weathered a crippling abundance of dowagers, the earl's mother still required another £200. These deductions left a disposable income of approximately £900. As a youth, he had lamented that, unlike continental nobility, the English peers 'are noe more but bare tityles and peradventure scarce possess a penny of revenew in the place from whence they take their titles'.[18] Unfortunately for him, the rest of his life was simply a gloss on this text.

The transition from Tudor magnate to early Stuart administrator haggling over a few pounds is too stark to be taken in at once. Yet the evidence of the family's decline was everywhere to be seen. In the sixteenth century, glorious matches had linked the family with the great dynasties of the realm: the Greys, the Devereuxs, the Dudleys, the Staffords, the Poles, and by extension, the Plantagenets and the Tudors. But the pattern changed with the fourth earl, who married the daughter of a Derbyshire knight. His son married Sarah Harington, the daughter of a Rutland knight. Although Huntingdon himself returned to the old pattern by wedding the daughter of the Earl of Derby, the new prescription ensured that Huntingdon's own son was to marry the daughter of a Welsh judge, Sir John Davies. A more dramatic sign of the family's financial decline can be seen in the marriages of the Hastings women. The third earl saw his sisters married off to the Earls of Somerset and Lincoln and to Lord Compton. By contrast, while the fifth earl managed to wed one of his sisters to Lord Stanhope, later the Earl of Chesterfield, the other one had to make do with a knight, albeit a prosperous one. So too did both of his daughters. The key to these less than enviable marriages was money: Lucy Davies alone brought the Hastingses £7,000 and 'the expectation of the whole state of the said Sir J. Davys'.[19] By contrast, no lavish dowries went with Alice and Elizabeth Hastings, the earl's daughters.

With the family's decline came the quips. Thomas Pestell, a Leicestershire clergyman and poet, had a stormy relationship with the fifth earl that included an extended law suit in which Huntingdon charged Pestell with failing to treat him with respect. This background makes it hard not to see Pestell's short couplet, 'Missdemeanours', as a barbed commentary on his erstwhile patron:

> On MissDemeanours why shou'ld great ones stand?
> They missdemesne themselfs that sell their land!

However much Pestell's admirers applauded the appalling pun, Huntingdon himself doubtless felt less amused, especially when Pestell took to 'abusinge' the earl from the pulpit 'for sellinge house and land'. What made this sally even more painful was the regularity with which it dogged Huntingdon. Hence, when the earl denied a local opponent permission to hawk in Donnington Park, it was all too easy to cut Huntingdon to the quick with the retort, 'I am glad hee hath no more land [than he does] to hawke on.'[20] Occasionally, of course, straitened circumstances were useful. In 1626, the 'great Burthen of debt' and the expense of a son at university covered his absence from Parliament. Shaky personal finances also could make the Corporation of Leicester at times generous; in 1617, the Mayor and his brethren thoughtfully sent up £6 when James I came to Donnington Park, 'His Honour then beinge att greate charge in makinge provision'.[21] Yet on balance, such financial embarrassment was especially galling to a man as proud as Huntingdon.

The implications of his well known financial distress were far-reaching. His poverty first of all forces a reconsideration of his standing as a 'Country' peer. While unquestionably sincere in his aversion to courtly life, he was essentially rejecting what he could not have, and if the situation had been slightly different, there is every reason to believe that a wealthier Huntingdon would have gladly joined the other peers at court. Knowledge of this fact dominated his mother-in-law's attempt to lure the earl and countess to the metropolis. 'Men long experienced in the course and charge of living in London,' she argued, 'are of a confident opinion that your Lordship (with a fit traine) maye live at as little expense heare for som season of the yeare as where you doe.' Since business drew him regularly to London anyway, he might as well save the travelling expenses and stay there. The tenor of his reply can be seen in his response when Worcester relayed the councillors' surprise at his irregular court attendance; 'your Lordship knoweth I want meanes to performe this service'. Then came a recitation of Huntingdon's 'poore estate', whose poverty should be too well known at Whitehall for anyone seriously to expect his attendance.[22] In short, necessity at least as much as theology dictated Huntingdon's austere lifestyle; poverty, much more than ideology, made him a 'country' peer.

The earl's tortured attitude can most clearly be seen in his bitter anecdote about suits at court. First, the petitioner must begin lobbying 'those of the greatest power' near the king in the full knowledge that the chances of success were entirely fortuitous. To collect a majority of such power brokers was not to guarantee success, for 'one or two of the great ones will crosse all the rest ... not soe much out of hatred to the person that sues as the spleene to the contrary faction that are for him'. Yet there was no option but to pursue not simply the 'great ones', but 'his freinds and servants' as well. So all-consuming was the eagerness to please that if the petitioner inadvertently slighted one of this number, 'he shall not be able that night to sleepe'. After a few weeks, his suit would be so well known that the petitioner became prey to any manipulation. A minor official could then secretly report that 'the king is leaning his way'. A few bouyant weeks would then give way to gloom with the information that the king had balked at the request. Nevertheless, the intermediary was hopeful of better results in a few weeks. Even such faintly happy news, which required at least 'some guifte' of 'a sute or two of fine apparrell', delighted the long-suffering petitioner who 'if he be married gets her jewels or plate if she have none', and it persuades him 'to sell a peice of her Joyncture which she hath for her life thinking after a moneth thye busines will be done'. In fact, one month turns into several before the suit is finally handed to a Master of Requests, who in due course directs it to a Committee of the Privy Council. For these developments, 'more guifts must be presented'. Further time passes before the petition finally receives the king's approval before languishing in further committees where it appears to die until 'very fainte Aurum Notabile revives it'. Consequently, by the time a petitioner finally receives his grant, 'it is not soe much as he hath spent in his attendance by halfe', and the suitor finally appreciates that he was like 'the Dogge in Esopes fables' who 'looseth the flesh and catcheth the Shaddowe'.[23] Although Huntingdon did not claim this horror story as his own, parts of it like selling off jointure lands certainly ring true. This administrative nightmare suggests that the earl rejected Whitehall, not in disgust over its inherent evil, but in frustration over his own inability to bend it to his advantage.

Given these financial disasters, both great and small, it is no wonder that contemporaries had doubts about his stewardship of public funds. This is not to say that the earl was defrauding the county; it is merely to note that such allegations seemed plausible. Sir Henry Hastings plainly knew this, when in his outrage at having been presented for poaching in the Forest of Leicester, he struck back at Huntingdon's vulnerable spot. The parts of the forest, Sir Henry charged, which the earl had enclosed for his own use, he had overrun with sheep and horses. Similar corruption explained the disappearance of the bricks ordered to build a new hunting lodge; Huntingdon had quietly sold them off. Such fraud was only natural with a keeper and his creatures who

> made sale and spole of his Maiesties Woods within the said Chace by cuttinge downe carreinge awaie and stocking up of great Timber trees, Cropping of others at unseasonable tymes whereby the[y] dye and by sellinge the springe woods at lowe and under valluable pryces.[24]

Although nothing ever came of the charges, Sir Henry had deftly exposed his noble cousin's administrative Achilles' heel.

This financial background casts a different light on the earl's commitment to royal service. A well developed sense of *noblesse oblige* could account for his assurance to Charles I that 'I have ever been carefull to doe my dewtie'. So too did a sober calculation that the best means out of the fiscal morass lay in dogged devotion to duty. Some rewards of office were immediate; with the Lieutenancy of the Forest came fees worth £500 a year, prodigious amounts of deer, fish and birds as well as the right to have poets dub him, as Marston did, 'the high siluan that commaundes thes woodes'.[25] Others were more long-term, for only after several decades of faithful service could the earl seriously request extraordinary bounty from the Crown. By 1625 diligent service had put him in serious contention for the Garter, and in 1626 only a sudden round of budget cuts stopped a grant reducing his considerable royal debts. As a result of his loyal service he was able to spend much of the 1630s in almost constant mediation over 'some suite to move the King for recompence for service done'.[26] But dominating all schemes for rewards was the memory of the third earl.

Family tradition recalled how the third earl's estate would have 'beene lefte in farr greater quiet then now it is' if only 'the Lord had pleased to gyve hym leave to see London agayne'. As the fifth earl struggled with his great-uncle's debts, the possible result of a final trip to the queen must have haunted Huntingdon. Yet notwithstanding this lost opportunity, the third earl's brother had been confident that God 'will raise up some good meanes to repay[r]e the ruynes and decayes of our honorable house'.[27] His great-nephew, it is safe to say, never abandoned the search for 'some good meanes'.

A PRECARIOUS FOOTING

The pain which this acute financial embarrassment caused Huntingdon came from much more than wounded pride; shrinking estates and crushing debts also made him highly vulnerable to political attack. Along with the importance of honor and family, the brutal realities of life figured prominently in his advice to his son. While 'thou shalt finde the most parte of the world to esteeme thee as thou hast power to doe them good or hurt', power had only a modest relation to a distinguished pedigree. Instead, money 'will make thee more freinds and doe thee good turnes then all the Allies thou hast'; in fact, 'unlesse the matter be notoriously evill, it will carry thee out in any thinge'. While in this mode, he had no time for more metaphorical definitions of wealth: 'they be the Richest that have the most gold'.[28] The opposite situation he passed over in silence – and with good reason, for it was too grim to contemplate. The lack of gold translated into a paucity of friends and a diminution of any ability to do good or ill. This impotence was particularly acute, because Huntingdon simply could not afford anything more than the odd fleeting visit to Whitehall. Precisely how defenceless poverty left him was not an idle academic concern. In the first decade of the century, Leicestershire witnessed a frightening demonstration of the Hastingses' vulnerability, which no contemporary could have soon forgotten.

The apparent solidity of the Hastings' hegemony over the county masked the fact that it had been comparatively brief and certainly contested. Their chief rivals had been the Greys of Bradgate, who in the mid-sixteenth century launched a determined bid for local control. During Northumberland's regency of Edward VI, the Hastingses' eclipse seemed final as Henry Grey, who had married Henry VIII's niece, rose from Marquis of Dorset to Lord Warden of the Marches and Duke of Suffolk and ultimately, albeit briefly, to the father of the queen. In 1554, however, his involvement in Wyatt's rebellion doomed him and his ill-fated daughter, Lady Jane. At the end of his bid for power, the duke had the galling experience of watching as local feuds intertwined with national politics; the person who eventually arrested him and brought him to the scaffold was the second Earl of Huntingdon, whose action saved England for Queen Mary and Leicestershire for the Hastingses. Suffolk's debacle opened a power vacuum in the shire which the Hastings clan obligingly filled for the rest of the century. In fact, the third Earl of Huntingdon controlled matters so tightly that for decades, he effectively ruled Leicestershire from York. Meanwhile, all was quiet at Bradgate Hall; Suffolk's fall halted his grand building projects there as the remnant of his family relocated to Essex.[29]

The Greys' defeat, while crippling, was not decisive. While Elizabeth ensured that Suffolk's children all died without issue, his nephew and namesake escaped retribution under Mary and even flourished under Elizabeth, serving as Lieutenant of the Gentlemen Pensioners for the last fifteen years of her reign. A prominent position near the monarch enabled Sir Henry Grey to rebuild much of his family's lost position. Hence in the 1590s, when the fourth Earl of Huntingdon was locked in an apparently losing battle with moneylenders and dowagers, Sir Henry understandably judged the time auspicious to return to his uncle's mansion at Bradgate.[30]

The fourth Earl of Huntingdon, although scarcely delighted with the revival of his father's old rivals, was too concerned with other matters to oppose Sir Henry's return or even his appointment to the bench. Letting him serve as Knight of the Shire, however, was another matter entirely. In 1601, Grey launched an early campaign for the county seat, apparently on the understanding that Huntingdon would not oppose him, but the earl in fact advanced his nephew, Sir Henry Hastings of the Abbey, and a protégé, Sir William Skipwith. Rather than undergo the vagaries of a contested election, Grey withdrew. Although a Cornish borough eventually returned him, he understandably regarded the belated Hastings campaign as a personal affront. The electoral results were equally upsetting for Huntingdon. Notwithstanding his triumph in the county, he had to digest the fact that Leicester had defied his express command and returned Sir George Belgrave. His prohibition against electing Belgrave had been received well in advance of the election, but Belgrave negated it by appearing at the hustings in Hastings livery and proclaiming himself the earl's man. Insult promptly gave way to injury when Belgrave reacted to his election by tossing the livery in the gutter with the words 'Thou hast served this turne thou shalt never serve more.' The earl's complaint eventually secured Belgrave's public apology and his removal from the bench, but it could not unseat him from the Commons.[31]

Amid these aggravations, the fourth earl had some consolation in the fact that his power, if unable to thwart Sir George Belgrave, was sufficient to drive Sir Henry Grey to Cornwall. Yet, as subsequent events revealed, all he had succeeded in doing was irritating a formidable opponent and poisoning the political atmosphere. Sir Henry did indeed leave a county, but it was Essex, where he sold his lands in order to concentrate on developing his Leicestershire holdings. James's accession only increased the Greys' influence; although the new monarch rejected the Greys' claim to the title of Marquis of Dorset, he was impressed enough to raise Sir Henry Grey to the peerage as Lord Grey of Groby, and he brought Sir Henry's son, Sir John Grey, into the Privy Chamber. Meanwhile, the new peer and his son busily organised those disgruntled with the Hastings hegemony like Belgrave and the Beaumont brothers, Sir Henry and Sir Thomas.

As the Greys steadily consolidated their position, their opponents appeared on the verge of disintegration late in 1604 when the fourth earl's death left a minor to head the family. While the earl's grandson immediately succeeded to the family titles, the fifth earl's 'under yeares' prevented him from executing the customary family offices as Lieutenant of Leicestershire, Rutland and the Forest of Leicester as well as *Custos Rotulorum*. 'To misse these places,' the young peer protested to James, 'might make my house lesse esteemed,' and for precisely that reason Sir John Grey lobbied for those offices, claiming them as compensation for resigning his post with the Gentlemen Pensioners. In the end, James sided with the fifth earl, placing the lieutenancies of Leicestershire and the Forest into a commission full of Hastings loyalists until the earl's majority. Yet Grey's strenuous lobbying was not entirely fruitless; the lieutenancy of Rutland went to Lord Harington, while the custos-ship came to Sir Henry Beaumont of Coleorton, a protégé of Lord Grey. Although Beaumont only held the post pending Huntingdon's majority, he had enough time to show the county what a new local regime would look like. Thanks to Beaumont's influence, several gentlemen, long frozen out by the Hastingses, at last found themselves nominated to the bench, and every Liber Pacis during the Hastings interregnum saw Sir Henry Hastings of the Abbey, the senior member of the family, slip lower in precedence.[32]

In subsequent months, both sides warily eyed one another, searching for the most advantageous point of attack, and the earl's opponents thought they had found it in his Catholic relations, Walter Hastings, the younger brother of the third and fourth earls, and his son, Sir Henry Hastings of Braunston. In the new political climate, Sir Henry's neighbours at last felt safe enough first to increase his subsidy assessment, then to return him as recusant and finally to denounce him as a co-conspirator in the Gunpowder Plot. Never known for a cool head in the best of circumstances, Sir Henry was so enraged by these indignities that he was willing to strike back with anything, even the malicious reports of disgruntled servants. Thus in 1607 when Sir Thomas Beaumont of Stoughton, a Knight of the Shire and brother of the *Custos Rotulorum*, dismissed John Coleman, Sir Henry welcomed him at Braunston. Once armed with the servants' tales of wild sexual disorder in Stoughton depicting Sir Thomas as a cuckold and his son as a whoremonger, Sir Henry busily spread the stories to all and sundry and even taunted Sir Thomas in person. From these confrontations came a messy suit in Star Chamber, which involved both factions as witnesses. The case might have blossomed into a general fracas had not the fifth earl and Sir Henry Hastings of the Abbey been eager to dissociate themselves from their cousin's morally dubious attack on Sir Thomas.[33] Nevertheless the incident clearly exposed the mounting tensions within the shire.

Earl Henry did nothing to ease the rivalry when he came of age in 1607. Although Lord Grey and the Beaumonts represented a sizeable proportion of the local elite, Huntingdon blithely ignored them when appointing his new Deputy Lieutenants, all of whom were Hastings loyalists. Likewise the new *Custos Rotulorum* restored the Hastings domination of the bench in a fashion which was as obnoxious to his opponents as possible: he arranged to have Walter Hastings named to the bench, and as the son of a peer, this notorious church-papist vaulted over all the knights and baronets in order of precedence. Sir Thomas Beaumont, the Knight of the Shire, objected even to sitting next to 'a man given to bloode', who in any event 'by the statute ... could not beare office'. Such an outrage, Beaumont promised, would be reported to the Council and to the Commons. Two years later Huntingdon responded to his critics by naming 'uncle Walter' as one of his Deputy Lieutenants. By this time, the political temperature can best be gauged by observing the sudden decision of Sir John Grey and Sir Henry Hastings of the Abbey to visit the Dutch Republic in 1610. Unable to think of any other alternative, they left the country for a final attempt to resolve their differences – with cold steel.[34]

Although friends soon intervened before any blood was shed, this encounter did have the effect of convincing Lord Grey that the best prospect of humiliating his rivals came not from melodramatic affairs of honour, but from mundane complaints of mismanagement and fraud. The result was a series of allegations, any of which, even if only partially correct, would have struck a crippling blow against Huntingdon. Since contemporaries found royal forests and administrative abuses almost synonymous, Sir John Grey launched the campaign by complaining to Lord Treasurer Salisbury of grave problems in the Forest of Leicester. Shortly afterwards, another duel nearly developed over purveyance when Walter and Sir Henry Hastings of Braunston attempted to gather Sir John Grey's composition arrearages. Not only did Grey reject their order, but he pointedly denounced Huntingdon's controversial great-uncle, who could command 'neither himself, his friends, servants nor doggs'. This scene escalated to a protest against the earl's handling of the purveyance composition, whose size, critics alleged, inefficiency and corruption had inflated. Consequently, the collection of the composition halted. Almost simultaneously the Greys organised another public complaint, this time against Huntingdon's appointment of Sir John Bale to the bench. Huntingdon liked to advance men of humble origins to local prominence, but with Bale, a scarcely literate man of dubious integrity, many felt that the earl had gone too far. Sir John, they protested, brought 'scandal and contempt' on the magistrates, who had to associate with 'a man altogether unfitt for the place and most unworthy'. Yet their objections to Bale made transparently clear that they actually sought to humiliate Bale's patron.[35]

Thanks to these charges, the young earl labored in heavy political seas for much of 1611. The councillors took the protest against Bale seriously enough to appoint a special inquiry into the matter, and pending the hearing in Leicester, the county elite polarised quite sharply. Meanwhile the purveyance protest rapidly eroded the earl's authority. As the impasse continued, Lord Grey began to negotiate on the county's behalf; eventually the Green Cloth officials began to address their letters to Lord Grey as well as to Huntingdon. At the same time, Sir John Grey reported out of the bedchamber James's irritation with officials like Huntingdon, whose sloppy collection had sparked the protest. These intimate contacts with the monarch made Sir John sound quite plausible when he confidently spoke of trimming the county's assessment almost by half, down to £500. Such influence and such favourable deals strengthened the Greys' hand so impressively that Lord Grey soon began pressing Huntingdon to accept a settlement of their feud, which would have converted Leicestershire into a condominium carefully monitored by the two families.[36]

To his credit, Huntingdon responded warily to the compromise, and events soon proved the wisdom of his caution. To counter the Greys' petition against Bale, he organised a larger one denouncing 'those envious and malignant Criminations wherewithall his [Bale's] adversaries have sought to wounde his credit'. Bale himself responded by pointing out that some of 'the obiectors' on the bench were actually 'of as meane and base parentage as my selfe'. Illiteracy moreover could scarcely be a serious issue since 'some of their fathers that could neither wryte nor red and yet was in Commission of the peace'. To

counter Sir John Grey's influence in the bedchamber, Huntingdon marshalled his relatives, from the Earl of Worcester, Lord Privy Seal, to his
mother-in-law, who assured him that Lord Chancellor Ellesmere 'will not be
easily persuaded to beleeve any reportes made by your opposites concerning
the busines of Mr Bale'. Finally, the Hastings' long run of bad luck ended late
in 1611 when Sir John Grey suddenly contracted smallpox and died. With his
son's passing Lord Grey buried his best county connection. Further bad news
came early in 1612 at the long awaited hearing in the Bale case; notwithstanding Belgrave's vigorous indictment of Sir John, Huntingdon managed to
depict Grey and his allies as a malignant faction and ultimately to clear Bale
and by extension himself.[37]

In subsequent months the feverish atmosphere abated, and Huntingdon's
agents again began collecting purveyance compositions. The challenge to the
earl's authority had collapsed so completely that he was able to go on the
offensive by serving Lord Grey with orders from Whitehall to allow
Huntingdon's men to rescue the royal deer that Grey had long impounded on
his estate. By that time, Lord Grey was too ill to care; indeed, by 1614 he and
Sir Thomas Beaumont of Stoughton would join Sir John Grey and Sir Henry
Beaumont of Coleorton in the grave. Bereft of leadership, the rest of the Grey
adherents either made their peace with Huntingdon, as the Dixies and
Skipwiths did, or accepted their ostracism. Admittedly in later years, the old
Grey faction occasionally disturbed the county; in 1620, for example, the
sheriff abruptly disqualified Huntingdon's brother, Sir George Hastings, as a
non-resident and returned instead another local gentleman. Although historians have been astonished at the sheriff's action, much of the mystery disap-
pears once it is appreciated that one old Grey supporter, Sir Alexander Cave,
the sheriff in 1620, was simply advancing another, Sir Thomas Beaumont, the
son of Sir Henry Beaumont of Coleorton.[38] Such surprises notwithstanding,
Huntingdon by 1612 found himself at last in undisputed command of the
shire.

Although this extended struggle between the two families came to an
anticlimactic conclusion, it had a profound effect on the earl and the county.
The running battle with the Greys transformed Huntingdon's interest in
advancing worthy allies into an obsession. Immediately after the crisis, he
honourably refused to discuss the matter in his advice to his son, 'charity
teachinge me both to forgive and forgett'. Yet the sole exception to this
resolution was an ominous one for the county's later history: after firmly
cautioning his heir to 'carye a vigilant eye' on 'those that have binne enymies
to thy sealfe or thy Auncestors', he added that 'I never found any faithfull unto
me that loved not my Auncestors and my house'. This hard attitude made
Huntingdon operate on a sharply polarised view of the world. Any toleration
of criticism, constructive or otherwise, having vanished, Huntingdon's

primary consideration in assessing the local elite was loyalty. In 1616, for example, when he promoted Sir Thomas Hesilrige to command the horse troop, he rated 'your lovinge affection unto me and my howse' at least as high as 'your worth and sufficiency'. Plainly Sir Thomas was well aware of the earl's priorities, for he took pains to assure the Lord Lieutenant that he was 'ever prayinge for the longe continuance and prosperous increase of your Honors honorable familie'.[39] In short, the prolonged struggle to establish his control over the shire only reinforced Huntingdon's already pronounced tendency to esteem personal loyalty above all other considerations. Consequently, the administration of Leicestershire later resembled much more a closely held family corporation than a collegial affair where consensus decided all.

The more damaging legacy of this feud was simply the memory of how effective a few local gentlemen had been in employing court contacts and open challenges to undermine Huntingdon's authority. The chief drawback of such an autocratic system was that in a crisis, the disgruntled had no trouble deciding where to lay the blame. To minimise any difficulties, Huntingdon could have scrupulously avoided the least hint of favouritism and corruption, while at the same time courting the local elite so sedulously that none of them would exploit his plainly visible liabilities. Unfortunately Huntingdon was capable of neither policy, much less both, and this failure was particularly dangerous. Conspicuous poverty and his own family members significantly tarnished his august public persona, and the memory of how narrowly the family had dodged disaster corroded it further.

NOTES

1 GEH's petition, [1603–4], HAP 14/9.

2 'A note of such money', 1612, HAF 7/11; and Hastings to H, 3 December 1605, *Hastings Letters*, p. 107. On Worcester's protection, see [Skipwith] to Grey, 3 January 1606, *HMC Salisbury* XVIII, p. 5.

3 'A lybell of Leicestershire knights 1606', BL Harleian 6,383, fols. 71v–3; John Gerard, *The Autobiography of an Elizabethan*, translated by Philip Caraman (London, 1951), pp. 194, 215, 215; and 9 May, *PP 1614*, p. 185.

4 'The Case of Sir Henry Hastings', [November 1605], *HMC Salisbury* 17, p. 523; Hackett's report, [November 1605], SP 14/16/71; and Hastings to H, 22 December [1624], HA Corr. 8/1097.

5 'The examination of Edward Goodgale, 8 November 1617; H to Conway, 20 August 1624, HAM 48/26 and 32; 'A note of all such Recusants howses', November 1625, *LRLB*, fol. 147v; and 'The names and summes of such as I returned', 1611, HAM 53/4.

6 PC to Hastings, 24 March 1624, *APC* 39/194; Covenant between Sir Henry Hastings and H, 28 August 1618, HAP 16/15; and Manchester to H, 4 September 1629, HA Corr. 13/9342.

7 'Kirby', n.d., HAM 48/9 ; Examination of C. Dorman, 12 May 1626; and Examination of G. Walsham, 24 February 1620, Leics. RO, BR II/18/16, fol. 118; and II/18/13, fol. 476.

8 H. Hastings to H, October 1624, *LRLB*, fol. 91; F. Hastings to E. Hastings, [1596], *Hastings Letters*, pp. 59–60; and 'Certaine Directions', HAP 15/8, fol. [18a].

9 [H] to Middlesex, 18 September 1623, Bodleian Library, Carte MS 77, fol. 286; same to same, 14 November 1623, Centre for Kentish Studies, Cranfield MSS, U269/1, OE 377; and H's petition and James's response, 2 July 1624, HAP 17/11.

10 'A booke of the sales of lands', HA Misc. 9/3; Cross, *Puritan Earl*, pp. 316; and GEH's petition, [1603], HAP 14/9.

11 William Dugdale, 'Historical and Geneologicall Collections', HA Misc. 13; and 'The Account of ... the Administration', 10 February 1607, HAP 14/16. See also marriage settlement of H and ECH, 20 June 1603, HAP 14/3; Mathew to Carleton, 13 February 1605, SP 14/12/75.

12 'A note of such money', 1612, HAF 7/11; Dugdale, 'Historical and Geneologicall Collections', HA Misc. 13, fol. 70v; and Settlement of the Countess's jointure, 14 January 1617. For early efforts, see the proposed settlement of 27 November 1615, 27 May 1616, 10 November 1616, HAP 16/2, /7 and /10.

13 'Certaine Directions', HAP 15/8, fol. 20v; and H to Ellesmere, 24 October 1609, HA Corr. 6/5432. On his mining activity, see Beaumont to H, 26 January 1618, HA Corr. 7/672; 'Articles agreed upon', 26 March 1625, HAM 62/11; and 'Thinges for mee', 24 September 1624, HAP 17/6.

14 'Outwood Sale', 1628, HAF 9/1; and [Sir H. Hastings], 'Instructions for the Bill', [early 1620s?], Leics. RO, Winstanley MSS, Second Deposit, DG 5/863.

15 'A note of my lords Annual present revenue', 31 October 1620, HAF 8/5; and 'The Scedule debts', 1621, HAF 8/11. For a careful analysis of debts 'uppon use and without use', see 'A note of my lords debtes', 1621, at the end of HAF 8/5.

16 Certaine Directions, HAP 15/8, fols. 20v and [21A]; and Dugdale, 'Historical and Geneologicall Collections', HA Misc. 13, fol. 70v.

17 'Certaine Directions', HAP 15/8, fols. [21A]–22v; 'A rent rolle ... and to what uses appynted', 6 October 1621, HAM 55/3; and J. Murray, *English Dramatic Companies* (London, 1910), II, pp. 47–9.

18 'A note of such money', 1612; and 'A note of my lords present revenue', 31 October 1620, HAF 7/11 and 8/5; and 'The Kingdome of England', Commonplace book, [*c.* 1600], HA School Exercises 1/10.

19 TEH's notes, HA Genealogy 1/12; and Sir John Davies to H, 1 December 1623, Bodleian Library, Carte 289, fol. 20.

20 *The Poems of Thomas Pestell*, pp. 32 and 138; and HA Legal 2/11. Professor Collinson will soon present a detailed analysis of Huntingdon *v.* Pestell.

21 H to Pembroke, 18 January 1626, HA Corr. 12/5510; and Chamberlain's Accounts, Michaelmas 1617–18, Leics. RO, BR III/2/77, fol. 28.

22 Countess of Derby to H, [n.d.]; and H to [Worcester], 21 July 1606, HA Corr. 5/2511 and 5417.

23 'Certaine Directions', HAP 15/8, fol. 8–8a.

24 [Sir Henry Hastings], 'Instructions for the Bill', [early 1620s?], Leics. RO, Winstanley MSS, Second Deposit, DG 5/863.

25 H to PC, 14 June 1627, SP 16/67/2; and 'The Entertainment', *The Poems of John Marston*, p. 193. See also 'The Contents of the things granted unto my Lord'; and 'To the Kings most Excellent Majestie', Bodl. Carte 78, fols. 119 and 188.

26 Davies to H, 1 April 1625; and Segrave to H, 16 March 1635, HA Corr. 12/1930 and 15/10725; and 'Grants and warrants stayed', 8 July 1626, SP 16/31/36. On Leicester Forest, see Levi Fox and Peter Russell, *Leicester Forest* (Leicester, 1948).

27 F. Hastings to E. Hastings, [1596], *Hastings Letters*, p. 60.

28 'Certaine directions', HAP 15/8, fols. 7Av and 21Av. For what follows in this section I am indebted to Richard Cust for many discussions of this period, and for allowing me to read in typescript the following articles: 'Purveyance and Politics in Jacobean Leicestershire', *Regionalism and Revision: English Provincial Society 1250–1650*, ed. by P. Fleming and A. Gross (London, forthcoming); 'Honour, Rhetoric and Political Culture: the Earl of Huntingdon and his Enemies', *Political Culture and Cultural Politics*, ed. by S. Amussen and M. Kishlansky (Manchester, 1995), pp. 84–111; and 'Concepts of Honour amongst the Jacobean Gentry: the Star Chamber Case of Beaumont *v.* Hastings', *Past and Present*, forthcoming.

29 Cross, *Puritan Earl*, pp. 14, 18 and 20; and Nichols, *History and Antiquities*, III, pp. 660–674.

30 *House of Commons, 1558–1603*, ed. by P. W. Hasler (London, 1981), II, pp. 222–3; and Nichols, III, pp. 674–5.

31 *House of Commons*, I, pp. 192–5; J. E. Neale, *The Elizabethan House of Commons* (London, 1949), pp. 166–8; and Cust, 'Honour, Rhetoric and Political Culture', p. 5.

32 H to James, [late 1604], Hatfield House MSS 197/10; Grey to Salisbury, 30 December 1604, *HMC Salisbury* IV, p. 387; and Cust, 'Honour, Rhetoric and Political Culture', pp. 7–8.

33 'Sir Henry Hastings', [late 1605], Hatfield House MSS 112/170; and Cust, 'Concepts of Honour', pp. 4–14.

34 'The coppies of the Wryting I wrote unto the Judges', 25 March 1612, HAP 15/7; Chamberlain to Winwood, 24 May 1610, *Memorials of Affairs of State* (London, 1725), III, p. 175; Browne to Lisle, 19 and 28 May 1610, *HMC Dudley and de l'Isle*, IV, pp. 200 and 204; and Cust, 'Concepts of Honour', pp. 9–10.

35 Sir J. Grey to Salisbury, 16 June 1609, *HMC Salisbury* XXI, p. 57; Lord Grey *et al.* to Ellesmere, 17 September 1611, HA 6/4328; and Cust, 'Honour, Rhetoric and Political Culture', pp. 21–25.

36 [Grey's settlement], [1611], FSL, V.a. 402, fols. 5–6; Grey to H, 8 and 12 October 1611, HA 6/4329 and 4330; and Cust, 'Purveyance and Politics', pp. 13–20.

37 H *et al.* to Ellesmere, 8 February 1612, HA 6/5437; 'The Answer of Mr Bale', HAM 53/5a; Countess of Derby to H, [1611–12], HA 6/2512; and Cust, 'Honour', pp. 26–38.

38 'Instructions for Sir Thomas Lake', 18 February 1613, HAM 48/20; J. K. Gruenfelder, 'The Electoral Influence of the Earls of Huntingdon', *TLAHS* l (1974–75), pp. 20–1.

39 'Certaine directions', HAP 15/8, fol. 14; H to Hesilrige, 20 June 1616; and Hesilrige to H, 22 June 1616, *LRLB*, fols. 22v–23.

Chapter 4

Critics anatomised

The earl's political liabilities became a serious problem only if some of the local elite were willing to exploit them. Unfortunately for Huntingdon, he had no dearth of critics. Resentment steadily kept pace with the Lord Lieutenant's achievements until by the middle of the decade it had reached a dangerous level. Early in 1627 it boiled over in public, and over the next decade the county elite struggled with the controversies which the burden of war had generated. Looming large in the crisis were grand issues like loyalty, efficiency and public accountability, to say nothing of Parliament and the constitution. In the impending conflict, these issues were to be the cudgels, but why individuals employed them as energetically as they did had at least as much to do with personal motives and crochets as it did with ideology. Since it is difficult to understand these personal factors once the accusations began to fly, this chapter will first explore the deeper background of the disputes.

A NATIVE SON

Analysis of the aristocratic struggles in early Stuart Leicestershire are fairly straightforward. The Earls of Rutland, notwithstanding their residence at Belvoir Castle, were largely concerned with their standing elsewhere, and as a result, Huntingdon lacked any serious local rivals. Contemporaries in the 1620s would have quickly spotted the glaring error in this analysis, an error which can best be seen in William Burton's dedication of his pioneering county study, *The Description of Leicester Shire*. In the dedication, Burton humbly implored a 'Great Lord' to 'grant a protection to her [the book] and to the Countie, and take them both under your Honours Tutelage, sith by birth they doe belong to you, and none alike can make the like defense'. But the virtues and talents which Burton praised were not those of the Earl of Huntingdon, but rather belonged to George Villiers, Marquis and shortly

Duke of Buckingham. At first glance, Burton's dedication seems illogical. Although Buckingham had been born in the county, the focus of his attention was Whitehall. He was Lord Lieutenant of Middlesex and Buckinghamshire, and of the dozens of manors that James I had showered on his favourite, only one, that of Dalby on the Wolds (Old Dalby), was in Leicestershire. In short, the Villiers interest in the county would appear to have been succinctly stated in the advertising slogan of the main Leicester–London carrier: he was 'the man with whom many of the duke of Buckingham's kindred had come up' to the metropolis.[1] Yet, on closer inspection, it becomes clear that the traffic was far from one-way.

Burton had chosen his patron well, for Buckingham's presence loomed over the shire and over Huntingdon. Both of his parents had come from old county families, and his father's stature and wealth made him a logical candidate for Sheriff in 1591. As befitted a native son of Brooksby, Buckingham thought of himself as a Leicestershire lad, even after he had vaulted to the greatest heights at court. In fact until he was twenty-one, he had lived exclusively in the shire, except for a short stay in France. Consequently when the favourite hailed someone as a 'schoolfellow', it was invariably another pupil of Anthony Cade's school at Billesdon. Not surprisingly, savvy beggars in the metropolis quickly learned how to open the passing grandee's purse; for a steady earner, they had simply to mention that they hailed from Leicestershire, thus doubling Buckingham's normal hand-outs.[2] Even if he had wanted to forget his origins, he would have found it impossible to do so. The county had witnessed the births, marriages and other notable events in the lives of his wife, Katherine Manners; his father-in-law, the Earl of Rutland; his mother, the Countess of Buckingham; his brothers, the Earls of Anglesea and Viscount Purbeck; his sister and brother-in-law, the Countess and Earl of Denbigh; and his Brett cousins, the Countess of Middlesex and Arthur, a potential new royal favorite.[3]

These relatives had eventually followed him to court, but Buckingham left behind a host of kin and well-wishers. His elder half-brother, Sir William Villiers, was a JP, and on his mother's side there were a host of Beaumonts from the Greys' friends, Sir Henry and Sir Thomas Beaumont, to the court poet, Sir John Beaumont of Gracedieu, as well as her Babington kindred. For them, it was an easy enough matter to visit their distinguished relative either at court or at his Rutland country seat, Burley on the Hill. Consequently, it is scarcely surprising to see that Buckingham and his family still took an interest in often minor matters in the county. When the position of Recorder of Leicester came open, the Countess of Buckingham lobbied the Corporation on behalf of a Babington kinsman. Likewise she pushed to get a relative's old servant a place in the Hospital.[4] Given the family connection, it is equally unsurprising where the Corporation turned for assistance in a crisis. When the Crown's sale of the Forest of Leicester in 1626 threatened the town with 'great and inevitable losses', the Corporation petitioned the duke for help for 'your native Countie'. They had chosen well. While Buckingham did not stop the sale, he did see to it that the Corporation was compensated for the loss.[5] In short, however much national and international affairs occupied his attention, he always had time for his 'native Countie'.

He had less for Huntingdon. As early as 1616, Buckingham's mother assured the earl that 'I knowe my lord my sonn will doe your Lordship any service that layeth in his power'. These courteous sentiments could not veil a reversal of roles which the parvenus enjoyed just as much as the Lord Lieutenant abhorred it. The reversal, moreover, was quite personal. As befitted two prominent county families, the Hastingses and the Villierses had known each other, albeit with the latter in a decidedly subordinate position. While the wife of Sir George Villiers, a local JP, Buckingham's mother had mixed socially with the young earl and countess, who had invited her daughter to dance in the grand masque which they presented in 1607 to welcome the Countess of Derby to Ashby Castle. Their kindness was soon repaid. In the controversy over Sir John Bale, the favourite's elder half-brother, Sir William Villiers, loyally backed the earl. Even after the young George Villiers had begun his ascent at Whitehall, he remained helpful. Hence in 1616, when Huntingdon sought to be excused from service on the Overbury trial, the 'rising favorite' kindly intervened on his behalf.[6] After this point, however, relations between the two families rapidly deteriorated.

Tormented by his own thwarted ambitions, Huntingdon understandably had trouble digesting the rapid rise of the younger son of one of his JPs from baron, viscount, earl, marquis to duke. Even more galling was the elevation of the favourite's family, Buckingham's mother and sister quickly found themselves countesses; with equal speed, his brother-in-law and a brother became earls, and the other brother, in spite of intermittent madness, had to settle for a viscountcy. Yet the bitterest pill to swallow was the inexorable rise of Buckingham's half-brother and his former Muster Master. In 1614 Edward Villiers served under Huntingdon as a foot captain and, for a time, as Muster Master. He held these positions only briefly, resigning them in the following year after a scandal involving some of the regiment's scant funds. The money was soon recovered, and afterwards Huntingdon may have observed that such behaviour was only to be expected from such a feckless family. Unfortunately for Huntingdon, any satisfaction on this score quickly vanished as Edward rose on his brother's coat-tails. In a matter of months after his resignation, Huntingdon's erstwhile Muster Master received a baronetcy, the offices of Master of the Mint and Comptroller of the Wards, and an appointment – with a suitable expense account – as an ambassador extraordinary. Even more painful was watching as royal bounty rained down so heavily on the man who had attempted to pocket the militia's small change that Villiers was soon able to invest £4,000 in a lucrative royal patent. After that, it scarcely mattered that his old captain metamorphosed into Lord President of Munster.[7]

Meanwhile the earl's relationship with others of the duke's kindred turned equally sour. In the mid-1610s Sir Thomas Beaumont, the son of Sir Henry Beaumont of Coleorton, had briefly served as Huntingdon's horse captain until he abruptly resigned in 1616. While the reasons for his departure are obscure, the earl's irritation at his action can be seen in his testy reaction to the news. Huntingdon's final overture to the family came in 1618 when he attempted to persuade Sir Thomas Compton to serve as his Deputy Lieutenant. Regrettably the second husband of the Countess of Buckingham and the stepfather of the favourite had better things to do than to serve as Huntingdon's subordinate.[8] Any hope that the two families might later reach an understanding did not survive the county election early in 1621.

After seeing the Beaumont brothers occupying both of the county seats in James's first Parliament, Huntingdon laboured to re-establish his family's customary influence over these selections. In 1614 he had the satisfaction of seeing the county endorse his younger brother, Sir George Hastings, and in 1621 he hoped for an even greater triumph in persuading the county to return his brother again as well as his cousin, Sir Henry Hastings of the Abbey. The majority of the electors approved of the slate, but the Sheriff did not; in a legally dubious move, Sir Alexander Cave disqualified the earl's brother as a non-resident, returning instead Sir Thomas Beaumont. Cave's action was a delight for Buckingham and his mother as well as a belated *coup* for the Grey stalwarts. Not only was Sir Thomas's great-great-uncle the countess's father, but Sir George Villiers had first met and courted her at Coleorton while she was serving in the household of Sir Thomas's father. The family connection made it natural that Buckingham should have intervened, pleading with Huntingdon's brother not to appeal against Cave's decision. Such a favour would be taken 'kindely', and Buckingham himself would 'be readie to imbrace any occasion to requite it' in the future. In the event the family refused the deal and lodged an appeal, which eventually ejected the Beaumont intruder. While the earl's decision speaks well for his independence, it did nothing to advance a reputation for political acumen. The price was to prove quite high; having rejected the opportunity to come to terms with the royal favorite, the Lord Lieutenant had to face the prospect that if he ever fell into trouble, Buckingham might well be interested in settling accounts for having shown his mother's family 'much disgrace'.[9]

The Hastingses for their part appeared oblivious to possible danger. In the Commons, the new county knight for Leicestershire played an instrumental role in toppling Buckingham's adviser, Lord Chancellor Bacon. Meanwhile Huntingdon himself practically shadowed Southampton as the two men moved from Virginia Company meetings to the House of Lords. Not surprisingly, when a majority of peers from the Prince and Buckingham to Arundel and Pembroke pleaded for lenience in Bacon's case, Huntingdon and Saye insisted on the most humiliating possible punishment. At the end of the first session, James had Southampton, Oxford and Sandys detained and interrogated for their opposition to 'the King, Government or any other person neere them'. Had the net been cast a little wider, it could in truth have landed on Huntingdon.[10]

In the following year, antipathy between the two families burst into plain view of everyone in the county. As a local history, William Burton's *Description of Leicester Shire* is noticeably unimpressive. William Dugdale sniffed that Burton 'performed briefly', and even that was disappointing, given the numerous printing errors and Burton's wobbly Latin. As for his pedigrees themselves, the College of Heralds plumped against publication since 'many of them will scarcely be proved'. Such coolness was nothing compared with that of the author himself, who spent the next two decades correcting and expanding the first edition. Why Burton brought it out at all in 1622 is profoundly mysterious until it is appreciated that he would never have done so if 'a higher power' had not drawn it to press with 'scarce an allowance of time for the furbishing and putting on a mantle'.[11] Licensing a book was generally a perfunctory task left to royal chaplains, but in a remarkable exception to the rule, the Earl of Arundel himself approved Burton's work. What interested the Earl Marshal was not so much a sudden passion for the Midlands as his political ally in 1622 and Leicestershire's favourite son.[12] Amid the tedious recitations of medieval charters and abbreviated pedigrees, the book's most salient aspect is its regular rhapsodies about Buckingham and his family. Burton could not say enough about Brooksby, the birthplace of a man

> whose sweet disposition and excellent gifts of Nature make manifest to the world, that his Maiesty hath beene guided by his accustomed sharpe understanding, and solid iudgment, in choosing such a subiect ... to communicate his maiesties goodnesse to all worthy persons.

Likewise Lutterworth was worthy of extended praise for simply being the ancestral home of a man 'who married the noble and worthy Lady Susan, Sister of the illustrious George Marquesse Buckingham'. With the Beaumonts, Burton was equally reverent, from noting the excellence of Sir Henry Beaumont's tomb to praising the splendour of his son's estate. Even the Greys of Bradgate received respectful coverage.[13]

Burton's readers could have easily reached the conclusion that the Hastingses had precious little to do with the county. Ashby de la Zouch managed only a fleeting reference, and Donnington Park none at all. Burton was equally terse when discussing the family. While he praised the Countess of Huntingdon as 'a worthy Lady, descended of Royall Blood', he said nothing about her equally well born husband unless to record embarrassing information like a manor which 'is lately sold by this Earle of Huntingdon'. Similarly in Burton's account it is hard to know what is more peculiar about the earl's great-uncle, Lord Loughborough: his obsession with chess or his devotion to Queen Mary. Hastings protégés are scarcely better served. Sir John Bale's difficulties, Burton suggested, were not educational but environmental, stemming from the foul air and water of his estate at Carlton Curlieu which made everyone there have 'an harsh and wratling kinde of speech, uttering their words with much difficulty and wharling in the throate, and cannot pronounce the letter R'. Likewise Sir John Skeffington had the satisfaction of seeing Burton parade his parents' marital difficulties in public and of suggesting in several languages that Sir John himself might not be his father's son. Yet the pain of these jabs was nothing to that of Burton's treatment of the family's most distinguished member. The third earl never appears except to drive Sir William Fawnt's father to an early grave by ejecting him from a prominent militia post in 1588 to make way for his crypto-Catholic brother, 'Master Walter Hastings'. So somber was the abuse of power in this incidence that Burton could only 'referre the Reader to the *Anatomy of Melancholy*, penned by my brother Robert Burton'. If anyone had failed to glean Huntingdon's fundamental insignificance from over 300 pages of text, Burton added an additional list of 'those Knights of the Garter which were of this Countie of Leicester'; needless to say, while Huntingdon had not merited this distinction, Buckingham had.[14]

Burton's achievement was quite remarkable. In a county which often appeared more a Hastings satrapy than a royal shire, he had constructed a vision of its past in which the earl and his family, when not petty and vindicative, were generally irrelevant. Burton had managed this audacious feat by generously presenting the county as well as his book to the 'Great Lord' to whom 'by birth they doe belong'. This daring performance, in spite of a cool response from Donnington Park, served notice of the fact that the long-standing Hastings hegemony was not without powerful antagonists.

Buckingham's position in county politics must be clearly understood. He did not represent a direct challenge to Huntingdon; given his very limited land holdings in the shire, he would have been an unlikely candidate to replace Huntingdon as Lord Lieutenant. Yet if someone else wanted to make trouble for the earl, Buckingham might well be sympathetic, and if anyone aspired to replace him outright, the favourite would almost certainly be the deciding voice in any council about his 'native Countie'. Unfortunately for Huntingdon, by the mid-1620s, several gentlemen were irritated enough to try both of these options. Even more embarrassing, they were all Huntingdon's colleagues on the bench.

THE JUSTICES

The Council's decision to reform the militia had activated a level of local administration which had been dormant for well over a decade. With erratic musters and militia assessments, the office of the Lord Lieutenant had become largely honorary. Meanwhile all of the important business in the shire had been decided in the quarter sessions before the Justices of the Peace. There, as *Custos Rotulorum*, Huntingdon exerted great influence on the proceedings; he did not, however, dominate them. Rather, he had to act with the assent of roughly two dozen other JPs. In order to ensure co-operative and congenial colleagues, Huntingdon regularly lobbied the Lord Keeper to rearrange the composition to his liking, omitting those whom he thought 'may bee well spared' and inserting others 'very able for that service'.[15] Yet as the realm slid into war, Huntingdon's attention to the composition of the bench dwindled as the duties of the lieutenancy multiplied. The earl and his Deputies of course represented a subset of the entire bench. Yet their actions were in no way dependent on the approval of the rest of the Justices. Thus in the 1620s, the earl discovered that warfare, in addition to allowing him to equal his great-uncle, also gave him near absolute powers over the county. Warfare created a potentially explosive situation as it summoned into existence two powerful governing bodies, which technically had no relationship with one another.

At the end of the long Elizabethan war, tension was readily apparent between the magistrates and the deputies. In Norfolk, for instance, 'the majority of the justices, denied any opportunity to influence these developments and to cushion their impact upon the county, increasingly resented' the lieutenancy's demands. Meanwhile the Lords Lieutenant across the realm 'rapidly assumed the role of overlords'.[16] Although the importance of this Elizabethan precedent in later turmoil has largely been ignored, the same tension between the bench and the lieutenancy was increasingly evident in the 1620s. In their eclipse, the neglected JPs grumbled about a mixture of the petty and the suggestive, but at least until 1626, there were no apparent smoking guns. But this fact did not quell early criticisms of Huntingdon's actions, which at times resembled those of Lord Hastings of the late fifteenth century more than those of the third earl of the late sixteenth. When he fussed over the proper attire of the 150 pressed men for the Cadiz expedition, he was largely fretting over 300 yards of blue cloth. When he could not find enough in Leicestershire, he sent a rush order to Coventry. Anyone who was familiar with the Hastings family knew why he went to such trouble; it was the colour of their livery. As one supplier noted about blue cloth, 'there is noe Cullor redier to fitt your honor then blew'. An early Stuart lieutenancy, Anthony Fletcher aptly observed, 'fulfilled the same functions as retaining: it could be seen as a way of keeping horses and armour at the cost of the county'.[17] Liveried retainers could easily be added to his list. Incidents like the blue coats, so obviously associated with fantasies about earlier family glories, suggest that the expanded power of the Lord Lieutenant may have gone to his head. Certainly there were those who thought so. One of the reasons Sir William Fawnt had such trouble with his militia assessment was that he, as a JP, normally expected a little more consideration from his fellow magistrate, the Lord Lieutenant. The worsening relation between the two men could only make Fawnt look back wistfully on the time when 'I still remayned faire in your lordshipes opinion'.[18] Thomas Pestell also had difficulty with Huntingdon's new attitude, which eventually drove him to inform Huntingdon of the fundamental fact that 'you and hee were all come from Adam and that there was no such difference betweene you and his Lordship'.[19]

Part of the resentment stemmed from a sense that Huntingdon used his expanded powers to bypass members of the county elite whom he found awkward. It would have been hard to argue with his selection of Deputy Lieutenants early in the 1620s: Sir Henry Hastings of the Abbey, Sir Thomas Hesilrige and Sir Richard Morison were all mature, experienced local administrators. The ones who had replaced them by 1625 were more questionable. The earl, as we have seen, had a fondness for promoting men up through the ranks. Nevertheless, his choice of Francis Staresmore must have not rung entirely true with some in the county; however talented he was, the fact remained that he was not even a knight. Sir John Skeffington, Sir Henry Skipwith, Sir Wolstan Dixie and Lord Grey had no problems on that score, but they were, on the whole, quite young. In 1625, Skeffington would have been the greybeard among them at forty-one, while Dixie was barely twenty-three.[20] There was of course something to be said for learning on the job, but given their inexperience, who were the Deputies to learn from?

The answer to this query was of particular interest to Sir Thomas Hesilrige and his son, Arthur. By 1625 the other members of Hesilrige's initial cohort of deputies had lost interest. As the pressure of the war mounted, Morison had less and less time to act as Huntingdon's London agent, and Sir Henry Hastings of the Abbey had developed a career as the family's parliamentary representative, sitting in the 1614, 1621, 1624 and 1626 sessions. Their absences meant that the bulk of the actual field work fell on Sir Thomas's shoulders. All of the the extensive correspondence indicates that his performance was exemplary and deferential. Yet in 1625 Huntingdon abruptly dismissed him. The decision left Hesilrige in shock, and his mood can best be seen in his evocative endorsement of the letter to Huntingdon – 'livinge though despised'. Once he had accepted his disgrace, he celebrated it by complaining about his assessment in the horse troop, vowing to protest even 'to the lords of the Counsell'.[21] It was no idle boast. His earlier experience as a

Deputy Lieutenant had left him well acquainted with the route to the Council and the personnel there. Hesilrige was distressed for his family as much as for himself. In 1623, on the death of his eldest son, Huntingdon invited Sir Thomas's second surviving son, Arthur, to succeed his brother as captain of the horse troop, a post which brought young Arthur considerable prestige and £20 a year. Thus a man who would later gain distinction for his bold cavalry tactics in the Civil War learned the rudiments under the Earl of Huntingdon in the 1620s. Yet after two years of leading the county's troop without controversy, Arthur Hesilrige fell with his father. To be sure, some belated compensation came several years later, when Huntingdon asked a younger son, Bertine Hesilrige, to lead one of the foot companies. Nevertheless the earl's initial judgement of Sir Thomas and Arthur cannot have improved the family's opinion of the earl's administration immediately after the 1625 purge.[22]

This shuffle of the earl's administrative personnel obviously angered the Hesilriges and their friends. It could not, however, be expected to attract the attention of a wider audience. What could were allegations of corruption, and regrettably for Huntingdon, these were becoming more common as the decade progressed. Take for example the 150 men in blue coats who marched down to Plymouth in the spring of 1625. There were, as we have seen, unauthorised substitutions, from which the conductor personally profited; one man gave him a horse; another, £5. This practice sometimes proved to be a problem for the replacements. Those who were quietly replaced occasionally went off with their press money and coats, thus defrauding the county as well as depriving the king of fit men. This fact helps explain the company's shabby state at the coastal rendezvous where four men arrived without coats. But the substitutions cannot entirely account for the seventy-five men out of the 150 who arrived without shoes, the fifty-one without shirts, the thirty-three without stockings, the twenty without breeches, the nineteen without doublets, and the one poor soul without a hat. Even more embarrassing, the money to clothe each of these men had been collected in the county. In fact the county had paid far more than necessary for this. The village of Congeston, for example, had paid £5 14s. for three men. Yet only one man from the village actually made it to Plymouth, and he in threadbare shape. The same phenomenon of disappearing public funds occurred with the money allocated for their maintenance on the eleven-day march to the coast. The journey quickly became particularly awkward when, in front of the pressed men, one of the conductors accused his colleagues of defrauding the troops and the county. What made this episode doubly suspicious was that such problems were rare in other English counties: only in cases from Norfolk and Gloucester did the councillors also demand a full investigation. Quite understandably, the central government was eager to get to the bottom of the problem.[23]

Although blame came to rest squarely on a few constables and conductors, the allegations of skimming public funds were, Sir George Hastings protested, 'undesarved aspersions' and a 'great wrong'.[24] Such accusations, while almost impossible for someone notoriously cash-poor to shake, also prompted the earl's critics to scrutinise his actions, and amid a considerable amount of smoke, the search for the fire at the heart of the administration was soon to lead to a most devastating critique. Its author, Sir William Fawnt, deserves some introduction, in large part because he does admirable service as the archetypical disgruntled JP. Huntingdon's attorneys later portrayed Sir William as a malignant man 'of a perverse and factious disposition not affacting his Majesties happy government and an opposer of the demands and directions of his Majesties and the lords of the council'. Most others in the county found Fawnt to be less disagreeable, albeit cranky enough. The family emerged into prominence with Sir William's grandfather, whose election as Knight of the Shire in 1555 crowned a long career as a local attorney. Fawnt's father and uncle subsequently devoted themselves to the Dutch military service, and thanks to his considerable experience, Anthony Fawnt was heartbroken when the third Earl of Huntingdon suddenly removed him from a local militia post. Notwithstanding the brothers' dedication to the Protestant cause, the Fawnts had had a difficult time sorting out their religious allegiance. The grandfather had remained a loyal Catholic, and another of Sir William's uncles had actually been a Jesuit. Yet in spite of such Catholic leanings, Fawnt himself was a loyal member of the Church of England. Born in 1576, he had received his knighthood in the orgy of creations at James I's accession, and his 'long experience ... of the publique service' on the bench stretched back to the enclosure riots in 1606, when his ruthlessness had earned the popular epithet of Fawnt 'the Gunner'. In subsequent years he had less controversial, although equally important, assignments. In 1610–11, he loyally supported Huntingdon over the Bale case, and in 1625, he sat on the select commission that reported to the Privy Council on the problems with the pressed men.[25] In contrast to many of the county elite who lived in northeastern Leicestershire, Fawnt was one of the dominant figures in the southern hundred of Guthlaxton. There he enjoyed a repuatation for diligence and honesty, arguing here on behalf of local artisans and there against Leicester's attempts to dump a pregnant woman on a rural parish. It followed, therefore, the Corporation of Leicester felt good enough about his integrity to press to have Fawnt named as their subsidy commissioner in 1621.[26]

The most distinctive feature of a man who owned over 3,000 acres, which William Burton described as the 'most fertile, rich, and fruitful soil ... in the whole country', was his wealth. In a later law suit, the earl's attorneys asked several dozen people 'whoe at that tyme had soe greate or a greater estate in lands' than Fawnt; no one made any suggestion. Given his financial resources, Sir William had no trouble in moving his family into the front rank of the local elite. His youngest sister was married to Huntingdon's Deputy Lieutenant, Sir Wolston Dixie, while his brother, Anthony, served as an royal equerry. More importantly, Fawnt was connected with Huntingdon himself; his sister married Sir Henry Hastings of the Abbey, and he himself had wed Lucy Harington, first cousin to Huntingdon's mother. For his eldest son, Arthur, Sir William moved outside of the county for a splendid match with Elizabeth Coke, daughter of the Secretary of State, Sir John Coke.[27] Therefore, while Huntingdon's attorney was able to depict Sir William as 'perverse and factious', he could not easily term Fawnt as insignificant.

A long-serving JP with considerable wealth and his own lines of communication to the court represented a potent adversary. Fawnt was also someone whom Huntingdon had just embarrassed. The game in the local royal forests, far from the normal routes of summer progresses, was comparatively underutilised. The local inhabitants, ever eager to assist their monarch, were keen to correct this oversight. Yet in 1624, rather than overlook the matter, Huntingdon launched a major poaching dragnet, which pulled in culprits like the Plumb gang, who were not above pulling a knife on a constable and threatening to make him 'stinke a bush'. It also ensnared Sir William Fawnt. Since one of his estates, Cold Newton, bordered the Forest of Leicester, Fawnt and his servants had regularly figured in earlier complaints, and by 1624, Huntingdon's patience was at an end. When citing Fawnt for poaching, the earl complained that Fawnt's men had repeatedly slaughtered royal deer which had wandered on to his property. Privately Fawnt conceded that twice when his wife, tired of salt meat, had asked 'to eate a peece of flesh', he had ordered a servant to kill one of the smaller royal deer on his property. But he flatly denied going into the forest, where 'neyther I nor any [of mine] hath nor shall come', and as a character witness he cited the earl's own treasurer, Walter Rudinge. Yet rather than have the matter come to this, Fawnt asked the earl to drop further proceedings against a man 'very loath to give your Lordship any iust occasion of offence'.[28] Earl Henry responded by adding Fawnt's private letter to him to the official indictment, and the matter ended with a sharp rebuke from the king, who told Sir William of 'his dislike of such destroying his Game and his displeasure for it'. Fawnt's revenge doubtless came a few weeks later when a group of JPs, who had gathered in Leicester to discuss the subsidy assessment, unexpectedly examined and then released the Plumbs, whom Huntingdon had taken such pains to apprehend.[29]

Since this forest business simply led to another rebuke in the following year over Fawnt's contribution to the militia troop, it was becoming increasing obvious to all involved that Huntingdon had set his face against Sir William. The earl's hamhanded relations with Buckingham undercut a case for Huntingdon's shrewd political skills, and his handling of Fawnt does nothing to alter this judgment. Admittedly by Huntingdon's lights, Sir William had far too much of the brash parvenu about him. Yet he was also well informed; his service on the investigation of the pressed men in 1625 afforded him more than a few hints about corruption within the Hastings regime. Furthermore, Sir William had an ear for scandalous gossip, as he made abundantly clear in one of his recurrent complaints about his assessment. His problem with an additional horse, he assured Huntingdon, was nothing compared with the denunciations circulating elsewhere in the county of 'so extreame a charge in payment of monies' for the militia. The scale of the Lieutenant's demands had not attracted as much criticism as the fact that the assessments were 'but unnecessarily exspended'. Yet the worst charge, he warned Huntingdon, was outright fraud; 'it is said that there hath beene formerly and att this present so much moneyes gathered upp and nott laid out for the good and benefitt of the cuntrie'.[30]

Fawnt's talent for collecting awkward information and his independent position on the bench made him potentially dangerous. And yet, thanks to the 1624 forest crackdown, Huntingdon had personally seen to it that Fawnt received a royal chastisement, followed quickly by an increased militia assessment. In short, the disgruntled JP had both the motive and the means to repay the earl's kindnesses; by 1625, the only real question was not whether, but when 'the Gunner' would open up.

THE CATHOLICS

The earl's devotion to militia reform earned him antagonists on the bench. Yet the JPs' ability to cause trouble paled beside the confusion that the recusants, technically pariahs in the county, could call down on the earl's head. When Huntingdon reported on the results of his Catholic searches, there was, he conceded, almost nothing to report on Rutland, 'there being very fewe Recusants in that Countrye'.[31] The contrast with Leicestershire, which had a significant number of open Catholics, could not have been more striking. With recusants came church-papists, secret Catholics who went through the motions of conformity in order to protect small groups of the faithful. The most threatening thing about the local Catholic community was not its size; the wildest estimates might place Catholic sympathisers at a tenth of the population. Rather, it was their power and influence. No one ever said the Catholics dominated the local government; Huntingdon made that unthinkable. Nevertheless those who made the most perfunctory obeisance to the Established Church had served as Sheriff and some even as JPs, and their presence within the government threatened the effective implementation of any new measures against the old faith.

To fervent Protestants, the already infuriating situation became positively dangerous during a war against the Most Catholic king. Yet any attempt to root out the closet Catholics would only bring out their many prominent friends. Sir Kenelm Digby, a prominent courtier, was plainly interested in his manor and family at Tilton, just as the Earl of Rutland was concerned about what happened around Belvoir Castle. While their intervention would have been awkward for Huntingdon, Buckingham's would have posed an exceedingly ticklish problem. The favourite, to be sure, never wavered in his conformity to the Church of England. But when Henry Burton exhorted the duke to root out Catholic sympathisers, he urged him to begin 'in your owne howse and in all the skirts of it' where, as everyone knew, the favourite would find his wife, his sister and his mother. The Countess of Buckingham, in particular, had a profound and at times suffocating influence over her son; who else but that redoubtable dowager could have elicited reports from her son at the Ile de Ré that he was saying his prayers at night? Their Catholicism had made the 1623 trip to Madrid even more horrifying; 'wee knowe,' Thomas Scott observed, 'who was his wife, who was his mother.'[32] While the Villierses were generally loyal Anglicans, the Beaumonts and the Babingtons on his mother's side abounded with recusants and church-papists. This fact alone made Huntingdon's raid on the Catholic residences late in 1625 rash indeed.

The order for the the searches was designed to convince the Parliament men of the government's solid Protestantism. Yet public policy could not easily overrule personal sentiment. Hence, immediately after the raids, the Earl of Carlisle hastened to inform the duke that 'there was as much respect had of some who have relacion to your Lordship as you yourself would desire'. Nothing in Leicestershire rivalled the scene in neighbouring Northamptonshire where Richard Knightley's search of the Vaux residence ended in a punch-up when Knightley fined Vaux's brother for swearing. Variations on the affray and the subsequent Star Chamber suit occupied contemporaries for weeks. Yet the raids in Leicestershire were actually every bit as dramatic. Along with Sir Henry Merry and Sir Francis Smith, the family of Sir Kenelm Digby received one of the earl's posses. So, too, did Sir John Beaumont of Gracedieu, Buckingham's kinsman.[33] The earl, of course, operated well within the letter of the Council's order, but on the night of the raid, a shrewder man might have forgotten the way to Gracedieu. After all, Sir John Beaumont was a poet, not a frondeur, and none of the dark reports of Catholic plotting ever named him. Nevertheless, Huntingdon's public zeal led him to deepen the animosity between the duke and himself.

Presumably the earl calculated that, court influence or not, the Catholic gentlemen were scarcely in a position to challenge the dominant local magnate, who was committed to the Spanish war. Such reasoning, however, contained a crippling flaw in the assumption that the war effort would follow the pattern set by the 'Blessed Revolution' of 1624. If it did, Huntingdon could compensate for Buckingham's coolness with the warm support of his fellow

'Patriots', Pembroke, Southampton, Warwick, Essex and the Countess of Bedford. Unfortunately the Parliament of 1626 shattered the war coalition. By then, Southampton was dead; paranoia had so overwhelmed Buckingham that only his 'creatures' had any hope of office; and while Warwick, Essex and Bedford had fallen out with Buckingham, Pembroke had made a cynical *rapprochement* with the favourite in return for new court appointments. After the turmoil in the first half of 1626, Huntingdon doubtless echoed the Earl of Clare's lament about the Villiers–Herbert reconciliation: 'I wishe therfore it hath been sooner ear a Parlament, ear the whole Kingdome had been a party.'[34] Consequently, the Council's glowing commendation at the end of 1625 quickly become more qualified as Huntingdon's political position rapidly eroded.

In the new political environment, his decision in the Catholic searches increasingly was the wrong one, and confirmation of this suspicion came on 4 July 1626 when Buckingham exacted vengeance. Afterwards, the duke's animosity was apparent for all to see four times a year, when Huntingdon led his colleagues into the quarter sessions. There, before the entire county, all of the JPs below the rank of baron had to defer to Sir Henry Shirley of Staunton Harold.[35] In a society obsessed with precedence, a Deputy Lieutenant and baronet like Sir Henry Skipwith could not have enjoyed yielding to the new-comer. Yet it was something he and Huntingdon would have to grow accustomed to, for in the coming years Shirley and Buckingham were to give them fits.

Although contemporaries heard rather more than they wanted about murkier figures far distant on the Shirley family tree, the real founder of the family's fortune was Sir Ralph Shirley, whose greatest achievement was not so much to have survived both the battle of Stoke and Henry VII's expedition against the French as to outlive three wives. Whenever they could, his de-scendants wisely followed his lead; thus both Sir Henry's father and his grandfather married either widows or heiresses. By the time Sir Henry did so, it was only to be expected, but his match heralded for all to see the family's financial and social triumph.[36] Although Sir George Shirley had set no mean mark by marrying Lord Berkeley's daughter, his son handily surpassed it. Scholarly yawns would greet the Earl of Hertford's description of himself and the Earl of Essex as 'two soe neerely linked in freindship and alliance'. What would guarantee immediate attention is the realisation that Sir Henry Shirley could, and did, greet both peers in such terms, for in 1615 he had wed Lady Dorothy Devereux, the daughter and co-heiress of the second Earl of Essex. While Lady Dorothy unquestionably brought tremendous prestige with her, the attraction of the match for the Shirleys went well beyond snobbery; it might also prove a shrewd investment. Financial windfalls in this family were a way of life; in 1586, for example, Thomas Lovett left Sir Henry's already comfortable father another four manors. An even greater bonanza loomed if the third Earl of Essex's embarrassingly public problems with impotence eventually allowed Lady Dorothy to inherit still more of the Devereux estates. In that event, he promised her the centrepiece of the Devereux lands, Chartley in Staffordshire. To console her in the interim, Essex settled on Sir Henry's wife an annuity of £1,000 in 1623.[37]

These wise marriage alliances and careful husbandry gave the Shirleys extensive estates in Derbyshire, Northamptonshire and Warwickshire as well as Leicestershire, and an annual income estimated in 1621 at £4,000. It allowed Sir Henry's father to bequeath £2,000 each to his younger son and daughter; and it further explains why no less than Huntingdon's grand-mother, the fourth countess, named Sir George Shirley as the executor of her will. When William Sampson came to eulogise Sir Henry's passing in 1633, he found it easy to transcend the traditional tropes about the departed's honour and virtue; after noting Shirley's burial on Breedon Hill, he asked

> Can suche a slender hill keepe in command
> Him that could tread o're leagues of his own land?

What made this couplet especially uncomfortable for Huntingdon was the recollection that much of the Shirleys' 'leagues' had once been part of the Hastings demesne; Sir Henry and his father had been avid purchasers in the earl's periodic land sales.[38]

As distinctive as the Shirleys' wealth was their religion. At first glance, they appeared unremarkable members of the Church of England. Sir Henry's house was not searched in the 1625 raids, and his father received a testimony from four clergymen about 'his conformitie in coming to the Church and heareing divine service and Sermons there upon Sundays and holy days'.[39] Contemporaries, however, had their doubts. After all, Sir Ralph's son, Francis, saw in the Henrician sack of the Church an excellent opportunity to acquire the old priory church of Breedon on the Hill. During Elizabeth's reign, his son Francis then positioned the family to move into leading recusant families, marrying one daughter to the Brookes of Shropshire and another to the Brooksbys of Leicestershire. The family's religious affiliation became even clearer in the next generation; Sir George's brother died fighting in the Elizabethan wars in Flanders – on the Spanish side – and a sister corresponded with Father Garnet on the eve of the Gunpowder Plot and died a nun in Louvain. With such relatives, well might contemporaries have wondered about the Shirleys' true faith.

Like many families, they found the Reformation traumatic. After two generations, intense pressure to conform brought most local families to terms with the national Church; thus only in the late 1590s did the Fawnts convert. It may well have been so with the Shirleys. Notwithstanding a brother in Span-ish service, Sir George Shirley served with Leicester in the Dutch Republic, financing six lances and leading them 'many tymes in the field against the enemy being Spanishe'. Nor was this youthful exploit his last for the regime. To repel Spanish invasion attempts, he raised fourteen cavalrymen in 1588 and a cornet of horse in 1599. His close relationship with Lord Burghley, Secretary Walsingham and Lord Knollys eventually earned him appointments as a Northamptonshire JP and as Sheriff in 1603. Finally while other Catholics balked at taking the Oath of Allegiance, he proudly noted that 'he was as forward and diligent to doe his service as other of his fellowe Justices'.[40] Hence Sir George might well have rejected the old faith altogether, if not for his first wife, Lady Frances Berkeley. Her death in 1595 proved a pivotal moment, for she made her husband promise 'that he would have a Care that they [her children] mighte be Instructed and broughte up in the fere of God and true Catholicke Religion'. This vow was decisive in the deciding the family's religion. Although he remarried another wealthy widow, he erected in Lady Frances's memory a massive alabaster memorial, which still dominates the Breedon church.[41] More importantly, he honoured his promise. Consequently in 1614 when the Council ordered all recusants to be disarmed, his colleagues on the Northamptonshire bench searched his house and seized his weapons. This action produced protests about the 'great aspersion ... causeleslie cast upon this petitioners creditt and estimation' as well as the testimonial of four friendly Protestant divines.[42] Nevertheless as his health began to fail, Sir George found the moral ambiguities of even occasional conformity too much to bear. By 1620, he had abandoned all pretence and begun paying recusancy fines, dying two years later 'in the bosome of his Mother the Romayne Catholique Churche'.[43]

The family's wealth and religion encouraged the Shirleys to cultivate an extraordinary sense of themselves. Following a stint at Oxford and abroad, the young Henry Shirley attached himself to the court of Prince Henry, where John Davies of Hereford celebrated Shirley's merits. Davies had chosen well, for Henry's future was indeed bright until the prince's unexpected death dashed it. 'Soe deeply strucke' was the young man, his brother recalled, that he 'retired himself into the Cuntrie to live a solitarie life determining not to thinke of Courtly Pompe or glorie'.[44] Family pomp and glory were another matter entirely. In his retirement, Henry and his brother, Thomas, sought to legitimate themselves through genealogy. One of the few satisfactions that recusant gentlemen could savour was that they often could sneer at the conformist parvenus who had assumed their traditional commanding roles in society. Hence Sir Thomas Shirley devoted his life to *The Catholicke Armorist*, a mammoth work in which heraldry served as the basis of an extended religious and political polemic. Coats of arms led him to a detailed justification of the old faith and a glorification of its recent English martyrs; it also inverted the standard Protestant history, making 'the Blessed Queene' Mary, and 'the cruell' one Elizabeth.[45]

These forays into their past also led the Shirley brothers to a happy discovery about themselves. Although their father regularly trumpeted the fact that he was 'the XIXth heyre male of his house by lineal descent', the precise dimension of such a vast family tree remained vague until his sons clarified it. Patient research managed to get them only back to Sewalus, who died in 1085. That was enough, however, for them to establish descent from

> the Barons of Berkeley, dukes of Norfolcke and Buckingham, Earles of Arundell, Oxforde, Northumberland, Shrewsburie, Kent, Darby, Worcester, Huntingdon, Pembrooke, Nottingham, Suffolck and to most of the Antient, famous and florishing families of the Nobilitie and Gentrie in this whole Monarchye.

And then there was the Shirleys' royal blood, from 'the Royall stemm of England, both Saxon and Norman; as likewyse of that of fraunce, Scotland, Denmarke, Arragon, Leon, Castile, the Sacred Romayne Empire and allmoste to all the Princely Howses of Christendome'. In their passion for tricking out their family tree, Sir Henry and his brother, like other aspiring gentlemen of substance, were simply establishing their genealogical *bona fides* in order to justify their return to where the family always belonged, the peerage. Their father made an impressive down-payment on the family's dreams by being the fourth person in the realm to purchase a baronetcy. Until they managed the next leap upwards, they could console themselves with the knowledge that their pedigree had few equals in the county, and in the meantime, their father's prompt investment gave Sir Henry precedence over the entire non-noble population of Leicestershire.[46]

By the time Shirley reached the bench, his well developed sense of superiority had produced an imperious, impulsive man in his early forties. Sir Henry Skipwith was to learn this fact a few years later when he refused to yield his seat in a quarrel over precedence. Sir Henry responded with a peaceful resolution: he would sit in Skipwith's lap. Some contemporaries understandably found him insufferable; certainly his wife soon did. Less than a decade of marriage was enough for Lady Dorothy to begin proceedings for a divorce. Naturally Sir Henry opposed the idea, and at one point, in his desperation to halt the proceeding, he resorted to the extreme measure of denouncing her as a recusant, 'indicted and convicted', and so unworthy of the court's sympathy. Such information failed to persuade the archbishop, who eventually granted the divorce, and by 1629 she was back on the aristocratic marriage market. These prolonged hearings allowed Abbot to see a lot of Sir Henry, and he was underwhelmed. Shirley, he remarked, was a man 'of more livelihood than wisdom'.[47]

Yet Sir Henry was more than an unpleasant poseur. The divorce proceedings brought the Leicestershire baronet to court, where he soon became thick with the county's favorite son. Buckingham, in contrast to Abbot, fancied Sir

Henry, and precisely how well they got on became increasingly obvious late in
1626. Then the archbishop was amazed to hear the first word of the duke's
plan to suspend him from office from Sir Henry Shirley, who characteristically taunted him with the news. The perplexed archbishop again encountered
the blossoming Shirley–Villiers connection in Lady Dorothy's divorce proceedings. By any rational formula, Sir Henry's wife with her aristocratic
relations held a distinct advantage over her husband. Yet on 3 December 1626
Shirley upset this equation with a royal warrant halting proceedings, an action
which Lady Dorothy then laboured two months to reverse. Consequently Sir
Henry's sudden acquisition of influence with the duke was the most ominous
development in county politics during the 1620s. Huntingdon for his part
acknowledged that in the feud which would soon erupt, he had to struggle
against 'Shirlies powerful freinds' as much as with the baronet himself.[48]
Oddities notwithstanding, Shirley represented a deadly threat to Huntingdon
with his wealth, his 'powerful freinds' at court, and his frustration with the
Protestant upstarts who had usurped his position. With ample motive, all
Shirley needed was the right issue.

When well past middle age, Shirley was finally called into local administration in 1625. Admittedly most contemporaries found the office of Sheriff an
expensive honour that they would just as soon avoid. For Shirley, however,
years of exclusion made the post exceedingly welcome. He also had the good
fortune that James's timely death suddenly loaded his otherwise mundane
office with ceremonial significance. The scene on 4 April 1625 at the High
Cross in the center of Leicester was one which Shirley can only have relished.
There, surrounded by the Mayor and the Corporation, a host of Justices and
Deputy Lieutenants, and a guard of honour from the trained band, Sir Henry
Shirley, Baronet and Sheriff of Leicestershire, proclaimed the accession of
Charles I amid peals of trumpeters. He then presided over a banquet cele-
brating the new reign.[49]

From this triumph Shirley's tenure as sheriff came within an ace of ending
in ignominy, for the Lord Lieutenant very nearly included Staunton Harold in
the list of Catholic residences to be searched. Central to the report of secret
Catholic musters were 'loads of Ammunition ... brought to Sir Henry
Shirlies'. Consequently, Huntingdon initially planned to search the Sheriff's
house. Word of the danger soon reached Shirley, who, much to the earl's
disgust, reacted with sudden enthusiasm for the Established Church: 'hee
went to Church with the Judges and hath come to sermon and divine service
himself twice since'.[50] Notwithstanding such conformity, grounds of suspicion renained, as the raids in Derbyshire uncovered. Local reports there held
that the Charnwood midnight musterers would move to either of two places in
Derbyshire. At one of these, the JPs discovered 'great preparations of Bedding
and victualls'; the house belonged to Sir Henry Shirley's bailiff, who freely

confessed that the preparations were for Sir Basil Brooke, Sir Henry Merry and 'Sir Henry Shirley his master'. Brooke was Shirley's cousin and, like Merry, a prominent Catholic gentleman. Although the bailiff confidently predicted their arrival the following day, the posse waited in vain to interrogate them. Nevertheless, the Derbyshire justices complained about their uneasiness in dealing with recusants who had grown 'very insolent and kept Companie amongst themselves, as scorning us'.[51] And in the midst of these 'great troopes' was Sir Henry Shirley, baronet and sometime Sheriff of Leicestershire.

NOTES

1 William Burton, 'To the Illustrious and Right Honourable George Villiers', *The Description of Leicester Shire* (London, 1622); and William Lilly, *The History of his Life and Times* (London, 1715), quoted in Nichols, *History and Antiquities*, III, p. 749.

2 Buckingham to Chetwynd, 12 November 1622, William Salt Library, SMS 565/19; and 'Sir Sackville Crowes Booke of Accomptes', BL Add. MS 12,528, fols. 11v and 21. See also Roger Lockyer, *Buckingham: the Life and Political Career of George Villiers, First Duke of Buckingham, 1592–1628* (London, 1981), p. 4.

3 Nichols, II, p. 199; III, pp. 1 and 473.

4 Mayor to Countess of Buckingham, 27 October 1624; and Beaumont to Mayor, 25 August [1622?], Leics. RO, BR II/18/15, fol. 449; and II/18/14, fol. 208.

5 'To the duke of Buckingham', [1626]; and Fleetwood's warrant, [1626], Leics. RO, BR II/18/16, fols. 163 and 223.

6 Compton to H, 13 October 1616, HA Corr. 7/1576; *The Poems of John Marston*, p. 43; 'The aunsweres of those gentlemen', [1610], HAM 53/5b; and Dugdale's notes, HA Genealogy 1/26/15. See also J. Knowles, 'Marston, Skipwith and *the Entertainment at Ashby*', *English Manuscript Studies*, III, p. 175.

7 The 1614 Militia Certificate; H to DLs 31 July 1615; DLs to H, 5 August 1615, *LRLB*, fols. 11v, 14v and 15; and Lockyer, *Buckingham*, pp. 38, 86, 93 and 216.

8 Beaumont to H, 11 June 1616; H to Beaumont, 13 June 1616; and H to DLs, 24 September 1618, *LRLB*, fols. 22–2v and 37.

9 Buckingham to Sir George Hastings, 23 January 1621, HA Corr. 8/12993; and Lockyer, p. 6. See also J. K. Gruenfelder, 'The Electoral Influence of the Earls of Huntingdon', pp. 20–1.

10 *Notes on the Debates in the House of Lords*, ed. S. R. Gardiner (London, 1870), pp. 15–17; C. C. Stopes, *The Third Earl of Southampton* (Cambridge, 1922), pp. 407 and 428; and Colin Tite, *Impeachment and Parliamentary Judicature in Early Stuart England* (London, 1974), pp. 111–14.

11 Burton's preface to the proposed second edition of 1641; and [College of Arms] to Burton, 23 July 1622, quoted in Nichols, III, p. xx; and II, p. 842. See also Daniel Williams, 'William Burton's 1642 revised edition of *The Description of Leicestershire*', *TLAHS* L (1974–75), pp. 30–6.

12 *A Transcript of the Register of Stationers' Company*, ed. by E. Arber (London, 1874–94), IV,

p. 37; W. W. Greg, *Licensers for the Press* (Oxford, 1962), pp. 6–7 and 31–2; and K. Sharpe, 'The Earl of Arundel, his Circle and the Opposition to the Duke of Buckingham', *Faction and Parliament* (Oxford, 1978), pp. 214–20.

13 Burton, *Leicester Shire*, pp. 55, 120, 123, 187, 209 and 217.

14 *Ibid.*, pp. 17, 67, 105, 181, 185, 260–1 and 320.

15 H to Coventry, 13 February 1626, HA Corr. 12/5509. See also same to Williams, 20 May 1623, HA Corr. 9/5471.

16 Smith, *County and Court*, p. 129.

17 Legge to H, 12 May 1625; H to Legge, 12 May 1625; and same to Holland, 11 May 1625, *LRLB*, fols. 114 and 111v; and Fletcher, *Reform*, p. 291.

18 Fawnt to H, 8 June 1638, HA Corr. 15/3150. For Fawnt on the bench, see C66/2310, back of membrance 19.

19 'A booke of the proceedings' in H *v.* Pestell, 1632, HA Legal 5/8.

20 On the ages of the DLs, see Nichols, III, pp. 368 and 449; and IV, pp. 187 and 506; and *Complete Peerage* under Stamford.

21 Hesilrige to H, 18 June 1625; and Staresmore to same, 26 June 1625, *LRLB*, fols. 127 and 126v.

22 H to A. Hesilrige, 4 September 1623; same to Skeffington, 18 June 1625; and same to B. Hesilrige, 14 September 1625, *LRLB*, fols. 74, 125 and 130; and Nichols, II, p. 756. For payments to him, see H to Rudinge, 30 September 1623, *ibid.*, fol. 77.

23 'A note of the Souldiers returned', [1625], Leics. RO, BR II/18/15, fol. 595; and PC's letters to Leicestershire, Norfolk and Gloucestershire, 31 August 1625, *APC* 40/153. See also H to Noel, 21 July 1625, *ibid.*, fol. 128; and the Investigation of John Everard, [1625], SP 16/22/5.

24 FEH to Corporation, 8 July 1625, Leics. RO, BR II/18/15, fol. 596.

25 H's Bill, and Fawnt's demurrer, 1635, in H *v.* Fawnt, HA Legal 7/1 and 6/3; H *et al.* to Ellesmere, [1612], HA Corr. 6/5437; and 'A lybell of Lestershire knights 1606', BL Harleian 6383, fol. 72. See also Nichols, IV, p. 175. See also *The House of Commons, 1509–1558*, ed. by S. T. Bindoff (London, 1982), II, p. 121–2; and Burton, *Leicester Shire*, pp. 104–6.

26 [Corporation] to Heyricke, [1621]; Fawnt to Mayor, 10 August 1625; Fawnt *et al.* to Corporation, 29 May 1626; Fawnt to Mayor, [1626]; Fawnt to the Corporation, 14 December 1629; and Fawnt and Roberts to the same, 3 December 1629, Leics. RO, BR II/18/14, fol. 42; II/18/15, fol. 617; and II/18/16, fols. 119 and 158; and BR II/18/17. fols. 437 and 461.

27 Burton, *Leicester Shire*, p. 106; and H's Interrogatories, H *v.* Fawnt, HA Legal 6/2, p. 145. For a description of his lands, see Nichols, IV, pp. 169–70; and his family, see IV, p. 175.

28 H to Manchester, 22 November 1624, HA Corr. 10/5494; H to Chancellor of the Duchy, 16 August 1609, HA Corr. 6/5429; Fawnt to H, 18 August 1624, SP 14/71/63.I. See also Fox and Russell, *Leicester Forest*.

29 H to Conway, 20 August 1624, SP 14/71/63; Conway to Fawnt, 26 August 1624, HAM 48/33; and H to May, 22 November 1624, HA Corr. 10/5494.

30 Fawnt to H, 25 June 1624, HA Corr. 10/3147.

31 H to PC, 30 November 1625, *LRLB*, fol. 147. On the local Catholics, see T. B. Trappe-Lomax, 'Roman Catholics', *VCH Leicestershire*, II, pp. 57–8.

32 Henry Burton, *The Baiting of the Popes Bull* (London, 1627), dedication to Buckingham; Buckingham to Countess of Buckingham, [autumn 1627], Warwick County RO, Fielding of Newnham Paddox MSS, CR 2017, C1/30; and [Thomas Scott], *Vox Dei* (Utrecht, 1624), pp. 61–2. See also Nichols, III, pp. 464–5; and the sixth Earl of Rutland, *Complete Peerage*.

33 Carlisle to Buckingham, 20 November 1625, BL Harleian 1580, fol. 201–1v; Conway to Buckingham, 30 November 1625, BL Harleian MS 1580, fols. 342–3; and 'The Presentment of the Grand Jury of Constables', Michaelmas 1625, *LRLB*, fol. 142v–143. See also Star Chambers Reports, [1620s], FSL, V.b, fols. 23v–24v; Quintrell, 'Recusant Disarming'; and Cogswell, 'Parliament and Foreign Policy: the Case of La Rochelle, 1625–1626', *EHR* XCIX (1984), pp. 241–67.

34 Clare to Saye, 12 September 1626, *Holles Letters*, II, p. 334. See also Cogswell, *The Blessed Revolution* (Cambridge, 1989).

35 4 July 1626, PRO C231/4, fol. 204v. For a 1626 *liber pacis*, see PRO C193/12/2.

36 Thomas Cololeimon Philopatron [Sir Thomas Shirley], 'The Genealogicke Historie of the Howse of Shirleys', BL Add. MS 4928, fols. 90–7; the Shirley pedigree in Nichols, III, pp. 717*–18*.

37 Hertford to Essex, 16 July 1629, BL Add. MS 46,188, fol. 114; Leics. RO, Ferrers MSS, 26D53/2573; and Essex's settlement, 8 July 1623, Longleat House, Seymour MSS, Box 16/60. See also [Shirley] to [Hertford], [1610s?], Longleat House, Seymour MSS, Volume 6, fol. 20.

38 Sir George Shirley's will, Leics. RO, Ferrers MSS, 26D53/1958; anon. to Mead, 1 June 1621, *CT James I*, II, p. 256; Dorothy Hastings's will, 26 January 1606, HAP 14/15; William Sampson, 'On Sir Henry Sherley of Stanton', in *Virtus Post Funera Vivit* (London, 1636), [sig.] h2; and Vernon Snow, *Essex the Rebel* (Lincoln, 1970), p. 84.

39 Lewis *et al.* to Lambe, 23 January 1619, Leics. RO, Ferrers MSS, 26D53/2598b.

40 Sir George Shirley's petition, [1612?], HAP 14/10; and his conveyance in trust to Finchpoole Lovett, [1584?], Leics. RO, 26D53/2572.

41 Shirley's agreement with Sir Henry Poole *et al.*, 23 August 1598; Inventory of Farringdon House; and Shirley's agreement with Richard Royley, 9 August 1585, Leics. RO, Ferrers MSS, 26D53/735, 2583 and 2571.

42 'Agreement made by the Iustices of the peace ... in Northamptonshire', 11 January 1614; and Lewis *et al.* to Lambe, 23 January 1619, Leics. RO, Ferrers MSS, 26D53/2598a and 2598b.

43 'The Genealogicke Historie', fols. 106v and 108; Nichols, III, pp. 717*–718*; and Philip Caraman, *Henry Garnet 1555–1606 and the Gunpowder Plot* (New York, 1964), p. 320. See for example, recusant fines in Heyricke's accounts, Michaelmas 1621–Easter 1622, PRO E401/2434 Exchequer.

44 John Davies of Hereford, 'To my right worthy and truly generous gentleman Henry Sherley', *The Scrouge of Folly* (London, 1611), epigram 163; and 'The Genealogicke Historie', fols. 109v–110.

45 [Sir Thomas Shirley], *The Catholicke Armorist*, Queens College Oxford, MS 142, book 8.

Fragments of this work also survive in Sir Joseph Williamson's papers at the PRO. I am grateful to Richard Cust for bringing this document to my attention.

46 Petition of Sir George Shirley, HAP 14/10; and 'The Genealogicke Historie', fols. 2v–3. See also 'The Lineal Descent of the most ancient Family of the Sherleys', BL Harleian 4028; and the Book of Baronets, 1632, Huntington Library, HM 3134, fol. 1.

47 Judge Hutton's certificate, December 1632, HA Legal 2/11; [Shirley's statement], [*c.* 1625–28], BL Add. MS 46,189, fol. 30; and 'Abbot's Narrative', *State Trials*, II, p. 1455. See also Countess of St Albans and Clanricard to Essex, 6 December 1629, BL Add. MS 46,188, fol. 124.

48 Abbot's Narrative, *State Trials*, II, p. 1455; [Charles] to Abbot, 31 January 1627, PRO SO 1/1, fol. 5, and SO 3/8, unfoliated; and H to Lightfoot, 29 April 1636, HA Corr. 15/5542.

49 Hall Book, Leics. RO, BR, II/1/3, fols. 481–3; and Chamberlain's Accounts, Michaelmas 1624–25, BR III/2/78, fols. 186 and 204.

50 Grey to H, 5 October 1625, and H to PC, 30 November 1625, *LRLB*, fols. 134v and 147.

51 F. Coke to J. Coke, 17 November 1625, [Coke MSS], BL Add. MS 64,885, fol. 63v–4.

Chapter 5

Iron and gold

The cost of efficiency

With war engulfing the continent early in the 1620s, Samuel Buggs urged a congregation in the Midlands to abandon the peacetime mentality which enshrined scrupulous accounting and revered handsome cash balances. 'Bee well assured of this,' he told them,

> that if matters should come to tryall, and dint of sword come to decide our Countries cause, it is not plate or cash that shall secure us, not the glory of Shops that can defend us, nay more, more your good Angells [i.e. coins] will not guard you.

Instead his audience should prepare for the hour of decision when 'will iron be of more worth then gold'. Consequently, 'whosoever comes to reason the Case with the enemie, his best Logicke will be to conclude in ferio'. While Buggs's reasoning made increasing sense, a flood of unexpected financial levies nevertheless made it hard for many obdurate minds to abandon the old verities of the golden age. Sir Thomas Nevill was one of these stubborn souls, and by 1625, several years of unprecedented financial demands had left him in a querulous mood. Repeated subsidies and various benevolences had combined with an expensive wedding to deplete his cash reserves. Yet what made his mood especially dark was not so much his five unmarried children as his obligation to contribute to the horse troop. He found this burden so heavy that 'if I be taxed in such sorte as formerlie I have ben I shall not be able to keepe open my doores'. Unless the Lord Lieutenant listened to his plight, Sir Thomas would have to move to Essex.[1]

When set against Buggs's exhortation to abandon the customary obsession with 'good Angells', Nevill's complaint highlights the obvious question about just how badly pressed the local ratepayers actually were. A clear answer is essential, because in the subsequent months, a chorus of other gentlemen were singing variations on Sir Thomas's tune. Confronted with this rustic cacophony, modern scholars find it hard to take the complainers seriously.

For one thing, provincial gentlemen were notorious whiners, and for another, the amounts which prompted such bitter laments appear entirely inconsequential. Take Sir William Fawnt's objection to the apparent necessity that 'I and others as good as my selfe [must] be skrued out of our money at every becke'. Such passionate rhetoric naturally excites our sympathies – until it becomes clear that what was at issue was 'tenn shillings and nyne shillings and seaven shillings'.[2] Nevertheless the sheer volume of the complaints requires a careful examination of the fiscal costs of the war, and a thorough examination reveals that there were surprisingly ample grounds for complaint. Ironically the segue from the Age of Gold to that of Iron left the state more avaricious than ever. To be sure, most of its fiscal demands were modest, but when taken together, the amounts quickly rose to such heights that by 1626 Nevill was far from alone in his indignation. Since Huntingdon's critics had a field day with these taxes, it is well worth understanding how the local elite felt that they had been little-thinged to distraction.

COAT AND CONDUCT MONEY

When the government required pressed men, the lamentations were not confined to the immediate families of the ill-fated soldiers. The Crown readily acknowledged its obligation to provide every man with a heavy coat and to maintain him on the march from induction to embarkation. Unfortunately, its perennial lack of cash forced local authorities to advance 'coat and conduct' money. Sometimes this arrangement was not vexatious; in 1616, for example, only four months separated the loan and repayment. Prompt action, however, was the exception rather than the rule with such an irresponsible debtor; thus the loan for all intents and purposes often became a national tax. The memory of infinite delays in repayment during the 1590s moved the Parliament men in 1624 to forestall a repeat performance by insisting that all 'coat and conduct' money would be taken out of parliamentary taxes. Such careful planning worked to perfection with Count Mansfelt's levy when a letter from the Council of War was sufficient to handle the matter without incident.[3]

The satisfaction with this arrangement was not universal. In particular, royal administrators disliked a procedure that limited their hitherto absolute control over expenditure. Therefore in 1625, when the outbreak of the plague made the apprehensive Parliament men forget to revive these provisions, royal officials did not remind them. Consequently the levying for the Cadiz expedition reverted to the earlier pattern; smoothly citing 'presidentes of former tymes', the Privy Council asked the counties to advance 'coat and conduct' money on the promise that the money 'shalbe repaide to the Cuntry againe, out of his Maiesties exchequer'.[4]

This request created some confusion for Huntingdon. Initially he ordered each pressed man to bring £1 18s. from his parish. Maturer reflection revealed that since the 150 men would be selected out of a larger pool, some areas might avoid any contribution while others laboured under a disproportionate load. To correct this inequity, Huntingdon revised the old method funding scheme by which a set formula divided the total to be raised across the hundreds, where the constables collected it 'equally and indifferently'. Since this system invited rating disputes, Huntingdon abandoned it in 1615 for a more precise system. It remained a rough-and-ready assessment of the county's wealth, which Huntingdon revived in 1625, and after some tinkering, largely for the benefit of the Corporation of Leicester, this proportion guided the collection of £285. The central government meanwhile acknowledged its debt, and three years later, £102 16s. of the total finally reached the county. The remaining £182 4s., however, never was repaid.[5]

Table 1 **Assessments by hundred**

	1614		1615		1625	
	£	%	£	%	£	%
Gartry	42	21	26	22	60	21
Framland	22	11	18	15	46	16
Sparkenhoe	28	14	20	17	50	18
East Goscote	36	18	20	17	44	15
West Goscote	24	12	14	12	30	11
Guthlaxton	28	14	16	13	45	16
Leicester	20	10	6	5	10	4
Total	200		120		285	

Source LRLB, fols. 5v, 17 and 115v.

The experience with 'coat and conduct' in 1625 reveals only part of the reason for the contemporary dislike of the practice; the other was that the 'loan' represented only about half of the total expense. The 'national' obligation covered only the cost of a coat, generally about 18s., and the *per diem* expenses of 8d. from induction to embarkation. Getting the potential recruits to the selection point in a presentable state was the exclusive responsibility of their localities. The experience of the twenty-one men whom Leicester sent out with Mansfelt and Wimbledon illustrates the seriousness of this liability. Since these men were selected out of the forty-two candidates, the Corporation had to underwrite the expenses of the forty-two on the two-day march out to Ashby and of the twenty-one 'rejects' back to Leicester. Furthermore, aside from the king's coat, the Corporation had to handle the rest of the apparel.

One group of six soldiers required no fewer than six pairs of shoes, four shirts, four pairs of stockings and three knapsacks. Finally, there was the social expense of levying; since Mr Tinker, a pressed man, was married, the Corporation gave his wife 2s. to ease her distress. All of this cost the city £38 8s. 3d., of which £21 6s. 8d., approximately 56% of the total, eventually came back from the Crown.[6] In other words, the Corporation's shortfall was £17 1s. 7d., just under £1 for each pressed man.

Nor was the Corporation's experience unique. Although responsible for a lone pikeman in the trained band, Branston presented a dozen men for various selections in 1624–25. Fragmentary records do not reveal the full financial burden of impressment, but one figure that does survive is chilling enough; the travelling expenses of six of these men to the rendezvous came to £4. Since other local authorities must have faced similar bills and shortfalls, the 300 men raised for Mansfelt and Wimbledon likely cost the county some £250 in addition to the £285 which Huntingdon levied, and a sum in excess of £500 was not inconsequential in a county where a parliamentary subsidy brought in some £750. The figure was all the more ominous because in 1625, the Stuart war machine was far from through with the county's young men and its ratepayers. Against this financial background, we can begin to appreciate Edward Alford's depression when he considered the subject in 1628; he asked his colleagues in the Commons, 'how we shall be able to go on' after '[w]e have had four or five payments of coat and conduct money?'[7] His assessment of the situation was exaggerated – but not by much.

THE MILITIA ASSESSMENTS

The costs of coat and conduct, while annoying, were simply one-off exactions. More regular and more onerous were the militia assessments. In reforming the militia, Huntingdon's most formidable opposition came not from the 1,100 soldiers but rather from the local ratepayers. Hence he was obsessed with devising a method of underwriting the local regiment which 'I hope will not be distastfull to them'. When the militia's 'vacation' ended in the 1610s, the earl first used a set formula to divide the amount among the six hundreds and the borough of Leicester.[8] (See Table 1.) Unfortunately this arrangement practically guaranteed inequities. Walton on the Wolds, for example, presented three men and Branston one to the trained band, but while Walton in 1614 contributed 20s., or 6s. 8d. per man, it gave nothing the following year when tiny Branston supplied 10s.[9] To correct this irregularity, Huntingdon shifted in 1616 to a more precise system; after careful consultation, he set a sum which was then divided by 500, and the resulting fraction the constables collected from each parish for every trained man. The beauty of the system was that it spread the burden so wide that the charge was comparatively light.

Difficulties nevertheless remained, given the questionable legal basis of the levies. A local governor eager to forge a consensus wisely struggled to keep the sums low and to phrase his requests less as a legal demand than a plea 'to contribute with their neighbours to this Charge'.[10]

The major exception to this policy came with the earl's ill-fated 1614 attempt to reform the regiment. By 1616, however, it had collapsed entirely; instead of raising more money, the earl desperately attempted to slash the budget. These economy measures soon left the Muster Master's pay hopelessly in arrears and two of the five foot captains in unexpected retirement. In all, this three-year experiment produced local assessments totalling roughly £600, a tidy sum when a subsidy netted only slightly more. Yet two factors made this amount less daunting. First of all, two years without musters and assessments flanked this activity, and by including these, the average annual assessment falls almost half, from £200 to £120. More importantly, Huntingdon's requests bore little relation to the amount actually collected. The earl in these years was not zealous in tracking down defaulters, few of whom found themselves before the Privy Council. Consequently other ratepayers were free to follow the Corporation of Leicester's defiant reaction to Huntingdon's call for 9s. for each trained man. Rather than pay their share of £19 7s., the Mayor and his brethren offered the Lord Lieutenant only £6, or 3s. a man, along with the advice that the earl was asking for 'more then ever the Towne paid att any of the former Musters and more then ever was knowne or harde of before'. Further negotiations produced a further £6 in return for a promise to excuse the Corporation from another county project. Leicester's ability to evade a significant percentage of its militia assessment furthermore was not unique; in the preceding year, when the earl had called for 4s. per man, the Corporation blithely offered up £6 instead of its assessment of £8 12s.[11] In short, the ratepayers were unlikely to have felt too badly pressed before 1618.

Table 2 **Militia assessments in Leicestershire, 1614–17**

Year	For each trained man	Total	Source
1613	–	–	–
1614	–	£200	*LRLB*, fol. 5v
1615	5s. approx.	£120	*LRLB*, fol. 16v
1616	9s. plus 15s. for each horse	£300 approx.	*LRLB*, fol. 21–21v
1617	–	–	–
Total		£620	

The comparative ease with which the county bore these assessments made the new administrative world after 1618 all the more unsettling. Huntingdon at last could fulfill his dreams, and the county in short order found itself committed to annual fees of £50 to a Muster Master, £6 to an assistant Muster Master, £13 6s. 8d. to the Captain of the Horse troop, £10 to each of the foot captains, £10 to a secretary, £5 to a clerk and £4 to a treasurer. Smaller sums went to each of the twenty-two constables, six bailiffs, various clerks, a trumpeter and a tent-keeper. Meanwhile Huntingdon could afford to expand the number of foot captains from three to four and eventually five. Likewise tolerance of defaulting ended, and some ultimately made the expensive and humiliating trip to Westminster. As assessments came into line with collections, the memory of Leicester's loud protests over paying more than £12 must have seemed almost comical; in 1619 the Corporation quietly parted with £42. Finally, the absence of musters did not forestall militia assessments, as the county discovered in 1621.[12]

The cost of these changes was hard even for Huntingdon to comprehend. In 1618, he levied an assessment of £340, easily the largest since James I's accession, and in early February 1619, he followed it was another for £290. Nevertheless a fiscal crisis loomed. Much to the earl's dismay, 'the Cuntry' proved to 'be wonderfull slacke in payment of money', and so the shortfall in the militia accounts rapidly expanded. The obvious solution was a second levy, but the additional funds, he judged, 'would be very difficult nowe to raise for it would discontent the Countrey more that warrants went out for the collecting of this Some then twice soe much would have done in the former'.[13] Instead he allowed arrearages to grow in the officers' fees and deferred all non-essential outlays. The deficit nonetheless continued to grow, as did the clamour of the unpaid London armourers. Meanwhile, a trip to Westminster allowed Sir Thomas Hesilrige to discover that in many other counties 'men are generally more deeply taxed and charged then with us'. This precedent, together with absolute necessity, stiffened Huntingdon's resolve, and although he had asked in February for 10s. for each trained man, he requested another 11s. in September. In levying more than £600 in a year, he was mindful of appeasing public opinion. While he had hoped to defer these expenses, events on the continent left him no time; as he explained to the constables, 'I cannot leave it to a sudden Alarum when thinges by the straightnes of tyme cannot possibly be supplied.' Lest the county think him profligate with their money, he also instituted a cap on the daily expenses of the trained men.[14]

The lessons Huntingdon had learned in 1619 guided his later actions. In the following year, although the Privy Council ordered a muster, Huntingdon did not hold one. When Dohna's benevolence raised over £1,500, the Lord Lieutenant was loath to add additional 'money payments' to the ones 'which the cuntry hath had of late'.[15] The second levy of 1619 eventually produced a

Table 3 **Militia assessments in Leicestershire, 1618–25**

Year	For each trained man	Assessments (approx.)[a]	Collections
1618	9s.		
	plus 4s. per musket		
	plus 6s. per horse	£358	–
1619	Feb. 10s.	£300	–
	Sep. 11s.	£330	–
1620	[no muster]	–	–
1621	2s.	£60	–
1622	6s.	£180	–
1623	7s.	£210	£184 18s. 0d.
1624	7s.	£210	£180 5s. 4d.
1625	8s.	£240	£197 0s. 0d.
Total		£1,888	

Note a Figures are based on a trained band of 500 men, with 290 musketeers, and 100 horsemen.
Sources LRLB, fols. 34v–5, 42v, 54, 56v, 65v, 69, 135–5v, 5; SP 16/70/70, fols. 110, 110v and 112.

healthy surplus, which the earl drew down in the following year. By that time, economising had become second nature to Huntingdon, whether cutting the soldiers' *per diem*, haggling with tentmakers or limiting the gunpowder allocation. Such cheeseparing, together with the completion of the rearmament programme, allowed him to reduce the militia fees to more manageable levels; after the dangerous highs of 1618 and 1619, which nearly totalled £1,000, he managed to run an exemplary regiment on about £200 annually.

While not inconsequential, a total of some £1,900 in militia fees from 1618 to 1625 initially excites little sympathy for the ratepayers. To be sure, they paid out the equivalent of 2¹/₂ subsidies, but they did so over a period of eight years. Yet it must be remembered that this figure represented only a small percentage of the cost. As with the pressed men, there were local as well as national obligations. The militia treasurer's records reveal that the militia levies covered the purchase of gunpowder, match and a host of little extras ranging from prizes for the best marksmen to an attending preacher. By and large, however, it went to pay the Lord Lieutenant's large and expanding staff; hence in some accounts these assessments are recorded simply as 'officers fees'.[16] To understand the expense of a well functioning militia unit is to appreciate what the assessments did not cover. They did not cover equipment; each man was responsible for providing his gear, and if any part of it was found defective, the soldier had to make it good before the next muster. They covered neither the *per diem* expenses of the trained men while travelling to and from the muster, nor the costs of transporting the pikes, muskets and armour. Finally they did not cover the equipments' maintenance. In short, although each of the 580 trained men had to pay the Muster Master a set fee ranging from a few shillings to almost half a pound, this money did nothing to cover the costs of putting that man in the field.

While the exact financial details are sparse, what has survived presents a somber picture. Late in 1622, for example, when Huntingdon required 6s. for each trained man, Waltham on the Wolds sent up its three men who duly paid their 18s. This payment, however, was only the beginning of the village's expenses. Before the rendezvous, an earlier poor estimation of the town's equipment doubtless accounted for the decision to buy two swords, a pike and a musket's scourer and rest, which came to 14s. 8d., with another 3s. 11d. in delivery charges. Then the gear had to be prepared for inspection, edges sharpened and armour polished, which required 1s. 10d. Carting all of the equipment to and from the muster was an additional 7s. 7d. Yet notwithstanding the new swords, their scabbards failed to pass muster, thus necessitating another 1s. 8d. in repairs. Finally the food and drink for the three men came to 11s. 5d. Thus the visit to the muster cost the village £2 19s. 1d., of which only 18s. went on the officers' fees. Waltham's expenses were not atypical, for a few miles away, Branston also wrestled with the fact that the officers' fees represented only a third of a muster's expense. In September 1619, for instance, the village duly paid Rudinge the officers' fees of 11s. after having to underwrite another 19s. 6d. for food, transport and weapon repairs. The same pattern held true in 1623 when the officers' fee of 7s. paled against the other expenses which came to a further 14s.[17]

Although these records suggest that some of the additional expense came from journeying to distant meetings, the Corporation of Leicester found that, even without travelling, the additional expenses did not decline dramatically. In 1622, the Muster Master's judgment on the Corporation's men was devastating, and the city suddenly had to buy thirteen pikes, one musket, twenty-five scourers, seven ramrods, three musket rests, thirty-nine belts, twelve buckles, seventeen bandoliers, two swords and three caps. Not surprisingly, the Corporation's militia charges in 1622 nearly topped £50, of which only £12 went to the officers. Although these purchases reflect the Lord Lieutenant's new insistence on modern weapons, the Leicester accounts reveal that the relatively low percentage of officers' fees in the total militia expenditure for 1622 was not unusual. The Corporation's long-running wrangle with Huntingdon makes these figures even more remarkable, for its men did not muster at all for three years in the decade, and rarely outside of Leicester itself. Leicester's men moreover were not only comparatively well rested; they were

Table 4 **Leicester's militia expenses, 1618–30**

Year	Total £ s. d.	Officers' fees £ s. d.	Source
1618–19	51 15 6	32 0 0	BR III/2/27, pp. 149–51
1619–20	29 9 0	22 0 0	*Ibid.*, p. 196
1620–21	–	–	
1621–22	48 8 5	4 0 0	BR III/2/28, pp. 74–5
1622–23	–	–	
1623–24	–	–	
1624–25	–	–	
1625–26	43 3 0	5 10 0	BR III/2/29, pp. 52–4
1626–27	13 16 6	[damaged]	*Ibid.*, pp. 104–5
1627–28	35 7 5	9 0 0	*Ibid.*, pp. 148–9
1628–29	31 2 7	18 0 0	*Ibid.*, p. 192
1629–30	13 1 4	–	*Ibid.*, p. 246
Total	266 5 11	90 10 0	

also distinctive. Intent on underscoring its unique standing, the Corporation bedecked its men with finery; in 1620, its forty men wore 156 yards of scarlet and white ribbon. This policy inflated the militia expenses, but only some-what; after all, the 156 yards cost only £2. 1s.[18] Yet more than offsetting such frills were the comparatively low *per diem* expenses which came with Leicester's insistence on mustering only at Leicester. On balance, therefore, the Corpora-tion's militia expenses were, if anything, less than those of other towns.

Of the bill of £266 5s. 11d., officers' fees represented only £90 10s. 1d., or about a third of the total, and even by dismissing the expenses of 1626–27 and 1629–30, when the officers received nothing, the percentage rises to less than 40%. These figures therefore suggest that the assessments recorded in Table 3 represent *at the very least* only about half of the militia's burden. Consequently the county's militia assessments between 1618 and 1625 of approximately £1,900 must be doubled. The figure went higher still to account for the 500 'private' men and the 100 cavalry. Half of the infantry was comprised of 'private men', whom the wealthier gentlemen presented. The exact expense of appearing at musters with approved weapons and armour and with their own powder is now almost impossible to uncover. Yet we do know that their liberty from officers' fees did not make the purchase and maintenance of their equipment any less expensive. When the drive to perfect the regiment began, some private men thought that 'they can buy their Armes cheaper' than the trained men could; painful experience taught them otherwise.[19] Nor can the expense of *per diem* maintenance or the transport cost have been significantly less than that of a trained man. And for the musketeers at least, any savings they may have gained would have literally vanished in a puff of smoke with the cost of powder and match. It is difficult to see how their expenses could have been less than that of the trained men, another £1,800, thus raising the total to over £5,000.

Grumbling among the private men, however, was nothing like the noise coming from the horse troop, and at the bottom of their complaints was the heavy cost of involvement in the horse troop. While a new musket cost £1, the regulation gear for a mounted soldier easily came to £10. The greatest expense, however, was not what the trooper wore, but rather what he sat on. While horses were plentiful enough in the shire, the breed of 'great horse', necessary for military purposes, was not. The money involved in maintaining one can be seen in an aggrieved gentleman's sarcastic taunt about the heavily indebted Lord Lieutenant who was not 'soe ill an husband as to keepe greate horse'. Consequently, in the troop, a 'defective' report from the Muster Master represented a significant financial setback.[20] Calibrating the fiscal burden of the horse troop is now impossible, but it is equally impossible to ignore either the volume or the intensity of the complaints about it. The cost was the ostensible reason behind Sir Thomas Hesilrige's decision to move into Northamptonshire. Those gentlemen whom Sir Thomas left behind represented an even greater problem for Huntingdon, for the charges of favouritism or outright corruption within Huntingdon's administration almost all originated from complaints about the horse troop. From Sir George Manners protesting that he was more highly assessed than any other of the county's knights, it was only a short jump to Sir Henry Hastings, the earl's own cousin, arguing about 'others of far greater estate being not deepelier charged and some not at all'.[21] Given that much of the political turbulence in the shire was directly related to the troop's assessments, it seems safe to assume that the financial burden must have been substantial indeed.

These figures allow general discussions about the burden of the war to become quite specific. England at last entered the continental war late in 1625, but the figures from Leicestershire reveal that by then, the provinces had already been labouring under a significant burden for almost a decade. Parliamentary grants in 1621, 1624 and 1625 had drawn roughly £6,300 from the shire, and various benevolences extracted an additional £2,100. In most discussions, these contributions rightly dominate the foreground, but they should not obscure local military expenses. Levying Wimbledon's 150 men cost the shire, in local as well as national obligations, more then £500. Furthermore the militia regiment called for assessments of another £1,800, a figure which the 'local' cost of putting a trained man in the field easily doubled. The local elite meanwhile shouldered the additional cost of the private men and the horse troop, which at the most conservative estimate equalled the militia assessments. Therefore, the local military expenses would easily have totalled at least £7,000, if not more, a figure which came close to the £8,400 from subsidies and benevolences.

The implications of these figures are worth lingering over. By the time the hostilities had actually begun, Leicestershire had already paid well over £15,000 towards the war effort. Admittedly the burden was widely shared. A subsidy roll for the hundred of West Goscote has survived which lists 199 people, and since this hundred was consistently rated as containing about 12% of the county's wealth, it seems likely that parliamentary grants were the responsibility of around 1,650 people in a shire with fewer than 13,000 men between the ages of sixteen and sixty. An even larger number were involved in the militia assessments, which were far more regressive; in Market Harborough, for example, when the town's four trained men required £5 0s. 2d. for the 1619 muster, the constables had to call on 102 men and five widows.[22] Therefore, given the broad distribution of the burden, the weight of £15,000 over nearly a decade was far from crushing. Nevertheless it is worth considering if the collective burden represented a hardship, either real or perceived. For almost everyone involved, the latter situation certainly obtained; the most striking aspect of the period before 1618 was the near-total absence of any demands from Whitehall. Given this extraordinary withering of the central government, the rapid escalation in the number and sheer scale of Whitehall's demands after 1618 represented a drastic alteration of the prevailing relationship.

Burdens widely perceived as heavy really were, in some cases. The Corporation of Leicester largely financed its operations from rents and fines and only rarely from direct taxation. After 1618, however, the occasional event became a regular occurrence. A special levy in 1618 to support the trained band called for £25 19s. 10d., and after that, the demands came thick and fast: in 1619 first for £37 14s. 10d. and then for £27 3s.; and in 1622 for £44 17s. As Huntingdon knew all too well, these levies would succeed only if defaulters were handled roughly. As early as 1620 the Mayor asked the Recorder's advice about how to deal with 'those Townemen that refuse there taxation for and towards the charge of the last Musteringe and Trayninge'.[23] Yet even though the Corporation began seizing the goods of defaulters, the number of those in arrears continued to grow, as did the turbulence within the town. After these measures, one man followed the Mayor through the streets 'usinge many disgracefull speeches against the government of the Magistrates in Leicester'; another, a butcher, accompanied his 'uncivill termes and usage' with flourishes from his knife; while a third trumpeted 'reproachfull speaches against the government of the towne'.[24] Anxious to restore order, the Corporation in 1625 ordered the recalcitrant to be imprisoned. Against the mounting unrest, the Corporation's defence of its charter and its refusal to muster outside of

Leicester appears in another light. What lay behind its willingness to challenge the Lord Lieutenant was not just its devotion to abstract rights; after all, the city's men had regularly mustered outside the town earlier in the decade. Rather it was the fundamental fact that musters 'lead to our great Charge and trouble'.[25]

Expenses in excess of £15,000 admittedly did not touch off any riots. They had, however, raised the political temperature to a dangerous level, and the source of a potential explosion was all too obvious. The parliamentary levies had never produced any controversy, and their ease of collection rendered the contrast with militia assessments even more striking. Notwithstanding the earl's best efforts at fairness, the rates which he and his Deputies set had attracted mounting criticism. What made these particularly explosive were the charges of corruption, which his own financial difficulties made it impossible for him ever to stop.

TO THE BREAKING POINT

Late in 1625, when Huntingdon directed the anti-Catholic campaign, the state's steady intrusion was prompting many in the local elite to scrutinise their normally harmonious relationship with the Lord Lieutenant. What finally shattered this arrangement was a series of administrative decisions in 1626. The 'great levy' galvanised Huntingdon's opponents into open defiance, but it was three other matters earlier in the year that brought the shire to the breaking point.

The first of these can be seen when the Mayor of Leicester and his brethren retained a brave soul to inspect a woman who had suddenly collapsed at the Town Cross; it cost them 2s. to learn that the plague had entered their city. At first, contemporaries attempted to soldier on, and this spirit accounts for Ashby de la Zouch's advertisements for its June fair. A group of local ministers headed by Arthur Hildersham assured potential visitors that of the fifteen deaths since March, the plague had claimed only nine of them; on that basis, all were heartily urged to attend.[26] Such blandishments having only a limited appeal, all activity in the county quickly ground to a halt. Once the disease entered Huntingdon's lodgings in Westminster, the earl was understandably 'very loath' to attend the 1625 Parliament. In his alarm, he strictly prohibited his son from writing to his new wife at court, lest her response bring the infection to Donnington Park.[27] His harsh attitude was only an extension of his position on anything or anyone from the metropolis. On his orders, the constables banned the reception of Londoners or anyone from infected areas; scofflaws would be punished by being 'locked up' with their guests indefinitely.[28] The Corporation of Leicester eagerly followed Huntingdon's lead. A prohibition on any trade with London and the seizure of contraband goods quickly gave way to a passionate desire for an antiseptic environment. Any stray cow, pig or dog was liable to face immediate execution, lest it foul the road surfaces which the Corporation insisted on completely repaving. To enforce these decrees, the Mayor set a dozen watchmen at the town gates and another for good measure before the Town Hall.[29]

In the event, stringent measures failed to halt the epidemic, and in their frustration, local officials turned on one another, Hinckley blaming Leicester for its misfortune, and Leicester denouncing Blaby.[30] The worst aspect of the outbreak was its duration. As late as July 1626, the Corporation was still attempting to lure the assize judges back to the city with the soothing information that the plague was responsible for only thirteen of forty-four recent deaths. The judges had every reason for caution, for by then, the plague was so virulent in eleven villages that Huntingdon excused their trained men from musters. Three months later, the situation was so uncertain that he abruptly shifted the muster out of Leicester where 'the plague is lately encreased'.[31] The tenacity of the disease made the epidemic painful for the ratepayers and the infected alike. Through Michaelmas 1625, Leicester's corps of watchmen cost a modest £14 10s. 6d., but the next fiscal year, the Corporation was not so lucky, the watchmen calling for £36 6s., and the dogkiller another 1s. 8d. Provision of the pest houses demanded a further £15 4s. 8d., and the maintenance of 'visited' people £100 16s. 4d., one street alone requiring £40. Finally, the expense of repaving the city came to £63 13s. 2d. In all, out of a total income of £943, £216 1s. 10d., or roughly 23 per cent, went on plague-related expenditures.[32] It goes without saying that neither the citizens of Leicester nor their local leaders were in a particularly buoyant mood at the end of 1626, and when the subject turned to money, they could become truculent indeed.

Along with the plague, the shire had to cope with three unexpected worries – Sergeants Basil Cave, Richard Smith and John Bowden. As the realm entered the war, the militia, Charles proclaimed in 1626, became 'a thing which wee have placed our owne eye and expectation upon'. The result of his cogitations was the dispatch of veteran sergeants out of the English regiments in Dutch service to ensure that at future rendezvous 'the Souldiers may not bee distracted with diversity of Termes but men finde the same wordes which they learned at home'.[33] These NCOs, whose labours 'soe much enabled and instructed the Souldiers in their Postures for the well usage of their Armes', naturally earned Huntingdon's praise. Yet if their accomplishments were undeniable, their funding was less certain. While the government paid these men on their journey to Leicester, once there they became the county's responsibility, since Charles 'would not doe the Gentlemen of the Counties that wronge as to question their readines to give these officers kinde entertainment ... and some smale allowance'. The king's gallantry was especially irritating in Rutland, where the local elite was baffled by the logic which held that its tiny company of fewer than 200 men required two sergeants, the same number as Leicestershire. Fortunately for them, Sergeant Cave's illness soon allowed Huntingdon to transfer John Bowden, one of Rutland's two men, to the larger shire's payroll.[34] With their wages the Lord Lieutenant was characteristically generous; while Charles suggested at least 6s. a week, Huntingdon gave half again as much. On their departure, decency required the county to give them each £5 'for their paines' and 'a nagg' of equal value. Consequently, by the time the militiamen saw the back of these three men, the experiment had cost the county £74 7s.[35]

This episode, although minor, did much to wreck the Lord Lieutenant's budget for 1626. Persistent economy measures had left the militia with a surplus of over £100 from 1625, and since the previous budgets had required slightly less than £200, he reckoned in February 1626 that all the regiment required was a mere £71 6s. 8d., the smallest amount since 1621. Had 1626 been a fairly routine year, the ratepayers would have applauded his probity. But by late spring, not only had the regiment run through the £180 which Huntingdon had carefully gathered, but it was in the red for another £135 7s. 6d. In addition to the sergeants' wages, their emphasis on 'oftener exercisinge and trayninge' also cost money. For example, after '5 monethes drilling' under the tutelage of Sergeants Cave, Smith and Bowden, it only stood to reason that the salaries of five foot captains had to double, their bill thus jumping from £50 to £100, and similar cost overruns occurred throughout the regiment.[36] In an ominous re-run of 1619, Huntingdon found himself struggling to check expenses, only to have Whitehall destroy his plans with each new order.

As expenses skyrocketed, the harried Lord Lieutenant came to see the county's fiscal salvation in the humble knapsack. In describing this humble item to the constables, Huntingdon waxed rhapsodic: 'noe one thinge will ease and abate the same [the expense] more then in causinge of knapsacks to bee made'. The private men could carry food from home, while the trained men could 'with the monie allowed them for their meales at each exercise and trayninge provide themselves in their owne Towne with victualls' at a better price than at the muster. The knapsack would also eliminate extended lunch breaks at local inns. Finally, if 'carefully kept', the earl's economic wonder-weapon would last 'for many yeares'. The trouble was, all the economies Huntingdon envisioned would apply only after the private men and the individual parishes had bought the knapsacks. In keeping with the earl's well developed sense of decorum, they could not be purchased just anywhere, or even sewn together at home. Rather, the regiment's latest piece of equipment had to be secured exclusively from Mr Thomas Astlyn of Hinckley, who alone could produce them from 'two severall and very differinge collours', which Huntingdon had personally selected to prevent confusion between the private and the trained men. Each one cost 3s. 4d. After examining one of Astlyn's products, one of Huntingdon's deputies pronounced that 'considering the goodness of them, the valew is reasonable'.[37] To be sure, the Lord Lieutenant's order was not another militia assessment. Yet that was too fine a distinction for the men to grasp as they paid Astlyn £166 1s. 4d. for 1,000 knapsacks.

Between the knapsack, the sergeants and the militia assessment, the rate-payers earlier in 1626 had to produce £311 when the costs of the extended epidemic were becoming heavy. Meanwhile, the mounting debt of the regiment made a second levy almost inevitable. Earl Henry nonetheless refused to yield to this logic, the interval since 1619 having only hardened his belief that a second levy 'would be very difficult nowe to raise for it would discontent the Countrey'. Thus the Lord Lieutenant struggled into the summer of 1626, squeezing out any possible revenues. Defaulters soon discovered a nasty shrillness in his demand that they should produce either their assessment or 'sufficient sueries to bee bound for your apparence for this your contempt before the lords'. Meanwhile the constables had to do their duty, lest 'every one of you will answere the contrary at your uttermost perills'. Even the tardy who belatedly paid their rates were bound over anyway 'for their Contempt and neglect that they paid not their monie upon the last warrantt'. With his new rigour, the earl meant well. All the same, in early June, whatever money he gained from harrying defaulters literally collapsed with the beacon at Buckminster, a critical link in the chain connecting the county with the coastal defences. Detailed reports from the scene made it clear that only a new stone foundation and warehouse could repair the vital connection with Lincoln-shire.[38] With this disaster, Huntingdon had to bow to the inevitable. The only remaining question was the size of the second assessment, and the answer came when the Privy Council's order of 10 July 1626 reached Donnington Park.

THE GREAT LEVY

For the English war effort, the Parliament of 1626 was a vital watershed. Ever since the 1624 session, Charles and Buckingham had assumed that since they were working with the Parliament men, they could expect generous funding. The 1625 Oxford session cast considerable doubt on this proposition, but the official line ascribed the turmoil to a handful of wreckers, not the majority. The 1626 session exposed the folly of such optimism. When an array of speakers criticised Buckingham's handling of the war, a majority predicated new supply on an end to the duke's vice-like grip on the administration. In response, royal spokesmen conceded that there had been early mistakes, but these paled in significance before an imminent Spanish invasion. Unfortunately for the government, it paid the price for having employed the same argument in two preceding Parliaments. Already in 1625, Sir Francis Seymour had blithely dismissed 'the rumor of flat-bottom boats we heard the last meeting'. By 1626, although the danger was then quite real, the Parliament men were even more sceptical. Thus the session and the nascent war effort headed for disaster.[39]

With the session's dissolution, despair overwhelmed the government. Given the vital importance of new funds, Secretary Conway's first response was understandably hysterical: 'I cannot see any other helpe then that which they use to say in the plague time every man to himselfe Lord have mercy upon us.' He soon got a grip on his emotions, altering the sentence to read '... then Vive le roi'.[40] Conway's reaction captured his colleagues' mood. Although the Commons had lost confidence in Buckingham's regime, this development did not change the fundamental fact of England's state of war. One way or the other, the realm had to prepare and, more importantly, to finance its own defence. The best-known outcome was the forced loan project of 1626-28, but this would require months of effort before significant amounts of money began to flow into the Exchequer. In the interim, the Council focused on defensive measures and decided to shift much of the financial burden of the war effort onto the localities. Part of the new policy required coastal counties and towns to loan the Crown ships at their own expense, and since this prefigured the ship money, scholars have had considerable interest in it. But there was another part of this emergency measure: on 10 July the councillors turned to the militia, 'the sure and constant bulwark and defence of this kingdome', and issued a stream of new instructions. While scholars have generally overlooked their action, contemporaries could not, for this order represented the most significant alteration in the militia since its creation.

The Council's directions called for a revolution in the county administration and, more importantly, in its budget. Over a decade later, Sir Wolston Dixie still vividly recollected the scene at Donnington Park when the new order arrived; the earl 'then and there read over the said letter to him [Dixie] ... divers times and gave the same unto him ... to reade'. In addition to a drastic increase in powder stocks and a stern prohibition against anything other than 'moderne' arms and armour, the Leicestershire regiment had added a company of 100 pioneers, fully furnished with 'spades, pickaxes, shovells, hatchetts, bills and the like'. The expanded force moreover had to be ready to march at an hour's notice with food stocks sufficient for ten days' campaigning. Given the formidable difficulty of moving this logistical tail, the councillors also required the county to purchase a fleet of 'carts with geares'. Rather than leave the county defenceless in the event of the regiment's mobilisation, Huntingdon was to select a second regiment from the remaining able-bodied men. To outfit this new unit, the Council suggested using the arms seized in the raids on Catholic households late in 1625. These requirements were startling demands, but the councillors scarcely noticed in their obsessive search for increased security against internal subversion. This paralysing fear accounted not only for the second regiment, but also for their insistence on a Provost Marshal to protect against those who 'by tales or false rumors distract the people's myndes' and for their command that all involved in both regiments must take the oaths of allegiance and supremacy.[41]

Hitherto the earl had responded to Council edicts with a minimum of protest, a practice which accounted in no small part for Leicestershire's status as a model county. But the 10 July order exceeded the limits of Huntingdon's deference to royal commands. So intemperate was his initial response that on 'second consideration' he drafted a more circumspect reply. The notion of raising a second regiment, when the county could barely afford one, attracted the bulk of his ire. Since the county maintained the customary proportion of one 'private' man for every trained one, the county, he argued, had effectively maintained a second militia regiment for over thirty years. Therefore, while he agreed to assemble all able-bodied men, he unilaterally refused to organise a second unit. Having rejected one order, Huntingdon then altered another; to reduce the expense, he appointed a joint Provost Marshal for both Rutland and Leicestershire. Finally, he could not help reminding the councillors that local officials could not administer the oath of supremacy without a commission from the Lord Keeper.[42]

Having vented his frustration, Huntingdon settled down to implementing the rest of the Council's wishes, and directives poured out from Donnington Park. In short order, the new pioneer company boasted an array of equipment worthy of the contemporary master of military engineering, Prince Maurice of Orange: a hundred spades, fifty shovels, fifty pickaxes, thirty hatchets, thirty handbills, twenty axes, twenty handsaws, twelve framing saws, ten hammers, ten pincers, six whipsaws as well as 100 swords. To move this material, the county transport pool expanded to ten carts pulled by sixty horses, which in turn required a mass of wood, iron bands, tar, harnesses and collars. Since such a small mountain of equipment would not fit into the county powder magazine, the pioneer company acquired its own warehouse, replete with a lean-to to keep the vehicles out of the weather. While the Lord Lieutenant and his staff handled the formation of the pioneer company, they had to work closely with the local authorities on other items. First the mayors and constables had to gather truly mammoth amounts of victuals, since ten days' food supply came to a ton and a half of butter, two tons of bacon, over two tons of hard cheese, and no less than eight tons of meal. Next, the local officials had to establish a rota of their 'best inhabitants' to guard each of the three beacons. Finally, several market towns had to establish an express mail service, able to send riders galloping to Whitehall at an hour's notice. Such orders, which would have been awkward enough at the best of times, were nearly impossible when the plague was still present in four of the six hundreds and in eleven of the towns, Leicester included. Yet the earl refused to relent; instead he adopted the Council's harsh tone in his dealings with local magistrates, ordering the execution of his commands 'upon pain of death'.[43]

Such an uncompromising attitude was vital if Huntingdon was to have any hope of getting the shire to implement even part of the Council's order. Thanks to the sergeants and the regular training, the militia was already significantly in the red. Meanwhile the equipment for the pioneer company required a further £130, and the new Buckminster beacon another £85. The price tag rose so high, so fast that even Huntingdon became apprehensive about the magnitude of his requests. His initial response had been to dispatch Muster Master Everard to the London armourers with an enormous shopping list. On second thoughts, he and his deputies decided that 'in regard of the great charge the Cuntrie will be putt to at this tyme', the purchase of some equipment could be deferred until the following year, among them 200 new belts, 100 corselets and pikes, thirty pistols and twenty saddles. Such last-minute budget-slashing notwithstanding, the second militia assessments broke all records. The record hitherto belonged to 1619, when Huntingdon had called for over £600 in two assessments; in 1626, however, he was demanding £1,220 in one levy. Needless to say, this money did not cover the purchase and storage of the regiment's victuals, a responsibility which lay wholly on the parishes and the private men. This was furthermore on top of the £71 which he had collected at the beginning of the year, and the £166 1s. 4d. which Mr Astlyn was gathering for the knapsacks. In short, in the name of a more perfect militia, the ratepayers were dunned almost £1,500 in addition to horses for the courier service, rotas of watchmen at the beacons and literally tons of food. The scale of these demands alarmed even the Lord Lieutenant, who carefully explained that the money would be employed solely for 'the buyinge of the aforesaid powder, Match, Bullet, watchinge of the Beacons and buildinge the Beacon and watch Tower at Buckminster Cariages with Geares and the like, halbeards, Spades, pickaxes, shovells, hatchetts, Bills and other instruments fitt for war'. None of the new funds, he assured the ratepayers, would be used for officers' fees, 'only for the Souldiers dyett'.[44]

Amid these demands, the ratepayers could have comforted themselves with the thought that this was the end of the Council's demands for the year. Vain hope! Early in August, only a few weeks after having been paid off, Sergeants Cave and Smith marched back into Leicestershire with new orders assigning them to the Leicestershire regiment. Given 'the great benefit that hath alredy bene receaved', it seemed a shame, the Council explained, to deprive the militia of their services. Therefore, the government seconded Cave and Smith to the Leicestershire regiment, not for a limited tour of duty, but indefinitely. Nor was the Council through. In August, the Council launched another Privy Seal loan, replete with detailed instructions to the local authorities. Such careful plans, however, could do little, for when the JPs called the meeting at Loughborough in mid-August, the constables were moving through the shire collecting the second massive militia assessment. The presiding JPs dutifully followed the instructions about heading off 'all secret combinations', but there was nothing secret about the resistance. The audience was positively rude; 'most crying a parliament, some pleading want and divers the pressure of other payments'.[45]

By the end of 1626, Samuel Buggs's fond dream had come to pass. By an involved political alchemy, England was finally involved in the continental war, and at last gold had been transformed into iron. Yet the cost of the metamorphosis had been high. By focusing on national taxation, most previous scholars have failed to comprehend the full scale of Whitehall's demands. In Leicestershire at least, however freely and insincerely contemporaries voiced pleas of poverty, they had ample grounds for 'pleading want and ... the pressure of other payments'. The only real question was how they would react to the new demands.

NOTES

1 Buggs, *Miles Mediterraneus*, p. 8; and Nevill to H, 13 October 1625, HA Corr. 11/9579. On Nevill, see Nichols, *History and Antiquities*, II, p. 730.

2 Fawnt to Dixie, [November 1626], HA Corr. 12/3148.

3 Council of War to the Leicestershire Subsidy Commissioners, 3 November 1624, *LRLB*, fol. 96v. See also Young, 'Revisionism and the Council of War'.

4 P to H, 5 May 1625, *APC* 40/42–4.

5 H to Constables, 11 and 14 May 1625, *LRLB*, fols. 112v–113, 114v and 115v; and payment to William Whalley, 5 February 1628, PRO E 403/2804, p. 67. On the earlier system, see above, pp. 15–16.

6 'Chardgs about the pressing and setting forth of Soldiers', Michaelmas 1624–25, Leics. RO, BR III/2/78, fols. 185 and 193–6.

7 Leics. RO, DE 720/30, fols. 22v–23; and 11 April 1628, *PP 1628*, II, p. 418.

8 H to Head Constables, October 1614; 'The Rates of the Hundreds', October 1614; and 'The Particuler Rates of each Hundred', September 1615, *LRLB*, fols. 5, 5v and 17.

9 Leics. RO, DE 625/60, pp. 17–18 and 22; and DE 720/30, fol. 10v.

10 H to DLs, 7 June 1616; and same to Constables, 4 September 1623, *LRLB*, fols. 21v and 73v–74. See also H to Bradshaw, 6 August 1624, HA Corr. 10/5487.

11 Leics. RO, BR III/2/77, fols. 35–6 and 33–4.

12 Rudinge's Accounts, SP 16/70/70; Leics. RO, BR III/2/77, fols. 150–1 and 196; and H to Constables, 22 November 1621, *LRLB*, fol. 65v.

13 H to Morison, 19 May 1619; and same to DLs, 13 March 1619, *LRLB*, fols. 71 and 45.

14 Hesilrige to H, 20 May 1619, HA Corr. 8/6743; and H to Constables, September 1619, *LRLB*, fol. 54–4v.

15 PC to H, 31 May 1620, *APC* 37/215; and H to Constables, 22 November 1621, *LRLB*, fol.

65v.

16 See, for example, Leics. RO, BR III/2/79, pp. 148 and 192.

17 Leics. RO, DE 625/60, pp. 50–1; and DE 720/30, fols. 16 and 21.

18 Leics. RO, BR III/2/78, pp. 74–5; and BR III/2/77, p. 196.

19 H to DLs, 9 March 1619, *LRLB*, fols. 43v–44. On the private men, see H to PC, 28 July 1626, SP 16/32/64; and Fletcher, *Reform*, p. 310.

20 Hesilrige to H, 18 June 1625, *LRLB*, fol. 127. On the cost of the equipment, see 'Cuirasser, Harquebuzier, Carabyne', 15 June 1625, HEH Bridgewater, EL 7617. See also Edwards, *The Horse Trade*, pp. 38–46.

21 Hesilrige to H, 18 June 1625; and Staresmore to same, 26 June 1625, *LRLB*, fols. 126v and 127; and Manners to H, 20 March 1619, HA Corr. 8/9137. See also Grey to Conway, 4 September 1627, SP 16/76/27; and Hesilrige's appointment to the Northants bench, 8 March 1628, PRO C231/4, fol. 242.

22 'Subsidy Book 1625', Bodleian Library, Engl. Hist. C483 [Herick MSS], fols. 12–17; 'A note of the particulars', 10 May 1627, HA Military, Box 1/12; and *Market Harborough Parish Records*, ed. by J. E. Stocks (Oxford, 1926), pp. 137–8.

23 Leics. RO, BR III/2/77, fols. 130 and 175; and BR III/2/78, fol. 50; and [Queries for Mr Recorder], [1620], Leics. RO, BR II/18/13, fol. 496. See also 'The Submission' for defaulters, *ibid.*, fol. 527.

24 Mayor's Court, [1620]; 4 February 1624; [1625], Leics. RO, BR II/18/13, fol. 499; and BR II/18/14, fols. 305 and 616.

25 Common Hall Resolution, 15 April 1625; and [Corporation] to May, 22 June 1625, Leics. RO, BR II/18/14, fols. 541 and 582.

26 Leics. RO, BR III/2/78, fol. 190; and Hildersham *et al.* to Corporation, 1 June 1625, Leics. RO, BR II/18/15, fol. 586.

27 H to Pembroke, 28 June 1625, HA Corr. 11/2514; same to Staresmore, 2 July 1625, *LRLB*, fols. 127; and ECH to LCH, 17 November [1625], HA Corr. 11/4835.

28 H to Constables, 27 July and 4 October 1626, *LRLB*, fols. 175v–6v and 185v. See also same to Heather, 27 July; same to Loughborough, 9 August; and same to Sparkenhoe constables, 15 October 1625, HAM 47/6, 53/20 and 51/26.

29 Resolution, 15 July 1625 and [1625–6], Leics. RO, BR II/18/15, fols. 593; and II/18/16, fol.112; and accounts, BR III/2/79, fols. 28 and 43–7.

30 Mayor of Hinckley *et al.* to Corporation, 1 and 8 September 1625, Leics. RO, BR II/18/15, fols. 627 and 625; and Fawnt *et al.* to Corporation, 29 May 1626 and n.d.; Corporation to Fawnt, n.d. and Common Hall's resolution, 15 September 1626, Leics. RO, BR II/18/16, fols. 119, 158, 120 and 132.

31 Corporation to Assize Judges, 16 July 1626, Leics. RO, BR, II/18/16, fol. 109; and H to Constables, 27 July and 4 October 1626, *LRLB*, fols. 175v–176v and 185v.

32 Leics. RO, BR III/2/78, fols. 197–8; and BR III/2/79, fols. 28, 43–51, and 57–60.

33 Charles to PC, 24 May 1626, *LRLB*, fols. 162v–3; and same to same, 14 January 1626, SP 16/18/55. See also PC to H, 24 January 1626, *APC* 40/321–4.

34 Certificate for Sergeant Salmon, 20 June 1626; Cave to H, 1 March 1626; and H to Palmes, 3 March 1626, *LRLB*, fols. 165v, 158v and 159.

35 H to [Palmes], 2 June 1626, *LRLB*, fol. 161v; and Rudinge's accounts, SP 16/70/70.

36 H to Constables, 3 February 1626, *LRLB*, fols. 154v–5; and Rudinge's accounts, SP 16/70/70, fols. 112v–113.

37 H to Constables, 24 February 1626; and same to Skipwith, 27 February 1627, *LRLB*, fols. 157v–8 and 188.

38 H to Dixie, 26 June 1626; same to Constables, 26 June 1626; and Glover to H, 4 July 1626, *LRLB*, fols. 164, 164v–5 and 167–7v.

39 5 August 1625, *PP 1625*, p. 394. See also T. Cogswell, 'Parliament and Foreign Policy: the Case of La Rochelle, 1625–1626', *EHR* XCIX (1984), pp. 241–67.

40 Conway to Carlisle, 5 June 1626, [draft], SP 78/79/64; and BL Egerton MS 2597, fol. 13.

41 PC to H *et al.*, 10 July 1626, *APC* 41/72–4; and Dixie's testimony in H *v.* Fawnt, HA Legal 6/2, p. 15. See also Andrew Thrush, 'Naval Finance and the Origins and Development of Ship Money', in *War and Government in Britain, 1598–1650*, ed. by M. C. Fissel (Manchester, 1991), pp. 133–62; and Robin Swales, 'The Ship Money Levy of 1628', *BIHR* L (1977), pp. 166–7; and Boynton, *Elizabethan Militia*, pp. 248–50.

42 H to PC, 28 July 1626, SP 16/32/64.

43 H to Constables, 27 July 1626, *LRLB*, fols. 175v–176v; and Rudinge's accounts, SP16/70/70.

44 H to Everard, 28 July 1626; and H to Constables, 27 July 1626, *LRLB*, fols. 175–176v. See also same to Knight, 28 July 1626, *LRLB*, fol. 177.

45 PC to H, 19 July 1626, *LRLB*, fol. 179v; JPs to PC, 18 August 1626, SP 16/34/4. See also R. Cust, *The Forced Loan and English Politics, 1626–1628* (Oxford, 1987), pp. 35–9.

Analysis

The height of glittering honour

The irony of Huntingdon's formidable skill in fashioning an efficient county machine was that it only served to increase his political vulnerability, and Part II has simply produced variations on this somber theme. For any local official, magistrate as well as Lord Lieutenant, the wisest policy was to balance Whitehall's demands against the locality's resources, and the shrewd local governor, confident in Whitehall's celebrated inability to keep three dozen administrative balls in the air, generally erred on the side of his neighbours.[1] By his own lights, Huntingdon employed his good offices with the Council to secure the most favourable treatment for the shire. Yet a number of his neighbours increasingly wondered if he was not in fact more interested in currying favor with the privy councillors. Such an uncharitable assessment logically followed from the fact that the execution of the regime's orders required a substantial outlay of money, all extracted, not by statute, but by prerogative. The grumbling from the ratepayers only increased as they saw their money flow into the hands of a peer who would have likely been bankrupt, if not for his noble lineage. Carping along these lines, while disquieting in alehouses, became particularly dangerous once broad segments of the local elite came to voice them. All of these developments, when taken together, made it quite possible that the hour of the earl's triumph, when he seemed within reach of the 'height of glitt'ring honour', might actually herald his disgrace.

Having earlier analysed the potential sources of trouble, there is no need to rehearse the danger posed by the earl's Catholic kinsmen and his own poverty, by his critics on the bench and in Whitehall, and by the cost of the local rates which he had imposed. Yet there are aspects of each, which are well worth further contemplation, and not the least of these concern the militia's impact on the local rates.

After reading about the South Battalion of the Hampshire Militia in its extended campaign during the Seven Years War against English taverns and French prisoners of war, a campaign which included sporadic attempts to stumble through 'such rare and superficial practise' as drill, the reader may well follow Edward Gibbon's advice and 'may smile'. Certainly most scholars have, and this reaction may explain their unwillingness to consider that the early Stuart ancestors of Gibbon's militiamen may have been expensive as well as droll. Such considerations as we have had of militia finances have focused on the continual rows of muster masters' fees and the furore over billeting along the south coast.[2] Anything else which the Lords Lieutenant may have levied must have been too minute for serious consideration. Furthermore this accounting game cannot have been worth the historiographical candle, for even these derisory sums appear to have been rarely paid; 'evasion of these taxes', Boynton concluded, 'was one aspect of the more efficient technique of modern landownership'. Holmes represents the honourable exception to this trend by discussing a novel scheme to levy a militia rate of 1d. an acre on the Lincolnshire gentry and by noting that the cost of weekly musters in 1626 'came to represent a considerable charge'. Yet after observing that the levy prompted protests, even he abandoned the topic.[3] To be sure, much of the oblivion into which the militia rates have fallen doubtless relates to the erratic coverage of the subject in most lieutenancy books, and here the detailed one which Huntingdon kept for these years proves its value.

Once a local community's first line of defence – studied inactivity – had fallen before the Council's relentless pressure, its leaders would customarily flood Whitehall with complaints and excuses, all displaying the inventive possibilities of epistolary fugues based on the common themes of endemic poverty, current hardship and previous generosity. In these performances many gentlemen proved themselves accomplished virtuosi. Yet scholars arguably have been more apt to applaud their skill as grumblers than to listen to their complaints. This tendency reverses itself after totting up the basic cost of Huntingdon's military levies, after calculating the additional expenses of towns and parishes, and after figuring the staggering charges of the horse troop and the 'private' men. This sobering exercise transforms the early modern ratepayer from a *grogneur*, for ever protesting about twopence ha'penny, to a civil martyr, resigned to suffering in comparative silence. Regrettably, as will shortly be seen, the patience of the mildest man has limits, and even the admirers of Sir Henry Shirley and Sir William Fawnt would have conceded that neither man was temperamentally suited to portray the early modern Job.

Further trying their forbearance was the earl's conspicuous financial problems. Aristocratic laments about imminent financial collapse, while heartrending, are also commonplace; hence the fifth earl's tale of woe is not especially remarkable. More astonishing, however, is the primary means which he adopted for saving himself. In earlier discussions of the value of the lieutenancy, issues of reputation and honour have loomed large. Granted, local governors with an active militia had some financial patronage to dispense, but that generally went to their loyal subordinates. In Huntingdon's case, however, the lieutenancy was essential to his fiscal as well as his psychological well-being; indeed, this office produced somewhere between a fifth and a quarter of his annual income in the 1620s. Lawrence Stone has argued that the comparative poverty of the early Stuart monarchs made it impossible for them to offer sufficient financial inducements to control the peerage, particularly when a few courtiers effectively monopolised the limited royal bounty.[4] His logic is flawless – except that he failed to consider the possibility of a peer so strapped for cash that a few local offices might represent the difference between a bare existence on an aristocratic subsistence economy and utter ruin. This is not to argue that financial considerations dictated Huntingdon's actions as a local governor; as will be seen, he could act against his economic self-interest. Nevertheless, far more than was the case with most Lords Lieutenant, the earl's dependence on the Crown's favour circumscribed his range of political options.

The inherent fascination of the spectacle of a distinguished peer frantically clinging to local office should not obscure the equally remarkable breadth of his critics. After Hassell Smith's work, there is little surprise in discovering that some local magistrates regarded an active lieutenancy as a serious intrusion on their authority. In Leicestershire in the 1620s, as in Norfolk thirty years earlier, they were understandably nonplussed to find their broad powers reduced to 'the formidable and unwelcome task of providing adequate funds to finance schemes which the Council propounded ... and the lieutenancy readily put into effect'; meanwhile they were 'denied any opportunity to influence these developments and to cushion their impact upon the country'.[5] Little wonder then that by 1626, Sir William Fawnt and the Hesilriges, *père et fils*, were simply awkward political incidents ready to happen.

So too was Sir Henry Shirley, but nothing in Smith's work, or indeed in that of any other historian, prepares us for the spectacle of a notorious crypto-Catholic gentleman publicly attacking a staunchly Protestant peer of the realm. Although Whitehall and isolated rural estates had long harboured Catholic sympathisers, a county bench generally did not make a congenial home for them, given the number of oaths which a magistrate had to take, all of them expressly designed to flush out devotees of the old faith.[6] Yet it was not simply Sir Henry's cheerful willingness to abjure Catholicism which accounts for his rise; there is also his timing.

Behind Huntingdon's eagerness to bully the shire into compliance with the latest decree lay a desire to curry favor with the Crown, and so much the better for him, if Whitehall's orders demanded implementation of aggressive Protestant policies, to which the earl was personally committed. In his zeal, the earl assumed that he was working for the king; Buckingham was simply a royal favourite from whom local governors could maintain a safe distance. Yet as the decade progressed, it increasingly became impossible to separate the duke from the king, and with the accession of Charles I, Buckingham's influence so pervaded the regime that, as the Parliament men soon discovered, the two were inextricably intertwined. Consequently, the net effect of the criticism which members poured on Buckingham's handling of foreign and military policy was simply to drive the government into the hands of Arminian divines and Catholic sympathisers. By the summer of 1626, Charles's insistence on identifying his interest exclusively with that of the duke forced Whitehall to attempt to wage a major war with the help of a domestic coalition largely indifferent, not to say hostile, to the war aims.[7] The Crown's willingness to adopt such a fundamentally absurd position, and so forestall any diminution of the duke's power, flabbergasted and angered Protestant 'Patriots' like Huntingdon. The earl's dismay and wrath mounted higher still as he saw that the local manifestation of this shift in national politics was the inexorable rise of Sir Henry Shirley.

The emergence of this new irritant reminded Huntingdon of a final point, which historians have failed to appreciate. Buckingham, that most towering of all early Stuart 'court mushrooms', might at times appear to have sprung from an otherworldy spore nourished in the hothouse environment of the Jacobean court. Yet as we have seen, the duke in fact nursed a strong connection with his native shire as well as equally deep animosities there. Huntingdon's political problems in the 1620s stemmed from the fact that he had too little claim on the former and too much on the latter.

NOTES

1 Hirst, 'The Privy Council and the Problem of Enforcement in the 1620s'.

2 Lindsay Boynton, 'Billeting: the Example of the Isle of Wight', *EHR* LXXI (1950), pp. 23–40; and Esther Cope, 'Politics without Parliament: the Dispute about Muster Masters' Fees in Shropshire in the 1630s', *HLQ* XLV (1982), pp. 271–4.

3 Edward Gibbon, *The Autobiographies*, ed. by J. Murray (London, 1897), pp. 181 and 190; Boynton, *Elizabethan Militia*, p. 236; and Holmes, *Lincolnshire*, p. 105. See also Fletcher, *Sussex*, p. 196; and Barnes, *Somerset*, pp. 258 and 263.

4 Stone, *Crisis of the Aristocracy*, p. 503. See also, Cust, 'Honour, Rhetoric and Political Culture', pp. 84–110; Fletcher, 'Honour Reputation and Local Officeholding in Elizabethan and Stuart England', pp. 106–9; and Stater, *Noble Governors*, pp. 8–31.

5 Smith, *County and Court*, pp. 128–9.

6 It must be conceded that although the existence of Justices sympathetic to Catholicism, if not outright recusants, was more common in northern shires like Yorkshire, they remained markedly infrequent in the commissions of the peace further south. See Hugh

Aveling, *Northern Catholics* (London, 1966), pp. 202–7 and 228–9; and set against it, Hughes, *Politics, Society and the Civil War*, pp. 62–4.

7 Cust, *The Forced Loan*, pp. 23–9. I will also develop this point further in my forthcoming work on Crown and Parliament at War, 1621–29.

Part III

'Aspersions and indignities'

Huntingdon and Sir Henry Shirley 1626–28

I entended ... to have enformed your Lordships of some aspersions cast upon me and indignities offred me in the execution of the place I hold by his Matiesties grace and favour of Lieutenant.

[Huntingdon to the Privy Council, 27 February 1627]

Like other ministers in the 1630s, Thomas Pestell sought to explain the multiple disasters which had followed England's intervention in the continental war. For generations God had hovered over the English Israel, 'long preserving us, and extending over us as a floud, even then, when it hath beene a Sea, a red Sea of Bloud and ruine round about us'. Lest anyone had forgotten the signs of His protection, Pestell quickly rattled off the Armada, the Gunpowder Plot and Charles I's return from Madrid. Yet of late, God's attitude had unmistakably hardened; hence Pestell pointed to the sufferings of the godly abroad and to England's inability to relieve them, 'for a long time being able to doe no good there and our enemies able to doe us much mischiefe from thence'. The conclusion followed ineluctably: 'God is angry with his people', and He might even be preparing for 'the last Judgement'.

Pestell's application doubtless caused some squirming among his audience in Leicester; he drew this deduction not only from the enemy's successes, but also from 'our home-divisions, our great boughs beating one against another'.[1] Although Pestell may have been alluding to a series of increasingly tumultuous Parliaments, many listeners would have found a more immediate and more local application. They and the rest of the shire had witnessed one of the most remarkable examples of 'great boughs beating one against another' in early Stuart England. And in this dramatic contest, the weapons of choice were 'aspersions and indignities'.

NOTE

1 Thomas Pestell, *Gods* Visitation ... *Preached at Leicester* (London, 1630), pp. 23–5.

Chapter 6

In the face
of the county

For nearly two decades, Huntingdon had governed the county from an apparently unassailable position of power. To be sure, some had grumbled about his actions, but they wisely kept their complaints to themselves. In late 1626, however, criticism of the Lord Lieutenant, which earlier only the boldest would have dared to whisper abroad, was suddenly trumpeted across the Midlands. It was not an anomaly, but a beginning in which one public outburst only led to others. In short order, these 'aspersions ... and indignities' having been broadcast 'in the face of the county' represented a fundamental, and quite formidable, challenge to his once impregnable local position.

OPENING SALVOS

Scarcely had the orders gone out for the second assessment than problems arose. Rutland, for example, suddenly teetered on the brink of civil disobedience. Although Leicestershire and Rutland were autonomous, Huntingdon had long laboured to see 'these two Cunties soe symented togeather on one uniforme course that they may seeme to bee all of one piece'. The two militias thus co-operated in a host of areas and shared a Provost Marshal. On that sensible basis Huntingdon and the smaller county had operated through the 1620s to everyone's satisfaction. This sensible arrangement dissolved with the return of the two sergeants. While the Council's belief that Rutland was 'equall to other counties in quantitie five tymes as bigg' baffled Sir Guy Palmes, Sir William Bulstrode and Sir William Noel, the notion that Rutland's company of 170 men required the services of two sergeants positively boggled them, and any attempt to explain these mysteries only enraged Huntingdon's Deputies further. This furore had nearly erupted during the sergeants' first temporary assignment earlier in 1626, but tempers in Rutland had cooled with the transfer of Sergeant Bowden to Leicestershire's payroll. Given that the county had struggled to pay just Sergeant Salmon, the sudden return of Bowden as well as Salmon on permanent assignment was more than the ratepayers could endure in silence. The two, the Deputies insisted, could only be 'very distastfull and burdensom to the Cuntry', and from this axiom flowed near constant protests like that in December 1626:

> the many burthens of charge which lye upon this smale County and the generall complaints of the Inhabytants unto us makes us bould to intreat your Lordships favour to help us of one great unnecessary expence which this County doth grone under.

The earl's unsympathetic response simply brought on threats about taking 'an other course in appealing higher', and since Buckingham was a large land-owner in the shire, their message was not hard to decipher. Hence, after years of occupying only a tiny proportion of Huntingdon's time, Rutland and its two sergeants suddenly blossomed into a major crisis, and as Huntingdon proved unable to resolve it, his relations with his Rutland Deputies deteriorated.[1] The sudden flare-up of problems there only served as the backdrop for more vexing difficulties in Leicestershire. Tiny Branston with its one militiaman again affords the best illustration of the magnitude of the demands in 1626. In the preceding years, even Huntingdon's best efforts at revitalising the militia generally managed to increase the local budget somewhere between £4 and £6 per annum. Yet in 1626, the figure shot up to £12 15s. 9d. The plague in Hinckley garnered 12s. out of the public purse, and Mr Astlin's knapsack another 3s. 6d. But these expenditures were nothing compared with the 'great levy', which collected 14s. for the officers' fees and another £3 0s. 4d. in 'pickaxes'. In addition the steady pace of increased training caused the bands-man to claim reimbursements first for 5s. 4d., then for 12s. 6d. and finally for 27s. 6d.[2] No wonder then that increases on this scale produced a lengthening list of defaulters.

In previous years, the earl's diligence and the occasional councillor inter-ventions had made defaulting a comparatively rare practice. Of the levies for which we have both the assessments and the collections, the earl's low point came in February 1619, when out of an assessment of approximately £290, he collected £247, or about 85 per cent of the total. The highest proportional yield came in 1623 when a levy of approximately £203 netted £184, or some 91 per cent. Two other years, 1624 and 1625, averaged 89 per cent and 85 per cent respectively. Therefore, assuming 85 per cent compliance, Huntingdon could have expected well over £1,000 from his assessment of £1,220. Instead, he almost immediately encountered mounting resistance as defaulters multi-plied. In frustration, he prepared copies of the Council's orders to present to the recalcitrant, but by October there were so much resistance, he exclaimed, that 'I cannot see fully execute his Majesties pleasure'.[3]

Topping the list of problem cases was the Corporation of Leicester. The city had had an increasingly difficult time weathering the fiscal year with the plague draining a quarter of its budget. No less than three extraordinary levies were necessary just to keep the Corporation in the black. Between the possibility of a grotesque death and the certainty of heavy local rates, many citizens were in a foul mood, and in the face-to-face world of a densely populated town, the discontented had ample opportunity to express their displeasure. A prominent citizen like Henry Boome had to endure being awoken in the middle of the night to hear an aggrieved man deliver 'many uncivile and opproburous speeches against the sayd Henry Boome and his mother'. Meanwhile Mr Nasebey 'did shake his head and his bearde at Mr Maior in a most contemptuous and scornefull manner'. Mayor Ive also had to sit through public outbursts like that of John Gillum: 'if a man Come to Leicester he can have no right'. At least Gillum was more coherent in his criticism than Peter Platts, who displayed his 'contempt of authoritie' in front of the Mayor 'by puttinge his hatt upon his head several tymes' and by berating the town constable, 'calling him knave, base fellowe and many other very uncivill and reprochefull speeches'. John Lawe, a baker, had even less time for the authorities, national or municipal; 'I bake more bread in a yeare,' he maintained, 'then the kinge is worth.' Yet the most pungent abuse came from old Mr Sherman. When he and his son were leaving St Mary's church, the younger Sherman anxiously described his problems with Mayor Ive, until the old man loudly erupted: 'a fart for Mr Maior and a turd for Mr Maior.'[4]

The mounting internal criticism helps explain the Corporation's open defiance of the Lord Lieutenant. In late July Walter Rudinge, the militia treasurer, arrived in Leicester to collect the £50 assessment for the city, only to find ratepayers balking at turning over 2s. Even the customary sanction of preparing a list of defaulters failed to intimidate the Corporation, which offered the earl only £25, all that it could gather 'in a generall and equall tax' in a year which had been 'very chargeable unto us', thanks to 'the Countinewed Trayning and exercising of our men'.[5] Unmoved by these excuses, the Lord Lieutenant badgered the Corporation for almost a year until it proposed to pay the final £25 if the city could deduct £6 for Astlin's knapsacks. A few weeks later, the earl received some belated satisfaction for having been bullied into granting a 12 per cent reduction in the Corporation's assessment. On 27 May, the Mayor and aldermen agreed that in the future they would seize the property of all militia defaulters.[6] If only they had done so a year earlier, they would have spared the Lord Lieutenant an extended wrangle when he had trouble enough elsewhere.

FAWNT'S LETTERS

More ominous for Huntingdon than the ratepayers' grumbling was the hectoring of his fellow magistrates. By November, able to keep silent no longer, Fawnt vented his irritation in a letter to his cousin and Huntingdon's Deputy, Sir Wolston Dixie. It opened railing at Huntingdon's orders to collect food for the regiment: 'I perceave … that the warrants which my Lord graunted out for money butter and cheese and bacon and meale hath not brought in soe much as you did expect.' Having mocked one aspect of the earl's regime, he turned to another, much closer to his heart. Although Fawnt's loud complaints had first earned a reduction, Huntingdon had again raised Sir William's obligation back to two horses. This alteration brought forth the bitter allegation that the earl was 'pleased to spare you and others because you are his deputies that you shewe noe horses', even though 'you are the kings subiects as well as wee and therefore fitt to strengthen his kingdome by horses as well as I'. Then there was the matter of the militia levies. Although the ratepayers were willing enough to support the local regiment, the overbearing Lord Lieutenant had bullied plain country folk into accepting unprecedented taxes, since they were 'willinge to condescend to any thinge rather then be frightened otherwaies', which, Fawnt darkly observed, 'I will not name.' Hence in order to provide 'the Countrey with Powder, Match and bullet' the taxpayers had systematically been 'skrued out of our money at every becke … by tenn shillings and nyne shillings and seaven shillings'. Yet in spite of at least £2,000 in recent years, the militia was 'soe unfurnished nowe, nothing being spent that there is need of two thousand pounds at one slap'. Plainly the Council's order of 10 July had gained his attention.

Careful observers of Sir William would have noted that the violence of his rhetoric merely accentuated themes which had long obsessed him. As early as 1624, when the militia assessments were some £200, he was already reporting widespread complaints about 'so extreame a charge' and about militia funds either being 'unnecessarily exspended' or embezzled outright. Naturally, when the assessments topped £1,500, Sir William waxed apoplectic. What was more novel about his letter to Dixie was Fawnt's solution; a full public accounting was the only possible remedy. Otherwise, it was all too easy for ordinary subjects to assume that something unsavoury was happening with the comparatively massive amounts of money being collected in the name of the militia. Ideally Fawnt hoped that this bold letter on 'behalfe of the Countrey and myselfe' would make Huntingdon see through his 'complimentinge freinds' and realise that Fawnt's 'plain dealinge is a Jewell'. But he was not entirely sanguine that his hopes would come to pass. In his mind there was 'noe question' but that the Privy Council 'wilbe ready to approve of anythinge which my Lord hath done'. Against the councillors, however, Fawnt set the Parliament-men; 'alsoe I doubt not but upon complaint to a Parliament it will not give way that a whole Countrey should be ympoverished by taxations without callinge to an accompt'.[7]

Such a blistering letter produced a swift reply from Dixie, who reminded his cousin that nothing could excuse defaulting, and in any case, as Dixie patiently showed, the accusations were false. The Deputy Lieutenants were indeed assessed in the horse troop, and rather than the £2,000 yield that Fawnt had assumed for the 1626 militia assessments, 'I assure you the Charg cometh to little more then halfe soe much'. As for a large expenditure of powder stocks, he reminded Fawnt that 'a great part thereof hath beene spent in the often Trayneings'. More important, this would not happen in the future, because, thanks to Huntingdon's latest orders, 'there shall be noe more of the powder ... spent in that manner'. Above all, Dixie urged his cousin to appreci-ate that Huntingdon 'is as carefull not to wrong the Contrey (though forward to have every thinge fitt for the defence of the kingdome) as any noble lord can bee'. Since this was the case, Dixie warned that the charges could well be considered slanderous; therefore, he hoped Fawnt would withdraw them before Dixie presented the letter to Huntingdon. Fawnt did not recant. Instead he amplified the charges, reporting that the 'great levy' had stunned both Sir Thomas Hesilrige and Sir Henry Hastings of Braunston. As for forwarding the letter onto the Lord Lieutenant, 'your pleasure be don': 'there is neither Felony nor treason' in it. Indeed, if questioned, Fawnt vowed, 'I will prove what I say.' On receipt of this second letter, Dixie consulted his son, who had married Fawnt's daughter, and ultimately they decided to forward copies on to Donnington Park. Huntingdon naturally was 'much displeased' with Fawnt's allegations, but he did nothing more dramatic than to file the letters away.[8]

In the history of the shire, few letters were as controversial as these three; indeed, Sir William, the earl and their attorneys were still arguing about them well over a decade later. While some had doubted the earl's honesty, and others were to expand on this theme, no one set down these suspicions aside from 'the Gunner' Fawnt. Thus a senior JP alleged that Huntingdon was using the militia assessments to reward friends and punish the less favoured. Worst of all were the calls for a public reckoning of the money which had apparently disappeared into the earl's coffers. After the disgrace of Lord Treasurer Suffolk a few years earlier, no one could have been ignorant of the problem of public officials confusing public funds with their own. Fawnt's suggestions finally merely amplified the charges of fraud which had cropped up in the preceding year with the coat and conduct money, charges which were well known to a magistrate who sat on the investigating panel.[9]

In the long run, the charges of financial misconduct nearly proved fatal to Huntingdon's career. In the short term, however, the aspect of Fawnt's letter which doubtless produced the most anxiety in Donnington Park was the prospect that Sir William was not keeping such thoughts to himself. Plainly Fawnt's circle of grumblers included Sir Thomas Hesilrige and Sir Henry Hastings, both even better informed than Fawnt about the Hastings regime. And it was much bigger. Fawnt himself confessed that Huntingdon might well 'thinke I sett my selfe against him because I sometymes speake and write in the behalfe of the Country and myselfe', but he was only warning the Lord Lieutenant as well as the Justices 'before the Countrey complaine of my Lord and us' (i.e. the bench). The most ominous part of the letter came in the following line: 'assure your selfe they doe in private already'.[10] A few days after Huntingdon received these letters, an event fully confirmed that the circle of critics was indeed larger than Fawnt, a wayward Hastings and the superannuated Deputy Lieutenant.

SHIRLEY'S CHARGES

As a stage for embarrassing Huntingdon, there was none better than the quarter session held early in 1627. Although illness kept the earl at home, the rest of the county elite gathered to hear two well known councillors launch the forced loan project. The Earl of Exeter directed the neighbouring Northamptonshire militia from his seat at Burghley House, while Sir John Coke, one of the two Secretaries of State, was practically a Leicestershire man. His cousin, William Whalley, was a junior member of the county bench; his daughter had married Fawnt's son and heir; and Sir John's own house in Derbyshire was so close to the county line that as he himself noted, 'I am divided only by a pale'.[11] At the meeting in the Leicester Town Hall, these familiar figures clearly explained the necessity of the forced loan. All was proceeding admirably until Secretary Coke sat down and Sir Henry Shirley rose to speak.

It did not require detailed information on the local elite to know that Shirley was likely to say something provocative. Only a few months earlier, he had finally been named to the bench in the turmoil after the 1626 Parliament. For their refusal to vote supply in time of war, a number of peers and Parliament men had fallen into royal disfavour, and chief among them were Huntingdon's friends. Thomas Pestell, the local poet, had penned some buoyant verses to Saye and Sele, Warwick and Essex as they had ridden off to the session; a few months later, the earl's friends were in disgrace for their 'opposition'. In their place came 'hard-liners', either Laudian or crypto-Catholic, who were not about to quibble over the constitution in the middle of a war. One of those was the former Sheriff of Leicestershire. Given the stark contrast between Huntingdon and Shirley, it was only predictable that Shirley's first act as a magistrate would be to investigate Huntingdon's administration. Shortly before the meeting with Exeter and Coke, Sir Henry had privately interrogated the shire's constables. His questions were scarcely innocent: he wanted to 'what mony they had raised by my [Huntingdon's] warrant, to whom it was payd, and how bestowed'. The reason for such questioning became apparent one evening early in the session, when, after dinner at the Angel, Shirley summoned the head constables before himself and some other JPs. Although the constables thought that they were to hear some new orders concerning Leicester Forest, Shirley instead warned them that 'we should be called to an accompt of the Great Levy (and that the Countrey was wronged)'. In their defence the constables maintained that 'wee did nothing but what wee had warrant from my Lord of Huntingdon to doe'.[12] That defence was good enough for Sir Henry.

Afterwards, the constables uniformly denied telling Shirley anything, but, as became apparent on 15 January 1627, more than enough information had come out to fuel Sir Henry's suspicions about the 'great levy'. Then Secretary Coke's harangue brought the former Sheriff to his feet to argue that the plague and Huntingdon's recent levies 'made the people unable to give, thoughe the[y] were very willinge'. The 'great levy for Carts, spades and mattocks' which came to £1,200, he continued, was plainly excessive; for support Sir Henry turned to the other Lord Lieutenant, observing that 'my lord of Exeter knowes that Northamptonshire which is as bigge as two of this and it cost not that County 200 pounds.' In the end, Shirley conceded, the size of Huntingdon's 'great levy' had ultimately turned out to the county's advantage; since £500 of the £1,200 still remained in the earl's hands, Shirley proposed that 'the overplus of the mony might be payed to this loane'. Before he could develop the idea, Exeter called him down: 'you speake intemperative'. Dixie added to the turmoil by quickly defending his superior: the earl 'had done nothinge but what I [Huntingdon] had warrant to doe from the Lords of the Councell and coulde give a good accompt of that I had done'.[13]

Some order having been restored, the assembly returned to the loan, and Shirley himself promptly paid £20. Only Lord Noel, the fortunate heir of the London financier, Sir Baptist Hicks, and Sir Edward Hartopp exceeded this mark with contributions of £25 each. In spite of Fawnt's grumblings about the horse troop, Sir William equalled Shirley's generosity, and Arthur Fawnt, Coke's son-in-law, added another £2 13s. 4d. The rest of the sums, however, were considerably less. Dixie, the earl's defender, offered £12; Sir William Villiers, the duke's half-brother, £13; and William Whalley, Coke's cousin, another £10. To be sure, these sums were respectable enough. Yet what is striking about the yield was the paucity of the number, not its size; Secretary Coke recorded only fourteen contributors.[14] In time, the shire would boast a comparatively good record for the forced loan. In the short term, however, the damage had been done.

Shirley's boldness had transformed another royal plea for money into a sensational public attack on Huntingdon's management. Secretary Coke, no stranger to the shire, remained convinced that something was seriously awry: 'he doubted Sir Henry Shirley wold except against him [Huntingdon] for partialite'. More importantly, unlike Fawnt's private letter, Shirley's outburst 'in the face of the Countie' could not be ignored. Huntingdon might well regard the charges as ridiculous, but the councillors would have to treat them seriously if the forced loan was to get off the ground. Thus, immediately after Exeter and Coke returned, the Privy Council, acting on Shirley's 'complaint made in publique', ordered a 'perfect account' of the county's finances 'for the suppressing of unjust complaints'. For the councillors themselves, 'wee rest assured in your Lordship's care and providence in gouverning the service so as there shall be no just complaint made of any necessary grievance cast upon the subjects'. Therefore, in everyone's best interests, they ordered an accounting 'without delay' and 'with all speede'.[15]

Given Walter Rudinge's meticulous record-keeping, the question of precisely what Shirley was doing becomes compelling; thanks to the treasurer's labours, challenging the earl to produce records only played to his strong suit. Yet, exemplary records notwithstanding, Huntingdon was loath to defend himself. It eventually took five months of increasingly abrupt letters before the earl made his defence. Two months after the initial order, the councillors were astonished at the earl's inertia: 'wee cannot but lett you knowe that we much marvaile at the neglect therof'. After two more months, they reiterated the order, adding that this time they expected 'your Lordship faile not to performe this our directions'. In the meantime, unwilling and perhaps unable to defend himself, Huntingdon's standing plummeted. 'To make his Majesties service a Cullor to raise monney upon the Subiect,' Huntingdon protested, 'is a heavie imputation to an honest man.' Yet he did not hurry to remove this 'heavie imputation'.[16] The explanation for Shirley's attack and for his inaction was simple: Shirley had focused councillor attention on the Lord Lieutenant at the precise moment when he longed for obscurity. Underneath Shirley's accusation lay much more than a question about the correct use of public funds; it was also bound up with the forced loan.

The presence of two councillors at the Leicester quarter sessions was sign enough that all was not well with the Crown, which was teetering on the brink of insolvency in the midst of a major war. In spite of the failure of the Privy Seal loan in the summer, the Council had no choice but to try again, this time with all the whips out, and the key to success would be the public support of the local governors. Admittedly most of the aristocracy and the leading gentry eventually subscribed to the loan, albeit reluctantly. But some refused outright, as did the Earls of Essex, Warwick, Clare, Bolingbroke and Lincoln, and Huntingdon's brother-in-law, Lord Stanhope, thus earning a prominent entry in the government's 'black book' and losing them their local offices.[17]

To this select group Huntingdon must be added. At the same time as

Shirley called for an inquiry in his administration, the earl was drafting a belated explanation of his failure to subscribe to the loan. To guide him in this crisis, he had already dispatched his wife to Whitehall, from where she reported such important developments as 'Norfolke hath refused to lend' and that some who agreed to lend nonetheless 'aske security for the repayment'. Overall, in spite of the efforts of Exeter and Coke, 'little is yett gathered' in Leicestershire. Offsetting the government's new rigidity was a warm welcome for the wife of a 'backwoodsman' like Huntingdon. Not only was the queen quite gracious to her, but the king, who had not laid eyes on her in seven years, quickly picked her out of a crowd for an extended conversation about her family's health. Charles's friendly demeanour, the countess concluded, meant one of two things: 'the King is eather not angry with you, or hee thinkes you will give'. The last point was vital, for metropolitan newsgathers had already placed Huntingdon among his friends like Essex, Warwick, Lincoln and Saye and Sele, who all 'refused to subscribe'. In the event, neither of the countess's conclusions applied. Nathaniel Tomkins, an official at court, explained to Sir Robert Phelips in Somerset that in this matter, 'the middle way' would never be 'a good way'. Thus, 'if you deny faintly', he reasoned, 'and are not a leader of those who shall refuse, you shall hardly be held a meritor among them; if you doe not avowedly declare yourself to advance the work, you shall have no thanks from the king'. Huntingdon chose the problematic 'middle way'. Abject poverty made him beg to be excused, and his litany of burdens highlighted the fact that with 'my land intayled, three of my yonger children unprovided for and myself in many thousand pounds debts and the land that I have reserved for the payment thereof being but sufficient for that end', subscription to the loan would only 'plunge my self further into debt'.[18] To this position Huntingdon held fast.

Huntingdon's lament, although heart-rending, was not an ironclad excuse, for when necessary, Huntingdon could summon up significant amounts of cash. The Crown's request in 1627 moreover was scarcely crippling. While the earl's precise assessment is unknown, it was likely £200, his contribution to five subsidies. He regularly paid £40 in each of the parliamentary subsidies of the 1620s, and he was to pay as much as £200 in 1628–29 without any whingeing.[19] Unfortunately for him, Charles knew this as well. Therefore, it was almost impossible for Charles to accept Huntingdon's plea of poverty without opening a broad avenue of escape for the rest of the peerage.

It was not simply Huntingdon's example to the aristocracy that troubled Whitehall. Since Huntingdon had to play a pivotal role in the collection of the levy, royal officials did not even want to consider how a senior administrator, who was himself a recusant, would react to footdragging and outright refusal among his subordinates. While the 'Northampton and Warwicksheere infection' did not reach epidemic proportions in the shire, there were to be enough outbreaks for concern. How would the earl deal with men like Sir Roger Smith of Edmondthorpe? His 'conscience being stricter than other mens', Smith told Huntingdon that he was 'altogether unable to doe what eyther I would or should'. Therefore, although the earl had placed him on the bench and groomed him for higher office, Sir Roger asked to be removed from the bench. Smith was only one man, but in Guthlaxton hundred, almost two dozen men refused to make their second payment until they 'heare what course will be taken with those that absolutely stand out'.[20] Thus to let Huntingdon escape might well be to accept higher rates of recusancy in Leicestershire.

So it was that barely a year after the councillors had praised Huntingdon, an impasse had suddenly developed between Whitehall and its model local governor. At the same time, as the councillors insisted on reviewing Shirley's charges with Huntingdon in person, the earl was desperate to avoid the metropolis, where he would certainly have to explain, perhaps even to the king, his problems with the forced loan. The only solution for the earl was to delay the confrontation as long as possible. Unfortunately, as long as he did so, his standing in the county disintegrated.

NOTES

1 H to Rutland DLs, 27 June 1626; Rutland DLs to H, [August 1626], [December 1625], and 10 August 1626, *LRLB*, fols. 165v–6, 180 and 185v–6.

2 Branston Constables' Accounts, Leics. RO, DE720/30, fol. 24–24v.

3 H to [Rutland DLs], 2 October 1626, *LRLB*, fol. 185. See also Table 2.

4 Mayor's court, 11 August 1625, 16 and 24 June 1626, and 23 January 1627; examination of Richard Huseto[n], [1626]; and 'Misdemanour of Peter Platts', 11 November 1626, Leics. RO, BR II/18/15, fol. 620; and /16, fols. 93, 102, 197, 164 and 168. For the three levies, see Leics. RO, BR III/2/79, fol. 15.

5 [W. Rudinge], 'A noate of the names ... as doe refuse to pay', 26 July 1626; and Resolution of the 24, [early August 1626], Leics. RO, BR II/18/16, fols. 131 and 135; and Corporation to H, 15 August 1626, LR*LB*, fol. 131v.

6 Common Hall, 5 April and 27 May 1627, Leics. RO, BR II/18/16, fols. 209 and 219. See also H to Constables, 24 February 1627; and same to Skipwith, 27 February 1627, *LRLB*, fols. 187–7v and 188.

7 Fawnt to Dixie, [November 1626], HA Corr. 12/3148.

8 Dixie to Fawnt, November 1626; Fawnt to Dixie, [November 1626], HA Corr 12/2294; and 15/3149; and Dixie's testimony in H *v.* Fawnt, HA Legal 7/4, pp. 5 and 16.

9 On this, see below, pp. 41–2. On Suffolk, see Menna Prestwich, *Cranfield*, pp. 199–222.

10 Fawnt to Dixie, [November 1626], HA Corr. 15/3148 and 3149.

11 Coke to Holland, May 1640; and Whalley to Coke, 10 March 1627, BL Add. MS 64,921, fol. 99, and 64,890. fol. 105. On the Coke–Fawnt match, see above, p. 96.

12 'To the Earles of Essex and Warwick, going by the Lord Saye, and Earle of Hartford, to the Parliament 1625 [1626]', *Poems of Thomas Pestell*, p. 29; and testimony of Paulson and Alsop, 'Speaches of Sir H. Sherley', HA Legal 2/11. See also Cust, *The Forced Loan*, pp. 13–39.

13 'Speaches of Sir Henry Sherley', HA Legal 2/11.

14 'The names of such as are contented to lend', 15 January 1627, Coke MSS, BL Add. MS 64,890, fol. 81.

15 Skeffington to H, [June 1627], *LRLB*, fol. 208v; and PC to H, 31 January 1627, *APC* 42/43–4.

16 PC to H, 14 March and 11 May 1627, *APC* 42/131–2 and 270; and H to PC, 28 May 1627, *LRLB*, fol. 208–8v.

17 Anon. to Mead, 1 December 1626, BL Harleian MS 390, fol. 167; and H to Marlborough, 22 January 1627, HA Corr. 12/5514.

18 ECH to H, 18 January 1627, HA 12/4839; anonymous diary, Trinity College, Cambridge, MS o.7.3, fol. 7v; Tomkins to Phelips, 27 November 1626, Somerset RO, DD/Ph 219/35; and H to Marlborough, 22 January 1627, HA Corr. 12/5514. I am grateful to Richard Cust for stressing the importance of the Trinity College diary.

19 See H's payments, 5 July, 20 September and 19 November 1628 and 20 February 1629, HA Corr. 13/13,789–92.

20 Savage to Buckingham, 4 February 1627, SP 16/53/18; Smith to H, 15 February 1627, HA Corr. 12/10978; and Roberts to PC, 4 August 1627, SP 16/73/35. See also Cust, *The Forced Loan*, p. 121.

Chapter 7

Labouring
under a cloud

Huntingdon's most uncomfortable period in a long political career un-questionably was the first half of 1627. Rather than confront awkward questions, he delayed his hearing before the Council as long as he dared. But even a five-month respite brought him little satisfaction, for as he stalled the councillors the spectre of his enemies grew larger. His preoccupation in these months was clear to his Deputies; when Skeffington, for instance, related some awkward news, he begged that Huntingdon 'will never thinke me anie of those whom Sir William Fawnt calls your complimentall frends'. The emergence of 'friends' like Fawnt and Shirley signalled the erosion of his hitherto impeccable standing with the Council. If he ever doubted his new impotence, he had only to consider the problem of Rutland's two sergeants. After the Deputies there had grown strident over the 'great and unnecessary expence', which was 'very distastfull and burdensome to the Cuntry', Huntingdon vowed not to 'slack any fitt season when I may doe it, by anie other fitt meanes'. But, he added, 'I hould it not fitt as yett.'[1] The 'fitt season' to ask favours from the Council would not come until he had put Shirley's accusations and the forced loan behind him.

THE REQUIREMENTS OF WAR

As Huntingdon's stock tumbled at Whitehall, the earl had to endure the spectacle of Sir Henry Shirley lording it over the county, and the Easter assize almost appeared to be his triumph. The new JP energetically involved himself in the deliberations and courted his fellow Justices. For his pains, he was 'extremely graced' by no less a figure than the Lord Chief Justice of Common Pleas. Needless to say, Shirley displayed no uneasiness over the earlier scene before the councillors; 'there is none that goes about', Whalley reported to Coke, 'to mend aney of the fences that were overstepped at the sitting'.

Huntingdon meanwhile was holed up in Donnington Park trying to ride out the forced loan. Yet Huntingdon remained the Lord Lieutenant in a year which proved exceptionally busy for provincial governors. In this administrative maelstrom, he sought to avoid appearing disheartened; although 'some out of their inconsiderate Judgments seeme to except' against his rule, 'let several humors confuse things as they will, that shall not put me of the Byas to doe that befitts me in my place'.[2]

His administrative troubles in Rutland only worsened in 1627. As in 1626, the solution to the problem of two sergeants was Sergeant Basil Cave, whose ailments remained so serious that in February 1627 Huntingdon unilaterally dismissed him as unfit, and Cave's departure allowed the earl to shift Sergeant Bowden to the larger militia, thus leaving Rutland with one NCO. Yet by that time, this extended affair had badly strained Huntingdon's relationship with his Rutland Deputies. The survey of Rutland's able-bodied men, the earl complained, was very haphazard, and the county's munition stocks were 2,400 lbs short of the powder requirements alone. This news earned a stinging rebuke from Huntingdon, who reminded them that 'in my absence you have the sole mannaging of theis affayres by a derivative power from the authoritie I have from his Maiestie'. In more tranquil times, a direct order from the Lord Lieutenant would have ended the matter; now it only prompted protests that the Council had imposed 'a greate burden to this smale County, being proportioned to the halfe of Leycestershire, this County being in quantitie and qualitie about the fifth parte of the same'. Relations had deteriorated so much that the Deputies could not resist a mocking salutation from those who exercised 'derivative power from the Authoritie your Lordship hath from his Maiestie'.[3]

Equally troublesome was the Corporation of Leicester, which continued the tenacious defence of its privileges. When the Lord Lieutenant ordered Leicester to dispatch its candidates for foreign service to a selection at Market Harborough, he got another lecture on the city's charter and the demand either to change the site to Leicester or to excuse its citizens. Huntingdon had endured too much in recent months to haggle with the Corporation over fine legal distinctions. 'I would not goe about to deprive you of that righte the lawe gives you which is every mans birthright,' but no one could possibly confuse impressing with mustering. If the Mayor and burgesses wished to do so, then 'I will add this to the heape of your former neglects and contempts of his Maiesties service.' Very little broke in the earl's favour early in 1627. He could, however, find some quiet satisfaction in watching Leicester's contingent line up at Market Harborough.[4]

As this tangle revealed, the Lord Lieutenant had his hands full merely providing the county's share of manpower for a second round of military expeditions. The yields from the forced loan allowed Buckingham a final chance at proving his qualifications as a warlord. In February, the Council ordered another 150 men to replenish the four 'new' regiments, which volunteers had filled in the balmier days of 1624; once brought up to full strength, Colonel Morgan would lead them to assist Charles's uncle, Christian IV of Denmark.[5] The four units neatly serve as a microcosm of what had happened to the earlier war fever. In 1624, the Earls of Southampton, Oxford and Essex had led the troops against the House of Austria; three years later, Southampton and Oxford had died in the field, while Essex was in disgrace over the forced loan. The county, too, had wearied of the fruitless struggle. Yet for Huntingdon, this Danish levy offered an opportunity to redeem himself from the debacle in the Cadiz expedition.

His instructions for the impressment were those of a veteran administrator, well versed in the customary dodges. Some of the guidelines were by then routine, such as the strictures against choosing employed agricultural workers or vagrants and the admonition to focus on unemployed cloth workers from the market towns, which 'doe most swerm with uselesse people'. But this time, there was to be absolutely no alteration from the initial list of candidates; Huntingdon himself would review all problems at the time of the selection. Constables were also enjoined to fuss over the men's clothing; since the parish could not avoid underwriting the men's apparel, it might as well do so sooner rather than later. They were also to examine the men themselves; 'if anie doe alleadge they have Ruptures or anie other infirmity', the constables were to 'search the same party to see whether it bee true'. Finally, the earl laid down a stern line on runaways. The master or parent of the man selected was responsible for ensuring that the man arrived at the selection; otherwise such people would be 'summoned to appear themselves to be imprested in their steads'.[6]

The same concern to avoid a repetition of 1625 also dominates Huntingdon's orders for the actual impressment. He cautioned the Deputy Lieutenants against publicly overruling one another, for without a united front they could not control either the constables or the men. This time, defects in clothing mattered; after a careful examination of the men's apparel, and especially their 'shirts, hose and shooes', the Deputies were to replace all sub-standard articles at the parish's expense. Should the constables balk at this or anything else, the Lord Lieutenant enjoined his Deputies to 'reprehend them sharplie and publiquely', and if that failed, to imprison them. Yet underneath the tougher attitude was the earl's customary paternalism. Those whom the constables had presented out of 'malice or sperne' were to be passed over, as were all with wives 'neare the tyme of her deliverie'. Moreover, Huntingdon ordered that the pressed men should get a chance to settle their financial affairs. Finally, the new soldiers could immediately don their ultimate consolation, a brand-new coat. As before, the earl had fussed over this, demanding from Coventry merchants that the coat itself had to be 'very good, the prices reasonable'. This time, however, he did not fret over colours, and the new soldiers donned green broadcloth coats with yellow linings. The earl was resolved that the Leicestershire contingent would have 'such things as is needfull and fitting' and would not be 'poorly arrayed out of the Cuntrey'.[7]

Plainly the earl had learned from the earlier selections; unfortunately for him, so had the constables and the prospective soldiers. The messenger bringing the impressment warrant to Leicester, for example, revealed 'the contentes of it to divers of the Towne before the same was delivered to any magistrate' with the result that the likely candidates 'withdrew themselves from their habitations'. Meanwhile chaos reigned at the selections. Notwithstanding Huntingdon's presence, the results of a selection at Ashby were less than encouraging. The earl released two men whose wives were about to deliver and forced constables to scramble to find new 'shoes and stockings'. What was much more ominous was the failure of some constables to return *any* candidates. Furious, Huntingdon presented them with their own green coats and set them marching with the other pressed men to Harborough. It was a bluff; 'I did it *in terrorem.*' The earl soon ordered their release, confident that a brief stint in uniform would make them and other parish officers do their duty. In the event, terror made little impression at Harborough. First, the snail's pace of the this continguent forced the rest of the men to dally an extra day, and when they saw the paltry numbers from Ashby, this 'gave much discontent' to the waiting men from the other hundreds, who realised that they would be 'enforced to supply the remissnes of the former'. Further compounding the chaos was the 'extraordinary importunitie of Gentlemen and other Officers of the better sort' for the release of their retainers and neighbours, but this time the hard-pressed Deputies could not be so accommodating. In the confusion resulting from the 'unsatisfied', a number of the pressed men slipped away. In their report, Huntingdon's Deputies roundly denounced the deserters, whose actions exposed the levy 'to contempt and discourage those that have the imployment'.[8]

Less than three years separated the comparatively easy impressments of 1624 from this turmoil, and the contrast illustrates that the supply of surplus males was near exhaustion. In Mansfelt's levy of 200 men, over 130 of them, or approximately 65 per cent, were either labourers or husbandmen. Meanwhile, the clothing industry contributed twelve weavers, nine tailors, two hatters and a woolman, or almost 12 per cent of the total. The rest came from a broad array of local crafts ranging from a wheelwright to a bearward. The press for the Cadiz voyage a few months later followed the same pattern: husbandmen and labourers made up over 70 per cent and the members of the clothing trade another 12 per cent. With the Danish levy, however, the numbers suggest that the readily accessible pools of labour were drying up. Fortunately for Huntingdon, the depressed clothing trade remained more dependable, yielding enough manpower to make up its customary 12 per cent. But the ordinary staple of these levies, the labourers and husbandmen, offered up only seventy-seven men, or barely 50 per cent. Consequently, the earl and his Deputies had to dip much more heavily into more essential tradesmen. Thus Morgan marched with ten shepherds, six butchers, six blacksmiths, five carpenters, and three yeoman as well as assorted brewers, steelmongers and bakers.[9] The increased social pain of the 1627 levy, therefore, renders the turmoil which surrounded it more understandable.

The problems of impressment, grave though they were, should not obscure the solid accomplishment of Huntingdon and his Deputies. To be sure, some of the troops deserted, but the bulk of the 150 soldiers marched into Harwich without Morgan's officers noting a single problem: there was in short no repetition of the 1625 procession of ruptured, shirtless men limping in with complaints about massive embezzlement. For this, Huntingdon had reason to be proud. There were, however, very real limits to his satisfaction.

Morgan's officers made no comments simply because the troops arrived in the midst of a crisis which was rapidly becoming a nightmare. Since the ships to carry them to Hamburg had failed to arrive, and the officers lacked funds for provisions, the troops ran amuck in the town. Yet when the vessels arrived and the troops were marched on board, they mutinied, holding their officers prisoner. The revolt then took a terrifying turn for the citizens of Harwich when the soldiers announced their plans to come ashore, vowing 'wheareas they were lodged before in the worst bedds, as they say, they will now both command and have the best bedds'. In the end, the local militia restored order, and the men sailed for the continent, but not before a number of the Leicestershire men had unilaterally dismissed themselves.[10] The incident at Harwich therefore was truly appalling, but ultimately not Huntingdon's problem. He and his Deputies had done their part.

Afterwards Huntingdon's Deputies arrested some of the deserters, and if the earl wondered what to do with his prisoners, an answer soon came with a new order for another 150 pressed men for a desperate push to break the stalemate on the Ile de Ré.[11] A haunting sense of *déjà vu* hung over the fourth levy in as many years as Deputies, constables and candidates acted out well rehearsed roles. The Deputies found the scene at the selection so shocking that they composed a formal report to the Council reviewing all of the major problems. First of all, the mere 'fame of levyinge men' prompted 'a great part of them that it may concerne' to 'secretly transporte themselves into other Counties'. They had good reason to run, thanks to the corruption of the constables, who frequently selected some men 'for particular spleene conyvinge at such as are more able and sufficient either for their owne respects or of some superior neighbour'. Finally the business of the county 'loaning' the government its share of coat and conduct had to end immediately; otherwise they predicted that the next levy which depended on such local loans would 'fall and come to nothinge'.[12]

The Deputy Lieutenants rightly centred their protests on the finances, for the task of financing these 300 new recruits so soon after Shirley's outburst was one of Huntingdon's most delicate tasks. Thankfully, the orders for Morgan's 150 men arrived with a surplus left over from the 'great levy' of 1626, but it proved unequal to the task, which eventually required almost £250. Therefore, in March 1627 the earl called for another proportional contribution by hundreds which netted another £212. This amount of course simply covered the 'national' obligation; the localities had to get the men to the induction site in presentable appearance. Thus Leicester sent twelve men to march with Morgan, and the transport expenses together with multiple shirts, doublets, jerkins, hats, hoses and shoes ran up a bill of £11 11s. 3d., in addition to £16. 10s. which the Corporation paid for coat and conduct money.[13] Therefore, the two levies back to back drained something in excess of a parliamentary subsidy out of the shire.

Although these episodes left the Deputies uncertain of their ability to control subsequent impressments, the twin selections of 300 men represent, in the circumstances, an administrative triumph. This success should be set against Huntingdon's less exemplary performance in the forced loan. Given the earl's tendency to dominate the execution of all orders from Whitehall, the most striking aspect of the project was the extent to which it proceeded independently of Huntingdon. Since the county's location made its subsidy-men prime candidates for the 'Northampton and Warwicksheere infection', the central government sought to forestall an epidemic by announcing that the coat and conduct money still due from the 1625 levy could be deducted from the loan receipts. Yet notwithstanding such concessions, recusancy presented serious problems for the collectors. Whalley warned his cousin, Secretary Coke, that 'the kinges money comes but slowly' in spite of the best efforts of the increasingly frazzled collectors. Hence Sir Henry Skipwith justly dubbed the entire project 'such a trublesome busines I have seldome undertaken'.[14] Nevertheless Skipwith and his fellow collectors kept up the pressure. A few followed Thomas Burse's example; after a private conference with the collectors, he asked for a 15-minute delay during which he apparently skipped the county. Others like Francis Staresmore's widow pleaded poverty. Most, however, displayed, as they did in Leicester, 'the most willing and readie affections ... in that loane so as not one that appeared before us did denie to lend'. The worst pocket of outright resistance was in Guthlaxton hundred, where some were 'most refractory'. Since their obstinacy stemmed from their desire 'to heare what course will be taken with those that absolutely stand out', Sir William Fawnt, one of the local collectors, begged the Council to be ruthless.[15]

The result of their labours was impressive. In Leicester, the collectors gathered £171 13s. 4d. out of a total assessment of £182; and in Sparkenhoe hundred, £690 13s. 6d. out of £709 16s. 8d.[16] In all, Leicestershire paid into the Exchequer £3,386 3s. 2d.[17] From this £60 17s. came back in the form of collectors' fees and another £102 16s. in belated repayment from the Cadiz coat and conduct money.[18] Consequently the government cleared £3,222 10s. 2d. While Huntingdon's care of the 300 men levied in 1627 was laudable, Whitehall's attention was understandably fixed on the yield of the forced loan. All of this activity only prompts the question – where was the earl? While the collectors were moving through the county, the Lord Lieutenant was preparing his own explanations for the Council.

BALANCING IN THE SCALES

As the last of his evasive manoeuvres played out, Huntingdon finally had to answer Shirley's charges. In late February, the earl had been eager to refute 'some aspersions cast upon me and indignities offred me'. But he also requested a delay on the grounds of ill health; by Easter at the latest he vowed that he and his records would be in Westminster, 'God sparing me life'. Easter came, but not the earl, who most likely hoped that the Council would simply lose sight of him amid the other commotions. It did not, and in May the councillors demanded Rudinge's presence, if Huntingdon remained indisposed.[19]

The earl accepted this compromise, since 'it hath pleased God to afflict me this halfe yeare with an extreame acke and paine in one of my hippes and leggs as I am but few howres in a day able to stirr and cannot endure a long Jorney'. He entrusted to Sir John Skeffington and Walter Rudinge his financial records and his emphatic denial that he had had 'anie of the Cuntries mony for my private use, but onely for the publique affayres of his Majestie'; in fact, in twenty years of royal service, he had 'never receaved a pennie'. In addition, he could scarcely help reminding the councillors of their earlier judgement of his administration being 'an example for other counties to follow'. This accomplishment made Shirley's accusations 'a great affliction to me that through my absence my integritie long time since questioned by a publique Complaint is not yet made manifest both to your Lordships satisfaction and the Cuntries'. Therefore 'I humbly beseech your Lordships that I may by some publique meanes be righted except it can be proved I have Cozened the Cuntry of there money'.[20] With this defiant rhetoric, he committed his political fate to Skeffington and Rudinge.

In spite of such righteous rhetoric, his efforts to lobby his friends on the Council indicate that he assumed his response to the forced loan would cause as much trouble as Shirley's accusations. Before the Council hearing, Rudinge sought to rally the earl's allies, but the results were not comforting. The earl's brother-in-law, the Earl of Bridgewater, would not be back in town for the inquiry. The earl's uncle, the Earl of Worcester, could not hobble across the room, much less to the council table. From the Herbert brothers Rudinge received only characteristically vague support in which Pembroke and Montgomery promised that 'when the tyme served they wold be ready to doe their best'; the road to political ruin had been paved with such firm support. The only exception was the Earl of Manchester, Lord President of the Council. Thanks to the complications of the forced loan, Manchester warned Rudinge that only a convincing refutation of Shirley's charges could save Huntingdon; hence the Treasurer's confident assurances that his accounts would clear the earl 'much reioysed' the Lord President. Nevertheless, Rudinge's last-minute lobbying had thrown into brilliant relief the stark truth that this hearing would be rough sailing for his master.[21]

The hearing began well enough. In response to Manchester's questioning, Rudinge insisted that he would present 'such an accompt as I thought all the Lords of England cold not make the like', proving that 'never penny thereof came to your Lordships hands'. His denial of Shirley's 'greate and foule' accusations gave such 'good content' that the councillors deferred further discussion until Sir Francis Gofton, the Auditor of the Press, could inspect the records. This development led the Earl of Dorset, the influential favourite of the duke, to observe that 'Sir Henry Shirley had done your Lordshipp wrong, if that were true ... that tongue which had soe much wronged your Lordship should right you.' Any delight with his outburst was soon overwhelmed by a loud murmuring among the councillors, which dashed any hope of a quick vindication. On arrival in London, Skeffington had heard alarming reports that the Earls of Kent, Bolingbroke, Essex and Huntingdon 'shold be put out of ther Lieutenancies'. 'Ever slowe in believing rumors,' Sir John discounted this one until at the inquiry he 'heard divers of the Lordships whispering': 'some excusing your Lordship and others insisting that the Kings order was peremptory for putting your Lordship out of Commission'. During a recess, Skeffington buttonholed sympathetic councillors. The earl, he argued, 'had much and many uses for money' and for his long service 'had receaved noe benefitt under the king'. More importantly, the earl's decision not to lend 'had nether offended by example nor discouncelling of anie others'; indeed, 'the businesses had receaved as smooth a passage in your lieutenancie as in anie other part of the kingdome'. Such a frank explanation proved to no avail. When he asked Dorset 'whether it were not possible to decline that course by some other way', his answer was uncompromising: 'it was not possible'. Sir Thomas Edmondes, the Treasurer of the Household and the earl's stepfather, likewise held out no hope unless the earl compromised, for 'the king had Sworne that all such as were averse in the loane shold hold noe ymployment under him'.[22]

The Council's formal response only reiterated this hard-line position. Shirley's charges did not survive the careful scrutiny of Rudinge's account, and after a few queries Gofton concluded that the disbursements were all justified. But in the process Gofton also uncovered the awkward fact that Huntingdon had overestimated the expense of the 10 July order. Consequently, when Shirley had charged that £500 out of the £1,200 remained unspent, he had only got the amount wrong: in March 1627, the county had a surplus of nearly £250.[23] Nevertheless, if the Lord Lieutenant had erred, he had clearly erred on the side of the war effort and of a 'perfect' militia. Thus Skeffington reported that the councillors appeared 'much to commend your Care and diligence approving of all disbursements and parrelelling the plentifull provision of munitions and your readines in that Service with the deficiencies which were found in other Cunties'. In the end, however, Huntingdon's obsessive care could not balance out his intransigent position on the loan. The councillors informed Rudinge and Skeffington of 'the rigor of the kings resolution' not to retain recusants in positions of authority. But as a favour to Huntingdon 'they wold for 12 dayes suspend the execution of the kings command and of your continuance of ymployment in that charge untill they might receave some further answeare from you to take of the kings discontent'.

Skeffington relayed the news as well as his overall assessment of the situation. After noting the unexpected emergence of Dorset, a notorious 'hard-liner' in the forced loan, as a Hastings stalwart, Sir John observed that 'noe man can be soe happie to have his freinds in all places'. But even distinguished sympathisers could not help him evade the loan; either the earl could seek 'the conformitie of payment' or he could take his chance and argue 'in extenuation of your meanes to make payment, renunncing all resolution and wilfulness of denying the king'. If he clung to the poverty defence, Huntingdon ran a grave danger of dismissal, and 'at this time in the concurrence of 2 severall imputations the vulgar will hardly distinguish whether you loose your Commission for refusing or for inability for clearing accompts'. Whatever the true cause, Shirley certainly tarred Huntingdon with a reputation as a common embezzler.[24]

Years of distinguished service thus came down to one hurriedly written letter on which his political future depended. In it, Huntingdon held to his pleas of rectitude and poverty. The reports that 'his Majesties Commission of Lieutenancie shall shortly be taken from me' obviously distressed him, but, in response, he did not endorse the monarch's right to tax at will; all he said on this delicate question was that ill health had prevented him from attending the Leicester assembly launching the forced loan. Instead he dwelt on his family's long and faithful service to the Crown, which had 'consumed almost all of the Earldome' and made subscription to the loan out of the question: 'I owe many

Thousand pounds my Land seaven yeares since intayled except some fewe allotted for the payment of my debtes and my younger Children not yet provided for.' Therefore the choice before Charles was simple. If Huntingdon was guilty of embezzlement, then he begged for a signal punishment. If not, then the earl adroitly deployed Shirley's allegations to protect him from dismissal: his dismissal immediately after the formal review of Rudinge's books 'will I assure my selfe make the cuntry thinke I am discharged from the place for cozening them of their money'. Hence he begged the councillors to 'lett his Majestie knowe howe much my innocencie is like to suffer in the Worlds opinion being nowe in question and being a Peere of the Realme to be thus slandered for doing his Majesties service'.[25]

Huntingdon's gamble was a monumental one, but in the end, it paid off. In late June, Manchester and Lord Keeper Coventry met with the king to discuss 'those places of authority which you hold under his Majesty'. Since Charles was eventually satisfied with Huntingdon's argument, Coventry could report that 'I heare noe more of any alteration touching those places.'[26]

Huntingdon had achieved something quite remarkable. The rumoured dismissals had not been idle gossip, for while Huntingdon was penning his final letter the king supervised the most extensive purge in early Stuart England. On 21–2 June the Earls of Essex, Warwick, Clare, Bolingbroke, Kent and Lincoln, Viscount Saye and Sele, Lords Dacre, Deincourt, Stanhope, Cromwell and Grey of Warke were all removed from lieutenancies and commissions of the peace. Many had earlier been forced to wait in Westminster until the councillors found leisure to browbeat them for their obstinacy. Meanwhile several dozen gentry spent the month in jails where, among others, Sir Thomas Barrington of Essex contracted a fatal fever. The survivors often found themselves ejected from county commissions, and a few unfortunates were actually pressed into foreign service.[27] Amid this political persecution Huntingdon not only avoided an appearance in Westminster, but retained his high office.

How he managed this feat is worth pondering. First of all, his plea of poverty should not be taken too literally. Severely straitened circumstances were not destitution. While he was able to pay parliamentary subsidies without complaint, the earl offered an even more telling illustration of the financial resources at his disposal a few weeks after this crisis; then he spent a month at Bath and almost £500, more than twice as much as Charles had asked for in the forced loan. The need to soothe his hip, of course, justified the jaunt, but several minor gambling losses and £24 for a new suit suggest that he went as much to soothe his nerves. Rather than money, what lay behind Huntingdon's convenient poverty was his devotion to Parliament and the 'ancient constitution'. In all other attempts to collect extraparliamentary levies, he stuck to the absolute minimum necessary when he could not sit on his hands. The JPs in 1622 were effectively speaking for Huntingdon in their confession that 'whatsoever cometh from them in any sorte by waie of guyfte is procured with extreame difficultie'. Furthermore it was striking that in 1627, Skeffington's warning that Huntingdon should renounce 'all resolution and wilfulnes of denying the king' fell on deaf ears. His refusal to endorse the king's prerogative rights becomes less surprising once we remember that one of the few from outside the county to break bread with him in this period was the Earl of Warwick, a peer whose opposition to the forced loan was matched only by his commitment to the war effort.[28]

At the same time, Huntingdon was also discreet; if, as seems likely, he had reservations about the forced loan, he kept them to himself. Many of those who suffered for their recusancy had made more public nuisances of themselves; the Earl of Lincoln, for example, was implicated in a propaganda campaign to mobilise popular resistance to the loan.[29] Nor, as Lord Lieutenant, had Huntingdon hindered the service; Skeffington was only pressing home a telling truth by emphasising that 'the business had receaved as smoothe a passsage in your lieutenancie as in anie other parts of the kingdome'. To have dismissed Huntingdon therefore would have cost the government an effective local governor of admirable discretion when there were precious few others around. Hence his otherwise excellent record allowed him to turn Shirley's attack to his own advantage. If he was sacked, while the councillors would know that it was Huntingdon's response to the loan which had earned him this signal disgrace, many less knowledgeable subjects would interpret it as the just punishment of a corrupt local governor. Therefore, since Gofton's audit had clearly established the ridiculousness of that charge, dismissal would have ruined a provincial administrator whose crime in the eyes of the public had been 'doing his Maiesties service'. That prospect ultimately proved too much for a monarch who was in this matter otherwise inclined to vindictiveness.

NOTES

1 Skeffington to H, [June 1627]; Rutland DLs to H, 10 August and December 1626; and H to Rutland DLs, 2 January 1627, *LRLB*, fols. 209, 180 and 185v–6.

2 F. Coke to J. Coke, 20 April 1627; and Whalley to Coke, 10 March 1627, Coke MSS, BL Add. MS 64,890, fols. 52 and 105; and H to DLs, 2 April 1627, *LRLB*, fol. 203v.

3 H to Conway, 9 February 1627, SP 16/53/63; same to Rutland DLs, 22 March 1627; and Rutland DLs to H, 4 May 1627, *LRLB*, fols. 201–2 and 207; and Rudinge's accounts, SP 16/70/70. fol. 115v.

4 Corporation to H, 13 March 1627, HA Corr. 12/8525; H to [Corporation], 14 March 1627, *LRLB*, fols. 197v–8; and 'Charges of Mustering ... to Harborowe', Michaelmas 1626–27, Leics. RO, BR III/2/79, fol. 110.

5 Charles to H, 9 February 1627, *LRLB*, fol. 190v. See also E. A. Beller, 'The Military Expedition of Sir Charles Morgan to Germany, 1627–9', *EHR* XLIII (1928), pp. 528–39.

6 H to Constables, 11 March 1626, *LRLB*, fols. 192v–3v.

7 H to Legge, [March 1627]; and same to DLs, 17 March 1627, *LRLB*, fols. 193v and 198v; and Rudinge's accounts, SP 16/70/70, fol. 115.

8 Corporation to H, 13 March 1626, HA Corr 12/8525; DLs to H, 20 March 1627; and H to DLs, 17 March 1627, *LRLB*, fols. 199 and 198v.

9 Indentures, December 1624, May 1625 and March 1627, *LRLB*, fols. 105–6, 117v–18 and 200–200v.

10 Saltonstall to Coke, 30 March 1627; and Goodwin to Coke, 8 April 1627, BL Add. MS 64,891, fols. 10 and 24; H to the local officers, 2 April 1627, *LRLB*, fol. 203; Goodwin to PC, 26 March 1627, SP 16/58/32; and Gosnold and Saltonstall to same, April 1626, SP 16/60/51.

11 Charles to H, 28 July 1627, HA Corr. 12/1344.

12 DLs to PC, 10 September 1627, SP16/77/31.

13 Rudinge's accounts, SP 16/70/ 70, fol. 115; and 'Charges of Mustering … twelve soldiers to Harborowe', Chamberlain's accounts, Michaelmas 1626–27, Leics. RO, BR III/2/79, fols. 110–11.

14 Savage to Buckingham, 4 February 1627, SP 16/53/18; Whalley to Coke, 10 March 1627; and Skipwith to same, 1 February 1627, BL Add. MS 64,890, fols. 83 and 105. See also Marlborough and Weston to H, 2 March 1627, *LRLB*, fol. 192.

15 'Certificate of Leicester Borough Problems'; Sir Richard Roberts, 'A note', 4 August 1627; Fawsit and Skipwith to PC, 23 July 1627; Fawnt and Whalley to same, 4 August 1627; and Roberts to same, 4 August 1627, SP 16/71/80; 16/73/35; 16/71/80; 16/73/31 and /35.

16 Fawsit and Skipwith to PC, 23 July 1627; and [Leics. yields for the loan], October 1627, SP 16/71/80 and 16/83/56.

17 The source of this figure requires some explanation. £3216 3s. 2d. came from the Leicestershire payments in 'Mutuum a Laicis', [Abridged Receipts], Michaelmas 1626–Easter 1627, PRO E401/2322; 'Mutuum a Communalit-', [Abridged Receipts], Easter–Michaelmas 1627, PRO E401/2323; and 'Mutuum a laicis', [Auditors' Receipt Book], Easter–Michaelmas 1628, in Pitt's accounts, PRO E401/2443. The additional £170 derives from the list of rewards in the Auditors' Issues, Michaelmas 1627–Easter 1628, PRO E403/2804, pp. 5, 39 and 68. This figures suggest that the Abridged Accounts failed to list two payments by William Whalley and Sir Richard Roberts of £40 and £130 respectively. Since in all other instances the amounts recorded in this Issue Book corresponded precisely with the figures in the Abridged Accounts, it is likely that Whalley and Roberts did in fact pay in the additional £170, thus raising the total of £3,386 3s. 2d.

18 'Rewards to Collectors', Auditors' Issue Book, Michaelmas 1627–Easter 1628, PRO E403/2804, pp. 5, 39 and 68; 'Coat and Conduct Money', *ibid.*, p. 67; and entries for 27 April, 4 May and 8 June 1627, 'Rewards for collectors', Book of Certificates, Michaelmas 1627, PRO E405/226.

19 H to PC, 27 February 1627, *LRLB*, fol. 189; and PC to H, 11 May 1626, *APC* 42/270.

20 H to PC, 28 May 1627, SP 16/65/3.

21 Rudinge to H, 6 June [1627], *LRLB*, fol. 210.

22 Skeffington to H, [early June 1627], *LRLB*, fols. 208v–9v.

23 Rudinge's accounts, SP 16/70/70.

24 Skeffington to H, [early June 1627], *LRLB*, fols. 208v–9v.

25 H to PC, 14 June 1627, SP 16/67/2.

26 Coventry to H, 3 July 1627, HA Corr. 12/1676.

27 Crown office docquet book, PRO C 231/4, fols. 227v–228v; and Cust, *The Forced Loan*, pp. 187–218.

28 'A booke of my Lords expenses [at Bath]', 28 August–28 September 1627, HA Financial 8/32; and 'Mr Robies Accompts', HA Financial 8/36, entries of 3 May, 8 and 18 June.

29 Cust, *The Forced Loan*, pp. 170–5.

Chapter 8

The search
for vindication

Having backed Huntingdon into a tight corner, Shirley receded from the earl's consciousness as he focused on retaining his local offices. Only at the end of the summer, as Huntingdon's anxiety levels began to return to normal, could his attention turn to the man behind the scandal. Echoing through his mind was Dorset's observation that 'that tongue which had soe much wronged your Lordship should right you'. In fact there were legal grounds for compelling Shirley to do so. Yet in the event, the councillors simply cleared Huntingdon of all charges, leaving alone the question of Sir Henry's fate. The Lord Lieutenant wanted more, and he began searching for a sympathetic legal venue to finish the matter. Unfortunately for him, complete vindication was to prove extremely difficult to achieve.

ALONE WITH SHIRLEY

Huntingdon's victory in the matter of the forced loan came at a near Pyrrhic price. Before the crisis, his 'exquisite performance' had made the councillors vow to 'take speciall knowledge of it as you shall have occasion to expect the encouragement or make use of the favour of this Board'. By the summer of 1627, however, this fund of special favor neared exhaustion, and the normally phlegmatic Lord Lieutenant began to display visible signs of anxiety. 'I beseech you,' he begged his cousin Manchester, 'to stick close unto me that by this false report my honor may not be trampled under foote by my enimies.'[1] Yet his *cri de coeur* failed to move a majority of the councillors as a coolness verging at times on the glacial became noticeable between Whitehall and Donnington Park.

Illustrations of this abrupt transformation abound. While the earl's deteriorating influence at Whitehall often only cost the local ratepayers, his impotence sometimes translated directly into his own loss. Throughout 1626–27, as the earl struggled to counter Shirley, Sir Miles Fleetwood had been quietly surveying the royal forests in preparation for placing most of this land on the block for outright sale. During the extended preparations for this massive sale, Fleetwood assured everyone that the results would lead to 'the Universall Contentement and satisfaction of all', and his prediction was almost entirely correct. Huntingdon's errant cousin, Sir Henry Hastings of Braunston, profited handsomely from the deal, using it to expand his holdings. Even the Corporation of Leicester achieved laudable results from its petition to Buckingham for assistance in the matter so that the prayers of 'thousands of pore souls ... will never cease to be powred forth to god for your Graces long and happie Continueinge in this lyfe'. The duke in the end did not stop the sale, but he did ensure that the Corporation received forty acres.[2]

In this bonanza, the one notable exception was the Lieutenant of the Forest himself, who possessed a patent letter from James I conferring the office on him for life. The disafforestation scheme, which sold off the earl's charge without any compensation, troubled Fleetwood, who as an afterthought proposed soothing Huntingdon with a gift of some redundant royal deer, but nothing ever came of the idea after rioting villagers helped themselves to the animals. Consequently the earl was to spend years lobbying for compensation for the loss of this office, whose prerequisites were worth nearly £500 to him. The conclusion is almost irresistible that the Crown's insensitivity to the long-serving Lieutenant was linked with Huntingdon's recusancy in the case of the forced loan. Confirmation of this assessment came when 'rude people' produced 'a verye great disorder' in the midst of the disafforestation. To sort out the matter, the Council issued a commission to a panel headed by Lord Grey and including Sir Thomas Hesilrige. When Grey declined to execute the commission, the councillors dropped the matter, reasoning, so it seemed, that no investigation was better than one which involved Huntingdon.[3]

The pain of these actions were nothing compared with the Council's response to Sir Henry Shirley. After the councillors had dismissed his charges as groundless, Huntingdon had begged for much more, asking 'that I may by some publique meanes be righted'. In the event, however, the Council took no further action other than to impose a particularly cruel punishment of Huntingdon's recusancy. They left both shires in Huntingdon's hands, confident that the earl 'wilbe ever ready and carefull to dischardg the trust reposed in you to the advauncement of the publique service'.[4] Yet they made it nearly impossible for Huntingdon to execute his commission, because they left him in the shire with his enemy unchecked. Furthermore, it was almost impossible for the antagonists to avoid one another, since less than five miles separated Donnington Park from Staunton Harold.

Well might Shirley rejoice at this development, which led to the public 'vanting of himselfe' and to Huntingdon's profound chagrin. The earl, Shirley confidently gave out, had begged the councillors to arrest him, 'but it was staied and the kinge said I [Shirley] was an honest man'. Indeed, Sir Henry's friendship with the mighty led him to intensify his old dream of a peerage. It can scarcely be coincidental that in 1627 Shirley commissioned two grand pieces of art glorifying his family. The first was an elaborately decorated family tree on whose canvas Sir Henry's younger brother could display his formidable genealogical research. Since a peerage was, at least in theory, as much in recognition of the family's lineage as of its wealth, no one would carp at Sir Henry's promotion after examining such a pedigree. Contemporaries need not have gone into Sir Henry's parlour to see his confident expectation of imminent elevation; a visit to the Breedon church would have served the same purpose. There, Sir Henry commissioned a new family pew with the Devereux arms prominently displayed; his recent divorce notwithstanding, Shirley was intent on reminding contemporaries that his son was a co-heir of the Earl of Essex. Nor was all this self-induced fantasy, for there were confident reports in 1627 that Charles would soon raise three men to baronies, one of whom was 'a Shirley of Leicestershire'.[5]

As 'Lord' Shirley's dreams mounted higher, Huntingdon's pleas for retribution became more exercised. 'In soe publique and great a meting in a common hall before two Lords of his Majesties most honorable privie Councell and in the face of the whoale County', Shirley had wounded Huntingdon 'in my honor and reputation'. The public bearding of a Lord Lieutenant, Huntingdon reminded the councillors, was not simply a private matter; as long as Shirley went unpunished, 'I languish in my esteeme finding that my Commands upon your letters are not obayed and every day lesse regarded.' Yet his impassioned pleas left the Council unmoved, and its inaction in turn produced further 'vantinge' from Sir Henry. Little wonder then that Huntingdon equated Shirley's chastisement with the re-establishment of his hegemony over the county: hence 'I will never leave this matter till I bee righted.'[6]

If a spirit of charity suddenly overcame Huntingdon, he still could not have forgotten about Shirley, for Sir Henry would not be quiet as the earl's collection of Shirley's 'Speaches ... against me' rapidly swelled into a sizeable collection. Take what happened when Gilbert Barker, one of Huntingdon's tenants, went to reclaim his stray cattle from Shirley's property. Since Huntingdon had brusquely rejected Shirley's petition to hawk on his land, Barker's transgression only reminded Shirley of what 'a poore thinge' it had been 'to denie mee hawking in his grounds'. The result was a tirade in which the earl's dwindling estate especially attracted Shirley's ridicule: 'I am glad hee hath noe more land [than he does] to hawke on.' When the loyal retainer cautioned against slandering a gentleman, Sir Henry insisted 'hee knew not that'. When Barker tried to soothe Shirley by insisting that he was on no errand of 'My Lord', Shirley shot back that 'he cared for never a lord in England a farte (the lord of hosts excepted)'.[7] Once these tales reached Donnington Park, Huntingdon was irritated to learn that 'I were the onlie person for Sir Henrie to purge his spleene'.[8] Yet until the Council altered its low regard for the earl, he could do nothing except carefully record the latest outrage and hope for the best.

THE CHETWYND AFFAIR

After months of intolerable suffering, Huntingdon's endurance at last appeared rewarded in November 1627 when Shirley finally overplayed his hand and expanded his campaign against Huntingdon to include Philip Chetwynd. Although some uncertainties remain, Chetwynd was almost certainly connected with the Chetwynds of Ingestre in Staffordshire, one of whom had married Huntingdon's aunt, and he was probably the 'Mr Chetwin' in the 1609 list of the Hastings household. Yet for Shirley, Chetwynd's gentility was entirely obscured by the fact that he was simply 'my Lords man'. Chetwynd and Shirley came together on 25 October 1627 after Sir Henry had told several local gentlemen his considered opinion of Huntingdon's cousin; 'he would not take the said Phillip Chetwynds word for anie thing, because he would forsweare himselfe for a doggs turd'. On learning of this assessment, Chetwynd promptly rode to Staunton Harold to confront Sir Henry. When Shirley boldly repeated his opinion, Chetwynd lost control and began pummelling Shirley with a stick, shouting 'I will beat your honor out of your Arse.' Bystanders intervened to end the first round, but fisticuffs nearly erupted again with Shirley's remark that he could not possibly duel with someone as base as Chetwynd.[9]

So far, Sir Henry had simply been running true to his usual intemperate form, but then he played into Huntingdon's hands. News of the affray quickly reached Huntingdon, who wisely decided not to intervene himself; instead he ordered his Deputies, Sir John Skeffington and Sir Henry Skipwith, to 'compose the difference'. Chetwynd proved 'conformeable'; Shirley did not. Sir Henry waved off a formal summons to appear before his fellow JPs with the smooth reply that 'Sunday is noe fitt day to travell on'; instead he invited them over for a meal. As far as he was concerned, their task was pointless 'when the mischife is allready done'. The facts of the case were simply that Sir Henry had been 'walkinge in my ground' when 'this fellowe comeinge from his Lords house violently assaulted mee'. For his part, Shirley was interested only in legal retribution from Star Chamber, since 'I too well understand my Office [as a JP] and the disadvantage of breaking the peace.' Had Chetwynd been his equal, Sir Henry conceded, 'hee would not have breathed after such a great Iniury done unto mee'. But there was no danger of further violence, since '[I] scorne to sett my Condition in equall balance with my Lords man.' The Deputies thus could tell Huntingdon not to 'feare any further harme to his man from mee howe basely soever I have been used'. Shirley's careful calculations of personal worth and legal right had failed to appreciate the full authority of Justices of the Peace, for he had just given Skipwith and Skeffington grounds for a formal complaint against a man who denied 'himselfe anie wayes subordinate to our authority'.[10] In such a case, even powerful friends at court, who could easily shield him from a vengeful magnate, could not halt a summons before the Privy Council, and in short order, Shirley found himself committed to the Marshalsea.

Scarcely believing his unexpected good fortune, Huntingdon begged the Council for exemplary punishment. Since Shirley had long had it coming to him, 'I beseech your Lordships that seing hope deferred is a fainting of the flesh and dries up the marrow in the bones' not to delay further his richly deserved reward. Outwardly sympathetic, the councillors assured him that 'for the disrespects given your Lordship and the slighting of your deputy lieutenants ... wee have thought fitt to sensure and to punish him as the cause well deserveth'. They then volunteered the opinion that 'both your honor and your actions tending to advance the Kings services ... will ever be nobly esteemed and preserved by us'.[11]

Triumph at last appeared within Huntingdon's grasp – until the Council's idea of a fitting chastisement became clear. After spending seventy-two hours in prison, Shirley was confined to his London residence, pending a written apology. Two tries and ten days later, he found the right formula. Citing his ill health and 'manie other occasions of much importance', he first petitioned his release, asking forgiveness of the councillors. This construction failing to serve the turn, Shirley belatedly included Huntingdon in the apology. While the councillors' tender regard for Shirley was unsettling enough, much worse was their willingness to revive Shirley's earlier accusation. They reaffirmed their belief in Huntingdon's innocence, since 'all things are truely accompted for by your Lordship'. Nevertheless, further reflection on Rudinge's accounts and further discussion with Shirley led them to rebuke the earl; thanks to his excessive zeal in responding to the Council's order of 10 July 1626, 'the county were putt to some more charges then the occasions of the service did sense require'.[12] Inexplicably what had began as Shirley's apparent self-destruction had turned into an occasion to give Huntingdon a dressing down.

The most alarming aspect of a thoroughly frightening affair was that while the earl remained in the shire, the case brought Shirley back into personal contact with friends at court. By all lights what should have been the occasion of Shirley's disgrace and chastisement had the opposite effect. Sir John Beaumont of Gracedieu, the poet whose house Huntingdon had searched, died in 1627 leaving behind a son, who was a royal ward. In November 1627, when Shirley was allegedly under house arrest, Buckingham persuaded Charles to award Sir Henry Shirley with a yearly grant of £99 16s. for the remainder of the Beaumont minority. For good measure, Charles presented him with a cash gift of £500. Shortly after this extraordinary mark of favour, Shirley belatedly received a crushing punishment for his antics; on 8 January 1628, Lord Keeper Coventry removed him from the Leicestershire bench, although he left him on the commission for Derby. Huntingdon can only have exulted at the news, Derbyshire's misfortune being none of his own, and the removal of such a noxious presence might offset the irritation of Shirley's cash grant. But thanks again to Shirley's friends, the celebrations in Donnington Park were brief. As Sir Henry explained to all who would listen, Buckingham had brought him to kiss Charles's hand. A brief conversation ensued with the monarch, who eventually said, 'Buckingham Sir Henrie Shirley lokes angerly and bid my lord Duke send unto my lord Keeper to put him into the Commission of the Peace.' On 18 February 1628, Lord Keeper Coventry did so.[13] Probably never had Huntingdon witnessed a more telling demonstration of the power of the right contacts.

With the Chetwynd affair, the jockeying between Huntingdon and Shirley had dramatically escalated. Previously Sir Henry had bragged about his connections with the high and mighty; now he had made his boasts good. How else could anyone account for the wrist slap from the councillors? No other word could properly describe a private apology to the earl, a brief suspension from the bench, and a £500 gift from the king. Quite understandably, Sir Henry returned breathing fire, telling one local gentleman that 'for the wrongs my Lord hath done me he beinge a Christian perhaps he might forgive mee [Huntingdon]'. Shirley's children were another matter; 'he would leave it with his Children never to forgive mee nor myne but to doe me all the hurt and mischeife they could'. Far from ending the dispute, the Chetwynd affair had simply intensified it. Powerful parties were working not only to topple Huntingdon from the lieutenancy, but also to hoist Shirley into his place. Moreover, as the conflict intensified, the Privy Council steadily abandoned all pretence of being an impartial arbiter. Alarmed by these developments and frustrated that 'I doe verie clearlie see my honour not vindicated', Huntingdon retained his brother-in-law's councillor, William Noy, and began plotting a Star Chamber suit to gain the long-delayed 'satisfaction for the inurie Sir Henrie hath done mee'. No matter what happened, the earl vowed that 'I will never leave this matter till I bee righted'.[14] Such defiant rhetoric masked the fact that Huntingdon had no other choice, unless he was willing to give up his local offices without a fight.

BEFORE THE LORDS

Early in 1628, the feud between the Lieutenant and the Justice had reached the point where it was simply a political explosion waiting to happen, and they could have asked for no better occasion than the 1628 county election. Huntingdon advanced his son, Lord Hastings, and a militia officer, Sir Edward Hartopp. Shirley meanwhile offered his services to the county. Although no record shows that the issue was ever put to the poll, the energy with which both men lobbied for votes suggests that they thought it might well go that far.

Like an old professional, Huntingdon busily nailed down commitments from the leading county gentlemen, making certain that they would turn up with their tenants. Early canvasses revealed that while the Hastings grip on Sparkenhoe and part of Guthlaxton hundred was unshakable and that Leicester itself was 'also firme', other sections of the shire were more vulnerable. Shirley marshalled the Catholic gentry and, in particular, the Beaumonts, and from this solid base appealed to the Protestant freeholders, and to entice naturally apprehensive voters, served up red political meat. Earlier in the year, Shirley had simply insinuated financial irregularities in the county budget, but in his stump speech a year later, these hints became detailed accusations of fraud. 'In the face of my county,' Shirley told the waverers,

> I will prove by the handes of many hundred of the best freeholders, what unnecessary charge my lord hath put the Cuntry unto, as buying of a Tent which cost 200 pounds, and Staves of wood ... which cost the Cuntry X li. or XI li. I can buy as many for Xs. or XIs. And Knapsackes which cost seaven groats a peece and made the Cuntry to pay ten groates a peece.[15]

Against the corrupt power of a long-time political boss, Sir Henry offered himself as the champion of virtue and probity.

With a sensational platform, Shirley even entertained solid Hastings voters in the hope of weakening the earl's grip. Loyalty, he smoothly argued, was pointless to a man about to be dismissed; in fact, Sir Henry offered £100 wagers that he would replace Huntingdon in less than a year, and he boasted of his own imminent elevation to the peerage. To be sure, Shirley's hot temper sometimes undercut the force of his appeal; when some confused voters offered to split their votes between Lord Hastings and Sir Henry, the candidate raged at them as 'a company of poore foolish Rascalls that depend upon your Lieutenant'. Nevertheless, the mere fact that Shirley secured one of the two votes from the earl's own retainers amply illustrates the seriousness of his challenge. As the election day approached, Sir Wolston Dixie anxiously requested Huntingdon's presence at the hustings, 'lest any cratchet shall soddainely arise to breake and sunder the forces conceived to be united or any stratagem unthought upon be put in action to cause a distraction'. Such care paid handsome dividends, for the county returned the Hastings slate. Yet in the end, even this triumph did not bury the issue that Shirley had hoped to ride to Westminster; the earl, he explained, had engineered his defeat by bullying wavering voters into line with threats of swingeing reassessments in their militia charges.[16] Even a resounding defeat could not stop Shirley from spreading allegations of the Lieutenant's corruption.

Having scandalised county politics for over a year, the Huntingdon–Shirley quarrel now spilled into the House of Lords. Although the constitutional fireworks in 1625 and 1626 had not lured the earl from Donnington Park, the prospect of finding a sympathetic venue led him to Westminster as soon as the weather warmed up. As an old member of this most exclusive club, Huntingdon could at last neutralise Shirley's court connections, and this was especially true in 1628, when a cash-starved government was willing to put up with quite a lot to obtain subsidies. Unfortunately, the administration had no shortage of critics, thanks to Charles's hard line over the forced loan: after all, the Crown could deny obstinate peers their local offices, but not their seats in the Lords. Consequently in the 1628 session, Charles and Buckingham had to confront the fact that they had created an 'opposition' group in the Lords.[17]

Huntingdon had long been quite close to Warwick, Saye, Lincoln and Essex, and his narrow escape from their humiliating fate only strengthened the bond, which remained quite close throughout the session. When the earl contradicted no less than the Duke of Buckingham himself, Saye backed him up. When Charles threatened to dissolve the session, Huntingdon and Essex attempted to form a committee to report on 'the present state of the kingdom'. Lest anyone had overlooked his devotion to the recusant lords, Huntingdon made it public on 19 May, when he moved that since 'the king had removed many lords lieutenants, justices or other officers upon this refusal [of the loan], they might be set in the same state as before'. Although his motion failed, Huntingdon had highlighted a fundamental grievance of his friends. Two weeks later, in a conciliatory gesture, Buckingham sought to soothe 'those Lords who had bin long in disfavour', among them Essex, Lincoln, Warwick and Saye, by leading them to kiss Charles's hand. Thanks to his actions, it is easy to place him in the great conflict between the 'ducal party' and the 'Peeres of the side that stood for freedome'.[18]

Since the regime would willingly sacrifice almost anyone in return for a subsidy Bill, the House of Lords was a decidedly hostile environment for Sir Henry. Nevertheless Shirley remained characteristically buoyant to the end, telling all who would listen in Westminster Hall, he 'braggs ... he was respected and my lord of Huntingdon was sleighted'.[19] Such bravado in retrospect may appear almost lunatic. Yet this seemingly demented man came within an ace of one more triumph. His powerful friends still stood by him, and while they were not prepared to hazard all to save him, they were certainly willing to minimise any damage. More importantly, time was on Shirley's side.

Huntingdon's decision to wait over a month before opening his parliamentary campaign against Shirley nearly proved disastrous. He appeared in the Lords on 28 April, almost in time to have seen the Hastings team in the Commons open the offensive against Sir Henry. The county knights were responsible for reporting the names of all Catholics in local government, either confirmed or suspected, and in Leicestershire, Hastings and Hartopp could think of no one worth mentioning except Shirley. Huntingdon lost no time seconding their actions. On 1 May the House named him to the committee for petitions, which in less than five days was hearing Huntingdon's own petition. In the formal charges, Sir Henry's various accusations of fraud quickly gave way to his pungent assessment of the peerage: 'hee cared not a fart for never a lord in England'. Having quickly gained an attentive audience with this one line, the earl apologised for using such coarse language, but 'hee would not charge him with other then the verie words hee spake'.[20] The House ordered Shirley to testify two days later, on 8 May. When Sir Henry pleaded a prior engagement before the High Commission, the bishops in the House assured him that another time for his case could be arranged; Archbishop Abbot for one was doubtless eager to see Sir Henry get his come-uppance. After Shirley's testimony, the first of over two dozen witnesses were heard.[21] The swift pace of the proceedings must have delighted Huntingdon, until on 8 May, the Parliament men sent up the Petition of Right.

Notwithstanding the peers' prestige, their legislative routine was generally mundane. Important Bills tended to originate in the Commons and to arrive in the Lords in a great flood towards the end of a session. In the interim, the Lords spent much of their time considering individual petitions for redress, and in 1628, aside from two non-controversial requests from Warwick, Huntingdon alone had lodged a petition, which the Lords were only too happy to expedite. This happy world, however, vanished once the Petition of Right reached the Lords. The resulting 'tongue-combat' amazed contemporaries, for 'the like ... was never heard in the Upper House'. As priorities shifted, the pace of the Shirley case abruptly slowed down, waiting for a bloc of time between the grand debates. After speeding through the House, Huntingdon's petition struggled to gain the House's attention, if only for a few hours.[22]

When set against 'the great business', the dozen witnesses whom Huntingdon carted down to testify about a thousand knapsacks and a fart can only have sounded more than faintly incongruous. From debating the 'liberties of the subject' the peers turned to listening to Rudinge and Skipwith recount the scene at Leicester on 15 January 1627. Discussions about the legality of billeting shaded into Bryan Knight insisting that the pioneers' equipment did not exceed £40 and Skeffington maintaining that Shirley's 'ill example' had encouraged defaulters. Momentous debates over the prerogative suddenly gave way to John Skarrat recounting Shirley's boasts in the electoral campaign.[23] Even one of Mr Astlyn's knapsacks made an appearance in the Palace of Westminster. And so for two weeks, the ridiculous jogged along aside the sublime, until 24 May when the Lords promised a final resolution of the case.

In these proceedings, Shirley was far from dejected, for reasons which became obvious when the Lords discussed his punishment. Huntingdon's cousin, Lord President Manchester, reported the committee's assessment of the case. In addition to allegations about the 'oppression of the county', Shirley had voiced 'many other words of asperity and scandal', many of which had been 'proved by witnesses'. Among the latter was the Earl of Exeter, who apparently never tired of relating how he had called Shirley down. Huntingdon then rose; his recitation of 'this scandal and the grief thereof' ended with his demand for 'justice as he was his Majesty's lord lieutenant and a peer of this realm'. After announcing his desire for 'nothing but reparation of his honor', the aggrieved peer left his colleagues to their deliberations. The nobility of Huntingdon's parting speech, however, could not entirely over-come the legally awkward aspects of his case. Manchester himself conceded there had been 'other words of asperity', but these were 'not duly proved'. Furthermore Huntingdon's platoon of witnesses had not proved that Shirley was the author of the scandals, a fact which Sir Henry heatedly denied. Worse yet was the House's response to the earl's final request to listen to his attor-neys, Mr Leveringe and Mr Noy; Lord Montagu, another of Huntingdon's cousins, blithely and successfully argued that Exeter's testimony made such formality unnecessary. Thus without counsel, the House debated the case.[24]

Since everyone agreed that Shirley had erred, the only question was the appropriate reparation. On one extreme was Lord Noel, who, in spite of problems with Rutland's two sergeants, supported his Lieutenant in the matter; at the very least, Shirley should 'make satisfaction at the assizes in the country and here at the bar'. Equally sympathetic was Dorset; although Huntingdon had insisted that he wanted 'not money for recompense', Dorset knew enough about the earl's financial difficulties to suggest a hefty fine. Unfortunately for the earl, other neighbours argued against stern measures; both the Earl of Westmorland, who lived in Northamptonshire, and Bishop Williams, Hunting-don's diocesan, insisted that if there was to be any hope that 'love and neigh-bourhood should be maintained', Shirley then 'should make a recognition of his faults here [in Westminster], not in the country'. Another neighbour, the Earl of Clare, alternatively suggested that after Shirley had submitted to the Lords, a record of his submission should be read at the Leicester assize. As a serious difference of opinion had developed, Buckingham intervened with the winning compromise. While the duke conceded that 'the offense was great', he also thought 'the punishment ought to be equal to the offense'; thus while Buckingham thought Shirley should apologise both before the bar and in the county, he asked in the name of the 'continuance of love and friendship' that Huntingdon 'be moved that latter part may be omitted'. The peers swiftly approved the duke's proposal, which aimed 'to lay no heavier censure ... than such as there might ensue a reconciliation between him and the said Earl'. Thus they resolved that Shirley should 'give the Earl of Huntingdon satisfaction' in the House. In addition, the circuit judges were to read his submission at the next assize, but before that happened, the earl, his colleagues hoped, 'shall be contented to have the same forborne'.[25]

By this time Huntingdon was in no mood for an exercise in neighbourliness. After the embarrassment Shirley had caused him, nothing less than a stern and humiliating chastisement seemed appropriate. Yet the councillors had not seen it that way; they had refused to rebuke Shirley for his outburst in January 1627 and given nothing more than a wrist slap over the Chetwynd affair. Now Huntingdon's fellow peers appeared equally charitable. Thus a few days before the verdict was to be formally delivered, the earl begged his colleagues for a thorough reconsideration. To support such an extraordinary action, he cited 8 Rich. II, No. 12, the statute against *scandalum magnatum*, under which the House of Lords punished Walter Sibille for slandering Henry de Vere, the Earl of Oxford. He also offered another, more recent example of Sir Henry's ability to 'speak intemperative'; Sir Henry Skipwith and Thomas Gerard recounted how just outside the Parliament House Shirley 'braggs' about 'he was respected and my lord of Huntingdon is sleighted'. Plainly the House was impressed. Huntingdon's invocation of *scandalum magnatum*, a statute more common in Star Chamber, underscored his seriousness in the matter as well as his desperation. Equally impressive was the latest report of Sir Henry's failure to accept the Lords' magnanimous efforts to restore peace in the shire. Hence the House swiftly approved Huntingdon's latest motion.[26] The only problem was time.

Huntingdon's success in reversing the initial judgment did little to make the ensuing two weeks any less agonising. The additional information only required two witnesses and a minimal amount of the time. Nevertheless, Huntingdon constantly battled to keep the issue before the House. Immediately after the decision for a reconsideration, Arundel reminded it that in its priorities 'salus reipublica' had to come before Shirley's antics. As Huntingdon was reduced to waiting his turn in the queue, he became a zealous advocate for the swift resolution of all other matters.[27] Yet days of energetic labours still left him on 30 May pleading with the House to return to his case. Arundel then confessed to some confusion, since the House had already agreed on a verdict on the 24th. Warwick repaid the earl's friendship by patiently explaining that the initial judgment had been 'waived' after Huntingdon had produced additional charges.[28] Victory at last appeared within reach when the House agreed to resolve the case on 4 June, almost a month after Huntingdon had first introduced it. But the peers promptly forgot their promise as turmoil over Charles's threatened prorogation forced the Lords to move the Shirley case first from 4 May to 6 May and finally to 7 May. In this period, the earl had ample grounds for apprehension that Shirley might again elude judgement. Nevertheless, Huntingdon's persistence eventually paid off.[29]

On 7 June, while awaiting the king's response to the Petition of Right, the House turned to Huntingdon *v.* Shirley. The first line of Sir Henry's defence was that the Privy Council had already punished him for the offences, and among others, Clare found this argument telling. Manchester, however, quickly assured them that this had involved 'other scandals', not the matters now before the House. Next, when confronted with Huntingdon's litany of complaints, Sir Henry 'denied that he uttered those speeches in the same sense they are charged against him'. This promising approach unfortunately failed to reckon with the Earl of Exeter, who promptly rose to add his recollection of that extraordinary day in Leicester, swearing 'the said scandall to be true'. Admittedly Sir Henry managed to label one of Huntingdon's witnesses as 'a drunken fellow'; that left only another dozen witnesses, among them the Earl of Exeter, for him to discredit.[30]

As Shirley's defence came undone, the Lords quickly reached a decision to Huntingdon's liking. On 11 June, Shirley appeared on his knees at the bar of the House to give 'humble and full satisfaction'. He acknowledged 'his sorrow for the greate offences hee hath committed, in laying aspersions and scandals upon the honor of soe noble a person and peere of this realm'. He then asked the pardon of the entire peerage as well as of Huntingdon himself, vowing 'that by his future carriage hee will indeavour to make amends to the Lords in general and to the said Earl in particular'. Since the 'aspersions and scandalls' had been spoken 'in the hearing of many', the House also ordered Shirley's submission to be read at the next assize in Leicester so that 'all men may know how cleere from the least blemish the honor of the said Earle doth stand'. Rather than encouraging the earl to waive this part of Shirley's punishment, the peers now simply left the matter to Huntingdon's discretion 'to stay ... if he please'. They also left Shirley's further imprisonment to him. On 7 June, the Bishop of Norwich recalled that such offenders customarily were committed; the House agreed, and Shirley spent the next four days in prison. After such a public humiliation, Huntingdon could afford to be generous. After an extended celebration over three nights with Warwick, Stamford, Sir Benjamin Rudyerd, his Stanhope nephew, and a host of local well-wishers, Huntingdon on the 11th felt gracious enough to ask the House to release Sir Henry. He was not so generous about the publication; at the next assize, a mass of citizens heard the report of Shirley confessing his guilt 'in laying aspersion and scandalls upon the honor of soe noble a person'.[31]

PARTING SHOTS

In a political universe which revolved around honour and virtue, Shirley's public humiliation can only have been seen as a heavy blow. It is vital to appreciate, however, that it was not a crushing one. Sir Henry's pretensions remained, as did the wealth to support them; in fact in 1631, he commissioned an even larger decorated pedigree roll than that of 1627. He certainly retained ample grounds to hope for a peerage; his connections at court remained, and the indignities meted out by Parliament had increased his claim on royal favor. After all, Huntingdon's triumph had simply placed Sir Henry in the elite company of those whom Parliament had punished: Auditor Sawyer, the accountant for the forced loan; the Cornish Deputy Lieutenants who had executed legally dubious Council orders; and Drs Maynwaring and Sibthorpe, who had exalted the prerogative from the pulpit. When Parliament rose, the Earl of Clare recalled wearily the old rule of thumb: 'to be censured by either hows, is a sure way of preferrment'. In short order, Charles made Sawyer a Master of Requests, promoted Maynwaring to an episcopal see, and showered on the Cornishmen knighthoods, baronetcies and even a peerage.[32] Therefore in spite of a humiliating experience on his knees, Shirley could still aspire to great things.

Lest anyone had doubted this point, the Star Chamber delivered a striking illustration of his enduring power. When the Chetwynd affair had erupted, Sir Henry had told the Deputy Lieutenants not to trouble themselves since he had decided to let the courts resolve the matter. As Philip Chetwynd discovered in November 1629, this was no idle boast. Although the affray had led Shirley to decline the JPs' mediation, the affray itself had never been examined until Shirley insisted on reopening the case. At the hearing Sir Henry conceded that he had called Chetwynd 'a base fellow'. Yet Chetwynd had little excuse for having 'mallice et waylay et dongs fait assault' on a knight and a JP. In contrast to Shirley's nominal punishment, Chetwynd, by no indication a wealthy man, had to pay a £200 fine and to present Shirley with a written apology, which was read aloud at the Leicester assize.[33] For Shirley, this decision was a tonic. A year after his own humiliation he had the satisfaction of witnessing the disgrace of one of Huntingdon's relatives. For the earl himself, the results of Shirley v. Chetwynd cannot have been an auspicious augury. While Shirley was in line for royal favour, Huntingdon, as a fellow-traveller, if not a charter member, of the 'opposition' in the Lords, was not. Furthermore earlier in 1629, the earl's parliamentary power base had dissolved in rancorous disorder, and without a sympathetic venue in the Lords, any renewal of the feud would almost certainly be in Sir Henry's favour.

After Chetwynd's disgrace, the conflict between the two rivals continued more as skirmishing than in any set-piece battles. Thus it naturally followed that when the Council asked Huntingdon to list those liable for fines in distraint of knighthood, Shirley headed the earl's return. Among the long list of Leicestershire 'offenders' were only two knights, one of which was Sir Henry, and while the earl set down practically everyone else for fines between £10 and £25, Shirley, in Huntingdon's opinion, owed the Crown £70. While more of the county elite were added to the list at the Council's insistence, none of them came close to equalling Shirley's assessment.[34] The stinging fine notwithstanding, the wind had not shifted to Huntingdon's quarter. Huntingdon's most fervent prayers could not make Shirley disappear, and the reason for his solidity can be seen on the first page of the contemporary work on baronets; there, among the arms of the first four in the realm, is the saracen's head of the Shirleys. Sir Henry's insistence on his right of precedence plainly galled Huntingdon's protégés, and this poorly concealed tension explains the remarkable scene at the 1632 winter assize. A row developed between Shirley and Sir Arthur Hesilrige; 'they multiplied words in Choller', and Sir Henry at one point dubbed the younger man 'but a silly or a poore fellowe'. In the midst of controversy, Dixie slipped into Shirley's seat at the head of the table. Another explosion thereupon erupted when Shirley moved to reclaim his position, politely offering, if need be, to 'sitt on his lapp'. In the end, after having repeatedly delayed the opening of the court, Shirley forced Dixie to yield the place.[35]

Mercifully for Huntingdon, this scene was to be Shirley's last, for serious illness and death were soon to terminate this most tumultuous 'home division'. Shortly after the scene with Skipwith, Shirley's brother recalled that Sir Henry was overcome with 'a longe lingegering [*sic*] disease', which forced him into 'abandoning all worldly things'. Although contemporaries had repeatedly dubbed him a Catholic, Sir Henry had dodged the accusation at critical times with timely displays of conformity. Now with no reason for such niceties, he summoned 'a Learned Catholick Spirituall Guide'. With the cleric's 'advice and holy instructions', which Shirley 'most diligently observed and practiced for the space of a Month', he died early in 1633 just as Huntingdon would have predicted, 'in the Lappe of his Holy Mother, the Catholicke Apostilike Roman Churche'.[36] Cynical modern readers might well suspect that Sir Thomas Shirley's devout Catholicism coloured this account, but no such suspicion can survive a reading of Sir Henry's will. To avoid the pressure even for outward conformity, Shirley asked to be buried in the middle of the night without mourners; and as befitted a reconciled son of the true Church, he left £500 to the English college at Douai, a bequest which his horrified Protestant executor refused to honor.[37]

While his own life had fallen well short of his expectations, Sir Henry's labours had placed his children on the verge of the greatness which he had so consistently pursued. In his will, Shirley left careful instructions conveying his genealogical records to his sons, but for them the family's greatest glories lay ahead, not behind. While Sir Henry and Lady Dorothy were plainly ill suited to one another, their marriage was Sir George Shirley's shrewdest investment, and on Sir Henry's death the Devereux connection began yielding impressive returns. His children went under the care and wardship of their uncle, the Earl of Essex, who lavished on them all the attention that his heirs deserved. The children in time repaid his care, and at the earl's funeral in 1646, Sir Henry's son was one of the chief mourners. Thanks to the earl's largesse, Essex House and other London properties immediately came to the Shirleys; Chartley in Staffordshire passed to them a few years later.[38] The political turmoil of the 1650s prevented him from receiving the other portion of his Devereux inheritance, the title of Lord Ferrers of Chartley. Consequently the family had to wait until the Restoration before Sir Henry's grandson was finally called to the Lords by that title. A few years later, when the grandson vaulted still higher in the peerage, the Devereux connection remained proudly displayed by the Earl Ferrers. Yet the keenest irony of this feud was not that Sir Henry's grandsons eventually gained the titles which he had so confidently claimed. Rather it was that in June 1728, almost a century to the day after Sir Henry appeared on his knees before the Lords, the ninth Earl of Huntingdon travelled to Staunton Harold, not to trade barbs, but to exchange vows with Selina Shirley, the daughter of the second Earl Ferrers.[39]

At Shirley's death, Huntingdon still had a decade of life ahead of him, time enough to settle scores with those who had challenged his rule in 1626-28. In the meantime, he savoured his triumph over Sir Henry Shirley. To be sure, retribution had not fallen as harshly as the earl might have liked, but it sufficed. In 1636, for example, he fondly recalled the scene when Shirley 'asked me forgivenes upon his knees in full Parliament in the higher Howse'. The old peer brightened at the recollection that 'a declaration of an Order by the howses Command was read at Leicester at the Assizes there in the publique Hall how cleare I was and that he was punished as he iustly deserved'.[40] He did not, however, boast about how long it took him to humble his adversary. Nor did he mention how uncomfortably close Shirley had come to bringing him to his knees.

NOTES

1 PC to H, 12 December 1625, APC 40/268; and H to Manchester, 14 June 1627, *LRLB*, fol. 212v.

2 Fleetwood to Conway, 13 June 1627, SP 16/66/84; and 'To the duke of Buckingham', [1626]; and Fleetwood's warrant, [1627], Leics. RO, BR II/18/16, fols. 163 and 231. See also Fox and Russell, *The Forest of Leicester*, pp. 105–18.

3 Fleetwood to Conway, 13 June and 18 July 1627, SP 16/66/84 and 16/70/49; Conway to

Manchester, 16 July 1627, SP 16/71/8; PC to Grey, 20 July 1627, *APC* 42/432; and Grey to PC, 4 September 1627, SP 16/76/27.

4   H to PC, 28 May 1627, SP 16/65/3; and Rudinge to H, 6 June [1627], *LRLB*, fol. 210.

5   Mr Gerard's testimony, 'Speeches of Sir H. Shirley', HA Legal 2/11; and anon. to Mead, [2 March 1627], BL Add. MS 4177, fol. 261–2. See also Nichols, *History and Antiquities*, III, p. 688; and the 1627 pedigree, formerly deposited, but now withdrawn, in the Ferrers MSS, Leics. RO, as 26D53/2884.

6   H to PC, 6 November 1627, SP 16/84/27; and H to Leveringe, 7 February 1628, HA Corr. 13/8537.

7   'The Humble Petition of ... Huntingdon', 6 May 1628, Main Papers, House of Lords RO; and 'The Abreviation of the materiall thinges', HA Legal 2/11.

8   H to Levinge, 7 February 1628, HA Corr. 13/8537.

9   Chetwynd's testimony, 29 October 1627, SP 16/83/29; and Shirley *v.* Chetwynd, Michaelmas [1629], in 'Reports of Cases in the Star Chamber', Harvard Law School, LMS 1128, fol. 32v. See also Nichols, III, pp. 608 and 599; and Fowke to Chetwynd, 5 December 1642, quoted in S. A. H. Burne, 'Chetwynd Papers', *Collections for a History of Staffordshire* (1941), p. 94.

10 DLs to Shirley, 27 October 1627, SP 16/83/29; Shirley to DLs, 27 October 1627, Main Papers, 7 May 1628, House of Lords RO; and DLs to PC, 30 October 1627, SP 16/83/29/II.

11 H to PC, 6 November 1627, SP 16/84/27; and PC to H, 27 December 1627, *APC* 43/201.

12 PC warrants, 8 and 28 November and 21 December 1627; and PC to Huntingdon, 27 December 1627, *APC* 43/134, 161, 197 and 201; and Shirley to PC, [November 1627], 'Speaches', HA Legal 2/11.

13 Grant to Shirley, November 1627, Signet Office Docquet Books, PRO SO3/9, unfoliated; 8 January and 19 February 1628, PRO C231/4, fols. 238–9; and Savile's testimony, 'Speeches against me', HA Legal 2/11. See also 3 Charles I, C66/2449, reverse of membrane 36 and 29; and 4 Charles I, PRO C66/2495, reverse of membrane 15.

14 Savile's testimony, 'Speeches', HA Legal 2/11; and Huntingdon to Levinge, 7 February 1628, HA Corr. 13/8537.

15 Dixie to H, 2 March 1628, HA Corr. 13/2295; and Gerard's Testimony, 'Speeches', HA Legal 2/11. See also Ashebie to H, 20 February 1628, HA 13/251.

16 Testimony of Skarrit and Savile, 'Speeches', HA Legal 2/11; 'The Causes', H v. Shirley, House of Lords RO, Main Papers, 7 May 1628; and Dixie to H, 2 March 1628, HA Corr. 13/2295.

17 C. Russell, *Parliaments and English Politics* (Oxford, 1979), pp. 323–40.

18 14 May, 6 June, and 19 May *PP 1628*, V, pp. 429, 589 and 469; and Mead to Stuteville, 31 and 3 May 1628, BL Harl. 390, fols. 406 and 398.

19 Gerard's testimony, H *v.* Shirley, House of Lords RO, Main Papers, 7 May 1628.

20 23 April, *PP 1628*, III, pp. 63–4 and n. 23; 'The Names of ... Recusants', *HMC Portland*, I, p. 1; and 'The humble petition of Henry Earle of Huntingdon', House of Lords RO,

Main Papers, 6 May 1628.

21 7, 8 and 10 May, *PP 1628*, pp. 389–1, 394–6 and 406. See also Shirley's summons, and the warrant for both sides to summon witnesses, House of Lords RO, Main Papers, 7 and 10 May 1628.

22 Anon. to Mead, 3 May 1628, BL Harleian MS 390, fol. 398. See also J. S. Hart, *Justice upon Petition* (London, 1991).

23 'The Causes betweene ... Huntingdon and Sir Henry Shirley', 7 June 1628, House of Lords RO, Main Papers, 7 May 1628; and 8, 10 and 16 May, *PP 1628*, pp. 394, 405 and 445.

24 24 May, *PP 1628*, pp. 520–8.

25 24 May, *PP 1628*, V, pp. 520–6.

26 26 May, *PP 1628*, V, pp. 531, 533 and 535; the examination of Thomas Gerard, House of Lords RO, Main Papers, 7 May 1628; and Sibille v. Oxford, December 1384, HAP 1/24. See also *Select Cases on Defamation to 1600*, ed. by R. H. Helmholz (London, 1985), pp. lxxii–lxxiii; and Elizabeth Foster, *The House of Lords, 1603–1649* (Chapel Hill, 1983), p. 140.

27 26 May, *PP 1628*, V, p. 535. See also H's actions in the Durrand case, 28 May, *ibid.*, V, p. 548.

28 30 May, *PP 1628*, V, pp. 566–7.

29 4 and 6 June, *PP 1628*, V, pp. 583–4, 590–2.

30 7 June, *PP 1628*, V, pp. 595–600.

31 The Lords' order, House of Lords RO, Main Papers, 10 June 1628; and 11 June, *PP 1628*, V, p. 620; and 8–10 June 1628, 'Mr. Robies Accompts', HAF 8/36.

32 1632 Pedigree Roll, Ferrers MSS, Leics. RO, 26D53/2681; and Clare to Vere, 2 July 1628, *Holles Letters*, III, pp. 383–4.

33 Shirley *v.* Chetwynd, Michaelmas 1629, 'Reports in the Star Chamber during the Reign of King Charles I', Harvard Law School, LMS 1128, No. 116, 124–6, fols. 32v, 35v–6v. See also pp. 164–6 above.

34 'The names', 30 September 1630, Bodleian Library, Carte 78, fols. 94–8; and 'Book of Compositions', 1630–32, PRO E407/35, fol. 107.

35 Book of Baronets, HEH, HM 3134, fol. 1; Judge Hutton's certificate, December 1632, HA Legal 5/7; and Coventry to H, 28 December 1632, HA Corr. 14/1677.

36 Thomas Cololeimon Philopatron [Sir Thomas Shirley], *The Genealogicke Historie of the House of Shirleys*, BL Harleian MS 4928, fol. 110v.

37 Sir Henry Shirley's Will, 5 September 1629, Ferrers MSS, Leics. RO, 26D53/1961; and Essex's memorandum, [1633–34], *Calendar of the Clarendon State Papers*, ed. by O. Ogle *et al.*, (Oxford, 1872), I, p. 81.

38 Inquisition post mortem, 18 April 1633; and royal grant of wardship, 9 November 1633, Ferrers MSS, Leics. RO, 26D53/2042 and /2605; and Snow, *Essex the Rebel*, pp. 189–90, 311–12 and 491.

39 Nichols, III, pp. 712–14; and *Complete Peerage* under 'Huntingdon' and 'Ferrers'.

40 H to Lightfoot, 29 April 1636, HA Corr. 15/5542.

Analysis

———————◆———————

The functional breakdown

A lthough Sir Henry spent less than two years on the centre stage, his brief
performance remains one of the most remarkable ones of the early
seventeenth century. Scholars, to be sure, have not been completely oblivious
to its importance. Lawrence Stone's work on the aristocracy as well as Felicity
Heal and Clive Holmes's study of the gentry have noted Sir Henry's comment
about hawking and his unflattering evaluation of the peerage. Heal and
Holmes went even further, citing one of Sir Henry's mammoth pedigree rolls
and highlighting his family box in Breedon church, which flaunts the
Devereux arms.[1] Aside from passing references, however, the profession has
passed over Sir Henry almost completely. If nothing else, the present study
hopes to end this lamentable state of collective amnesia. At the most basic
level, scholars struggling to comprehend a society otherwise noticeable for
decorous restraint can only welcome details of a gentleman whose political
stock-and-trade was imprudence and effrontery on a colossal scale. Nevertheless without downgrading the inherent attractions of Sir Henry's audacity, the
Huntingdon–Shirley row merits careful attention, sprawling as it does over
the intersection of several major historiographical issues.

The Leicestershire material, first of all, forces us to expand our notions of
how contemporaries conducted disputes. The bitter quarrels which often
broke out among provincial elites have long attracted scholarly attention. Yet
while this extensive body of work has made some of the Huntingdon–Shirley
row somewhat predictable, it does nothing to prepare us for other aspects of it.
Frequently these furores centred on a contested election as they did in Somerset in 1614, when Phelips first crossed Poulett, and as they did in Yorkshire
during the 1620s when Savile repeatedly battled Wentworth.[2] The Leicestershire fracas ran true to form, with Sir Henry challenging the Hastingses' grip
on the county seats. Likewise recent work on the importance of honour and
reputation in the local community has reminded us that 'men and women at

The search for vindication

all levels of society showed extreme sensitivity over slights against their good name'. Such touchiness, Anthony Fletcher maintained, was only natural when a gentleman's 'standing among the people could sink if gossip about his conduct, whether malicious or well founded, was allowed to spread un-checked'.[3] Shirley's weapon of choice therefore was a battery of 'aspersions and indignities' all directed against the earl's good name, and Huntingdon's emotional response to the assault stands as eloquent testimony to Sir Henry's skill with the instrument.

The variations on well established themes are in fact so predictable that the entire Huntingdon–Shirley controversy may appear thoroughly routine, but this early judgement is quickly overturned once the dispute veers off in unusual directions. In struggles between local gentlemen, less was often more. Indeed, gentlemen of roughly equal rank often took offence and con-ducted quarrels without ever openly trading sharp words; the real slights were frequently delivered, not in hysterical exchanges, but simply by standing for election or by quietly arranging an opponent's removal from office. In con-trast, Sir Henry's campaign against Huntingdon was astonishingly verbal. Admittedly he did attempt to outmanoeuvre the earl at Whitehall. Yet along with this customary strategy went a campaign of public vilification almost without equal in either rhetorical vehemence or sheer volume. At the assizes and before Privy Councillors, he implied that Huntingdon had defrauded the ratepayers, and at the hustings, he repeated the charge more bluntly. For months, Hastings loyalists were regularly berated as fools, and one of their number found his personal integrity equated to canine excrement. Such abuse was nothing compared to the earl's treatment. Throughout the shire, in the council chamber, before the Palace of Westminster, and in all points between, Shirley traduced the Lord Lieutenant. Given the importance of maintaining an unblemished reputation, Huntingdon was not over-reacting when he insisted that 'it is a great affliction to me' to see 'my integritie long time since ques-tioned by a publique Complaint'. The affliction moreover was far from psycho-logical; as he protested to the councillors, 'I languish in my esteeme' with 'the vulgar sort'.[4] This is not to minimise the vehemence with which other, equally bitter quarrels were conducted. It is simply to suggest that, when set against Shirley's almost compulsive ritual defilement of Huntingdon, these other controversies appear, publicly at least, more like squabbles between petulant Cub Scouts.

The very violence of the quarrel reveals another unsettling aspect; Shirley was assailing a peer of the realm whose lineage contained a plausible claim to the throne. Meanwhile, throughout Sir Henry's extended public battering of the earl's reputation, the central government, which was normally quick to resolve disputes, remained wilfully ignorant. After nearly a year of the Privy Council's studied indifference, the earl protested that 'hope deferred is a fainting of the flesh and dries up the marrow'. It is worth recalling precisely how faint and dry Huntingdon had become before the matter was finally resolved. Recently Richard Cust has stressed 'the vital role of court contacts when it came to the point of appealing to the centre for support or arbitration', and here we can see the vital role of Shirley's court contacts, which rendered Whitehall nearly impervious to Huntingdon's repeated pleas. That Bucking-ham should have supported Shirley's antics is not out of character. Charles, however, is another matter; it is hard to absorb that a prince, whom a recent scholar has described as 'obsessed with order and morality ... [and] with almost a sense of mission and energy to put his principles into practice', rewarded a man who proclaimed, 'I care not a fart for any lord in England.' The best explanation is to ascribe it more to the times than to unsuspected quirks in Charles's personality. The king, as some have suggested, may have enjoyed a little rude humour.[5] Nevertheless what is certain to have vastly increased the royal delight with Shirley's boldness was the crisis atmosphere which hung about Whitehall between the Parliaments of 1626 and 1628. In short, what would likely have found little favour in less stressful periods was welcome in 1627, especially when directed at a local governor who firmly declined to support the forced loan.

Along with exposing the extraordinary strains of 1626–28, this controversy presents telling evidence of the regime's 'functional breakdown'. Assess-ments of the government's attempt to cut an impressive figure in the Thirty Years War have been unflattering. Since the Crown was asking 'too much at once', Boynton concluded his study of the 'perfect militia' by noting, 'its collapse was predictable'. The evidence from Sussex led Fletcher to the same conclusion: the entire scheme was an 'impracticable programme'. Barnes concurred; too many awkward factors ensured 'that the "perfect militia" would never exist, save in the wishful thinking of the King and his Councilors'. Thus, in a celebrated line, the point of Barnes's study was not to explicate 'why the men of Somerset would not fight to the death for the King in 1640' but rather 'why, even if they had the will to fight, they could not have fought effectively'.[6] The deficiencies of the militia have subsequently been seen as a telling symp-tom of a larger 'functional breakdown'. Since 'an effective war effort was incompatible with the self-governing counties which were the ideal of Stuart England', it followed in Russell's judgement that early seventeenth-century England was 'a country which could not fight'. Confident that the limited financial resources of the monarchy made generous parliamentary funding indispensable, 'localist' Parliament men and their provincial constituents were able to shirk their responsibilities when confronted with the enormous cost of a creditable campaign. In short, as Roger Lockyer has argued, 'it was the will [to fight] that was lacking, and not, in the last resort, the wealth'.[7] These arguments both about the imperfections of the 'perfect militia' and about the 'functional breakdown' are powerful ones; they are also ones which sit uneasily with the details of the Huntingdon–Shirley furore.

First of all, if the ratepayers of Leicestershire attempted to shirk their obligations, they failed miserably. Out of a population of less than 13,000 able-bodied men between sixteen and sixty, 700, or roughly 6 per cent, marched off to war, and some made the ultimate sacrifice, as illustrated by Branston's payment to a woman who 'had her husband slaine in the Ile de Ree'.[8] Admittedly the task of levying troops became increasingly awkward, but the regime remained able to produce a flow of conscripts at will. In addition to the 700 men who marched off to war, another 1,100 militiamen remained behind; hence some 14 per cent of the 13,000 men were under arms. These trained bands, as we have seen, were neither shabbily armed nor casually trained. While it is uncertain whether they would have eagerly died for their king and his Lord Lieutenant, they would likely have given a good account of themselves if matters had ever come to the push of a pike.

The shire's co-operation with the war effort was equally impressive in terms of money. To appreciate this fact, it is necessary only to glance at two charts. Previous studies have focused on parliamentary subsidies and major extraparliamentary levies like the forced loan, and the compilation of the county's contribution in these categories (Fig. 1) apparently depicts the triumph of the localist malingerers. Yet if we include the other benevolences and loans, coat and conduct money, and militia rates in addition to the steady purveyance payments, the picture of the county's financial sacrifice (Fig. 2) changes dramatically. In 1620–21, the shire contributed £3,000 directly to the war effort, and the continental conflict roused the militia from its slumbers and extracted another £1,500 in the five years after 1618. These impressive levels were soon surpassed later in the decade, when the amounts raised are impossible to dismiss as notional. Between 1624 and 1628, the ratepayers produced almost £19,000, 74 per cent of which went directly to the war effort. The totals, furthermore, include neither the 'local' costs of militia assessments nor the expense of presenting 'private men'. The contribution of the equivalent of some nineteen parliamentary subsidies makes it difficult to see how tightfisted country gentlemen managed to sabotage the war effort.

If England's inability to get anywhere in the continental war cannot neatly be ascribed to mean-spirited 'localists', who then was responsible? Here the Shirley case speaks volumes. By all rights, if Buckingham was serious about the war, then he should have done everything in his power to support a local governor whose lineage, education and religion led him to welcome a Spanish war. Huntingdon's passion for his militia regiment admittedly verged on monomania, but Buckingham could only have hoped that his neurosis might infect other Lords Lieutenant. Nevertheless the duke sought to topple him. Although Huntingdon merited this disgrace for his refusal over the forced

Figure 1   **Parliamentary subsidies and the forced loan, 1614–29**

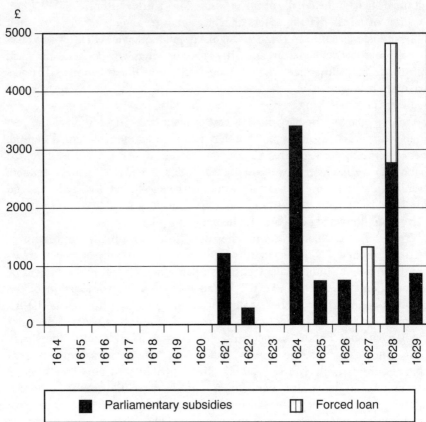

Sources: (the 1621 subsidies) PRO E401/1906 and 1907; (the 1624 subsidies) the discussion of estimating this yield, above p. 38; (the 1625 subsidies) PRO E401/2441 and 2442; (the 1628 subsidies) PRO E401/2445–6; and (the force loan) PRO E401/ 2322, 2323, 2443 and E403/2804.

loan, there was more to this episode than crude power politics. By 1626, most devotees of the Protestant cause had come to believe that even modest success would inevitably elude the realm as long as Buckingham directed the war, and so the Parliament men in 1626 adamantly refused to waste any more public money until something was done about the duke. While some had by then thoroughly demonised the favourite, others, more realistically, simply wanted to check his power. Hence plans early in 1626 called for turning the war over to a joint-stock company, which would have limited the power, if not the

Figure 2   **Collections from Leicestershire, 1614–29**

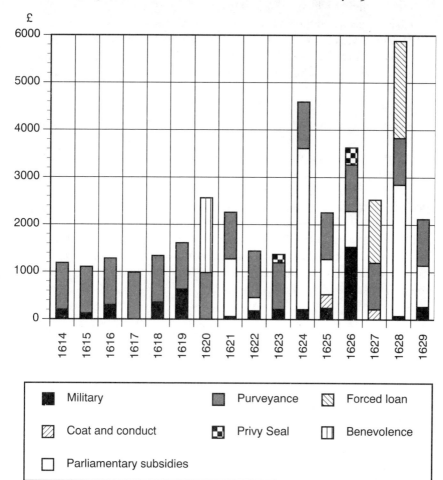

£

Military

Coat and conduct

Parliamentary subsidies

Purveyance

Privy Seal

Forced loan

Benevolence

Sources: (the 1621 subsidies) PRO E401/1906 and 1907; (the 1624 subsidies) the discussion of estimating this yield, above p. 38; (the 1625 subsidies) PRO E401/2441 and 2442; (the 1628 subsidies) PRO E401/2445–6; (the forced loan) PRO E401/2322, 2323, 2443 and E403/2804; (the Benevolence) *LRLB*, fols. 60 and 60v-61; (coat and conduct) *LRLB*, fols. 112v-3; and SP 16/70/70, fols. 115–115v; (Privy Seals) PRO E401/2323 and 2435; and E405/226; (the military charges) *LRLB*, 34v-5, 42v, 45, 54, 56v, 65v, 69; SP 16/70/70, fols. 110–110v, 112–3v and 115; and Leics. RO, BR III/2/79, fol. 192; and (purveyance), see the discussion above, pp. 16–17.

profits, of the Lord Admiral. Charles, however, rejected any compromise and instead pushed the loan project. Meanwhile, as Protestant interventionists increasingly detached themselves from the government in the course of 1626, Catholics like Colchester, Savage and Maynard took their place at Whitehall.[9] This background circumscribed Huntingdon's position over the loan and the timing of Shirley's public attacks within the fundamental realignment of 1626–28.

In that case, what was tactically expedient was also strategically insane, and the absurdity of the situation cannot better be captured than in Buckingham's decision to continue the Anglo-Spanish war by replacing zealous Protestant interventionists like Huntingdon with Hispanophile recusants of Shirley's ilk. In short, it is vital to remember that the crucial moment in the history of the war effort came in the spring of 1626 when Charles I refused to weaken his total commitment to the duke. His decision eloquently testifies to his devotion to his friend. It also reveals the reason for the chaos that reigned in England and Leicestershire for the next few years. Notwithstanding pleas from many in and out of Parliament, Charles I willingly confused Buckingham with the war effort. If there was a 'functional breakdown', the structural problem was not so much in the state as in Charles's mind.[10]

NOTES

1 Stone, *Crisis of the Aristocracy*, pp. 265 and 748; and Clive Holmes and Felicity Heal, *The Gentry of England and Wales, 1500–1700* (London, 1994), pp. 36, 291, 338–9.

2 Mark Kishlansky, *Parliamentary Selection* (Cambridge, 1986), pp. 85–101; and Richard Cust, 'Politics and the Electorate in the 1620s', *Conflict in Early Stuart England*, ed. by Cust and Hughes (London, 1989), pp. 134–67; and 'Wentworth's "change of sides" in the 1620s', *The Political World of Thomas Wentworth, Earl of Strafford, 1621–1641*, ed. by J. Merritt (Cambridge, 1996), pp. 63–80.

3 Fletcher, 'Honour, Reputation and Local Officeholding', p. 92. See also Cust, 'Honour and Politics in Early Stuart England'.

4 H to PC, 28 May 1627, *LRLB*, fols. 208–8v; and same to same, 6 November 1627, HA 5518.

5 H to PC, 6 November 1626, HA 12/5518; Cust, 'Honour, Rhetoric and Political Culture', p. 99; and Kevin Sharpe, *The Personal Rule of Charles I* (New Haven, 1992), p. 197. On Charles's taste, see Sharpe, *Criticism and Compliment* (Cambridge, 1987), pp. 44–8.

6 Boynton, *Elizabethan Militia*, pp. 269–70; Fletcher, *Sussex*, p. 200; and Barnes, *Somerset*, pp. 244–5.

7 Russell, *Parliaments*, pp. 81 and 83; and Lockyer, *Buckingham*, p. 472. See also C. Russell, 'The Poverty of the Crown', *The Causes of the Civil War*, pp. 161–84.

8 Leics. RO, DE 720/30, fol. 26v.

9 'Project for defence of the kingdome', [1626], HEH, EL 7004; and Cust, *The Forced Loan*, pp. 200–7 and 248.

10 For a fuller development of this, see Cogswell, 'A Low Road to Extinction? Supply and
    Redress of Grievances in the Parliaments of the 1620s', *HJ* XXXIII (1990), pp. 283–
    303.

Part IV

'A serpent and scorpions'

Huntingdon
and
Sir William Fawnt
1629–38

As all governments have their beginning from time, so too time
puts an end to them. The government, continuing so long, it had
contracted rust. The people groaned under great oppression, both
as men and christians. The Council Table bit like a serpent: the Star
Chamber like scorpions. Two or three gentlemen could not stir out,
for fear of being committed for a riot.

[Sir Arthur Hesilrige, speaking in the House of Commons,
7 February 1659]

Hesilrige's impressive indictment of the Personal Rule contains more than a touch of self-justification. By 1659, he had earned a reputation as a man who would do anything in order 'never to be troubled with a king or a bishop'. His speech certainly aimed at this goal, labouring to stiffen the devotion of his colleagues to the 'Good Old Cause'. For that purpose, what better method than trotting out the old Stuart bogeymen? Doubts about Sir Arthur's credibility have only deepened with the most recent detailed investigation of the 1630s. Exhaustive research has prompted one scholar to insist that Charles I, far from being a tyrant, 'was only a conservative: he was also what some in modern politics might refer to as a "wet", committed to the traditions and norms of English government and suspicious of radical change'. Nor have the financial schemes of the Personal Rule, so beloved in earlier accounts, proven on closer examination to have been particularly odious. Indeed, 'for all the novelty of the Caroline levies and county discontent, the financial expedients of the personal rule cannot be held to have contributed greatly to the failure to arrive at a peaceful settlement in 1642'. Likewise Star Chamber, hitherto the engine of Caroline repression, is pronounced a popular court whose judges were devoted to the rule of law. In this new prescription, the most astonishing aspect of Star Chamber is why anyone would have ever abolished it. These conclusions only confirm the validity of Clarendon's recollection of the period as a halcyon world disturbed only by the 'froward and peevish humours' of a few malignants, of whom Hesilrige was a charter member.[1]

And yet Sir Arthur arguably was not demonising the royal administration. By 1640, Hesilrige and his friends in Leicestershire had ample warrant for fearing the sting of Whitehall's scorpions and serpents. In light of the recent glowing assessments of the Personal Rule, details of their sombre and at times chilling experience in the 1630s are timely as well as illuminating.

NOTE

1 Sharpe, *The Personal Rule of Charles I*, pp. 931 and 929; and 'The Personal Rule of Charles I', *Before the Civil War*, ed. by H. Tomlinson (London, 1983), pp. 53–78; and the Earl of Clarendon, *The History of the Rebellion* (Oxford, 1843), p. 880.

Chapter 9

Repeat performance

In the spring of 1631, the Privy Council ordered a muster, a command which would ordinarily have produced at Donnington Park a response that was almost Pavlovian. In 1631, however, Huntingdon did nothing. An outbreak of the plague initially explains such uncharacteristic inactivity until it is recalled that never before had the plague kept the earl from exercising his favourite administrative plaything. Furthermore, in 1630, 1633 and 1634, when there was no epidemic, similar orders reached Donnington Park, and in none of them did the Leicestershire regiment stir. Such peculiar inaction certainly owed nothing to a sudden aversion to the military; in 1634, Huntingdon lovingly described to his son the various uniforms of a visiting Swedish military delegation.[2] Instead the answer can be found in the fall-out from his extended contest with Sir Henry Shirley.

Granted, against a wealthier antagonist openly backed by the royal favourite the earl had not only held onto his lieutenancy when others were losing theirs, but he eventually humiliated his rival. Nevertheless the price of success was painfully high, for victory had come only at the price of transforming a model local governor into an administrative pariah, barely tolerated by Whitehall. The restoration of the government's favour would be labourious and sometimes base, but a vulnerable Lord Lieutenant had no other option. And until he achieved this feat, the militia regiment required the most delicate handling.

A NEW WORLD

Early in 1629 a local minister pressed home the importance of England's role in the continental war. Solidarity with European brethren came first and foremost: 'Say not thou art a member of the Church of England, thou are not a member of the Church of France, or of Germany, or of Bohemia: for all the

Churches of the world that professe the same faith and religion, are but one body.' Consequently his audience should have readily rallied to the relief of the godly abroad. 'How canst thou be a member of the same body with them,' he inquired, 'if thou have no fellow-feeling of their miseries?' Unfortunately this was not an idle question. 'We heare and talke of the miseries and troubles of the Churches,' the irate minister noted,

> as if a matter that concerneth not us at all. We read the Currantoes, and listen after this as we do after other newes, but are no more affected with it, then Marchants use to be when they heare of the casting away of a ship, that themselves have to share in.

'Alas how few are there of us,' he noted, '... that are at all affected with this matter.' Lamentations were in order, for 'marke how wee provoke God against us by our profane stupidity'. But rather than labour a point that the audience had by 1629 heard for over a decade, he simply noted that 'our general senselesnesse in such times as these are, is a most dangerous signe of some fearefull ruine determined against us'.[3]

This frank sermon is all the more remarkable because it was not preached to a sophisticated metropolitan congregation; rather Arthur Hildersham delivered it at St Helen's in Ashby de la Zouch, a parish church full of Huntingdon's retainers. Such a blistering performance was certainly in order, for defeatism had managed to infect even the Lord Lieutenant himself. In later years, the earl remained concerned about the continental brethren, carefully following the latest developments in the Thirty Years War; the worst news that Lord Hastings offered his father at the end of the 1629 session was that Charles could not 'sende any ade or reliefe to the protestants in France'. Yet there was little that the earl himself could do, especially after the Shirley affair. The triumphant conclusion of this furore owed much more to the sympathy of his fellow peers than to any firm support at the Council table, and after the turbulent 1629 Parliament, his aristocratic sympathisers had little hope of gathering together in the near future.

His cousin, the Earl of Manchester, illuminated the depths that Huntingdon had reached in his political free fall after 1627. The Lord President acknowledged Huntingdon's struggles with 'your Lordships kinsman and myne', Sir Henry Hastings of Braunston, with whom 'I know your Lordship is not well pleased'. Nevertheless Hastings's extensive purchases in the disafforestation had enhanced his stock at Whitehall, for having 'paid well for that he hadd', naturally 'he was thought to do good service to the king'. Wisdom therefore suggested a reduction in Hastings's assessment in the horse troop, lest he default; if the matter ever came up before the councillors, Manchester warned that, given Huntingdon's recent eclipse, Sir Henry 'would perhaps be excused'. So dramatically had Shirley altered the situation that the government preferred a Catholic militia defaulter to a diligent Lord Lieutenant. Far from being a passing fluke, Sir Henry's elevation was a political fact of life for the next few years, during which Huntingdon had to get used to his awkward cousin joining him on important royal commissions.[4]

Painful though this realisation clearly was, Earl Henry could only carry on and hope for the best. The first task at hand was to supervise the militia regiment as it stood down. At first, neither the fall of La Rochelle in 1628 nor the Anglo-French peace treaty of 1629 halted the regiment's cycle of training and musters. While precise figures have not survived, Leicester's payments for officers' fees suggest that the militia assessments in 1628-29 collected roughly £400. Meanwhile Huntingdon remained assiduous with the militia-men, as the Corporation of Leicester could have testified; during these two years they had to replace nineteen caps, eleven swords, twenty-five scabbards, two bandoliers and a pike as well as pay for extensive repairs to twenty-one swords and four pikes. Thus, although the war was winding down, the Corpor-ation still paid £39 10s. in 'local' expenses in addition to its £27 bill for officers' fees. Likewise Branston's one soldier cost the village £1 3s. in officers' fees and another £1 9s. in 'local' expenses.[5] By 1630, however, all activity suddenly ceased as Huntingdon began to relax his grip on the county.

Signs of the new peace were visible everywhere. Take for instance the pioneer company's equipment, which had caused so much fuss. Three years after Huntingdon's controversial 1626 assessment, Rudinge was still attempt-ing to collect the shortfall. The councillors, while endorsing the effort, had no illusions about the likely result; hence they authorised him to make up the deficit by auctioning off 'so many of the utensils ... at the higheest rates that can be gotten'. Those remaining after this sale were quietly loaned out to the county's deserving poor. Likewise in the summer of 1629, Rutland finally saw the back of Sergeant Bowden. The Deputy Lieutenants' initial gambit of letting arrearages mount simply earned them a reminder of their obligation. Unfortunately for the long-suffering sergeant, when the Deputies finally is-sued the necessary warrants, they discovered that the money came 'in so slowly as wee are not able by farre to answere his expectation'. The matter ended with Bowden receiving a lump sum of £8 in exchange for his promise 'noe more to troble the Cuntryes'.[6] In the new atmosphere, Leicester's trained band could once again concentrate on its customary duty of leading proces-sions. Richard Braithwaite discovered the new lax attitude when Robert Oliver, a Leicester militiaman, escorted him to the gallows. After a promise to bring Braithwaite 'to the ground like a man' had extracted the condemned man's remaining cash, Oliver 'gave his halbert to another man and said he would goe to make water'. Regrettably Braithwaite's vigourous protests over this breach of contract gained him only a short reprieve, but before he stepped off, he at least had the satisfaction of seeing one of Huntingdon's trained men arrested. Oliver was not alone in his casual attitude. Even an old warhorse like

Huntingdon relaxed, as John Jackson discovered in 1631, when he appeared before the Privy Council for defaulting. Much to everyone's surprise, neither Huntingdon nor any of his Deputies appeared to press the case, leaving the Council to dismiss the jubilant Mr Jackson.[7]

While the end of the war brought on a host of transformations within the county, it did not change one crucial matter – turmoil on the bench simply continued to be an administrative fact of life. Just as contemporaries soon learned that Buckingham was not responsible for all of the kingdom's difficulties, so too Huntingdon quickly appreciated that Shirley's humiliation and death did not end his problems.

Ominous strains, for example, began to appear in Huntingdon's entente with Lord Grey, who was becoming restive with his elevation as the Earl of Stamford in 1628. Although Huntingdon's trademark was the promotion of humble protégés, Stamford in 1631 complained about having to sit on the bench with the earl's latest find, Sir Thomas Gerard. Faithful service to the Hastingses had earned Gerard a knighthood in 1628 and a place on the bench two years later. Then things went sour. Gerard's refusal to sell Stamford some land irritated the earl, as did Sir Thomas's willingness to report him to the Council for depopulation. Finally a land deal between Huntingdon and Stamford turned so unpleasant that for a time the earl and countess dared not face Stamford, and the person whom everyone accused of queering the deal was Sir Thomas. Not surprisingly, Stamford objected to Gerard's presence on the bench so strenuously that the Lord Keeper removed him from the Commission of the Peace. The furore was soon smoothed over; a petition reciting Gerard's lengthy services to the state eventually secured his restoration, and Stamford soon was the earl's 'very lovinge frend' and a house guest at Donnington Park once again.[8] Nonetheless the episode gave fair warning of stormy weather ahead.

More immediate problems for the Lord Lieutenant came from the gentleman whom even Sir Henry Shirley found 'a silly ... fellowe'. Sir Arthur Hesilrige proved able to nurse a grudge so effectively that the earl may well have repented ever having dismissed his father from the lieutenancy and Sir Arthur himself from the horse troop. In the final years of Sir Thomas's life, Arthur had had to witness his father's eclipse from once respected local governor to disgraced outcast. Quite certain of himself early in 1625, the Deputy Lieutenant had pressed the Leicester Corporation to enroll Arthur 'in the best Schoole in Cristendome', the House of Commons. His request, which testifies to considerable confidence in his local standing, also underscores why his sudden translation a few months later to the status of 'livinge though despised' was so devastating. Admittedly Huntingdon's selection of Bertine Hesilrige to lead a foot company softened the blow. Nevertheless the shame soon drove the former Deputy Lieutenant out of Noseley Hall and into Northamptonshire.[9]

In his bitterness, Sir Thomas became a regular entry on any list of trouble-makers. Later in 1625 he unilaterally withdrew from participation in the horse troop and eventually found himself presented as a defaulter. Doubtless the irony of this reversal was lost on a man who had himself presented others only a few years earlier. Likewise, he appears among those who initially refused the forced loan. Having established his *bona fides* as a tart critic of Huntingdon's administration, Hesilrige was a natural choice when the councillors wanted to go around the Lord Lieutenant in the 1627 Forest investigation.[10] They knew what they were doing, for the last sighting of Sir Thomas in the official records highlights the metamorphosis of the once smooth Deputy Lieutenant into a difficult, headstrong old man. In 1628, acting on a Council decree, Hunting-don ordered the inclusion of the Catholic minority into the militia bands. But Hesilrige, convinced that the earl had exceeded his authority, refused to co-operate until the councillors issued him a direct order. Only death in 1629 brought Sir Thomas back to Noseley. There, his tomb celebrated the time when he had been 'trusted with the places of greatest honor and power in the county'.[11] It politely passed over the bitterness of his final years.

Arthur had his own grievances. His abrupt ejection from the horse troop can scarcely have pleased him any more than his brother's death in a duel in 1630. Since duelling was illegal, anyone who killed his rival on the field of honour was technically guilty of murder. At the same time, the successful duellist, John Hurst of the Inner Temple, was well connected at court, and no less than the court poet, William Davenant, urged the family to pass over the matter in silence. Exactly what happened is unclear, except that Charles eventually issued a full pardon.[12] Consequently the young baronet began the 1630s resentful of both the state and its local agent and intent on finding occasions for vengeance. Amid these reverses, Sir Thomas retained a seat on the Leicestershire bench, which his heir soon assumed. Indeed, irrespective of the Hesilriges' problems with the Lord Lieutenant, the Lord Keeper could not have easily excluded a wealthy baronet and a staunch Protestant. Thus in 1630, the young Sir Arthur vaulted over all the knights on the bench, save only the more senior baronet, Sir Henry Shirley, and on Shirley's demise in 1633, Hesilrige assumed the position of honour after the peers and judges, an ideal post from which to harass the Lord Lieutenant. While Huntingdon had flirted with the hard left of the Caroline 'opposition', Hesilrige married into it. His first wife was the daughter of Thomas Elmes, a protégé of Richard Knightley and John Pym and a loan refuser. On her early death, Sir Arthur married the sister of Lord Brooke, the head of a circle of 'Puritan Opposition' in the west Midlands. With such relatives, Sir Arthur naturally enough spent the 1630s in a running battle with the Laudian church courts for control of the Noseley chapel.[13] Such kinsmen and such grievances thus made Sir Arthur an awkward colleague for Huntingdon on the bench.

While scholars since Clarendon's day have appreciated the importance of older men like Pym in Hesilrige's intellectual development, they have all overlooked another father figure who, while less celebrated on the national scene, was all too familiar to the earl. In his disgrace, Sir Thomas kept interesting company. His companion in an otherwise small number of militia defaulters was Sir William Fawnt, who shared Hesilrige's objections to assessments in the horse troop. Similarly, when Fawnt in his epistolary 1626 attack on Huntingdon named the other gentlemen 'wronged', Sir Thomas Hesilrige came at the head of his list.[14] Their friendship is not surprising; both men were out of Huntingdon's favour, and Foston and Noseley were only a few miles apart. Almost inevitably, Sir Arthur assumed his father's place in these neighbourly meetings while the Personal Rule ensured that they would have more to discuss than the weather.

Together the two JPs made a formidable combination, who were only waiting for the right issue to challenge the Hastings regime. In 1631, for example, scandal rocked the summer session when it emerged that Joseph Newton, the Clerk of the Peace, and Sir John Skeffington had privately reversed a decision of the entire bench. Although the issue at hand – a licence for a cottage – was comparatively minor, Newton's revelation was not; 'in the face of the countie' he confessed that 'the like had beene done by other Justices'. The man exposing this administrative sleight of hand was Sir Arthur Hesilrige, who doubtless enjoyed publicly embarrassing Huntingdon's cronies.[15] The results of this affair only encouraged Hesilrige and Fawnt to look for other issues on which to strike more directly at Huntingdon.

SHARKING THE COUNTY

Between his precarious standing at Whitehall and the growing boldness of his local critics, the earl had no illusions about the strength of his position. In the circumstances, he could not afford the luxury of another paralysing bout of conscience. Nor could the beleaguered peer appeal to Parliament for redress. In 1634, confident reports of an imminent Parliament brought forth Huntingdon's earnest prayers for a new session, which would lead to 'the reformation of abuses' as well as 'the reducinge of all things that are out of order to a sweet and perfect harmony'.[16] Regrettably the news proved a chimera. With no other recourse to Whitehall, Huntingdon could only execute all orders, no matter how awkward, and gamble that the Caroline regime would place a premium on energetic local governors.

The first task during the Personal Rule was that remarkable example of fiscal feudalism, distraint of knighthood. In the event, this project proceeded smoothly, thanks in large part to the earl himself, to whom 'his Maiestie hath bene pleased to commit ... the charge and care'. To assist him in this troublesome business, Charles also appointed as Collector the earl's protégé, Sir Wolston Dixie. Ever efficient, Huntingdon sought to avoid making 'longe worke of that [which] might in short be dispatched'. The Corporation of Leicester admittedly rejected his idea of a general composition of £300 and ignored his advice that 'second thoughts are the best'; instead its members preferred to make individual payments.[17] In this otherwise wearying task of badgering £10 and £20 out of merchants and small farmers, one thing doubtless delighted Huntingdon; baronets who had not previously been knighted were also obliged to compound. Thus both Huntingdon and the Exchequer derived considerable satisfaction from squeezing £75 and £50 respectively out of Sir Henry Shirley and Sir Arthur Hesilrige. Most of the other work was less exhilirating. The most awkward case concerned William Bent and his fine of £10. After repeatedly avoiding the commissioners, Bent eventually met them, and when chided for refusing 'so smal a summe', he 'did then publickely refuse' and persisted in his obstinacy 'to the ill example and discouragement of many more'.[18] Yet in spite of the Bent case, a steady stream of money flowed into the Exchequer over 1630–32, which amounted to £2,320 13s. 7d. Not only was the percentage collected one of the kingdom's highest, but Leicestershire also boasted an impressive total, its £1,927 raised by composition comparing favourably with wealthier Northamptonshire's £1,538.[19]

While the knighthood project was an administrative triumph for Huntingdon, the militia presented a more intractable problem. With the return of peace in 1630, the Council's interest in a perfect militia became more fitful. Ordinarily even erratic interest would have been enough to set Huntingdon in motion; by 1630, however, he and many other Lords Lieutenant were finding the militia a distinctly awkward question. The root of the problem was the thorough scrutiny which the Parliament men in 1628 had given the lieutenancy. Having highlighted that royal prerogative, rather than statute law, justified the militia levies, the members passed the Petition of Right, whose prohibition of non-parliamentary taxation could well apply to all prerogative taxation. Since some merchants employed it in their campaign against tonnage and poundage, Lords Lieutenant understandably wondered if the chaos, then swirling around the Custom House, might well descend on their first order for a muster and an assessment. The militia's dubious legal basis gave new urgency to old questions about the necessity of a professionally trained band in peacetime. By 1630 Charles I had made his peace with the Catholic powers, and in spite of periodic reports of imminent English intervention, Charles's ability to sit still during 1630–32, while Gustavus Adolphus rolled back Habsburg power and even recovered Heidelberg, suggested that any involvement was an increasingly remote prospect. England's neutrality in turn made some contemporaries restive over militia rates. This logic guided the Hertfordshire grand jury in 1629 when it petitioned Charles to dispense during peacetime with a professional cadre of officers headed by a Muster Master and underwritten by local rates.[20]

What transformed this uneasiness into active protest was a careful consideration of what the ratepayers received for their money. The depths to which the militia units so quickly sank in the early 1630s sickened Gervase Markham, whose drill manuals had guided a generation of officers. Indeed, he soon found it necessary to remind his readers that training

> is not the calling together of Bands, one daye in a Yeare, and to spend half that daye, in argueing of grievances, and the other halfe in callinge mens Names and noting Downe of Defects, in wishing reformation, and threatening punishment, and then to let all things slepe, till that time 12 monthes; at which time, all things are worse then before.

At the same time, the increasingly casual musters did nothing to a Muster Master's financial demands: 'for this ease, and nothing Doeing', he facetiously asked, 'will he abate the Countrye, a penny of his fee?' Instead his greed will 'make him soe audatious, that he will not sticke to invent newe exactions'. This paradox explained how even the most enthusiastic could come to believe that military service 'will prove such an Intollerable Loade, that it will make his heart grieve, and his tongue cannot chose but Murmure'.[21]

These factors all combined to produce an extraordinary situation in the early 1630s. In Dorset, the local gentlemen unilaterally refused to pay their Muster Master, 'alledging that there is no lawe for such taxation'. By 1631, so many other counties had followed suit that the Council had to remind all shires of the necessity of employing one. Consequently the ratepayers of Cumberland, Westmorland and Northumberland, who had managed all throughout the 1620s without a professional Muster Master, suddenly found themselves lumbered with one.[22] Even counties with a Muster Master could not always persuade everyone to pay their share, and the delinquents ranged from corporations like Oxford and Northampton to a Hertfordshire militia captain and a Northamptonshire constable. Between the legal questions surrounding the militia rates and 'sundry refractorie persons' eager to challenge their authority, many Lords Lieutenant, the Council conceded, 'make difficulty (or at least make dainty) ... in setting their hands to the said assessment'. In their desperation, the Deputy Lieutenants of Herefordshire developed an alternative, and non-coercive, method of funding the militia; although the Council finally quashed the idea, their alternative illustrates the scale and complexity of the issue.[23]

A much more effective response was simply to avoid the issue altogether by not summoning the militiamen. The attractiveness of this reaction can be seen in a stinging rebuke which the Privy Council in 1634 sent to all Lieutenants who had failed to report any military activity in the preceding three years;

the letter went out to twenty men controlling twenty-two shires. Striking though this figure is, it pales before the fact that the list included councillors like the Earls of Dorset, Northampton and Salisbury, to say nothing of the Lord Treasurer, the Lord Marshal, the Master of the Horse and the Lord President of the Council of Wales. Baffled about how to proceed, these councillors effectively numbered themselves among the grossly negligent.[24]

Huntingdon was not on this list. Nevertheless his handling of the Leicestershire regiment was uncharacteristically cautious. Orders for a muster in 1630 and 1631 he let pass in silence, but rather than allow his authority to levy assessments dwindle through inaction, the earl ordered the constables to gather 6s. for every trained man, 3s. each for 1630 and 1631. This request for £180 in all, a relatively modest sum by the standards of the preceding decade, almost certainly fell short of the mark, Mr Jackson having discovered that defaulters had little to fear. Entire villages managed to evade this levy, an omission which in previous years would have brought down the Lord Lieutenant's wrath.[25]

Given the comparative ease of this levy, Huntingdon felt confident enough in the following year to push the question further, summoning the militia and requesting 6s. per trained man. For the most part, the results were hearteningly predictable repetitions of the 1620s. Leicester's band duly paid its share of some £13; Mr Newton, Branston's sole soldier, arrived with his 6s., while Waltham's three men managed to persuade Mr Rudinge to accept 1s. less than the village's share by belatedly paying their previous assessment. The local costs, as always, ran high. Thanks to its insistence on attending musters only in Leicester, the Corporation got off lightly with only an additional £8 12s. 2d. Expenditure rose, however, for more distant villages. Between repairs on his equipment and travelling expenses, Mr Newton presented Branston with receipts totalling 12s. 10d., twice the village's payment in officers' fees. The Waltham ratepayers had a similar experience with their three men, who required an additional £3 3s. 3d.[26] The situation was less happy in the horse troop where defaulting continued to be a common practice, and at the centre of the controversy in 1632 were Fawnt and his young protégé, Hesilrige. By then, Sir Arthur's arrearages totalled £4 4s. 10d., while Sir William was burnishing a reputation for having 'been divers tymes found and judged defective sometymes both in horse and furniture'.[27] Behind these two came a disquietingly long list of other defaulters. Since the foot soldiers' obedience represented only a hollow victory if the county elite were able to evade their responsibilities, Huntingdon had no choice except to report the defaulters in the hope that the Council would back him up.

There was every reason to assume that they would. In the late 1620s, urgent administrative chores had distracted the Council from the mundane business of bullying militia defaulters. The return of peace, however, made defaulting a more dubious business; the Council registers for the early 1630s are littered with sombre examples, all illustrating the councillors' eagerness to resolve any doubts about a Lord Lieutenant's authority. Consequently the corporations of Northampton and Oxford soon fell into line, as did the Herefordshire Deputies, who abandoned their alternative funding scheme. Likewise the unfortunate Suffolk gentleman who fled involvement in the county horse troop by moving to Ipswich found himself setting a national precedent, requiring support for the horse troop as well as the trained band.[28] This uncompromising stance led some on Huntingdon's list of defaulters to reconsider the wisdom of challenging the Lord Lieutenant. Sir Robert Barnestre quickly cleared his arrears while attributing the problem to his servant's neglect. Others like Robert Howcott and Thomas Gray rode up to Westminster and quickly conformed.[29] Meanwhile, Fawnt and Hesilrige remained unconcerned and made no haste to Whitehall. Their charge that Huntingdon was unnecessarily burdening the county effectively echoed Shirley's accusation, and they cannot have forgotten that in that earlier contest, the Council repeatedly failed to support the Lord Lieutenant. To be sure, Huntingdon's position was not as precarious as it had been in the late 1620s, but precisely how much it had improved remained a moot point. For their part, Sir William and Sir Arthur relied on their own standing as wealthy gentlemen and diligent JPs; and Fawnt's son hailed Secretary Coke as father-in-law. From such distinguished local governors, complaints about county administration, it was hoped, would receive an attentive hearing.

These calculations revealed their shrewdness in the initial hearings on 21 November 1632. Sir Henry Skipwith and Sir John Skeffington were there to argue the Lord Lieutenant's case, and in ordinary circumstances, this information would have earned these 'refractory' men a speedy punishment. Instead, after listening to Fawnt and Hesilrige's story, the Council in an extraordinary move appointed a subcommittee to 'examine particularly what the said Sir Arthur Heselrige and Sir William Faunt have to alleage against the aforesaid leavies'.[30] For Skipwith and Skeffington this outcome must have been depressing in the extreme; for the second time in less than five years, the councillors were plainly willing to believe something was fishy in Leicestershire. Their discomfiture was so obvious that Sir Arthur could not resist taunting them. As they filed out of the room, Hesilrige triumphantly told Skeffington that 'if such gentlemen as you shalbe suffered to sharke the Country of their money, it wilbe a very pretty thing'. In hopes of turning the tables, Sir John immediately informed the councillors of the incident, and in his defense Hesilrige smoothly replied, 'I doe not say so to the Lordes, but onely to you in private'. Yet however he explained it, the young JP had incontrovertibly violated the dignity of the Privy Council. Consequently, Hesilrige found himself in confinement, while Fawnt had to remain in Westminster, awaiting the Council's pleasure.[31]

Jubilation among the Deputy Lieutenants proved short-lived. A week later Hesilrige appeared on his knees to 'humblie crave pardon' of the councillors, who granted it and dismissed him. This resolution, however, left Skeffington 'unsatisfied for his owne particular', and he complained to the earl's old champion, the Earl of Dorset, about 'such unworthy speeches especially to a person of that ranck and qualitie'. He lodged his plea in the right place, for Dorset soon persuaded the councillors to recall Sir Arthur. When the baronet proclaimed 'his sorrowe for having used those wordes' to Skeffington, the council allowed Sir Arthur to return home. Fawnt joined him a few days later after his signature in the Council register guaranteed his agreement 'to pay such summes of Money towards the muster Masters entertainment'.[32]

News of these remarkable scenes left Huntingdon unsettled. However delightful the thought of his enemies on their knees before the Council was, such humiliations still left unanswered questions about Huntingdon's own position. Fawnt alone had solemnly promised to comply with future assessments; what Sir Arthur might do at the next muster was anyone's guess. In the interim, the two had ample opportunity to intervene, for the Council left them on the bench. More importantly, their charges had launched another investigation of the earl's administration. Hesilrige's gloating taunt only complicated the situation further, for it sidetracked any verdict and left Huntingdon uncertain about the Council's attitude. Troubled by the indeterminacy of the affair, he subsequently pressed the councillors for a clearer answer. After thanking them for 'how Nobly your lordships have dealt to vindicate the reputation of Sir John Skeffington' against 'the undeserved reproaches of Sir Arthur Hesilrige', he asked point-blank 'how farre aspersions of that nature throwne upon any of my Agents may be extended to my sealfe'? Since the experience with Shirley led Huntingdon to assume that there would be a formal investigation, he requested 'the obiections that are against me' as well the Council's orders about 'which way to tender my iustification'. Since the councillors could only expect him to be as zealous in the defence of 'my owne honor' as he was 'to obay your Lordships commands', he concluded 'beseeching your Lordships I may knowe your pleasures herein'.[33]

Behind Huntingdon's letter lay the hope that, like Skeffington, he too would receive belated vindication, but the councillors' reply shattered that fond dream. They readily understood his anxieties: 'we perceive your Lordship to be apprehensive that upon Sir Arthur Hesilrigg his late convention before us ... something by him let fall and obiected might reflect upon your Lordship'. His concern pleased the Council, whose members 'cannot but lyke well of your Lordships Care and tendernes to acquit your selfe and to give all satisfaction to this Table'. Yet having clearly ascertained the earl's almost desperate desire for their approval, they withheld it. All they could bring themselves to say was that if Sir Arthur 'had left a doubtfull ympression in us', Huntingdon 'should have understood it from our selves'. At the same time, lest he interpret silence as approbation, they informed him of Hesilrige's allegation that 'the Annual charge leavied for Armes and Musters and Officers in that County is farr greater then in other Counties'. On this they pronounced no verdict, at least not as yet. Nevertheless the councillors did refer it to the earl as 'a particular Worthie Your Lordships Care and enquirie'. Precisely what Huntingdon was to do with this information was unclear until the end of the letter when they expressed their confidence in 'your readines to give all iust ease and releefe to the Country in retrenching and takeing off all unnecessarie leavies and Contributons'.[34]

Far from a ringing endorsement, the Council's response was in truth scarcely an endorsement at all. All it succeeded in doing was confirming the earl's unsettling sense of *déjà vu*. In the 1620s, unwilling to support Huntingdon against Shirley, the Council had left him in the county with his opponent largely unchecked and thoroughly irritated. By January 1633 the earl had unmistakable evidence that the same administrative nightmare was being re-enacted. Try as he might in the preceding years to recover the councillors' favour, the Fawnt–Hesilrige affair of 1632–33 had simply made apparent for all to see how far he yet had to go. Given the distressing results of the 1632 muster, the Council's order for another one in the following year understandably produced no response from Donnington Park. Even when confronted with a similar order in the following year, Huntingdon was still loath to order his militia-men into the field.[35] By then, he had come to appreciate that zealous attention to the militia would not ensure his rehabilitation; indeed, with Fawnt and Hesilrige still in the county, it might well be his doom. Instead by then he belatedly came to accept the advice which friends had been urging on him for years.

NOTES

1 PC to H, 30 June 1630, 30 May 1631, 27 March 1633 and 31 March 1634, HA Corr. 13/4257 and 14/4258; and PRO PC2/42, p. 539, and 2/43, p. 570; and H to FEH, 29 March 1634, HA Corr. 14/5533. On the absence of any militia activity, see Leics. RO, BR III/2/80, fols. 1–62; DE 720/30, fols. 29v–32; and DE 625/60, fols. 73–79.

2 Lectures 112 and 113, 3 and 17 March 1629, Arthur Hildersham, *CLII Lectures upon Psalme LI preached at Ashby-delaZouch in Leicester-Shire* (London, 1635), pp. 562, 565–6 and 568.

3 Hastings to H, [1629], HA Corr. 13/4863; and Manchester to H, 4 September 1629, HA Corr. 13/[illegible]. See also H to Henry Hastings, 29 March and 2 May 1634, HA Corr. 14/5533 and 5534; and Charles I to H and Sir Henry Hastings *et al.*, 26 March 1632, HA Corr. 14/1347.

4   Leics. RO, BR III/2/79, fols. 148 and 192; and DE 720/30, fols. 27–28v.

5   PC to H, 1 April and 19 May 1629, HA Corr. 13/4251 and 4254; Rutland DLs to H, 14 June 1629, HA Corr. 13/10619; and Rudinge's testimony in H *v.* Fawnt, HA Legal 7/4.

6   Braithwaite's confession; Oliver's examination, 14 March 1633; and note, 1 August 1633, Leics. RO, BR II/18/19, fols. 428, 430 and 508; and PC register, 28 October 1631, PC 2/41, p. 281. On the processions, see Leics. RO, BR III/2/79, fols 148 and 192, and BR III/2/80, fol. 108.

7   ECH to H, [1630–31], HA Corr. 13/4843 and 4844; Gerard's answer to Stamford, 26 April 1631, HA Legal 5/3; and entries for 18 February and 16 June 1631, PRO C231/5, fols. 48 and 58. See also H to Stamford, 3 March 1635, HA Corr. 15/5540; and 10 July 1632, Daily Accounts, HAF 10/17.

8   T. Hesilrige to Corporation, 19 April 1625, Leics. RO, BR II/18/15, fol. 560; same to H, 18 June 1625, *LRLB*, fol. 127; and Grey to Conway, 4 September 1627, SP 16/76/27. See also H to B. Hesilrige, 14 September 1625, *LRLB*, fol. 130.

9   Staresmore to H, 26 June 1625, *LRLB*, fol. 126v; 'A note of such persons of quality ... being defaultors', [late 1620s], SP 16/72/59; and PC to Grey *et al.*, 20 July 1627, *APC* 42/432. See also List of defaulters, [1627], SP 16/89/5; and above, pp. 93–4 and 162.

10 PC to H, 16 February 1628, *APC* 43/300–1; H to PC, 11 February 1628, SP 16/92/1; and Nichols, *History and Antiquities*, II, p. 753. See also above, p. 162.

11 Sir William Davenant, 'Elegie on B. Heselrick, slaine in's youth, in a Duell', *The Shorter Poems and Songs*, ed. by A. M. Gibbs (Oxford, 1972), pp. 52–3 and 382–3; Charles to Heath, 28 October 1630, SP 16/174/93 and Nichols, II, p. 756, n 1.

12 Entry for 22 November 1630, PRO C231/5, fol. 43; Leicestershire Commission, 6 Car. I and 8 Car. I, PRO C66/2536 and C66/2598; and Indentures ... of Noseley chapel, 1 October 1635; 4 November 1636; and 8 February 1637, Leics. RO, Hazlerigg MSS, DG21/57, 58 and 59. See also Hughes, 'Thomas Dugard and his Circle in the 1630s'.

13 'A note of such persons of quality ... being defaultors', SP 16/72/59; and Fawnt to Dixie, [late 1626], HA Corr. 15/3149.

14 Newton to H, 9 June 1631; and DLs to H, 7 June 1631, HA Corr. 14/9669 and 8538.

15 'A praier for the parliament', 1634, HA Religious 1/16.

16 PC to H, 24 March 1631; Charles to H, 26 March 1632, HA Corr. 14/4257 and 1347; and H to Corporation, 13 November 1630, Leics. RO, BR II/18/18, fol. 25. See also H to Corporation, 5 November 1631; and Resolution, 27 April 1631, Leics. RO, BR II/18/18, fols. 37 and 140; H. H. Leonard, 'Distraint of Knighthood: the Last Phase, 1625–41', *History* LXIII (1978), pp. 23–67; and Sharpe, *The Personal Rule*, pp. 112–16.

17 'The names of such', 30 September 1630, Bodleian Library, Carte 78, fols. 94–8; 'Book of Compositions', 1630–32, PRO E407/35, fol. 107; and [the Bent case], [early 1630s], HAM 54/24.

18 This figure combines the compositions which Dixie collected ('Book of Composition, 1630–32, PRO E407/35, fol. 107) with the individual payments into the Exchequer contained in various Declared Accounts, PRO E401/2448 [Easter 1630]; PRO E401/2329 [Michaelmas 1630]; PRO E401/2330 [Easter 1631]; PRO E401/2331 [Michaelmas 1631]; and PRO E401/2452 [Easter 1632]. See also entries for Leicestershire and Nottinghamshire in the 'Book of Compositions', PRO E407/35, fols. 107–108v and 133–134v; and Leonard, 'Distraint of Knighthood', p. 29.

19 Linda Popofsky, 'The Crisis over Tonnage and Poundage in Parliament in 1629', *PP* 126 (1990), pp. 44–75; Reeve, *Charles I and the Road to Personal Rule*, pp. 99–117; Esther Cope, *Politics without Parliament*, p. 102; and Cope, 'Politics without Parliament'.

20 Gervase Markham, 'The Muster–Master', ed. by Charles L. Hamilton, *Camden Miscellany* XXVI (1975), pp. 59–61.

21 PC to LLs, 8, 21 and 29 July 1631, PC 2/41, pp. 89, 114 and 133.

22 PC Register, 28 February and 2 May 1632, PC 2/41, pp. 421, 423 and 442; and 2/42, p. 12.

23 PC to LLs, 22 October 1634, PC 2/44, p. 181.

24 Leics. RO, De 720/30, fol. 31; and DE 625/60, p. 73.

25 Leics. RO, DE 720/30, fol. 31; DE 625/60, p. 79; and BR III/2/80, p. 119.

26 'A note of such money as Sir Arthur Hesilrige is in arrere', 1637, HA Military 1/12; and Dixie's deposition, H v. Fawnt, HA Legal, 6/2, p. 25.

27 PC Register, 18 December 1633, 29 September 1631, and 28 February 1632, PC 2/42, p. 398; and 2/41, pp. 184 and 421. See also Hirst, 'The Privy Council'.

28 Banastre to Edmondes, 6 July 1632, SP 16/220/28; and PC Registers, 22 June and 9 July 1632, PRO 2/42, pp. 107 and 137. See also Jesson to PC, 6 July 1632, SP 16/220/23.

29 PC Register, 21 November 1632, PC 2/42, p. 283.

30 PC Register, 21 and 28 November 1632, PC 2/42, pp. 283, 287 and 299.

31 PC Register, 28 November and 5 December 1632, PC 2/42, pp. 299–300 and 322.

32 H to PC, 28 January 1633, SP 16/231/59.

33 PC to H, 18 February 1633, PC 2/42, pp. 456–60.

34 PC Registers, 27 March 1633, PC 2/42, p. 539; and 31 March 1634, PC 2/43, p. 570.

Chapter 10

———◆———

The countess's legacy

B y 1635, the years had taken a heavy toll on Huntingdon, who was then almost fifty, in poor health and in a worse mood. Understandably those apprehensive about troubling him looked to his children. In the late 1630s, a poet eulogising the Dowager Countess of Derby dedicated his verses, not to her son-in-law, the earl, but rather to his daughter; and William Sampson, a local poet, offered his latest efforts, not to Huntingdon himself, but rather to his daughter-in-law, Lady Hastings.[1] Even the central government appreciated the imminent generational shift in the 'House of Ashby'. In 1631, the Lord Keeper named Lord Hastings to the bench, and in 1638 Charles named him Lord Lieutenant with his father.[2]

Huntingdon's darkness stemmed in large part from the death of his wife, whose eulogies all praised her equanimity and charity, qualities sadly lacking in her husband. Little wonder then that her memory long haunted the earl. He remained oblivious to *her* mother's strident advice to remarry: 'a good and rich wife' would 'benefit your selfe and your Children'. In 1637 he politely rejected a rich one with a *cri de coeur*: 'I doe find the greefe for my deere wife hath taken so deepe an impression in me as I doe thinke I shall never marry whilst I live.'[3] While his rejection speaks volumes about his sense of romance, it does little for his financial acumen. For a family who appeared to have red ink in their veins, such devotion was something they could ill afford; indeed, it is almost incomprehensible. This chapter will suggest an answer to the mystery, whose solution lies in the improvement in Huntingdon's standing at court. In fact, his rehabilitation was so dramatic that a handsome dowry no longer seemed imperative.

SEARCHING FOR THE APPROPRIATE RECOMPENSE

Even by the impressive standards of that family, the Hastings' problems with liquidity became particularly acute in the early 1630s. Hitherto the earl, although hobbled by a meagre income, had been the soul of probity with others' money, but early in the 1630s, Shirley's accusations of fraud would have been much more telling, for the public funds that passed through the earl's hands increasingly stuck to his fingers. Although as a Receiver of the Duchy of Lancaster he was responsible for some £300 per annum, he had by 1632 repeatedly failed to see this money to Westminster and blithely ignored queries from Duchy officials. In the end, only pointed legal threats from the Chancellor himself managed to prise the money out of Donnington Park. Problems with public funds were only symptomatic of larger financial difficulties. Take for instance his stewardship of £500 which Jeanne Harington, a lady-in-waiting to Elizabeth of Bohemia, had left in his care. Someone as devoted to the 'Winter Queen' as Huntingdon had no trouble appreciating his cousin's dedication. Her annual interest payments, however, were another matter; when these repeatedly failed to reach The Hague, progressively infuriated letters from his cousin extracted a confession from him: domestic expenses had long ago consumed her money. Even after this embarrassing revelation, it took him eight months to make financial amends. Similar examples began to proliferate. Such stability as there was in the family's finances stemmed from the earl's lease of the royal manor of Loughborough, which gained the earl an income of some £600 in return for an annual rental of £120. The advantage of the deal was so obvious that 'the Checker men' could only watch in amazement in 1630 as he casually came within a few days of missing his yearly payment. With a flinty Lord Treasurer like Richard Weston, such a sweetheart deal 'never will be thus gotten agayne if this be forfeited'.[4] Nevertheless severe fiscal emergency forced him to take such dire risks.

The worsening financial problems provided the only faintly amusing aspect of Eton College's case against the earl's chaplain for embezzling £7 14s.; the Provost lodged his indignant protest about such scandalous behavior with a nobleman for whom disappearing balances and awkward arrearages were fast becoming a way of life. Against this sombre background, Huntingdon's quarrel with Thomas Pestell in 1631 appears in another light. When Pestell requested payment of a longstanding debt, the normally phlegmatic earl exploded: 'Begon poore scabb.'[5] On closer examination, Huntingdon's irritation had much more to do with his collapsing financial position than with his erstwhile client.

The sudden descent into financial irresponsibility was directly related to the maturation of his family. His second son, Henry Hastings, was by then busy amassing his own tiny estate, while in 1634 Elizabeth Hastings required a dowry and a suitable wedding. Meanwhile Huntingdon's dreams of financial freedom for his eldest son through a wealthy heiress had disappeared on Sir John Davies's death in 1627. First Lady Lucy's father left behind much less than expected, only £2,300, and after deducting for a host of bequests, Lord

Hastings could look forward only to £100 and his mother-in-law, that 'so fantasticall a cretier', Lady Eleanor Davies. The discomfort that her prophecies caused Charles I and Archbishop Laud was nothing compared with the aggravation that she brought the Hastingses. 'Long and tedious sutes' erupted between Lord Ferdinando and his mother-in-law over the manor of Englefield, and in 1633 he had to concede that 'the cause is gonn against mee'. In the process the family had acquired heavy debts and the hatred of Lady Eleanor, who in 1633 publicly dubbed the Countess of Huntingdon 'Jezebel'; lest anyone had forgotten what the Hebrews had done with that wicked woman, Lady Eleanor thoughtfully reminded her readers that they had stoned her. With ample reason, Alice Hastings in 1635 bristled at the mere report that Lady Eleanor might visit Donnington Park: 'when I call to mynde the dishonor and abuses shee most wickedly spared not to laye on my late and most deare deceased mother and yourself', the recollection 'makes my harte to gush out teares'.[6] If Englefield proved a poisoned inheritance, Lord Ferdinando found some consolation in his wife's Irish lands in Fermanagh and Tyrone, which by 1638 produced a respectable £780. Unfortunately the costs of stocking the estate and establishing its legality initially consumed almost all profits. Such painful investments were on the verge of bearing handsome fruit when the Irish revolt impoverished the young couple.[7] The Davies match therefore became simply another of the family's string of bad investments.

These mounting pressures on the earl's purse led to a host of humiliating manoeuvres. Persistent appeals for small cash loans became something to which Huntingdon's brother-in-law, the Earl of Chesterfield, had to grow accustomed. Likewise, for a family in such straitened conditions, the route to the pawnshop was all too well known. Cash became such an imperative that it drove the earl to the unthinkable; in 1633, he seriously considered selling the family's extensive collection of military equipment, which gave solid form to his vivid dreams of feudal glory.[8] An even more ominous development can be discerned in the leases which the earl began granting his tenants. Years earlier, Huntingdon had strictly cautioned his son against the temptation of accepting large entry fines for nominal rents; 'take noe fine for they beinge spent thou must long patiently abide, ere they gather any more fruite from them'. Yet in 1633, such sensible advice did not stop him from accepting £24 for a ninety-nine-year lease with an annual rent of 2s. By his own yardstick, then, this lease – and there were others like it – underscored the sudden erosion of the family's finances. This background makes more poignant Huntingdon's salutation to his second son: 'and soe good Harry praying to God to make mee as able as I am willing to doe you good'. The distinct difference between ability and willingness was also painfully evident when financial difficulties forced the countess to curtail an important trip to the metropolis. After recounting her crippling lack of cash, she concluded with perhaps the most devastating words she had ever written to her husband: 'I know you cannot helpe it'.[9]

In his anguish, the earl constantly brooded over 'some suite to move the King for recompense' for having dedicated his life to the royal service, and his thoughts always returned to James I's patent awarding him the lieutenancy of the Forest for life. Although he had been in the running for a free gift of 400 acres, Sir Henry Shirley ensured that he received nothing, not even the deer that Sir Miles Fleetwood belatedly awarded to him. The contemporary administrative maxim that officers should be compensated for loss of office gave Huntingdon ample grounds for believing himself ill used. Persuading the central government to rectify the error was another matter.[10]

Huntingdon first confronted this fact in 1628. His protest proceeded to the Privy Council, which in May 1628 advised him to petition the Lord Treasurer, who 'might find some meanes whereby to give the said Earle recompense and satisfaction according to equity'. 'Might' proved the operative word for hard-pressed financial officers, understandably reluctant to allocate scant funds to a recusant in the loan project. Huntingdon's best opportunity to break this log-jam came when local inhabitants petitioned the Lords to investigate Fleet-wood's work and to restore the royal forest. Eventually the House dismissed the petition, but not before Huntingdon had managed to air his own grievance; hence in the formal report praising Fleetwood, there was also a somewhat incongruous plea that Charles 'would be pleased to give the Earl of Huntingdon a recompense, as his Majesty had done to the lords lieutenants of his forests' elsewhere.[11] Unfortunately for Huntingdon, the House approved this resolution only moments before adjournment, and scarcely had calm returned to the Palace of Westminster before Huntingdon learned the hope-lessness of his position. A few days earlier he had outlined several possible settlements: the Crown could award him 400 acres out of the forest, or it could terminate his annual £200 rent to the royal fee farm, or it could sell its share in the manor of Donnington at a nominal price. But when he presented these ideas to Charles, the king referred the matter back to Marlborough and Weston. To them, he reported rumours of some 200 unallocated acres, and much to his relief, they acted swiftly, ordering an immediate survey of the remaining parcels. Yet any hope of an effortless resolution ended with the discovery that every acre had already been awarded.[12] At this point, bereft of funds and, more importantly, political capital, Huntingdon's campaign came to a halt.

For three years, the earl brooded over events until, late in 1631, his long stalled campaign reopened with a barrage of petitions creeping through Whitehall. First, in a series of drafts he carefully rehearsed his appeal, maxim-ising the magnitude of his claim. By juggling various fees, he managed to increase his annual loss from £76 6s. 5d. to £81 2s. 5d. in cash, which was in addition to the annual loss of eighty deer, forty does and innumerable fish and birds. Finally, because the royal deer had driven down the value of the Hastings estates adjoining the forest, the third earl had to let out the manors of Endesby, Kirby Muxloe, Braunston and Leicester Abbey on long leases at 'very cheape rents' to the tenants, who found the land after Fleetwood's labours 'is worth almost as much unto them as he had for the whole mannors'. Similar profits would come his way if Huntingdon had not sold his remaining forest manor at Lubbesthorpe shortly before the disafforestation, and this bad timing had cost him at least £1,000.[13] Along with this general plea went appeals to individual councillors. Some stressed that Huntingdon had 'never receaved other reward but that command of deere for the long service which I did', and others that he had 'never importuned his Maiestie or his most excellent Father for any swite Except his Liefenency'. The timing of Huntingdon's revived offensive was dictated by the knowledge that, as he explained to Dorset, 'if this my humble suit have not now an end being soe long after the loss of my office I shalbe out of hope for ever having anything'.[14]

Huntingdon's impressive case promptly hit a snag, as it had before, when it came to finding suitable compensation. In 1628, the councillors had 'bad me [Huntingdon] see if I cold find out any thing', and in 1631 he was as far from discovering 'any thing' as ever.[15] For one thing, the exact dimensions of Huntingdon's loss remained vague. While the best accountant could not have come up with annual losses in excess of £500, Huntingdon found it impossible to set a price of the loss of the additional title after his name. His worst problem, however, was his solicitor at court. While the earl's kinsmen were sympathetic, they could scarcely follow such a complicated suit to its conclusion. Meanwhile Huntingdon's customary legal agents like his brother, Sir George, and his solicitor, Mr Leveringe, lacked political clout at Whitehall. The earl of course periodically flooded Whitehall with his own impassioned letters. Unfortunately for him, bureaucrats, whether early modern or modern, find it easier to ignore letters than personal pleas. To proceed as he had, therefore, was simply to accept mounting levels of frustration. Luckily, late in 1631, he resolved on an approach which was for him quite novel.

THE ROAD TO WHITEHALL

At the Countess of Huntingdon's funeral in 1634, the minister highlighted one of her attributes. 'Her understanding,' he recalled,

> was of great perspicacity, and as she fayled not to imploy the same for the comprehending of such occasions and affaires, as might advantage and susteine the estate of her house, and procure and reinforce the content and comfort of her noble Lord.

This was no poetic conceit, for this task had consumed years of her time and ultimately her life itself. The countess dramatically illustrated her devotion to duty in the spring of 1631 when she climbed into the family's battered coach for a long journey, and over the next three years she regularly repeated this act of daring. Such high mileage brought the earl and countess into an intimate relationship with carriage-makers in Leicester, London and all points between. The first journey left the coach in need of £26 2s. 6d. in immediate repairs, and in 1632 a serious breakdown forced the family to welcome the 'coach-menders' to their table for the better part of a week.[16] Yet the trouble and money invested in the coach proved well worth the bother, for it performed its vital mission; it delivered the countess, a considerable amount of baggage and her husband's petitions to Westminster. Given Huntingdon's aversion to the court, his tolerance of such long absences and heavy expenses clearly indicates the depth of his desperation.

Fortunately the game was worth the candle. Once there, her ability to mix business and pleasure managed to impress even the hard-headed Lord Treasurer, who later told Huntingdon that 'any other Solicitor could not have advantaged you soe much'. Initially Portland responded to her case 'after the Court manner', his smooth assurance that 'he wold be readie to do you service' actually meaning that he might think about the matter. Yet the countess pressed for a firmer answer. Thanks to her persistence, the Hastings claim disrupted Council meetings, the vacations of individual courtiers and even Jerome Weston's wedding.[17] Meanwhile she badgered into line friends and relations like the Earls of Bridgewater, Dorset, Worcester and Manchester. Weston, not surprisingly, soon made the resolution of the question a high priority.

The settlement of the claim proved quite complicated. First of all, a committee of councillors set the loss at approximately £2,500; although the earl set a higher price on his damaged prestige, Weston patiently explained that 'the Kinge lost the forrest and soe to loose your place there was noe dishonor'. In any case, the lack of any suitable redress soon overcame the pain of this distressingly low evaluation. The outright grant of some royal land, a logical resolution, was also the least likely in the current economic climate. The family's hopes then fastened on an assignation out of the fee farm before foundering on the 'constant course he [Weston] hath held to deny all sutes in that kind since the Duke [of Buckingham] died'. A gift of some Irish land was quite acceptable to the couple, although the prospect of waiting in a long queue was not. Weeks of tiring and expensive lobbying therefore brought the countess to the same place where her husband had stuck three years earlier: Weston 'did not doubt but assoone as you could pitch upon a particuler shuit of that valew but that wee should speedely obtayne it'.[18]

From there she slipped into the murky twilight of informers and projectors. Concealed lands, that financial El Dorado of Stuart England, at first tantalised her until she appreciated that the chaotic records would likely send them pursuing fools' gold. Ineluctably the couple found themselves pondering the proposal of a friend of a friend offering 'some particulars that are convenient for the kinge to grant some of ten thousand pounds value and others of lesse value'; the only catch was the projector's insistence on receiving his commission in advance. Dubious proposals were not the exclusive property of shady operators; the Earl of Stamford repeatedly pressed the countess to merge their claims on royal bounty. She politely declined the offer, announcing that 'I will never be yoked in my business.' Extended exposure to such difficulties eventually wore down her indomitable spirit: the woman who in November remained 'very Confident I have not lost my labour' was less hopeful a few months later when she lamented, 'I have layne so longe at Great Charges and to little purpose.'[19]

Despair had nearly overwhelmed her in the spring of 1632 when the Promised Land suddenly opened up before her in the form of Sir Miles Hobart's estate. In the turmoil at the end of the 1629 session, Sir Miles had locked the door and pocketed the key while Denzil Holles held the Speaker in his chair. His action earned him considerable popular applause and a crushing royal fine, which caused his property to revert to the Crown on his death in 1632. Profiting from the government's humiliation of such a popular Parliament man must have given pause to a peer who had scarcely earned a reputation as a staunch royalist. Nevertheless, so precious were likely suits for recompense that he could not afford to be fastidious.

The most awkward aspect of the Hobart suit proved not its indelicacy but its popularity. While some contenders already eyeing the estate like Sir Miles's sister could easily be brushed aside, prominent courtiers like the Earl of Holland could not. Still the countess proved a formidable campaigner and soon extracted a tentative promise from the king himself. Meanwhile the earl's agents inspected the Hobart estates with indecent thoroughness. Huntingdon's brother found Sir Miles's country house at Marlow 'convenient' and the land 'pleasant', while Joseph Newton, the Clerk of the Peace, announced that Huntingdon would become the owner of the Castle Tavern in Wad Street and a row of London town houses. Altogether the Hobart property produced about £500–£600 per annum, almost exactly what Huntingdon had lost with the disafforestation. By July, it seemed that nine months of lobbying would produce an ample reward, and the countess, who had doggedly pursued the matter 'as carefully as I can', felt confident about telling her husband that 'I shall make a good jorney for you.' Success had come none too soon, for her health had sharply declined, and her unpaid debts to London merchants were making her stay uncomfortable. Therefore she had no regrets about a quick visit to Donnington Park before a final trip out to Greenwich to thank Charles and the queen for their generosity.[20]

Practically the last words in her extensive correspondence from court praised 'my very Noble frend', Lord Treasurer Weston. Sir George Hastings, who knew his way around Whitehall, had dubbed Weston the man 'from thence althings move', and she had tenaciously applied herself to winning his favour. Yet in this, she may well have mistaken the 1630s for the 1620s. Weston's power and influence, while extensive, could not match Buckingham's omnipotence. Rather, the Lord Treasurer had to share power with other powerful courtiers, one of whom unexpectedly discovered an interest in the Hobart case. Consequently after the countess had thanked the king and the Treasurer, Sir Miles's estates ended up not on the Hastingses' abbreviated rent rolls, but financing 'certaine Schollers in the Islands of Garsey and Jersey' at Oxford; Bishop Laud had stolen a march on Weston.[21]

This *dénouement* was a bitter blow. Aside from dashing the fondest hopes, his wife's campaign had cost hundreds of pounds which he could ill afford. To her credit, the countess had struggled to hold expenses down, from purchasing her own bedding to having a steady stream of victuals sent down from Leicestershire. Yet in spite of these economies, 'I lye at a very greate charge.' At the end of her stay, she was confident that 'if this should fayle of Hubberts I made noe doubt but that you shall have recompense som other way'. But given her expenses in 1631–32, Huntingdon might not be able to afford to ask again. The dearest cost of this failed venture, however, was not financial. She had first gone to London to spare his health, only in the end to lose her own, limping home with intermittent backaches and 'much payne' in her foot which 'hathe no intermission'. To warn her husband of the situation, she wrote ahead with news that 'I am not very well.'[22] A quiet convalescence at Donnington Park failed to mend her health, which collapsed altogether at dinner on 2 February 1633. By then, her back and feet were the least of her problems, for severe pains in her lower abdomen, probably the result of a uterine cancer, increasingly hobbled the countess. Her precarious condition notwithstanding, she remained doggedly devoted to the pursuit of recompense. It was fitting therefore that shortly after Christmas 1633, she died in London in the midst of another round of lobbying.[23]

Mourning over her death was intense and widespread. William Sampson, that omnipresent poetical chronicler of local life, celebrated the lady who 'knew Court Ladies faults, and did not tie / Her faith unto her fashion'. Even more impressive was Viscount Falkland's epitaph. In the turmoil following his marriage to Lettice Morison over his father's objections, Donnington Park proved one of the few places where the couple were warmly received. Thus his praise for 'A wisdome of so large and potent sway / Romes Senate might have wisht, her Conclave may' came not from some distant well-wisher, but rather from 'him who saies what he saw'. Such encomiums rang true enough to make the sermon preached at her funeral one of the more popular works of the mid-decade; it eventually ran through three editions, the last of which boasted a fine engraving of the countess.[24] The family consequently was far from alone in its grief over the 'Excellent Countess'.

With her death, the countess left behind an invaluable legacy, for she had re-established personal links between Donnington Park and Whitehall. She thus left her husband no choice. Too much had been invested for the idea of a thorough reconciliation with the central government to be abandoned. Hence in the spring of 1634, only a few weeks after his wife's interment, Huntingdon himself climbed into the family's rickety coach for the southward journey. There he had his best hats repaired, and once presentable, entered Whitehall to deliver his latest petitions to Charles.[25]

The magnitude of Huntingdon's action cannot be overemphasised. Except for visits during the Parliaments of 1621 and 1628, he had spent well over a decade without setting foot in the metropolis, to say nothing of Whitehall. Even the Council hearing in June 1627, when his fate hung in the balance, failed to lure him south. The death of his countess, however, forced him to reassess this policy; whether or not he actually liked the court was irrelevant if he wanted something for his lost Forest offices. So quickly did the earl adopt the rhythms of his wife's movements that by September 1634 he was making appointments with royal officers 'at my coming up to London in the terme'. From here, it was only a short step to a more dramatic development, one which Mr Thorpe discovered in the spring of 1635 when he went to conduct a thorough inventory of Donnington Park. Since all he found there was Henry Hastings, the earl's second son, and a nearly empty mansion, Thorpe could not complete his task, since 'my Lord is gone to live at London'. Shortly after the earl's marriage, the Countess of Derby had pleaded with the young couple to move to the capital.[26] Almost three decades later, the old widower belatedly followed his mother-in-law's advice.

With the new silence at Donnington Park came a host of new attitudes and friends. The most controversial aspect of the Personal Rule was Charles's adoption of a more ceremonial Arminianism. Huntingdon's moderate Calvinism made him unlikely to embrace such a shift. Yet he enthusiastically co-operated with Archbishop Laud's campaign to improve the fabric of parish churches, denouncing the 'headstrong' churchwardens of All Saints, Loughborough, who had ignored orders for 'the beautifying and decoring of the Church'; unless these men were made 'examples for theire Contempt and disobedience', he warned the Archbishop that 'it will make others to be too sawcie and presumptious'. Such concern seems to have been sincere, for even after the Scottish Revolt had called the Laudian reforms into question, Huntingdon still insisted that the desecration of churchyards had to be 'severelie punished'. These statements have led one scholar to interpret them as evidence of Huntingdon's wholesale adoption of an anti-Calvinist position. Unfortunately, pending firmer evidence, this interpretation must remain at best problematic. What is quite certain is that these comments are perfectly consistent with the earl's long-held conformism. Twenty years earlier he had lamented that disputes over 'thinges of indifferencie and ceremonie', over vestments, bowing and kneeling had ever been 'broched amongest us'. Since such matters were 'in the power of the kinge either to comand or to prohibite as he pleases', loyal subjects had no choice in the matter; 'it is a sinne not to conforme unto them'.[27] Since Laud's campaign to ensure the 'beauty of holiness' primarily concerned matters of 'indifferencie and ceremony', Huntingdon's support is quite logical.

His compliance was also reflected in a shifting pattern of friendships at court. By the 1630s, many old friends like the Earls of Southampton and Pembroke and the Countess of Bedford were dead, and with those who had survived like Warwick, Saye and Essex, the earl become increasingly distant. In their place, he strengthened his ties with relatives at court like Worcester, Manchester and Bridgewater and built new ones with Dorset and Weston. Yet the best illustration of his fundamental realignment can be found in his relationship with the Earl of Arundel and Surrey. Decades had gone by without any contact between the two men, but now their friendship blossomed. To be sure, the Earl Marshal, one of greatest snobs of his era, had to appreciate that his impoverished rural cousin possessed one of the more distinguished pedigrees in the kingdom, and the regular extinction of other ancient titles only burnished the lustre of the Hastings lineage. Yet for whatever reason, Arundel lavished honours on Huntingdon, calling him to Westminster to deliberate on cases before the Earl Marshal and at one point even naming him as his deputy. Huntingdon in response could only announce himself 'exceedingly bound unto your Lordship for many favours which have soe much obliged me to you as my greatest ambition is to strive to deserve to live in your memory and good opinion'. In his charge to the quarter session in 1639, he even managed to work in an encomium for Arundel, whom 'no kinge in Christendome hath an abler servant ... for warr and Counsell'. Given their mutual admiration society, they naturally took the waters together at Bath in 1634.[28] By this point the countess was already dead, but she had already well advanced her husband's reintegration with the ruling elite of Caroline England.

Incessant lobbying and extended residence in Westminster had allowed the earl by degrees to reverse the unflattering assessment of many there, who only a few years earlier had valued Sir Henry Hastings of Braunston more than Huntingdon himself. Thus, by the middle of the decade, the earl could find some relief in the fact that the likes of the Lord Treasurer, the Lord Marshal and the Archbishop of Canterbury were favourably disposed towards him. This list also included the king himself; Huntingdon for instance had long complained of the government's refusal to acknowledge that some of the third earl's smaller debts had long been repaid. Early in 1636, he finally persuaded the Exchequer officials of the fact.[29]

Contemporaries could have been forgiven if they missed this act of grace.

Yet there was no avoiding a more public sign of favour, which the monarch bestowed a few months after the countess's death. Early in James's reign, the royal family had regularly visited Leicestershire. Yet following James's visit in 1616, they had apparently blotted the county from their collective consciousness, although they continued to visit neighbouring shires. The royal memory suddenly improved on 9 July 1634 when Charles and his queen entered Leicester. From its roads and churches to the Corporation members themselves, the town gleamed, and Charles could scarcely do anything less, particularly after receiving £200 in gold plate. The Mayor and his brethren were eager to welcome a long absent monarch, but in their delight, they did not forget who had engineered the occasion. Thus the town sent a handsome gift to Huntingdon as well 'in respecte off his honors great care of this Towne … and his furtherance toward theire Majesties entertainment'. From this signal success, the earl promptly received an even greater one; the royal couple proceeded to Ashby Castle, where Charles and Henrietta Maria stayed four days.[30]

Arguably the best illustration of Huntingdon's restoration was the revival of his dreams of the Garter. For decades he had been unable to forget this distinction, for in the same box with his Parliament robes he carefully kept his great-uncle's robes as a Knight of the Garter, 'all of purple velvet lined with taffet'. In 1625, when his stock had stood so high, there had been discussion that he might soon don these, only to have such hopes swept away in the crises of the late 1620s. Yet significantly by 1634 such dreams had returned. Then Huntingdon went so far as to document his claim to a garter which four of his Clifford, nine of his Stanley and four of his Hastings ancestors had worn.[31]

For all of these reasons, bearding the Lord Lieutenant, a game which Sir Henry Shirley had so enjoyed and which Fawnt and Hesilrige were coming to appreciate, was rapidly becoming a dangerous pastime. Whitehall's unfavourable assessment of the earl had eventually faded, leaving Huntingdon with an increasingly clear claim on the Crown's largesse. The Hobart fiasco, far from burying the question of appropriate recompense, simply left the matter unresolved. Therefore, behind Huntingdon's rejection of a financially lucrative second marriage was something more than his wife's memory; by 1637 all the trouble of another wedding seemed needless, since he had at last uncovered the ideal suit, one intimately connected with his problems within the county.

KNEELING BEFORE THE LORDS

In January 1635, Huntingdon at last summoned the Leicestershire regiment before him. While this order would likely produce another incident with his two wayward JPs, enough had happened in the intervening two years to make the earl sanguine about the odds in another confrontation. Thus in spite of the Council's admonition 'to give all iust ease and releefe to the Country', the earl required 14s. from each trained man. Even by the standards of the 1620s, this was a heavy levy, calling for some £350. Rather obviously, if Fawnt and Hesilrige were in the mood for complaints, Huntingdon made matters easy for them.

Events proceeded as might have been anticipated. The foot companies duly mustered without serious incident. Mr Newton arrived with his 14s., later billing Branston for additional expenses totalling another 15s., including 4d. in repairs to one of the infamous knapsacks. The same proportion governed Waltham's expenses; its three men paid the militia treasurer £2 in fees, while later collecting another £2 10s. in travelling costs.[32] Fawnt and Hesilrige were also running true to form. After his last experience at the Council board, Sir William discovered a loophole in his promise; although he had vowed to pay his share of the Muster Master's fee, he had said nothing about the rest of the militia staff. Consequently, early in 1635 Fawnt, Huntingdon later alleged, 'did diswade and worke in the people a backwardnesse in his Majesties service'; he did so by announcing that

> he knewe the opinion of the lords of the privie council, saying publickly that there was money onely to be levied for the Muster Master his fee ... and that theire lordships intended there should bee noe more levyed for any other use whatsoever.

Fawnt's confidence notwithstanding, there were few, if any, converts, aside from the inevitable Sir Arthur Hesilrige. Indeed, out of the £32 levied on the hundred of Guthlaxton, Richard Jacombe, the collector, had trouble only with Fawnt's assessment. Eventually Sir William paid his share, but only after insisting that his money went to pay the Muster Master and to purchase munitions, 'not for any other Officers'. While Jacombe accepted these conditions and duly issued Fawnt a receipt, Walter Rudinge, the long-time county treasurer, flatly 'refused to accept thereof upon these Conditions'. Jacombe then returned the payment to Sir William, who pocketed the money as well as the receipt.[33]

In due course, their latest display of obstinacy and imagination earned them another command performance at the Council table, but they were not particularly alarmed. Fawnt and Hesilrige had mastered Shirley's old sport of taunting the Lord Lieutenant and his men, and by now these well-heeled gentlemen knew that they could expect no worse penalties this time than they had earlier suffered. Nevertheless, their pleasant sport was becoming more dangerous. Not only was Huntingdon's stock rising fast at Whitehall, but international developments had abruptly undercut any councillor support for defaulters. Since 1630, the diplomatic basis of the Personal Rule had been firmly anchored on continuing English neutrality. Yet early in 1635, as open war erupted between the Bourbons and the Habsburgs, pressure mounted on Charles to re-enter the war. What had seemed insane in 1630 had become more rational five years later after the Crown had an opportunity of tightened control over the realm and improved naval preparedness.[34] A major stumbling block to any bellicose policy, however, was the state of the militia, and the Council moved on 24 April to correct this deficiency.

After 1630, the Council's annual order for a muster followed the same formula of 30 April 1629, stipulating a bare minimum of activities. Given these notional requirements, many Lords Lieutenant had difficulty believing that Whitehall was seriously interested in the militia, perfect or otherwise. Consequently, as T. G. Barnes has noted, 'with the end of war had come the end of purposefulness, and all slid back into the easy carelessness of peacetime'. Casual routine gave way to urgent detail on 24 April 1635 when the Council suddenly revived the controversial orders of 20 July 1626. In light of 'the dayly Advertisements from parts abroade of the greate preparations both by Sea and Land of the Neighbouring Princes', Charles 'instantly' commanded a muster. Along with ensuring that all was 'according to the modern fashion', all Lieutenants were to see their Deputies 'sharply reproved' for 'the Connivance and Remisnes of late yeares' and to ensure 'a more severe and strict Account taken' of their officers. The men themselves had to be present, fit for service, trained and ready to march 'upon an hours warning'. In spite of the chaos that followed this particular command in 1626, all militiamen were again to swear the oaths both of allegiance and of supremacy. The Lieutenants were then to raise another unit of untrained men, armed out of the spare arms of 'the best sorte'. The 1635 order even followed its predecessor down to requiring Provost Marshals and a twenty-four-hour guard on the beacons.[35]

For Huntingdon, a man whose administrative strong suit was his zeal for the militia, this order was an answer to his prayers. Sucess with the regiment, as he had earlier discovered, depended on the councillors' willingness to back him up. Their attitude, which was questionable before April 1635, became unambiguous afterwards, and Huntingdon revelled in the new political climate. Hitherto on the rare occasions when he dared to call a muster, Huntingdon had limited himself to one-day affairs with nothing more than 'calling mens Names and noting Downe of Defects'. Now he indulged in a series of company drills culminating in a county muster at Leicester. Needless to say, since the ratepayers were no longer a paramount concern, expenses soared. The renewal of training eventually cost the Corporation of Leicester £50 1s. 1d. for its forty men, Waltham £5 19s. for its three, and Branston £1 18s. for Mr Newton.[36] The commotion among the trained men and the ratepayers consequently coincided with the hearing at the Council board. Unfortunately for Sir William and Sir Arthur, this new activity symbolised the sea change which had come over the councillors in their attitude to the defaulters.

This unexpected development, which ensured a sympathetic hearing, can only have heartened the earl, and as he pondered how best to handle his presentation, he brooded over the fact that Fawnt had an extensive record of contrariness and recalled the heavy fines which had recently come out of Star Chamber. Since adherents of 'the Policy of Thorough' were committed to ensuring obedience, their fear of the multitude led them to react forcibly to any perceived challenge to the *status quo*. The result was an extraordinary number of cases concerning the defamation of peers. The Star Chamber, for example, punished a gentleman for libelling the Earl of Northampton, another for denouncing the Earl of Suffolk as 'a Base lord', and a third for calling the Earl of Danby 'un shitten Lord, Lord danbie, Lord danturd'. Nor were the councillors themselves immune to criticism; early in 1635, a gentlemen spread baseless rumours about Lord Keeper Coventry. What would have especially attracted Huntingdon's attention was the size of the fines, some as high as £3,000. And since these defamation cases all dealt with oral testimony, so much the better, then, if written evidence could be produced. Consequently Huntingdon's thoughts turned to Fawnt's two letters to Sir Wolston Dixie late in 1626.

Shortly before leaving for Westminster, Huntingdon asked Dixie for the originals. It was a ticklish request; given the recent row, the earl was obviously interested in much more than Fawnt's epistolary style, and Dixie's son had married Fawnt's daughter. Predictably the Deputy Lieutenant argued the merits of forbearance. Since Fawnt was certain to receive a stiff fine for depopulation, Sir Wolston suggested that Huntingdon 'passe by or deferr his offence till that censure be past'; then he could 'heape Coales of fire on his heade'. Otherwise Dixie would regret 'the punishment of that offence should by him or his, be any way imputed to your Lordship'. He also counselled delay, not only for his son's sake, but for that of Fawnt's wife, who was after all Huntingdon's cousin. Yet in the end, he left the matter to Huntingdon's discretion and sent along the documents.[37] Consequently in 1635 Sir William and Sir Arthur blithely rode into Westminster, heedless of danger.

The importance which Huntingdon attached to this hearing extended well beyond assembling the most formidable case. Unlike the earlier councillor encounters with Shirley in 1626–27 and with Fawnt and Hesilrige in 1632, the earl this time resolved to leave nothing to chance. Hence, at least a month before the hearing, the earl loaded a dozen trunks onto the Ashby carrier's wagon, while he himself climbed into the family coach. Even breakdowns failed to dampen his resolve. Once there, he ordered new clothes replete with the latest style in cuffs, purchased new shoes and hired a coach while his own was being repaired. Decently attired, he proceeded down river to Greenwich. Consequently on 2 June, when the councillors confronted the two defaulters, they had in the preceding days regularly rubbed shoulders with Huntingdon.[38]

The money for such elaborate preparations was well spent, for the initial round was anything but mundane. After Huntingdon charged the two defaulters, Fawnt then produced Jacombe's receipt and opened a detailed discussion of what had happened to his 14s. When the Deputy Lieutenants next charged him with violating his earlier promise to the Council, Sir William reminded them that technically he had only promised to pay the Muster Master's fee. Finally in response to Huntingdon's attack on Fawnt as a major encloser, he replied that whereas the unenclosed village of Foston had presented only one man, the enclosed estate returned two horse and two men. His explanation led one councillor to announce that, thanks to Sir William, 'his Maiesties service touching militarie affaires was furthered and his forces encreased'.[39]

As the case appeared to be taking an awkward turn, Huntingdon produced his trump card – Fawnt's old letters to Dixie. These substantially altered the situation, for the two letters transformed the crusty old gentleman into a malignant, whom the councillors could not easily ignore. Obviously impressed, the Earl of Manchester asked his cousin if he wanted the Council to act on the letters. Drama as well as rhetoric informed Huntingdon's reply; the aged peer fell to his knees and 'humbly requested ... that hee might bee at libertie to take his legall course ... for that letter'. Confronted with such an emotional plea, the councillors granted the request. But lest anyone failed to see their mood, they also added their own parting touch. Notwithstanding their local prominence and Fawnt's long service, the Lord Keeper abruptly removed Sir William and Sir Arthur from the Commission of the Peace.[40] Then the councillors imprisoned the pair for violating the spirit, if not the letter, of their earlier promise.

This time it was no wrist slap. Hesilrige spent nineteen days in jail before his pregnant wife personally begged Charles to release her husband 'in the tyme of her extremity', and even then the king only approved the leave until her delivery. Later in the autumn, Sir Arthur returned to hear the Council's pleasure, only to find himself back in the Fleet, where he remained until 30 December 1635.[41] As he belatedly rode home, Sir Arthur doubtless sputtered with indignation. Yet in his righteous anger, there was one consolation; at least he was spared Sir William's fate.

NOTES

1 Robert Codrington, *An Elegie sacred to ... Alice Countess Dowager of Derby*, William Andrews Clark Library, C6715M1/E38 [1637]; and William Sampson, *Roomes his est ille Cicero* [1630s], FSL, V.a. 301.

2 25 May 1635, PRO C231/5, fol. 57; and Lieutenancy Commission, House of Lords RO, Main Papers, 27 December 1638.

3 Derby to H, 25 August 1635; and H to Brounker, 19 June 1637, HA Corr. 15/2516 and 5547. See also, I.F., *A Sermon Preached at Ashby-de-la-Zouch* (London, 1635).

4 Newburgh to H, 10 March 1632; Harington to H, 1 January, 2 February and 22

November 1636; H to Harington, 29 December 1636; and G. Hastings to H, 16 April 1630, HA Corr. 14/438; 13/5310; and 15/13875, 13876, 13877 and 5543.

5 Wotton to H, 7 October 1637, HA Corr. 15/13666; and Wright's deposition, Pestell *v.* Johnson, [1632], HA Legal 5/9, fol. 11.

6 FEH to LCH, [1633], HA Corr. 13/4864; [Eleanor Davies], *Woe to the House* (Amsterdam, 1633); and Alice Hastings to H, 12 July 1635, HA Corr. 15/[illegible]. See also seventh earl's biographical notes, HA Genealogy 1/12; Douglas *v.* Hastings, 1626–29, HA Legal, 2/12–13, 3/2–7 and 4/1–8; and Esther Cope, *The Handmaid of the Spirit* (Ann Arbor, 1993), pp. 43–65.

7 Mr Segrave's reports, May 1637, Michaelmas 1638, Lady Day and Michaelmas 1640, HAM 76/4, 6, 10–11.

8 Chesterfield to H, 8 September [late 1620s–early 1630s]; and C. of H to H, 21 September 1631, HA Corr. 12/12600 and 14/4846; and 'An estimat what the Earle of Huntingdons Armor is worth', 19 November 1633, HA Inventories 1/9. See also additional estimates in HA Inventories 1/7.

9 'Certaine Directions', HAP 15/8, fol. 21; 'A note', 1633, HAM 26/5; H to HLL, 29 March 1634; and ECH to H, [June–July 1632], HA Corr. 14/5533 and 4852.

10 Segrave to H, 16 March 1625, HA Corr. 15/10725. See also Aylmer, *The King's Servants*, pp. 106–25.

11 PC to H, May 1628, Bodleian Library, Carte 78, fols. 111–12; and 26 June, *PP 1628*, V, p. 704.

12 'The humble petition of ... Huntington', 31 May 1628; H to Charles, [late May]; and Charles to H, 9 July 1628; Marlborough *et al.* to Heath, 9 July 1628; same to Fanshawe, 15 July 1628; and Fleetwood to Heath, [summer 1628], HAM 48/38–40 and 10, and 49/9.

13 'The particulars of the Office', [early 1630s]; 'Leicester forest', [early 1630s]; and [a draft petition], [early 1630s], HAM 48/14, 15a and 15b.

14 H to Dorset, 10 November 1631; same to Weston, 9 November 1631; and same to [Weston?], [late 1631], HA Corr. 14/5531 and 4848.

15 ECH to H, 28 November 1631; and H to Weston, 10 September 1631, HA Corr. 14/4847 and 5531.

16 I.F., *A Sermon Preached at Ashby-de-la-Zouch*, pp. 34–5; and 'A Note of monies disbursed', 5 April 1631; and 30 August to 3 September 1632, Daily Accounts, 1631–33], HAF 10/17.

17 See for example her pressure on Secretary Coke, 26 September 1631, BL Add. MS 64,903, fol. 48.

18 ECH to H, 21 September and 28 November 1631, HA Corr. 14/4846 and 4847.

19 Gell to Ward, [1632]; ECH to H, [1632]; and same to same, [1632], HA Corr. 14/4313, 4849 and 4850. See also Walley to ECH, 10 January 1632; Gell to same, [1632]; Ward to same, 24 May 1632; and H's reply, 29 May 1632, HA Corr. 14/13041, 3414, 13,074 and 3413.

20 Hastings to ECH, 14 September 1632; Newton to same, 17 September [1632]; and C. of H to H, 7 and 11 July 1632, HA Corr. 14/5312, 9670, 4852 and 4853. See also Shepard to same, 9 July 1632; Walley to same, 8 September 1632; and Hewett to Bohenham, 15 September [1632], HA Corr. 14/10,798 and 13,042 and 7/6748. On Hobart, see Reeve, *Charles I*, pp. 85, 99 and 118–71.

21 ECH to H, 7 July 1632; Hastings to same, 14 September 1632; and H to Manchester, 19 June 1637, HA Corr. 14/4852 and 5312, and 15/5547. See also Sharpe, *The Personal Rule*, pp. 145–50.

22 ECH to H, 7 July 1632, HA Corr. 14/4852. See also same to Corbett, 16 September 1631; Sheppard to H, 9 July 1632; and Roby to H, 15 July 1632, 14/4845, 10,798 and 10,544.

23 2 February 1633, Daily Accounts, 1631–13, HAF 10/17 [unfoliated]; the Herald's certificate; and the Doctor's report, HEH, Bridgewater MSS, EL 6839 and 6840.

24 William Sampson, 'On the right honorable Elizabeth Countess of Huntington [*sic*],' *Virtus Post Funera Vivit* (London, 1636), pp. 14–15; and Viscount Falkland, 'An Epitaph upon the Excellent Countesse of Huntingdon', in I.F., *A Sermon Preached at Ashby-de-la-Zouch*. On the Falkland's visits, see 8 March 1630, Oats Delivered; and 20 October and 12 November 1632, Daily Accounts, HAF 9/11 and 9/17.

25 'Mr Beale his acquittance', 6 June 1634, HAF 11/14; and H's petition to Charles, June 1634, HAP 18/8.

26 H to Norgate, 10 September 1634, HA Corr. 14/5538; and Household Stuff at Donnington Park, April 1635, HA Inventories 1/11. See also above, p. 75.

27 H to Lambe, 8 September 1634, HA Corr. 14/5537; H's charge, 8 January 1639, HAM 26/6; and 'Certaine directions', HAP 15/8, fols. 2–2v. See also Sharpe, *The Personal Rule*, pp. 306, 321 and 739.

28 H to Arundel, 31 January 1636, HA Corr. 15/5546; and H's charge, 8 January 1639, HAM 26/6. See also Arundel to H, 10 July 1634 and 20 June 1639; Norgate to same, 19 July 1634; Maltravers to same, 4 July 1639; and H to Norgate, 10 September 1634, HA Corr. 15/6921, 6922, 9726, 6911 and 5538.

29 'A note of the fees', 29 February 1636, HAM 81/1. On the debt repayment, see for example H's petition to James, 2 July 1624, HAP 17/11.

30 Corporation Resolutions, 16 July 1634; and 'The Kinge and Queene', [1634], Leics. RO, BR II/18/19, fols. 653 and 611. See also BR III/2/80, p. 161; and William Kelly, *Royal Progresses and Visits to Leicester* (Leicester, 1884), pp. 388–92.

31 'Household stuffe at Donnington Park', October 1639, HA Inventories 1/13, fol. 16v; Davies to H, 1 April 1625, HA Corr. 11/1930; and 'A note taken out of the booke of St George', 28 April 1634, HA Genealogical 1/5.

32 Leics. RO, DE 720/30, fol. 36v; and De 625/60, fol. 46v.

33 H's complaint; and testimony of Richard Jacombe and Thomas Goddard, H *v.* Fawnt, 1635, HA Legal 7/1, p. 2; and 7/3, pp. 40–4 and 53–4.

34 Sharpe, *The Personal Rule*, pp. 509–36.

35 Barnes, *Somerset*, p. 262; and PC to LLs, 24 April 1635, PRO PC 2/44, pp. 536–8.

36 Leics. RO, BR III/2/80, p. 211; DE 625/60, fols. 47v–48; and DE 720/30, fols. 38–38v.

37 Cases from Easter, 7 Charles I, and Michaelmas, 9 Charles I, 'Reports of Cases in the Star Chamber', Harvard Law School, LMS 1128, fols. 56, 83, 85 and 93; H to Dixie, 6 May 1635; and Dixie to H, 9 May 1635, HA Corr. 15/5541 and 2296.

38 'Richard Skot the carrier ... his bill', 14 April 1635; and 'Mr Lovejoy the smith his bill', 15 May 1635; 'Laid out for ... Huntingdon', [1635]; 'Judeth Jollie her bill', 19 August 1635; 'Denis the Coachman his bill', [1635]; and 'William Alvie his bill', 25 June 1636, HAF

12/38 [Miscellaneous bills], 12/7, 12/4 and 12/18 [Miscellaneous bills].

39 Sir Henry Skipwith's testimony; and Fawnt's Interrogatories, H *v.* Fawnt, HA Legal 7/4, pp. 20–1 and 82–8.

40 In a 1635 *liber pacis*, the names of Fawnt and Hesilrige have been crossed out and the word 'ex' inserted; PRO C193/13/2, fol. 37.

41 'Lady Hesilriges Petition', 22 June 1635, HA Legal 6/5; and PC order, 30 December, PRO PC2/45, p. 314.

Chapter 11

Politics and the courts

The Court of Star Chamber had a fearful contemporary reputation. One anxious mother in a popular poem warned her son against such 'a dangerous court', and after the verdicts in several celebrated cases in the 1630s, the defendants would have endorsed her judgement. While modern scholars have not minimised the court's severity in these notorious incidents, they have sought to place them within the total volume of business before the Star Chamber. From this broader perspective the once awesome court assumes a more benign appearance. The bulk of the cases concerned non-political matters; most verdicts were reasonable; the massive fines were not generally collected in full. The new prescription in short has transformed Star Chamber into a thoroughly routine judicial body preoccupied with mundane disputes.[1]

What permits this stark contrast between the contemporary assessment and the modern reappraisal is the almost complete destruction of the records of the Caroline court; of the hundreds of cases which the Star Chamber deliberated after 1626, a bare handful can be followed from the initial pleading to the final sentencing. Within this select category, Huntingdon *v.* Fawnt arguably is one of the best documented cases. To be sure, the earl's legal contest with his erstwhile colleague on the bench cannot be ranked with the high-profile trials of the 1630s, nor can Fawnt be confused with Hampden, Prynne, Burton or Bastwick. Nevertheless the very ordinariness of the case makes it even more compelling, for in this routine trial the Star Chamber ran true to its older, more fearsome form.

HUNTINGDON V. FAWNT

Almost two weeks before Lady Hesilrige secured her husband's temporary release, the councillors accepted Fawnt's apology, and Sir William walked out of the Fleet. Sir Arthur, however, did not envy his colleague, since freedom in Fawnt's case simply meant the right to defend himself in Star Chamber. Although the trial was to last another three years, Sir Arthur's attention never wavered, for he had only narrowly avoided Fawnt's fate. After all, the charge of being 'a man of perverse and factious disposition not affecting your [Charles's] happie government [and] a common opposer' could have easily applied to Sir Arthur. Plainly Huntingdon's attorney felt that way; he alleged that when Fawnt 'did most maliciously wickedly and unlawfullie Plott and Resolve to incite and stirrup your Maiesties people', he had worked in concert with 'others to your subiect [Huntingdon] as yet unknowne whose names when they shalbe discovered your subiect praieth may bee incerted into the bill', thoughtfully allowing room for Hesilrige in the suit.[2] Yet in the end, notwithstanding frequent mentions, Sir Arthur never became a party to the case. Instead he watched from the sidelines as Huntingdon savaged his old mentor.

By 1635 William Noy, who had earlier advised Huntingdon in the Shirley case, was dead, and in his place, Huntingdon selected John Lightfoot of Grays Inn. Although less celebrated than Noy, Lightfoot proved himself adept in drawing the indictment so that the earl could appeal both to the recent defamation cases as well as to the legal campaigns against political malcontents. Thus Lightfoot began by setting out a clash between aggrieved virtue and malignancy personified. Both as a peer of the realm and as the 'Lieutenant of the countyes and principall officer of trust there' Huntingdon 'ought to have due honor and respect and not to be scandalized and traduced'. That Fawnt had failed in this obligation was scarcely surprising, since he was, Lightfoot argued, 'of a perverse and factious disposition not affecting his Maiesties happy government and ... an opposer of the demands and directions of his Majesty and the lords of the council'. For years Fawnt had spoken and written against the earl in words

> full of scandall and faction and tend to the fireing up of the like ill affected persons to mutinye and tumults and to sett the people in opposition against his Maiesties officers and to cause remissnes in performance and neglect of his commands.

From these devastating general charges, the Bill quickly descended to particulars, which were long on rhetorical denunciation and short on solid evidence. Starting in 1625 Sir William and an unnamed associate 'did most maliciouslie wickedly and unlawfullie Plott and Resolve to incite and stirr up' the county elite to evade their militia assessments. To achieve this end, Fawnt laboured to draw Huntingdon 'into dishonor scandall and disgrace' by attempting to 'invente frame contrive publish and divulge' reports which slandered Huntingdon 'most wickedly falsely unlawfully and malitiouslie ... by letter messages wordes and speeches to divers and sundrie'. Two particular examples of Fawnt's malice supported this contention. First, Huntingdon had called for 'treble that nomber of horse' which normally were levied on the county gentry; and second, the earl 'did charge and oppresse your said people with greater Impositions taxations and levies of money ... then was or could be necessarily Imploied'. The success of Fawnt's campaign, Lightfoot argued, was a shortfall of nearly £400 in the 1626 militia levy.

As proof positive of seditious discourse, the earl offered Fawnt's first letter to Dixie. So far Lightfoot had proceeded in a predictable, albeit heavy-handed, fashion. Yet with the dating of Fawnt's letter, he did something unexpected; he insisted that it had actually been written in June 1633. Furthermore, it was not, Huntingdon's attorney maintained, a private letter to his cousin. Rather 'in divers other Townes Villages and places' in Leicestershire, Rutland 'and elsewhere', Sir William did 'bragg and vaunt of the said Libell and Letter ... and gave out copies of the same and did tell publish and divulge the effects and contents thereof'. This letter thus was part of Fawnt's larger design to disrupt the 1635 muster where he did 'wickedly diswade and worke in people an Unwillingnesse and backwardnes'. There at the Leicester meeting 'in a publique manner' he told everyone that 'the opinion of the right honorable the Lordes of your Councell' was to levy money only for the Muster Master and 'that theire Lords intended there should bee noe more levied for anie other uses or purposes whatsoever'. The price for 'a malignant humor to his Maiestie his state and government' was steep; Huntingdon asked the court for damages of £10,000.[3]

The magnitude of this amount together with the gravity of the charges underscored the seriousness of the case. So too did Huntingdon's personal depositions. In other suits, the earl had simply retained solicitors to follow his business; in the Fawnt case, he did so himself. Three weeks after the initial hearing, he leased the Earl of Nottingham's house in Charterhouse Yard. There can be no better indication of his resolution than the £62 which the impoverished peer laid out in rent. In contrast, Fawnt was, as he confessed, 'crazie and aged', with 'a dangerous swelling in his Belly' and with a seriously ill wife who had not left her bed in six months; hence he could not possibly travel to Westminster without risking his life.[4] Nevertheless he chose his counsel well: William Holt and John Herne. Although Holt was scarcely a neophyte, having represented no less than Sir John Eliot and Alexander Leighton, Herne was one of the era's premier defence attorneys, who had moved from Sir Henry Shirley to William Prynne and Henry Sherfield a few years later. Herne's efforts, while not enough to save his clients, nevertheless impressed his opponents. Thus when both Strafford and Laud struggled before an equally packed court in the early 1640s, they placed their lives in Mr Herne's hands. So diligently did he labour on behalf of the archbishop that Laud requested his presence on the scaffold.[5] In short, the earl was not going to win by default.

In the face of Lightfoot's bombast, Holt and Herne did not flinch. Since the case, they rightly reasoned, hinged on the Dixie letter, they stressed the implausibility of Lightfoot's interpretation where they did not overturn it entirely. First of all, the notion of painting Fawnt as a malignant was grossly overdrawn; since Sir William had long served as a Justice and twice been Sheriff, it only made sense that a man with such 'long experience ... of publique service' should privately speak to another magistrate about administrative problems. And it was the privacy of these discussions which Herne and Holt stressed. Far from organising a mass protest, Fawnt 'did privately conceive write and send sealed' the letter in response to Dixie's note ordering a second militia assessment. Confronted with demands which exceeded 'all ordinary presidents and examples of this Defendants former experience', Sir William could not help discussing the matter. Far from stepping out of line by protesting, Fawnt would have been remiss as a JP if he had kept silent. There was no intention to oppose the Council's orders, nor to cast 'dishonor disreputation or detraction' on Huntingdon. Instead, Fawnt had written 'as a Loyal Subject', eager 'to prevent and avoyde any such misinformation by any such inferior Officers or Agents in those affayres'. Herne and Holt portrayed the letter, not as the work of a provocateur, but rather as a desperate attempt to 'prevent or divert any provocation or occasions of any such petition Complainte or suite for any moderation or Reformation' which might have come from 'some of the Common people'. Thus the letter contained 'noe such severall scandalls' but rather his plea to Huntingdon's Deputy Lieutenant for 'some such equall moderation of those affayres'.

From the first, Huntingdon and Dixie knew that Fawnt had had no seditious intent; otherwise, Herne and Holt argued, they would not have waited so long to proceed against him. And here Herne and Holt had a field day with Lightfoot's transparent attempt to misdate the letter. It was a subterfuge to let Huntingdon and Dixie conceal the fact that they had known about the letter for 'nine or tenn yeares'. In all that time,

> noe exception was to this Defendants knowledge taken, nor any complaint by the now plaintiff either as a Peere of the Realme or as a Lord Lieutenant of that County nor by any of his saide deputie Lieutenant thereof nor any pretence made of any supposed offence therein or of any such complaint thereof as is nowe after about Tenne yeares silence and Cestation of any such Complainte pretended in and by the said Bill.

Only now did Huntingdon and his men resolve 'to make some benefitt to themselves by the nowe Plaintiffes exception to the same letter'. Finally, came the clincher: in 1635 the Privy Council had rebuked and imprisoned Sir William for the same letter. Herne and Holt thus rested their case on the legal ban against double jeopardy. Everything else in Huntingdon's bill was beneath detailed refutation.[6]

Unfortunately for Fawnt, his attorneys overargued almost as much as Lightfoot had. On reading their demurrer, Huntingdon rejoiced; 'for any thinge I can discerne in it there are more words then matter'. The point at issue centered on the contention that the Council had already punished Fawnt for the letters, and here the earl faulted Herne's lack of imagination. Since Herne had entered a similar plea for Sir Henry Shirley in 1628, Huntingdon eagerly pointed out to Lightfoot, that 'you may see Mr Herne runs upon the same Byas in this Demurrer'. Given the results of this manoeuvre in 1628, the earl was delighted to see Herne deploy it again; notwithstanding 'all his [Herne's] Rhetoricke and Sir Henry Shirleis powerfull freinds', Herne's client had to 'ask me forgiveness upon his knees'. There was every hope of a similar outcome this time, since it was an easy matter to establish that the Council in 1635 had punished Fawnt for his behavior at the muster, not for the letters to Dixie.[7]

Lightfoot was equally unimpressed with the demurrer, dismissing it as 'a meere delay'. To assist Lightfoot's efforts to hasten matters 'as effectually as I can', Huntingdon quickly produced testimonials from his brother-in-law, the Earl of Bridgewater, stating that the Council had not earlier punished Fawnt for the letters. Herne and Holt, however, proved quite skilful at thwarting any attempt to proceed 'effectually'. Lightfoot next sought to persuade the judges that Fawnt's demurrer was inadequate, and they agreed with him, but only after agonising delays from May 1636 to February 1637. Eventually Herne and Holt submitted 'Further severall Answeares', essentially reiterating the original demurrer. Their major shift in tactics was the decision to focus the Court's attention on the immediate background of Fawnt's letters; their client's sentiments, which might have sounded inflammatory in 1635, were only a reflection of the extreme situation in 1626, when Huntingdon's second militia assessment exceeded all others not only in the county, but all others in the entire country.[8]

This task proved complicated and, more importantly, time-consuming. After Fawnt's attorneys submitted their second answer, only in August 1637 did the court issue a commission to collect depositions in Leicestershire. Aggravated by the slow pace, Huntingdon first pressed for hearings a month later before wiser heads convinced him to move the date back to January 1638. Meanwhile unexpected difficulties developed in another quarter. To head the commission Huntingdon asked two solicitors, Gervase Teney and a Mr Gilbert, 'to do me a Curtesie which may make me acount myself much beholden to you'. Confident of their agreement, he secured the Court's commission for them. Yet in spite of the earl's pleas that in this suit 'I am deeply ingaged in my honor,' Teney declined to serve 'in regard of some secret promise you [Teney] have disavowed such imployments'. This development agitated the normally phlegmatic peer, for finding a suitable replacement would take valuable time. A delay might make the judges think that Huntingdon harboured 'a tacite mistrust I shold have in the iustice of my Cause', and certainly his suit 'wilbe very much delaied, wherby my Adversary may gaine much advantage'. Teney nonetheless refused, leaving Huntingdon scrambling to fill a new commission in time for the January hearing. He succeeded in avoiding an adjournment, but as the margin of error dwindled down to a few days, the second half of 1637 proved particularly uncomfortable.[9]

Satisfaction for this frantic activity came on 16 January 1638 when several dozen witnesses gathered at Nathaniel Potter's inn in Loughbough. By then, death had claimed some of those who could have presented valuable testimony, like Sir Thomas Hesilrige, Francis Staresmore and Sir Thomas Gerard. Yet because most of their colleagues were still alive, the gathering took on the air of a reunion of superannuated veterans of county government. Huntingdon's shift to younger officers in 1625–26, while alienating the Hesilriges, did allow him a decade later to call on John Everard the Muster Master, Sir Henry Skipwith, and perhaps the crucial witness, Sir Wolston Dixie. The earl was equally fortunate that the former militia treasurer, Walter Rudinge, although retired and well into his sixties, was eager to discuss old administrative procedures. While their information was always illuminating and often telling, perhaps the most striking testimony came from the constables. In response to precise questions, their betters tended to reply vaguely, 'thereabout' being a recurrent phrase with the Deputy Lieutenants. In contrast, the constables' testimony revealed that they had absorbed the first rule of early Stuart administrative life: they kept careful records. Fawnt's attorneys consequently learned the rashness of putting words into the mouths of these obscure local officials; as often as not, it earned them scenes like that when John Rice, the sixty-seven-year-old former Chief Constable of Gartry hundred, quoted Huntingdon's exact orders and the precise yields of various assessments down to the last pence.[10]

From these witnesses, both sets of attorneys sought to extract evidence to support their clients. Mr Lightfoot's questions aimed at establishing the equitable nature of the Hastings regime during the war years. While the practice of paying the militia captains as well as the Muster Master ran up the assessments, Rudinge, Skipwith and Dixie eloquently justified the policy; they 'thought it very hard that they [the Captains] should bee putt to discharge and paye their under officers for his Maiesties service'. Likewise Huntingdon had never been arbitrary. On receipt of any Council order, the earl, Dixie reported, always called his staff together 'to consult with them and to receave and take theire opinions'. Given such careful administration, Fawnt's allegation that Huntingdon called for £2,000 in 1626 was a gross exaggeration. A phalanx of constables armed with a mass of facts and figures conclusively proved that while the 1626 levy was unprecedented, the earl had called only for £1,220 and had collected less than £900. Thus a chorus of local officials only echoed Skipwith's conclusion; far from impoverishing the shire, Huntingdon 'hath used his best endeavours ... at all tymes and upon all occasions to ease the saide Countie all that hee could from charge and trouble'.[11] After Lightfoot's interrogation, Fawnt cut a less than admirable figure. His query went unanswered about 'whoe at that tyme had soe great or a greater estate' than Fawnt did 'and were more easily charged with fynding horse'. None of the witnesses denied the proposition that Sir Thomas Burton, Sir Edward Hartopp and William Halford, although poorer than Fawnt, presented as many horses as he did. Even Dixie conceded that Fawnt 'hath been divers tymes found and Judged defective some tymes both in horse and furniture and especially in his furniture for his horse'.[12] After Lightfoot had finished, Herne and Holt faced an uphill struggle simply to redeem some modicum of respectability for Sir William.

When Fawnt's attorneys examined their witnesses on 19 March 1638, they shifted the focus away from Huntingdon's strong suit, administrative routine. First they sought to establish that Huntingdon and his Deputies had given some hundreds and some gentlemen preferential treatment. The witnesses thus were encouraged to report any grumbling about the rating system and to reveal 'what words did they or any of them use declareing their dislike'. Problems with taxation, Herne and Holt suggested, were only symptomatic of larger irregularities within the Leicestershire regiment. What, for instance, had happened to the county's extensive stock of 'Oatmeale, Meale, bacon, butter, Bullet, match, powder, pickaxes spades shovells ironbound Cartes and other ymplements'? More embarrassing still, Fawnt's attorneys pressed for details of what the paid officer corps actually did; how many times had the trained men 'attended untill late in the afternoone and had noe Muster Master or other officer to instruct and treyne you', and how frequently had the militiamen simply 'shewed your Armes and paid the moneyes ymposed on you or your towne and soe departed without any more service'? Even the question of the trained men's daily expenses attracted the attention of Fawnt's attorneys: 'was there not much money spent by the countrey ... and much drunknenes and disorder?'[13]

This line of questioning should have produced a flood of provocative responses, and some deponents obliged. William Earle came forward with his story of how the earl and the Muster Master had forced his master to buy new arms from the London armourer; and Rudinge confessed that much of the pioneer equipment had been lent to 'poore labourers'. Furthermore a constable, Thomas Goddard, conceded that often the militiamen 'have nott been trayned but onely have shewed their Armes paide their money and been discharged'. Goddard also testified that the 1626 levies collectively cost his village of Little Peatling, which presented only one man, £3 10s.[14] But along with this supporting testimony for Fawnt, a good deal for Huntingdon inadvertently emerged.

For example, Fawnt's defence revolved around the turmoil of the 1626 levy. Yet Francis Gilliam, the Chief Constable of Guthlaxton, where Fawnt resided, calmly reported that he and his under-officers had collected all of the £188 levied on the hundred without incident.[15]

If many in the shire were reluctant to criticise the earl, others outside it were less deferential. To prove that Huntingdon had erected an unusually burdensome military regime, Herne and Holt summoned constables from all the neighbouring shires, who all reiterated the often stark differences among county militias. In none of them were the militia fees anything higher than 4s. per trained man; indeed, in Lincolnshire and Nottinghamshire, the standard sum was a mere 12d. To be sure, the Council order of 10 July 1626 had produced some variations on this pattern; in Nottinghamshire, the figure skyrocketed to almost 9s. per trained man. But for most of the rest, 1626 was simply an ordinary year like any other. Some had extra training, and a few had ordered a rudimentary pioneer company, but none collected additional funds.[16] Herne and Holt meanwhile constantly stressed the sharp contrast with Leicestershire. For example, Thomas Worde, a High Constable of Northamptonshire, could not recall any 'command for provision of iron bound Carts geeres spades mattockes pickaxes meale bacon butter or cheese'. All of this, needless to say, only supported the defence's point that Huntingdon's levies actually 'exceede all ordinarye presidents of the same county or any of the counties in this realme'.[17]

Herne and Holt had even better luck questioning Dixie. Sir Wolston plainly was a man torn by his professional loyalty to Huntingdon and by kinship with Fawnt, and after both sides had interrogated him, Dixie doubtless rued ever having sent Huntingdon the letters in the first place. Carefully reconstructing the scene, Fawnt's attorneys queried whether Fawnt had not earlier told Dixie 'the Country people tooke notice of the said taxation and were much discontented'. On this point Sir Wolston was vague; 'he doth not well remember'. Could Dixie confirm that Sir William was simply replying to an earlier letter from Sir Wolston about military affairs? Dixie could, although he did not retain a copy of it. Then came the pivotal questions: had the letters arrived in Dixie's hands sealed, and had he ever heard Fawnt discuss these matters with anyone else? Sir Wolston was emphatic that they arrived sealed; indeed, so far as he knew, aside from his son, his secretary and Huntingdon, no one else had even seen the letters until 1635. He was equally certain that Fawnt had never spoken in this vein with anyone else. Finally, talking about a man he knew quite well, Dixie firmly ruled out any possibility that Fawnt had been acting 'out of malice, but meerely out of error'.[18]

All in all, Holt and Herne can only have been satisfied with the results. In the opening rounds they had made easy work of Lightfoot's attempt to misdate the Dixie letters, and against the prosecution's case that the earl's assessments were just and equitable, they had highlighted precisely how extraordinary they had been. Finally the heart of Lightfoot's case portrayed Fawnt as a factious person long intent on stirring up a mutiny; not only had none of many witnesses backed up the prosecution's description, but Huntingdon's Deputy Lieutenant had flatly denied it. Therefore, by the end of the depositions early in 1638, the case against Sir William effectively boiled down to having written two private letters to his cousin.

HUNTINGDON *V.* LEICESTERSHIRE

Hundreds of pages of depositions together with the bills and answers then went up to the judges, who brooded over the mountain of material for several months, and in the meantime, plaintiff and defendant manoeuvred for position. Notwithstanding the success of his attorneys, Fawnt was deeply apprehensive about the outcome. His reason for failing to attend the hearings was no polite excuse, for stomach trouble claimed his life in less than two years. While Sir William's interest in the case had waned with deteriorating health, what eradicated it altogether was the death of his only surviving son, Arthur Fawnt, who appears to have taken his father's pugnacity with him. On 8 January 1638, the day of his death, Fawnt attempted to resolve the dispute. Invoking bonds of blood, he begged Huntingdon as 'a poore kinsman' to call off the proceedings. All of their difficulties had stemmed from his cousin Dixie, who had 'either ignorantly or wilfully mistook my meaning ... whearupon your Lordship knoweth what troble hath come unto mee'. In hopes of ending the dispute, Fawnt explained how he had come to write the fateful letter. First, Sir William denied that he had 'intended or indevered aney manor of dishonor, prejudis or damage at all to your lordship'. Rather he had simply thought that Huntingdon had not known the actual size of the assessments and so had written to Dixie in hopes of 'reformation wherof and for noe other end'. Needless to say, the bleak repercussions of penning these letters made Fawnt proclaim that 'I doe hartily wish the letters had wranght [ranged] no further then I intended them then had thes unkynd sutes and great Charges bene spared'.[19]

Huntingdon never deigned to reply as the prospect danced before him of simultaneously crushing a prominent critic and mending his own fortunes. Before the depositions had even begun, the earl resumed lobbying for compensation. After years of searching, he had at last, he reported to his cousin, the Earl of Manchester, 'found out a reasonable sute'; it was almost certainly Fawnt's fine in the Star Chamber case. With the long awaited compensation almost in hand, Huntingdon had no time for a last-minute settlement.[20]

The success of Herne and Holt in deflating Lightfoot's case makes the earl's optimism appear unwarranted. Nevertheless his position had distinct advantages, and chief among these was the sheer weight of the evidence, the depositions alone totalling over 200 pages. To guide the judges through this information, Lightfoot produced an abstract, but even that ran to several closely written pages. The full tactical advantage of such extensive testimony was that it somewhat obscured the points at issue, especially to the busy Privy Councillors, and for them, Huntingdon thoughtfully prepared multiple copies of a one-page abstract of the entire case. Hence, although Fawnt had said in his letter that 'many thousand will be ready to prove what he hath said', Lightfoot noted that Herne and Holt were able to offer 'no proofe, not so much as by one witnes'. This was true enough, provided the judges ignored all the evidence from the neighbouring shires. This legal legerdemain was scarcely noticeable, because earlier in the precis Huntingdon still insisted the Dixie letters had been written in 1632, notwithstanding compelling evidence for dating them from 1626.[21] The extensive testimony, in short, simply allowed Lightfoot to juggle the facts of the case to his client's advantage.

Huntingdon's chief advantage, however, was the political climate. For once in his life, Huntingdon was in the right place at the right time. Had he brought the suit in the late 1620s, the Star Chamber almost certainly would have listened carefully to Fawnt. By the late 1630s, however, new precedents of punishments and fines regularly came out of Star Chamber, and in the bill Mr Lightfoot pandered to the government's obsession with order and due respect. Furthermore, the delays in the case, which had so irritated Huntingdon, ultimately placed him in an enviable position. Thus the most important factor in the case arguably had nothing to do with the law. Concurrent with Star Chamber suit ran another contest, which might appropriately be termed Huntingdon *v.* Leicestershire. On it everything turned.

Having successfully mustered the regiment and brought one critic before Star Chamber, Huntingdon would not willingly dismiss the militiamen on another vacation. Admittedly the professional gloss which his troops had earlier acquired could not be restored in a few annual meetings, but as he had earlier shown, even erratic musters, if carefully handled, could make the regiment more capable. In May 1636, the Council ordered another muster, noting that with 'his Maiesties fleet being now readie to put to Sea', the king could not relax the landward defences. The strict instructions of April 1635 were still to govern the militia, but 'for the ease of the Countrie', the shire could dispense with watching beacons, organising additional home guard units and underwriting a Provost Marshal. Such relaxation was too much for the Leicestershire elite; led by Stamford and Lord Hastings, and supported by no less than Sir William Fawnt, they petitioned the Council to retain the aged Captain Savile, whose office was 'soe necessary as the countrey thinke their money well bestowed'. Faced with such support, the councillors naturally agreed, making Leicestershire the only shire in the realm to retain its Provost

Marshal. Again in March 1637 came renewed commands for a muster, but this order fell victim to an outbreak of the plague. In fact, the infection in the East Midlands was so virulent that the councillors regarded the assembled Nottinghamshire militia as a serious health threat; hence they ordered the Earl of Newcastle *not* to muster his men. While the situation to the south was not as grave, it was enough to forestall any musters in Leicestershire.[22]

With this inactivity the councillors rested content until riots in Edinburgh jolted them out of their complacency. In August 1637, Whitehall's concern for public health abruptly gave way to frantic calls for immediate musters 'in these stirring and hostile times'. Gone too was the amnesia about the importance of powder stocks as the councillors suddenly decreed new minimum levels of powder and shot unheard of since the 1620s. The urgent new priorities sent the constables moving across the shire collecting funds 'towards the provision of powder'; Waltham contributed £1 15s. 3d. for its three men, and Branston £1 10s. as its share for Mr Newton. Even at Waltham's lower rate, payments on this order meant a levy of approx. 12s. a man, or £300 overall. Careful adherence to Huntingdon's instructions allowed the Rutland Deputy Lieutenants to 'boldly affirme that fewe Cuntries of England are better furnished in there Magazine then this is'. The same judgement doubtless applied in Leicestershire. Furthermore, early in 1638 Huntingdon also ordered a series of company musters, the first in over a decade. The results were predictably poor; in Captain Rooe's company, four soldiers presented by clergymen were inadequate; one pleaded a recent fire, another cited a quarrel between the two vicars whom he represented, and two simply disappeared. Even worse were the private men, fourteen of whom failed to turn up, and those who did were highly dubious: one was 'unlikely', two pikemen appeared without their armour, two more attempted to share one set of equipment, and a confused musketeer came attired as a pikeman.[23] While these soldiers *manqué* rightly attracted attention, they should not obscure the other 175 men whose weapons and armour passed muster.

Regimental training quickly followed as Huntingdon ordered a three-day meeting at Leicester in the summer. The officers' fees were relatively modest: Branston paid 10s. and Waltham on the Wolds 6s. per man, or a total levy of around £200. But the local expenses of such a long muster were comparatively high. John Newton cost Branston another 15s. 8d., and Waltham's three men called for a further £3 1s. 9d. The ratepayers' one consolation was that the training was not perfunctory; Waltham's higher expenditure reflected the need to purchase a new belt and scabbard and to repair a musket.[24] Therefore some £200 in officers' fees, together with the several hundred more spent only a few months earlier on munitions, signalled a return to the levels of militia expenditure common a decade earlier.

The militia's revival guaranteed an attentive audience for Fawnt. But the ratepayers were never able to concentrate on the questionable legality of the militia assessments, thanks to two other projects which Whitehall had launched in 1635. Formally the most prominent of these, the Ship Money levy, had nothing to do with Huntingdon, since it was entirely the Sheriff's responsibility. Reality was more complex, for this project prompted the regime to pay closer attention to the selection of these officers, and that development made it hard for contemporaries to dissociate the earl from the levy.[25]

Hitherto, the prestige of a sheriff bore little relation to the heavy financial obligations of the office, which in 1630 cost John Bainbridge £253 11s. 4d., mostly in hospitality at the sessions. Consequently, the honour, whenever possible, descended on wealthy merchants struggling with their awkward metamorphosis into gentlemen. So valuable was William Wollaston as a sheriff that the former London draper moved immediately from Leicestershire in 1629 to Staffordshire the following year. Aside from such logical choices, the office generally went to local gentlemen either vain enough to want the honour or powerless to forestall it. The only exception to this pattern came in the late 1620s, when Charles I pricked a succession of six JPs, and even then they could scarcely be termed the senior members of the bench. Nathaniel Lacy arguably was the most obscure member of the early Stuart bench; two others, Sir Thomas Hartopp and Sir John Bale, had barely come of age; the rest, George Ashby, Sir Erasmus de la Fountaine and Sir Henry Shirley, were too well-off to care.[26] Certainly none of them was among Huntingdon's inner circle who ran the county. In any event, with the return of peace in 1629, these magistrates once again returned the office to the local gentlemen and merchants.

This pattern meant that the first Ship Money writs went to Francis Saunders and John Pulteney, both mere esquires and Pulteney only twenty-five. In the end, notwithstanding their periodic complaints, both men succeeded admirably, but only at great personal cost; within a year of stepping down, Saunders had sold up and left the county, and Pulteney was dead. Moreover, opposition which had initially been sporadic solidified as the scheme became a regular annual event. These problems forced the government to reassess the ordinary method of selecting sheriffs, and in 1636, the councillors in an extraordinary move ordered the circuit judges to prepare a short list of 'the ablest most serviceable and well affected persons'. Little wonder then that in the fall of 1637 and 1638, Charles's pen came down on the names of Sir Henry Skipwith and Sir William Roberts. Both were JPs and Huntingdon protégés. A long-serving magistrate, Roberts had married into the Bales, the family of the earl's administrative creatures, and his son commanded one of Huntingdon's prized militia companies.[27] Skipwith meanwhile was one of the Deputy Lieutenants whom Hesilrige had denounced for sharking the county. With such men in charge, the notion of the Sheriff's autonomy became nothing more than polite fiction.

The regime's decision to deploy such administrative heavy artillery proved wise, for the difficulties grew with each levy. Late in 1636, Pulteney's major complaint concerned a number of poor ratepayers whose notional assessments totalled less than £30. Only a few months later, Skipwith was astonished to find 'soe manye complayners and opposers', along the county's southern border from 'some Puritans that are soe neare Northamptonshire that they savor too much of the disobedience of those partes'. By the time Roberts took over, the inability to agree on assessments paralysed many local officials.[28] For their part, Skipwith and Roberts responded as they would have with militia defaulters: they began bullying slackers into line by issuing a wave of warrants to distrain their property. Thus a group of Loughborough landowners had to pay £177 6s. 6d. to secure the release of twenty-seven cows and 185 lambs. Such a firm response raised the political temperature, and it brought Hesilrige back into the spotlight. Constables busy distraining goods near Noseley found themselves face to face with Sir Arthur. Eventually the officials withdrew in confusion, and their colleagues across the county downed tools.[29] After calming the constables, Skipwith ran into a more formidable problem a few miles away, in Fawnt's hundred, where Robert Lord and Elkington Kirke urged restive constables upset with the Sheriff's orders to disobey him and to argue their case before the Privy Council; they all soon got their wish after first cooling their heels in Westminster for a week. Unfortunately for them, any hope of an attentive hearing ended when the 'sauciness' of Lord and Kirke irritated the councillors. Such antics should not obscure the quite real problems of collecting the levy, as the plight of Edward Chamberlain reveals. A local officer of the Court of Wards, Chamberlain had become so notorious for his zeal in this project that he pleaded for, and received, a royal pardon to protect him against vengeful law suits from 'ill-affected' neighbours.[30]

These problems notwithstanding, the two magistrates pressed ahead. Roberts avowed that in spite of poor health, 'I will abroad and get in what money I can.' Skipwith meanwhile announced his ambition 'to be the first

Table 5 **Ship Money: percentage collected two years after each writ**

County	1635	1636	1637
Derbyshire	100.00	100.00	96.97
Leicestershire	100.00	100.00	91.11
Lincolnshire	100.00	100.00	76.34
Northamptonshire	90.54	85.83	70.12
Nottinghamshire	100.00	99.14	100.00

Source SP 16/364/23; 16/400/113; 16/431/62; 16/473/103.

Sherriffe that shoulde paye in his whole somme'.[31] Although that goal eluded Sir Henry, he and his colleagues managed to raise impressive amounts of money. In the first two writs issued in August 1635 and October 1636, the Sheriffs each paid in £4,500. Only in the third levy, begun in October 1637, did Roberts fall short of the mark with arrearages on May 1639 of £400. Nevertheless, even with this troubled third levy, Leicestershire from 1635 through 1638 paid into the Exchequer £12,900, or almost 96 per cent of the total assessments. While such success could not equal the flawless performances in Derbyshire and Nottinghamshire, the shire certainly shone in comparison with its neighbours in Lincolnshire and Northamptonshire. By any measure, Huntingdon's protégés had done well.

Unfortunately for the local gentlemen, neither Huntingdon nor the Exchequer had done with their purses. Early in 1631, the regime had given fair warning of its insistence on enforcing earlier regulations about poor relief, and this renewed interest in vagrants led ineluctably to rural depopulation and enclosure. Although such an initiative aimed at stopping a common practice largely responsible for the flood of vagrants, local gentlemen suspected that what attracted the government's attention was landlords' profits as much as the plight of the local poor. A few like Sir Henry Shirley reacted calmly on learning that they had been returned for depopulation; if he could not convince the councillors of the legality of his enclosure at Ragdale, then he promised to 'throw in his ditches againe'.[32] Others lacking Shirley's cash reserves responded to the news more excitedly, Stamford did when Gerard returned him. They all learned in 1635 that their apprehensions were well founded when a depopulation commission began assessing compositions.

A thorough survey of the Personal Rule has led Kevin Sharpe to conclude that 'whilst the benefit to the government of fines should not be discounted, the financial aspects of the commission were not the most important'. Perceptive though his observation may be, it would have prompted vigorous dissent from over 100 landowners in Leicestershire; out of the £40,000 collected nationwide, they had contributed £8,861, roughly 20 per cent of the total. In other words, in a county where all parliamentary assessments in the 1620s garnered only £10,000, Leicestershire paid the equivalent of twelve subsidies in less than five years. Furthermore, this total was not evenly distributed across the period; in 1636, the depopulation fines of £4,320 effectively represented another Ship Money assessment of £4,500. Little wonder then that the county's banner year with the Exchequer came in 1637 with receipts totalling £6,637. The magnitude of the demands concerned even Huntingdon. In order to set a favourable precedent, many of the JPs were the first to compound. Sir Henry Skipwith quickly paid in £500, as did William Halford's family and Sir Erasmus de la Fountayne. Behind them came others on the bench: Sir Edward Hartopp, George Ashby, William Whalley; and Sir Henry

Hastings of Braunston. Local misgivings were further eased by the Exchequer's willingness to arrange easy payment terms, stretching out installments over a year and, in a few cases, over eighteen months. Such thoughtfulness persuaded a host of prominent landowners to compound, from Lord Sherard, the Earl of Kent and the Countess of Thanet to a host of Villierses and Mannerses and even the retired county treasurer, Walter Rudinge. Those erstwhile JPs, Fawnt and Hesilrige, also contributed; as Dixie had predicted, coals did indeed rain down on Sir William's head, at least, of sorts, and in the end the fine was a comparatively tiny £100 and even that only landed in 1639.[33]

While this much was admirable, there were more unsettling aspects of these fines. Given the county's overall contributions, no major landowner appears to have escaped some composition, however notional. Yet Huntingdon did. His rapidly dwindling estate doubtless explains this omission, but the same excuse rings less true for his fellow JPs like Sir William Roberts, Sir John Skeffington and Sir John Bale. Likewise Sir Henry Shirley's appeal to the Council must have found favour, for his heir never had to 'throw in his ditches'. And notwithstanding Gerard's best efforts, the Earl of Stamford never paid a penny. How he achieved this coup is illuminating; with Stamford, Gerard had also named Sir Wolston Dixie, who in turn used backchannels to explain the entire matter privately to Secretary Coke. Needless to say, neither Dixie nor Stamford compounded.

The whiff of favouritism only became stronger as the less fortunate sorted out the details of their composition. William Billers, a Leicester merchant, had to travel to the capital, spend three weeks there and retain an attorney, all of which, he carefully calculated, cost him £14 10s.[34] At first glance, such additional expenses scarcely appear an impressive burden for members of the local elite, but Billers was only settling a small fine of £80. His experience moreover was increasingly common. In the first year of the commission's work, £3,610 of a total of £4,320 came from thirteen gentlemen, eighteen landowners with fines less than £100 accounting for the balance. But in the second year, when most of the large-scale offenders had settled their accounts, the characteristics of the average compounder abruptly changed. Then only nine men paid in £1,000; the remaining £1,136 came from another fifty purses. This trend became even more pronounced in the third year when three landowners contributed £500 and sixty-nine others £795 13s. 4d. Thus as the amount collected diminished, so the number of those fined increased. A few of these with modest compositions admittedly were from the local elite like the Earl of Kent. Nevertheless the bulk of this category was filled with a few gentlemen, many esquires and a number of yeomen. After all, no one would mistake John Parlby, Edward Story, Henry Redish, Robert Briggs, Arthur Cam, Thomas Moore and their collective £50 fine for the social equals of Kent.[35] Consequently while the commissioners had not gone lightly on the

Table 6 **Payments into the Exchequer from Leicestershire, 1635–38 (£)**

Year	Ship Money	Depopulation	Total
1635	3,679	1,110	4,789
1636	821	3,160	3,981
1637	4,500	2,137	6,637
1638	3,900	1,296	5,196
Totals	12,990	7,703	20,603

gentry, they had not forgotten to involve the lower orders.

By any administrative yardstick, Huntingdon's achievement was impressive, for between depopulation fines and Ship Money assessments, money poured into the Exchequer. The least productive of the four years between 1635 and 1638 netted almost £4,000, handily more than the forced loan had collected. Similarly any two of these four years easily equalled all parliamentary taxation in the 1620s. Indeed, the total from these four years exceeded the amount which the regime had collected in both parliamentary and non-parliamentary taxation between 1603 and 1635. Results from the militia regiment, while understandably less dramatic, were nonetheless characteristic of Huntingdon. Consequently, as the court pondered the evidence in Huntingdon *v.* Fawnt, the delays in the case, which had so aggravated the earl, worked to his advantage. By the end of 1638, when Whitehall was beginning to marshal men and money from the provinces, zealous Lords Lieutenant were indispensable, and if nothing else, Herne and Holt had only underscored Huntingdon's utility to the state. With Scottish rebels in arms, the central government would have gone to great lengths to avoid embarrassing a local governor whose crime, as Herne and Holt proved, was his eagerness to execute councillor orders. Precisely how far it would go became apparent on 10 October 1638 when the court rendered its verdict.

EVERY SUBJECT'S BIRTHRIGHT

Huntingdon had always been noticeably taciturn, and this fact renders it all the more astonishing that after decades of restraint, he should have found his voice in January 1639 and, of all places, at the Leicester quarter session. The task at hand was a delicate one; in the midst of the Scottish rebellion, he had to exhort his listeners to assume even greater burdens. Out of a number of rhetorical strategies, he eventually adopted a particularly striking one; he decided to hymn the late Caroline judicial system. Thanks to the labours of the king's judges, 'I thinke no people in the Christian world live under a happier lawe.' Lest this sentiment prompt any murmuring, Huntingdon boldly tackled the subject of Ship Money; it was completely unobjectionable, since 'the Judges have delivered their opinions that it doth of right belong unto him [Charles]'. By this point, the old earl was in full flood rhapsodising over Charles's devotion to the law. Under such a righteous king, justice, he proclaimed, 'doth give to everie man their owne, and is the Subjects birthright'. In fact, 'the poorest man that is may have right done him against the greatest Peere'.[36] For those who had carefully followed the case against Fawnt, this last sentiment must have rung a false note. Admittedly neither was Sir William especially poor nor the earl particularly great. Nevertheless, given what had just happened in Star Chamber, the pious notion that a man might have justice against a peer sounded strange indeed coming from Huntingdon's mouth.

On 19 October 1638, the court found the Dixie letters 'full of mutinous and seditious passages and soe penned as to stirre up the Gentry and others of the County to discontent and mutinie against the kinges service'. Since such 'a very great offence' merited nothing less than 'a severe and exemplary censure'; the only remaining question was its severity. Sir Francis Cottington first proposed that Fawnt should acknowledge his fault and ask Huntingdon's forgiveness as well as pay the Crown £4,000 in fines and Huntingdon £2,000 in damages and court costs. Sir John Finch seconded the motion, adding that Fawnt 'should not beare any office in the Common wealth herafter'. After that, Sir Francis Windebanke unsuccessfully attempted to raise Huntingdon's damages to £4,000 before concurring with Sir John Bramston, Sir Thomas Jermyn and Sir Edward Barret in seconding Cottington. Then the earl's friends and relatives attempted to drive the figures higher. Dorset not only raised both amounts to £5,000, but added, 'if any did goe any higher he wold agree with the most'. To this Arundel and Manchester readily assented. Fortunately for Fawnt, no one else did. After Pembroke plumped for Cottington's proposal, the Archbishop carried the day by proposing a fine of £5,000, damages of £2,000 and Sir William's public admission of guilt at the next quarter session.[37]

It is hard to know which was more flagrant – the miscarriage of justice or the harshness of the verdict. In the courtroom, an unnamed attorney jotted down his impressions of the trial. First the observer noted the importance of the correct date of the Dixie letters; as a result Fawnt's attorneys could argue that 'being so longe before the suit the Earle ought not to have damages in regard of the Statute of Limitations of Actions'. In support of this position, Herne and Holt cited Kingston *v.* Copley. On 14 October 1637, Justices Hutton and Crooke heard the Earl of Kingston's complaint that three years earlier William Copley had called the earl 'a base Lord'. Copley's attorney reminded the court of the 1624 statute limiting defamation actions to two years; after all, 'it was a difficult thing for the defendant and for the witnesses to prove or answere punctually to words 3 years before spoken when as omission, the alteration, the transposition of a word might change the sense'. Hutton and Crooke agreed. To buttress the case even further, Fawnt's counsellors also cited Shrewsbury *v.* Farmer. In this Star Chamber case of 1637, Sir Richard Farmer had uttered 'Scandalous words' against his lordship over two years before Shrewsbury eventually filed charges. Therefore Justice Jones ruled that while the earl could continue with the case, he 'should have noe damages in regard his action upon the Statute of Westminster and of R2 was gone by that of Lymittations'. But in Fawnt's instance, none of the judges found these cases telling. Thus the two precedents were 'overruled in open Court, And all this notwithstanding the Earle of Huntingdon had 2,000 li. damages'.[38]

In reaching this verdict, the judges seem to have found the most telling precedent that of Huntingdon *v.* Leicestershire. Although Huntingdon had made some embarrassing gaffes, a decade of energetic service had softened, if not obliterated, the memory of the earl's obstinacy over the forced loan. When set against such a long-suffering Lord Lieutenant, Sir William Fawnt cut a decidedly ambiguous figure. Hence at a time when the regime was preparing for a confrontation on the Tweed, the Judges faced a fairly clear-cut decision: they could either have Fawnt return to the shire praising their fine sense of justice or have Huntingdon diligently execute the Council's preparations for the Scottish Armageddon. In the circumstances, their decision was predictable. Fawnt's campaign to discredit Huntingdon they found particularly offensive, because the earl was

> well known to theire lordships to be very observant of his Majesties commaundes and of the directions given him by letters from the lordes of his maiesties privie Councell and to use greate integritie and diligence in the execution thereof.

Such language, easily equalling the Council's praise in 1625 for fashioning a 'model for other counties', doubtless sweetened the verdict for Huntingdon almost as much as the financial rewards of the verdict did.

With considerable assistance from his wife and friends, Huntingdon had transformed himself from an 'opposition' pariah to a paragon of loyalty, and the court's verdict illustrated this remarkable metamorphosis. Following hard on the heels of his triumph came a series of others, all heralding Whitehall's renewed admiration. The practice of employing the earl in court ceremonial, which Arundel had begun, reached its culmination a few weeks after the Star Chamber's decision. Then Charles asked Huntingdon to conduct the new Venetian ambassador, Giovanni Giustinian, from Lambeth to Whitehall. All of his life the earl had prepared himself for national service, and in expectation of performing as his great-uncle had, he had warned his son that since 'by thy birth thou art a publique person', it was 'likely thou shalt be called to publique place and imployment'.[39] Yet only at the end of his career, after decades of impatient waiting, was he at last given a part, albeit small and transitory, on the stage at Whitehall.

Decorum and gravity Huntingdon had always had in spades, and now, thanks to Sir William Fawnt's fine, he could at last act the part of a court grandee. New shoes, stockings and ruffs rained down on the earl and his entourage, and the old battered family coach, which Huntingdon had nursed along for years, received a long overdue refit. The suspension was well oiled, and the seats were recovered. Next Huntingdon embarked on a string of purchases: for all the coach horses new shoes, harnesses and bits, and decorative brasses with 'Coronets and Flower de Luices'; for the coach itself new mats; and for the postillions, new saddles. All this was merely preparatory to the *pièce de résistance*: after the interior and exterior had been thoroughly cleaned, a prominent London artisan painted the coach twice before gilding it with the arms of the Earls of Huntingdon.[40] Then in his glittering coach, surrounded by a resplendent retinue on horseback, he road with Giustinian through the metropolis to Whitehall where he escorted the envoy to the presence chamber.[41] Many about the court and the city could be forgiven for failing to follow legal decisions with great care; after this splendid display, however, they could not easily ignore Huntingdon's remarkable transformation.

More tangible rewards soon descended on Huntingdon. For the better part of three decades, the earl had served as the royal Master of the Hunt-hounds. Grand though the title sounded, its duties and prerequisites were modest, so modest in fact that the post appears to have been in abeyance for well over a decade. On 14 February 1639, however, the Master emerged from bureaucratic twilight with a royal order for £506 4s. 0¹/₂d. in back fees.[42] If the money ever touched the earl's hands, it immediately went back into the Exchequer to clear some of the family's royal debts. Nevertheless this grant was certainly the best the family had got from the Crown since the death of the third earl in 1595. The timing of the grant was particularly impressive; wresting even a cash credit from the Crown was a major accomplishment at the best of times, and to succeed when the regime was gathering every penny together to deal with the Scots was nothing short of miraculous. Therefore, even if the grant was simply a triumph of creative accounting, it testified to the new royal favour for the erstwhile Master of the Hunt-hounds.

In sharp contrast, Fawnt ended the trial in a parlous state, 'wasted by a flux of blood issuing both ways from me'. No polite excuse, this illness prompted him to draw up his last will and testament. The plea of poor health, however, could not stop the execution of the court's justice. By April 1639, Sir William had scraped together enough cash to pay Huntingdon £2,000 and Lightfoot £50. An even more humiliating punishment was in store at the Leicester assizes, where Fawnt publicly acknowledged that 'I have much wronged the right honorable henry Earle of Huntingdon' and then asked forgiveness since 'I did as much as in mee lay falsly scandalise and traduce the saide Earle.'[43] Under these hammer blows, Sir William's already precarious health quickly collapsed; by December he was dead.

Fawnt's demise spared the old man having to watch helplessly as the earl and his attorneys measured up the remainder of his estate. Scarcely had Star Chamber rendered its verdict before Huntingdon was lobbying hard for Fawnt's £5,000 fine to the Crown. In a petition to Charles, the earl rehearsed his loss from the 1627 disafforestation, and since all subsequent schemes for his compensation had fallen through, he mournfully concluded, 'your Subject had no recompense'. Meanwhile since a £5,000 royal fine 'hath accrued to your Maiestie by your Subiects meanes and prosecution', he asked for it all. Against these efforts, George Fawnt, Sir William's nephew and heir, pleaded for mercy. Pressing debts totalling some £12,000 and dowagers claiming £900 annually threatened to overwhelm the estate, which yielded only £1,500 per annum. Since payment of the fine would only ruin Sir William's innocent heirs, the nephew begged for a drastic reduction, while noting similar examples of mercy in other cases. Seconding his plea was Secretary Coke, who could only watch the plight of his youngest daughter's relatives with sympathy.[44] Caught between such strong competing claims, neither Charles nor the judges were eager to meddle with the case, and they successfully delayed a further decision for months.

In the meantime, Huntingdon found adequate consolation in his triumph. In his struggle with Shirley and Buckingham, only luck and the House of Lords had permitted the earl a narrow victory. In contrast, Fawnt had not fallen in spite of the central government; rather this time the most formidable court in the land had publicly vindicated Huntingdon. This knowledge only increased the pleasure of hearing his chaplain preaching in St Helen's, Ashby de la Zouch, that 'the children of wrath, when they see the vertues of good men reprove their vices, they rage like wilde beasts ... [and] they cast the darts of envy and malice against them'. Thankfully beastly men like Fawnt found that their darts 'doe oftentimes returne back on their own pates'. Furthermore, the spectacle of Fawnt's humiliation and destruction left many petrified at the prospect of crossing the earl. Fear was the dominant sentiment in Richard Howeth's plea that Huntingdon regard him as a loyal Hastings retainer with no relation to 'those that are your Adversaries'. Terror understandably gripped Isabell Bewlie, for she too was involved in a Star Chamber suit with the earl; thus she abjectly apologised for any offence and begged that he drop proceedings.[45]

The verdict's benefits were not entirely psychological, for Fawnt's fine made 1639 a jubilee year for a family otherwise awash with red ink. Admittedly the royal fine of £5,000 still eluded him, but for the interim, Huntingdon found ample solace in the windfall of £2,506. Consequently, indulgences, which had been unthinkable earlier, became commonplace. Along with the old coach's remarkable metamorphosis came a new look at Donnington Park. The estate appeared incomplete without a set of massive pots 'of a new fashion', which alone consumed almost £46, and 'a general Equinoctiall Ringe of Bras'. The Fawnt money also permitted him to dabble in portraits. From George Geldorp of Blackfriars, the curator of Charles I's pictures and a protégé of Van Dyck, he ordered a painting of his deceased sister, the Countess of Chesterfield. And in the hour of triumph the earl did not forget the person who had suggested the way out of his isolation in the late 1620s: he also ordered a 'Moell of gold with the Countess of Huntingdons picture in it'.[46]

After a prolonged meditation on Huntingdon's bleak lifestyle, it is impossible not to begrudge the old nobleman the belated ability to afford a few creature comforts. Nevertheless these same luxuries can only have heightened the incongruity that contemporaries at the quarter sessions felt as they watched the newly resplendent peer step out of the glittering coach to lecture them about how even 'the poorest man' could find justice against 'the greatest peer'.

NOTES

1 Nicholas Breton, *A Mother's Blessing* (London 1621), [sig. C2v]. See also H. E. I. Phillip, 'The Last Years of the Court of Star Chamber', *TRHS*, 4th series, XXI (1939), pp. 103–32; T. G. Barnes, 'Star Chamber Mythology', and 'Due Process in the late Elizabethan and early Stuart Star Chamber', *American Journal of Legal History* V (1961), pp. 1–11; and VI (1962), pp. 221–49 and 315–46; and Sharpe, *The Personal Rule*, pp. 665–81.

2 'Fawnt his Petition', 12 June 1635, HA Legal 6/4; and the Bill, Huntingdon *v.* Fawnt, 1635, HA Legal 7/5.

3 The Bill, Huntingdon *v.* Fawnt, 1635, HA Legal 7/5.

4 'Mr Price his acquittance', 23 November 1637, HAM 66/18; Christopher Townsend's affidavit, 8 February 1636; and 'Humble Petition of Sir William Fawnt', 12 July 1635, HA Legal 5/14 and 6/4.

5 On Herne, see H to Lightfoot, 29 April 1636, HA Corr. 15/5542; 'The Humble petition of William Laud', [23 October 1643], *The Works of ... William Laud* (Oxford, 1854), IV, p. 34; and *ibid.*, pp. 67, 349, 386, 398 and 401; Wilfred Prest, *The Rise of the Barristers* (Oxford, 1986), pp. 368–9; and his entry in the *DNB*. On Holt, see 'Diverse Cases [in the Star Chamber]', FSL, Xd 337, fol. 203v; and J. Forster, *Sir John Eliot* (London, 1864), II, pp. 479, 538 and 546.

6 Fawnt's Demurrer, 1635, HA Legal 6/3.

7 H to Lightfoot, 29 April 1636, HA Corr. 15/5542.

8 Lightfoot to H, 9 May 1636; and H to Bridgewater, 21 May 1636, HA Corr. 15/4594 and 5543; and 'Mr Lord Keepers Orders'; 'The Certificate of Mr. Hutton', 17 February 1637; and 'The Further severall Answeares', 1637, HA Legal 5/14 and 7/2.

9 [Draft warrant], August 1637; and H to Teney and Gilbert, 14 August 1637, HA Legal 8/
1 [miscellaneous]; H to Teney, 26 August 1637, HA Corr. 15/5548; and 'An order', 22
November 1637, HA Legal 5/13 [miscellaneous].

10 John Rice's testimony, Depositions in H *v.* Fawnt, [1637], HA Legal 7/4, pp. 34–6.

11 Testimony of Rudinge and Skipwith, H *v.* Fawnt, HA Legal 6/2, pp. 70–1, 45 and 58.
See also that of Dixie and Skipwith, *ibid.*, pp. 12–13 and 50–1.

12 H's questions; and testimony of Sir Henry Skipwith, [1637], *ibid.*, pp. 154–5 and 25.

13 Interrogatories in H *v.* Fawnt, 19 March 1638, HA Legal 7/3, pp. 77, 78 and 80–1.

14 Testimony of John Earle, Thomas Goddard and Francis Warde; and that of Walter
Rudinge, H *v.* Fawnt, HA Legal 7/3, pp. 20–8, 53 and 3–4; and 7/4, p. 30.

15 Testimony of Francis Gilliam, *ibid.*, p. 48.

16 Testimony of Thomas Sale [Derby], George Milford [Notts.], Francis Longland [Lincs.],
Thomas Thomason [Lincs.], John Maydwell [Northants.], Thomas Perkins [Northants.],
Nicholas Knight [Warwicks], HA Legal 7/3, pp. 6, 10–11, 13–15, 18, 20, 29–30, 32–4.

17 Testimony of Thomas Worde [Northants.], HA Legal 5/13; Fawnt's answer, 3 May [1637],
HA Legal 7/1, p. 3.

18 Interrogatories; and Dixie's Testimony, [1637], HA Legal 7/4, pp. 53–6 and 2–11.

19 Nichols, *History and Antiquities*, IV, p. 175; and Fawnt to H, 8 January 1638, HA Corr. 15/
3150.

20 H to Manchester, 31 January 1638, HA Corr. 15/5546.

21 Precis attached to the Bill and answer, HA Legal 5/12 and 7/1; and 'An Abstract of the
Bill', [1638], HA Legal 5/14 [miscellaneous]. On the production of copies, see 'Mr Hough
his Bill', 9 September 1642, HAF 14/22 [miscellaneous].

22 PC to LLs, 18 May 1636 and 24 March 1637; same to H, 25 May 1637; and same to
Newcastle, 9 July 1637, PRO PC2/46, p. 181; PC2/47, pp. 269 and 453; and PC2/48, p. 58.

23 Leics. RO, DE 625/60, fol. 55; and DE 720/30, fol. 43v; Rutland DLs to H, 29 December
1638, HA Corr. 15/10,622; and 'The Defaults of Captaine Roes Companie', 13 March
1638, Leics. RO, Winstanley MSS, DG5/895.

24 Leics. RO, DE625/60, fols. 55–57v; and DE 720/30, fols. 43–44.

25 Sharpe, *The Personal Rule*, p. 564; and Hughes, *Politics, Society*, p. 105. In what follows
on Ship Money I am indebted to Dr Alison Gill for sharing her wealth of information on
this levy.

26 Nichols, II, pp. 231–2, 267 and 540; III, pp. 299 and 875–6; and IV, p. 541.

27 PC to the Circuit Judges, 12 September 1636, PRO PC2/46, p. 347; and Nichols, II, 792;
and IV, 310, 314–15, 319 and 545–7.

28 Pulteney to Nicholas, 19 November 1636; Skipwith to Nicholas, 12 February and [March
1637]; and Roberts to Nicholas, 1 March 1638; SP 16/336/11, 16/346/109, 16/351/92 and
16/395/2.

29 'A Note of the Cattel ... destreined', 17 June 1636; and various acquitances, 9–14 July
1636, HAF 12/25; and Skipwith to Nicholas, 12 February and [March 1637], SP 16/346/
109 and 16/351/92. For details on distraining goods, see various warrants, [1637?] and
19 March 1638, Leics. RO, BR II/18/20, p. 300, and II/18/21, p. 399.

30 PC order, 5 May 1637, SP 16/355/78; and Chamberlain's petition, 3 April 1638; and Charles's response, 9 April 1638, *CSPD* XII, pp. 345–6. See also PC warrant [late April 1637] and order, 26 April 1637, PRO PC 2/47, pp. 331 and 338; and Skipwith's certificate, 2 May 1637; and Petition of Lord and Kirke, April 1637, SP 16/355/26 and 16/354/144.

31 Roberts to Nicholas, 1 March 1638; and Skipwith to same, 12 February 1637, SP 16/395/2 and 16/346/109.

32 Sir Henry Skipwith and George Ashbie to the PC, 28 April 1631, SP 16/191/10 III. See also the report on Frisby from John Bale, William Halford and Sir John Skeffington, SP 16/191/10 I and II; Brian Quintrell, 'The Making of Charles I's Book of Orders', *EHR* XCV (1980), pp. 553–72; and Paul Slack, 'The Book of Orders', *TRHS* 5th series, XXX (1980), pp. 1–22.

33 Sharpe, *The Personal Rule*, p. 473. For the totals, see 'A Booke of Receipts upon Compositions for Depopulation', [late 1635 to late 1638], PRO E405/547 under 'Leicester Shire'; and fines for depopulation in Abbrev. Pells Receipts, Michaelmas 1638, PRO E401/2341; Easter 1639, PRO E401/2342; Michaelmas 1639, PRO E401/2343; Easter 1640, PRO E401/2344; and Michaelmas 1640, PRO E401/2345. For an example of the payment plans, see the arrangement for Sir John Sidley, 'Entry of Warrants', [1630s], PRO E403/3041, pp. 87–8.

34 Willis to Coke, 7 April 1631, BL Add. MS 64,902, fol. 93; and William Billers, 'Spent in the Charge of the Composition for Depopulation', Hillary term, 1637, Leics. RO, Hartopp MSS, 8D39/1339. See also Juxon *et al.* to Billers, 11 February 1637; and Lawson to same, 15 March 1637, 8D39/1336 and /1337.

35 May 1638 and December 1637, Leicestershire, E405/547.

36 H's charge to the session, 8 January 1639, HAM 26/6.

37 'A Breefe of the Lords of the Star Chamber', 19 October 1638, HA Legal 8/3 [miscellaneous]; notes on the cover of HA Legal 5/12; Exemplification of the decree in Huntingdon *v.* Fawnt, 20 December 1638, HA Oversize 1/2; and William Dugdale, 'Historical and Geneological Collections of the Family of Hastings', HA Misc. 13/76–7.

38 'Reports of Cases in the Star Chamber during the Reign of Charles I by an eminent Practicer in that Court, formerly a Member of Grays Inne', Harvard Law School, Rare Book Room, LMS 1128, fols. 112v, #370; 109v, #356; 105, #335; and 112v, #370.

39 'Certaine Directions', HAP 15/8, fol. 13.

40 'Mr Alveys his bill', 12 November 1638; 'Mr Meatcalf the harnestmaker', 12 November 1638; 'Mr Smith the Smith his bill', 24 November 1638; and Mr Gomersall the gilder ... his bill', 12 November 1638, HA 13/39 [miscellaneous]; and 'Mr pilcher his bill', 10 December 1638, HAF 13/40 [miscellaneous].

41 Giustinian to the Doge and Senate, 16 November 1638, *CSPV* XXIV, pp. 472–3; and *Ceremonies of Charles I: the Note Books of Sir John Finet Master of Ceremonies, 1628–1641* (New York, 1987), pp. 255–6.

42 Docquet, 14 February 1639, *CSPD*, XIII, p. 461.

43 Fawnt to Coke, 9 October 1638, *HMC Cowper*, II, p. 197; and his will dated 21 October 1638, Nichols, IV, p. 175.

44 'The acknowledgement'; and H's acquittance, 20 April 1639, HA Legal 8/1 [miscellaneous] and 8/4; 'To the Kings most Excellent Majestie', [early 1639], Bodleian Library,

Carte 78, fol. 188; and George Fawnt to Laud, [1639?], SP 16/377/148. On Coke, see above, pp. 96 and 142.

45 William Parks, *The Rose and the Lily* (London, 1639), III, p. 16; 'The humble petition of Richard Howeth', 19 May 1638; and 'Isabell Bewlie her submission', 19 January 1639, HAP 18/14 and 15.

46 'Hroeford pottes', 8 December 1638; 'Mr Elias Allens acquit[ance]', 28 December 1638, HAF 13/40 [Misc.]; 'Mr Gildorp the picture drawer', 7 August 1639; and 'Mr Edward Perrin his acquittance', 1 June 1640, HAF 14/11 and 19. On Geldorp, see R. H. Wilenski, *Flemish Painters* (New York, 1960), p. 271; and *DNB sub* Geldorp.

Analysis

Assessing
the personal rule

The spectacle of a distinguished provincial governor struggling to rehabili-
tate his reputation with the central government is interesting enough on
its own. What makes this tale compelling, however, is its conclusion with the
legal destruction of the earl's opponent; after all, Huntingdon *v.* Fawnt was
fought out before a court and during a decade which controversy has long
surrounded. Before Huntingdon and Leicestershire slip into the Civil War, it
is worth considering the implications of this particular legal struggle for our
understanding of the Star Chamber and the Personal Rule.

The period from 1629 to 1640, long regarded as the penultimate section of
the whiggish 'high road to civil road', has recently become hotly contested.
Instead of having been a decade when the Crown flexed its prerogative
muscles and set the stage for the Civil War, the Personal Rule has recently
been presented in a more favourable light. Marshalling a staggering array of
sources, Kevin Sharpe has stressed that the decade was an extended period of
peace and prosperity. What grumblings there were, and they were few, were
all easily contained within the 'mundus politicus' which afforded the disgruntled ample opportunity to air their grievances. Thus the old *bêtes noires* from
Laudian church reforms to fiscal feudalism assume a decidedly benign visage.
The new prescription finds the best illustration of the decade, not in William
Prynne's denunciations of a corrupt court, but rather in the Earl of Dorset's
response to Prynne: 'When were our days more halcyon? When did the people
of this land sing a more secure Quietas?' Notwithstanding the considerable
skill and erudition with which Sharpe has advanced his case, many of his
colleagues nonetheless appear unwilling to accept the new interpretation
without first thoroughly scrutinising it. Critical challenges have been quick to
develop, and in this appraisal, the details of Huntingdon *v.* Fawnt are particularly relevant.[1] Yet before considering the case's implications for our understanding of Star Chamber, it is well worth noting that the financial burden of

Figure 3 **Collections from Leicestershire, 1630–38**

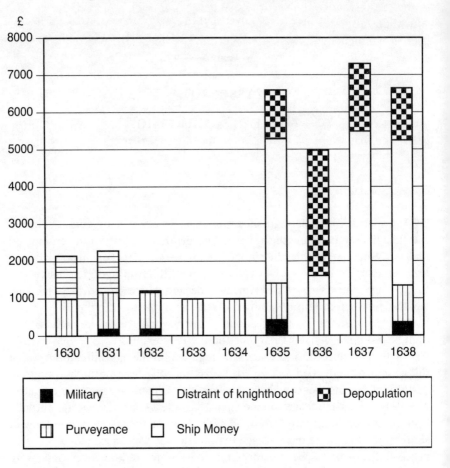

Sources: (military) see discussion of the estimates, above, pp. 111–19; (purveyance) see the discussion above, pp. 16–17; (knighthood) E407/35 and 401/2329–31, 2448 and 2452; (depopulation) PRO E405/547 and E401/2341–5; and (Ship Money) SP 16/364/23, 16/400/113, 16/431/62 and 16/473/103.

the Personal Rule on Leicestershire reveals some of the reasons for the bitter controversy over the decade.

The polarisation of the kingdom in 1641 baffled George Digby, who asked the Commons how rational people could arrive at two radically different conclusions. On one hand, some contemporaries regarded Charles as the monarch, 'firm and knowing his religion', who had kept the realm 'in a state of the greatest quiet and security that can be fancied'; and on the other, an equal number believed that under his rule, 'the property of the subject' had been 'fundamentally subverted, ravished by the violence of a pretended necessity'. The origins of this perilous situation perplexed Digby, and Sharpe concluded his massive study in a similar state of bewilderment; since none of the problems of the 1630s were beyond resolution, this polarisation must have been the comparatively late product of the Scottish rebellion.[2] While Sharpe's interpretation, as will shortly be seen, arguably is overly sanguine, both interpretations may well be accurate but, quite significantly, at different times in the decade (see Fig. 3). By 1632, after years of often hair-raising taxes, Whitehall had apparently done with the local ratepayers as levels of taxation dropped back to the happy days of the 1610s. In the following two years, the situation only became balmier as the rates sank even lower, thanks to anxieties about mustering the militia. Between 1632 and 1634, therefore, the local community did indeed sing their *quietas* with fervent devotion. Reality finally intruded in 1635 with a series of massive payments for Ship Money and depopulation, which were to continue for the next four years. In short, scholars might well make more sense of the 1630s – and of Digby's paradox – by dividing their analyses of the decade into distinct halves.

Regrettably, Huntingdon *v.* Fawnt does not suggest such an equitable solution for the new interpretation of Star Chamber. In a tantalising series of articles written almost forty years ago, Thomas Barnes dispelled the mythology which had long ranked this court 'with such proper nouns as "the Inquisition" and "Machiavelli" as one of modern history's few really dirty words'. Since it operated with procedures borrowed from common law, Star Chamber proved a thoroughly congenial venue for common lawyers like Sir Edward Coke, who acquired much of his fame and fortune from business in this court. Yet in spite of these important qualifications, he presented an unsettling picture of a less than benign institution in the 1630s. During the Personal Rule, the nature of the court's business dramatically changed, with a sharp drop in the number of cases not associated with the central government, and as it ceased being a friendly venue for ordinary plaintiffs, Star Chamber became 'a tribunal for the trial of cases of public import, involving profit for and the safety of the state'. In particular, Barnes highlighted the central government's enthusiastic adoption of the court's judgement against Sir Anthony Roper to launch the depopulation compositions. Consequently Star Chamber ended the decade with a firmly established role as 'a major vehicle' by which Charles 'raised much of the revenue that funded the "Personal Rule"'.[3]

Demythologising Star Chamber went further still with the publication of *The Personal Rule of Charles I* in 1992. Arguing against those who 'tended to think of Star Chamber as the early modern equivalent of the Gestapo, Latin

American trials, Middle Eastern tortures and mutilations, or some grisly combination of them all', Sharpe echoed Barnes's earlier indictment of casual assumptions that Star Chamber was 'an oppressive, unEnglish, irregular, extra-legal kangaroo court'. Likewise, *pace* Barnes, Sharpe described how the court's aversion to proceeding either 'arbitrarily' or 'precipitately' made it so obsessed with thorough documentation that it nearly drowned in paper, thus negating its earlier reputation for prompt judgements. The careful gloss of earlier work, however, quickly gave way to more problematic claims. With the 'fastidious scrupulousness of the judges at all stages of the trial' went a 'paternalism' which insisted on 'justice for the poor and humble as well as the rich and powerful'. Naturally 'victims of partial justice' regarded it 'as an important forum of redress', and no one, not even a defendant in the most controversial cases, ever denounced it 'as an agent of a tyrannous regime'. These propositions then allowed Sharpe to clarify its controversial role in the regime's fiscal policies. Large fines, he noted, were rare, and those few were generally reduced to more notional sums, if not dismissed altogether. Consequently, the Exchequer collected only £2,000 in fines from the decade's most productive year. Equally important was the discovery that the fines often 'sprang from a determination to reinvigorate local government rather than a plot to tax the gentry'. On balance, Lord Keeper Coventry had it right with his proclamation that 'the justice of this court has been to let justice flourish in her proper colours'. The allegedly ferocious court was so anodyne that Sharpe could account for the Long Parliament's hostility to it only by suggesting that Star Chamber had inadvertently became associated with Archbishop Laud and Arminianism.[4]

Qualifying where it does not overturn, the argument has an undeniable power. Nevertheless, since it rests on 'a preliminary perusal' of the documents which escaped the general destruction of the court's records for Charles I's reign, a 'full analysis' of the surviving information, Sharpe conceded, 'may enable us ... to piece together the history of the Caroline Star Chamber'. Among this small group of documents, Sharpe cites the extensive notes in the Hastings collection on Huntingdon *v.* Fawnt. As befits a book notable for its thoroughness, Sharpe's study does the honour of summoning Sir William Fawnt out of the historiographical oblivion into which he has fallen. Sharpe makes excellent use of Sir William's letters to Dixie; he faithfully chronicles his later campaign against the Muster Master; and the depositions in Huntingdon *v.* Fawnt buttress his case against 'the myth of the Star Chamber'.[5] And yet, for all that, he would have done well to consider this case much more carefully. Granted, a broad reinterpretation cannot afford to get bogged down in the details of a fiddly local squabble over militia rates. At the same time, when assessing a controversial institution whose records have almost totally disappeared, it is impossible to underestimate the value of a case like

Huntingdon *v.* Fawnt, whose lavish documentation contains arguably one of the fuller accounts, if not *the* fullest, of the 1630s.

What should have immediately attracted attention, in light of his assumption about Star Chamber producing less than £2,000 a year, was the size of the fine imposed on Sir William – £2,000 for Huntingdon and £5,000 for the Crown. The court of course regularly extended mercy to the guilty, a precedent which Fawnt's nephew duly invoked when he later begged the court to delete a zero from the fine. Sharpe rightly noted the heir's petition, but he would doubtless have been disturbed to learn that in Fawnt's case, the quality of mercy was noticeably strained; ignoring the nephew's suggested sum, the court, as will shortly be seen, instead lowered the total damages to £6,000. To be sure, this amount need not have crushed the family, thanks to the court's often cited willingness to extend easy payment terms. During the 1630s, for example, Mr Chetwynd, who had struck Sir Henry Shirley for slandering him, was steadily, if very slowly, paying off a Star Chamber fine of £200 at what can only be termed a generous rate of £2 a year. With the Fawnts, however, the court was in no mood for polite niceties. Late in 1639, the family paid £4,000 into the Exchequer, but when they failed to produce the balance, pleading poverty, the Crown seized one of Sir William's remaining manors. Any list of impartial witnesses able to testify about Star Chamber in 1640 would not have included John Pym. Nevertheless the financial agony of Sir William and his nephew underscores the folly of unilaterally dismissing Pym's protest that 'the nature of the Star Chamber is to protect not to bee a courte of Revenue'.[6]

Astonishment over such punitive damages only generates more nagging doubts about the court's purportedly evenhanded justice, doubts which reconsideration of Huntingdon *v.* Fawnt only feeds. Some of Sharpe's suggestions about Star Chamber fall into the category of nice, but immaterial. It is quite true that Fawnt never termed the court 'an agent of a tyrannous regime'; nor, for that matter, did anyone else in the decade. Then again, if they wanted to win their case, and more importantly, if they wanted to leave Westminster with their ears intact, they would not have. It is equally comforting to learn that even 'in the more political cases proper legal procedure' was not 'bent or laid aside'; thus the court violated its own guidelines by allowing plaintiffs to present their cases at often inordinate length. Herne and Holt certainly abused the court's kindness by producing responses so lengthy that they could have delighted only scriveners, who were paid by the paper, and later scholars. Yet while Fawnt and his attorneys doubtless were grateful for this concession, the real point at issue is not whether the court collected enough information; plainly it did. Rather it is what the judges made of the small mountain of evidence. After reviewing the record, they could have only agreed with Mr Lightfoot that Sir William was indeed an awkward magistrate, fond of offering unwelcome advice and of adopting troublesome public stances. It is, however, much harder to discover the firm evidence of his status as 'a man of perverse and factious disposition not affecting your [Charles's] happie government'. It is harder still, indeed nearly impossible, to follow the logic behind the court's decision that Fawnt's offences, whatever they might have been, justified fines of £7,000.

While it is unwise to generalise from one example, albeit a well documented one, the Fawnt case alone should breed scepticism about overly optimistic assessments of Star Chamber during the Personal Rule. It certainly overturns confident statements that 'whatever the fear, no one was prosecuted in Star Chamber for opinions expressed in correspondence'. After all, what did for Sir William were his two private letters to his cousin and fellow JP. Contemporaries, Conrad Russell rightly noted, were obsessed with ensuring that their letters did not fall into the wrong hands, but this exaggerated concern, he later implied, was unnecessary. In 1635, Sir Thomas Wroth penned a bitter lamentation about the Personal Rule, 'It tells us something about the 1630s,' Russell observed, 'not only that this letter was intercepted, but that no action was then taken on it.' Yet, as Fawnt doubtless would have remarked, Wroth was lucky. Sharpe, however, is quite right to note that the court 'took special cognisance of abuses of the subject by officials acting in the name of the government'.[7] But in the Fawnt case, the judges appeared to aid and abet the official. All of this suggests that behind the Long Parliament's assault on Star Chamber was much more than a general loathing of bishops. By the late 1630s, the yields from Ship Money and depopulation fines had dwarfed the size of the militia assessments, which had alarmed Fawnt a decade earlier. Yet all of these taxes shared a common problem – their dubious legal standing.

The verdict in Huntingdon *v.* Fawnt, coming on the heels of Star Chamber's verdict against Roper for depopulation, further excited apprehension about the state's increasingly arbitrary acts, and it forced contemporaries in the shire to ponder the continuing validity of the rule of law. And amid these reflections, the size and vigour of the local choir singing Dorset's *quietas* steadily dwindled as the decade progressed.

NOTES

1 Sharpe, *The Personal Rule*, pp. 953 and 610. For early responses to Sharpe's analysis, see Anthony Milton, 'Thomas Wentworth and the Political Thought of the Personal Rule', *The Political World of Thomas Wentworth*, ed. by J. Merritt (Cambridge, 1995), pp. 133–56; and David Underdown, *A Freeborn People* (Oxford, 1996), pp. 41–4.

2 Sharpe, *The Personal Rule*, pp. 951–2.

3 Barnes, 'Star Chamber Mythology', p. 1; and, 'Due Process and Slow Process', pp. 321 and 335–6; and, 'Star Chamber Litigants and their Counsel', *Legal Records and the Historian*, ed. by J. H. Baker (London, 1978), p. 17.

4 Sharpe, *The Personal Rule*, pp. 241, 666, 668, 670, 673, 675–7 and 679; and Barnes, 'Due Process and Slow Process', p. 225.

5 Sharpe, *The Personal Rule*, p. 671; and see also pp. 29–30, 495, 499, 677, 702 and 950.

6 17 April, *Proceedings of the Short Parliament*, ed. by Esther Cope and W. H. Coates (London, 1977), p. 154. For Chetwynd's regular payments in Michaelmas term, see for 1631, PRO E401/2331; for 1633, E401/2333; for 1635, E401/2336; for 1636, E401/2338; for 1637, E401/2459 [Savile's accounts]; for 1638, E401/2341; for 1640, E401/2345; and for 1642, E401/2347.

7 Sharpe, *The Personal Rule*, pp. 683, 674 and 681; and Conrad Russell, *The Fall of the British Monarchies* (Oxford, 1992), p. 21. For a similar caution, see A. Bellany, 'A Poem on the Archbishop's Hearse: Puritanism, Libel and Sedition after the Hampton Court Conference', *JBS* XXXIV (1995), pp. 137–64.

Part V

'The Fire of a Furnace'

The descent into civil war

1638–43

The banners of Henry, lord Hastings of Loughborough was, Gules; from the sess, and in the pale, nearly extending to the top of the chief, an arch, masoned proper, representing a burning oven or fiery furnace proper: in sess, or a little under it, on a scroll, its ends raised, and then bending inwards, points downwards and turned, Argent, shaed Vert, lined Or: in Roman letters Sable, QUASI IGNIS CONFLATORIS; fringed Argent and Purple.

[Sir John Prestwich, *Prestwich's Respublica*, 1787]

THE SOUTH VIEW OF ASHBY-DE-LA-ZOUCH CASTLE, IN THE COUNTY OF LEICESTER.

Along with Huntingdon's public triumph over Fawnt went a string of personal disasters, and before delivering the charge to the session in 1639, he lapsed into a lengthy recollection of these misfortunes, whose regularity in the preceding years made them seem 'like Jobs messengers bringing ill tideings, worse and worse, coming one uppon the head of the other'. Between the deaths of 'my most deare and incomparable wife, that was the better parte of my selfe, my mother, my mother in lawe, grandchilde, sister and divers others that were neare unto me and nowe verie latelie one of my two daughters', mourning clothes 'have never beene of me'.[1] His worsening health, together with these losses, only increased his introspection. Fortunately for him, his recent public successes allowed him to contemplate a comfortable retirement with considerable honour.

Such a peaceful conclusion regrettably was not in store. The earl's health was indeed poor and would give way entirely in less than four years. It left enough time for him to witness Fawnt's vindication and to see civil war engulf Leicestershire and his militia regiment. From the ensuing chaos he was to learn the bitter lesson that his efforts to retain his family's prominence had ironically only ensured a humiliation more abject than even Fawnt or Shirley could have imagined. And in his last days, the old earl had to watch as his son raised a fearsome banner over the shire on which he had so long doted.

NOTE

1 H's address, 8 January 1639, HAM 26/6.

Chapter 12

The price of
the Personal Rule

The earl reached the pinnacle of his success in 1639, when kudos, hon ours, and money descended on him, and this reversal of fortune at last allowed him to act the part of a magnate able to afford extended visits to court. To analyse Huntingdon's lodgings in the 1630s is to chart his steady rapprochement with the regime. He first kept a safe and comparatively inexpensive distance from Whitehall in Charterhouse Yard. Then he took up rooms along the Strand until he moved into one of the poshest addresses in the capital, Henrietta Street in Convent Garden. These shifts speak volumes about his finances as well as his politics; while Nottingham's house in the Yard only cost £5 3s. 6d., Covent Garden required three times as much. But thanks to the Fawnts, £15 a month seemed quite reasonable for a house within an easy stroll of the royal palace. Indeed, by 1639, Huntingdon's fondness for long stays in London was so notorious that when the Council ordered a select list of Lords Lieutenant back to their provinces, Huntingdon was on it.[1]

Unfortunately his triumph soon proved his undoing. By 1640, the Lord Lieutenant found himself so closely tied to Whitehall and its controversial policies that, even if he had wanted to, he could not have distanced himself from the regime. He had little choice but to endure in silence as his enemies turned his administrative and legal triumphs into reproaches.

THE LAST CAMPAIGN

At the quarter sessions, Huntingdon had proclaimed his eagerness to serve the king with 'a booke in his left hand as with a sword in his right'. A few weeks later, the Council gave him a chance to do so. In spite of his age, Huntingdon's reaction to the Crown's demands in the Bishops' Wars was entirely characteristic, but while the requests for men, materials and money were all familiar ones, their magnitude was more novel. The first sign of trouble was Whitehall's discovery of a renewed interest in the militia, and in December 1638, customarily a dead time for militia activities, the Council ordered a fundamental alteration of the regiment, almost as radical as that of 1626. First the number of infantry was to be increased from 1,000 to 1,250 men, all of whom had to be ready to march at a day's notice. Then the Council solved the traditional lack of outside examination by dispatching Captain Erneley to drill the troops before Colonel Jacob Astley arrived to inspect *his* work.[2]

As in the 1620s, terse orders often translated into significant financial burdens. Arms and armour marginally acceptable in peacetime now all had to be replaced. Erneley's presence checked any tendency towards leniency, and the passage of time had done nothing to reduce the price of arms. The misfortune of individual private men was nothing compared with that of local towns and parishes. First the local magistrates had to purchase the equipment of an additional 250 men and then to assume their recurring annual expenses, both of which were fearful. Over the winter of 1638–39, Mr Newton's travel expenses for six days of training in Leicester, Loughborough and Melton Mowbray came to £3 2s. 4d., and between the levies for the revived pioneer company, the powder magazine, and the inevitable officers' fees, Branston paid the militia treasure £1 18s. 4d. The anxiety in this village over a single militiaman's costs topping £5 was nothing compared with the near chaos in Leicester over the town's projected role in the expanded regiment. Since the Corporation had arguably got off lightly with its contribution of a mere forty foot soldiers, Huntingdon in 1638 thought the Corporation a likely source of sixty of the 250 new men. The logic of unilaterally increasing the militia rates by 150 per cent was lost in the sustained hysteria which descended on the Town Hall. Loud and repeated protests, as always, eventually forestalled this plan, but not until after an extended confrontation in which the waves of messengers dragged dozens of defaulters before the Privy Council.[3]

Since these alterations came as a serious shock to a county already labouring under the weight of Ship Money and depopulation fines, Earl Henry sought to soothe local nerves in his address at the sessions early in 1639. 'He were an undutifull childe,' Huntingdon argued, 'that would deny his father 'any thinge that is in his power to shewe his duty', whether 'with shipp money, lones or waies wherein we may expresse our dutifull and serviceable affections unto his Maiestie.' These new burdens therefore were actually opportunities to curry favour; 'Speake pleasinge things unto him [Charles] in these things,' he reminded his audience, 'and you winne his heart forever.'[4]

Unfortunately for the earl, one old administrative *bête noire* simply brought another in 1639. When some fretted over armed conflict, Huntingdon assured them by noting, 'I knowe noe certaintie thereof.' A few weeks later, in March, Charles removed all uncertainty by ordering the impressment of 230 men, eighty more than the largest levies in the 1630s. An overpowering sense of *déjà vu* pervaded this command; as in the preceding conflict, the Council asked local authorities to pay the Crown's share of the coat and conduct expenses, 'according to the presidents in former times upon other lesse occasions of service'. While the national and local obligations in levying troops came to roughly £2 a man in the 1620s, Branston's accounts reveal that its experience in 1639 was well off this mark; there, coat and conduct money from one man came to £1 10s., and the local expense of clothing the new soldier and of escorting him to the rendezvous called for a further £1 16s. If Branston's experiences were roughly typical, then this levy of 230 men called for roughly £750. To be sure, the Crown promised full repayment 'in such manner as in former times upon like occasions', a promise of which veterans of the earlier conflict knew the value. Precedent at least backed these distasteful demands. But Whitehall had novelties in store by ordering seventeen carters and fifty draught horses, which were to be selected at a six musters of the county's entire horse stock. Those owners upset with this innovation could find some solace in 12d. a day for each horse hired – provided they could draw it from an empty Exchequer.[5] Until that happy day, the local ratepayer again had to loan the Crown the necessary money.

The impact of all these schemes on local finances was dramatic. In small villages, where the bulk of the money went on various military charges, the ratepayers belatedly learned how much they had profited from Huntingdon's row with Fawnt and Hesilrige. From the eight years from Michaelmas 1629 to Michealmas 1636, Branston's annual total averaged roughly £6; with the outbreak of the Scottish crisis, however, the rates in the following year soared to £10 9s. 3d., and from Michaelmas 1638-39 the total more than doubled to £22 4s. 1d.[6] When confronted with increases of this order, even Huntingdon's eloquence failed. Certainly the Ship Money project ran aground on this fiscal shoal.

By early 1639, the levy had begun to encounter serious opposition. Although Roberts had already gathered £3,900 for the 1638 levy, the arrears of £600 remained elusive. Some flatly refused to co-operate, and a few even threatened him with legal counter-measures. His successor had an even harder time. A royal bedchamberman and local resident, John Whatton, strengthened his family ties with both court and county by marrying into the Heyricks, the prominent clan influential in the Corporation and the royal Jewel House. The enthusiasm of a man who would made his first payment of £600 entirely from borrowed money cannot be doubted. Such extreme measures had proven necessary when Whatton learned that the most ardent zeal could make little headway against 'the many taxes that have now lately bene for souldiours and horses'. After weeks of 'much ado', Whatton had prodded the constables into collecting nearly £400, only to see militia rates promptly consume this sum. Since 'the late taxes' had made cash 'very scant', he begged the councillors to proceed cautiously, lest 'any stricter course' might 'cause a murmurring amongst the Common people'.[7] Yet the councillors, finding murmuring among the Exchequer officials a more alarming prospect, issued a wave of new writs to destrain defaulters' property. By dint of such drastic measures, Whatton ended the year a mere £78 in arrears. Yet it is essential to recall that he only had to gather £1,650, a third of the earlier amount.[8]

Although costs and complaints had skyrocketed, the zeal and ardour of Huntingdon and his son remained undiminished. While some troops marched north with grossly inadequate arms, little training and few carts and horses, all in Leicestershire proceeded smoothly.[9] Some in the shire might well have grumbled that such dedication was easy for those who spent only public funds. But in late March 1639, the earl presented an impressive and expensive display of his own loyalty. Earlier in January, Charles individually ordered all peers to present themselves on 1 April at York with 'such forces as your birth, your honor and your interest in the public safety does oblige you unto'. Most peers greeted this request with dismay; in Northamptonshire, Charles's command plunged Lord Montagu into prolonged prayer before he reluctantly agreed to present six horse. His response moreover exceeded that of most of his colleagues, who pleaded the lack of either money or horses. In contrast, Huntingdon's reaction was almost automatic, being among the very first to reply of the non-metropolitan peers. 'My bounden duty,' he explained to Northumberland, 'shall make me study all the meanes and wayes I can to doe his Maiestie the best service my poore habilityes will enable me.' Thus he would appear with ten horse 'in such equippage as my fortune will give me leave'. His enthusiasm led him back into the arms market, purchasing a new sword for himself as well as full military regalia for his coachmen and grooms. Any lesser response earned his contempt; 'O Mores O Tempora,' he exclaimed on learning that 'any of his Maiesties Nobility of this kingdome should refuse to serve the kinge his Maiestie goinge in his owne person'. Those who 'should make a scruple of it', he snorted, 'must be of the newe stampe'.[10] A few days later, he and his newly armed coachmen rode north to join the soldiers, carters and horses he had earlier pressed into the royal service.

THE RECKONING

For Huntingdon, the greatest frustration of the First Bishops' War was that the county's contributions produced such ignominious results. A few weeks of brinksmanship brought on the Pacification of Berwick, which enabled Arundel to inform Huntingdon that 'our business is now ended'. Yet the abrupt conclusion only produced another echo of the earlier war; when marching the men south, the conductors systematically defrauded the troops of their daily maintenance of 8d., with the result that the government ordered another investigation, just as it had in 1625.[11]

Although not a war so much as a skirmish, the First Bishops' War had a profound impact on the county and its Lord Lieutenant. Huntingdon's contempt for 'those of a new stampe' who would not assist Charles can be seen as the authentic voice of a loyal 'backwoodsman' rallying to the colours. Yet it is worth remembering that he had been singing a much different tune a few years earlier, and only over the winter of 1638-39 had the regime given the Master of the Royal Hunt-hounds unambiguous marks of favour. Nevertheless more than Fawnt's fine made him exclaim 'O Mores O tempora'! When Huntingdon wrote to Northumberland, Charles had only a few days earlier given the earl his long sought prize. On 5 March 1640, he finally compensated Huntingdon for the lost Leicester Forest positions. Out of Fawnt's royal fine, Huntingdon received £3,000 on the understanding that £1,440 went to satisfy royal debts.[12] Admittedly the possibility of receiving the remaining £1,560 was remote as long as the Scottish crisis lasted, but a credit in the Exchequer had understandable advantages for a man whose largest and most insistent creditor was royal.

The importance of this grant can best be seen by reviewing William Dugdale's list of red-letter events in the family's history. Although he was one of the longer-lived Hastings peers, the fifth earl's entries in Dugdale's list were generally sparse and inconsequential. One of the few bright spots, however, came in 1639: 'Grant of 3000 pounds of Sir William Fawnts fine of 4000 to Henry Earl of Huntingdon reciting the grants of Forester of Leicester forest and the surrender of it.' While this passage may not sound as grand as the third earl's appointment as Lord President of the North, it nonetheless had a very pleasant ring to a family haunted by debtors. Therefore, when considering the division among the peerage in 1639, it is vital to remember that what separated Huntingdon from 'those of the new stampe' was a massive cash grant from the Crown as much as ideology. Since largesse was out of season in the Exchequer by 1639, why had Charles been so generous? Belatedly the king and his councillors had recalled what they had been so eager to acknowledge late in 1625; while the rigour with which Huntingdon ran the county verged on the excessive, not to say pathological, the pressure of war in 1639 as in 1625 transformed an awkward administrative shortcoming into a positive virtue. The chaotic situation in many other counties, where complaints and excuses had been institutionalised, only heightened the contrast in Leicestershire. Hence the councillors repented ever ordering Huntingdon, as they had in 1633, 'to give all iust ease and rellefe to the country in retrenching and takeinge off all unnecessarie Leavies and Contributions'; they had by then reverted to lavishing praise on an efficient and uncomplaining local governor.[13]

While his rehabilitation delighted the old earl, his joy may well have blinded him to the fact that Leicestershire might harbour a large number of those 'of a new stampe'. Rumblings of trouble had been frequent enough that they should have cautioned him against overly sanguine assessments of the shire. The Corporation of Leicester, as we have seen, had stubbornly resisted the attempt to increase the trained band, and Richard Howeth had cautioned Huntingdon about the existence of a sizeable number of 'your adversaries'. More troubling developments emerged as vocal opposition to the Scottish war became clearly audible in the county. In Ashby Magna, an argument over whether the conflict was the 'priests' war' or 'the king's' came to a sudden halt when John Owneby read out Jeremiah 5:30–1: 'A wonderful and horrible thing is committed in the land; the prophets prophesy falsely and the priests bear rule by their means.' More ominously, Fawnt's humiliation had not silenced Sir Arthur Hesilrige, who was back before the Council, this time over the Noseley chapel. Fair warning of imminent trouble was also apparent in Leicester's Christmas gift. For decades, Huntingdon and his immediate family could count on the Corporation for presents of wine and sugar worth about £4 to £5; Stamford at best had make do with gifts of about half that value. Yet at Christmas 1639, the earl and his sons received gratuities totalling only £1 19s. 8d., while Bradgate Park made merry with gifts worth £5 0s. 8d.[14]

Developments within Huntingdon's administrative elite shaded from ominous to frightening. Restive after over a decade of 'faithfull and acceptable service as well to his Maiesties satisfaction as to the content of my own contrimen', Stamford had begun lobbying hard for an appointment as Joint Lord Lieutenant, and at one point in the mid-1630s, Charles apparently agreed to his request. Huntingdon had other plans and pressed to have his son for a colleague. Unfortunately for Stamford, Charles resolved the issue in December 1638, at the zenith of Huntingdon's revival at Whitehall, and named Lord Hastings to the post. With good reason Stamford dubbed this decision 'an affront', and his irritation with the continued Hastings domination became plain a year later. When the county's horses returned from the Scottish campaign, Stamford retained six for his own use, and when other local officials protested, he unilaterally assessed their value at a mere £4 a piece. But then, in a none too subtle echo of Shirley's charge a decade earlier, he refused to pay their owners even this notional sum until Huntingdon presented a full accounting of the recent military levies.[15] Huntingdon for his part remained blithely unconcerned. Consequently the magnitude of his miscalculation became apparent only when writs for parliamentary elections reached Leicester in January 1640.

With the Anglo-Scottish negotiations near collapse at the end of 1639, rumours about a new Parliament became more insistent. As early as 30 December, Lord Hastings was lobbying his father to help a friend into one of the Leicester seats; 'the rarenes of them', he explained, 'makes many desirous to be of that nomber'.[16] His judgment proved all too accurate, for in 1640, an extraordinary number of people were eager for the honour. Huntingdon, however, ignored them all, confident in his exceptionally well oiled electoral machine. During the 1620s, a trip to the hustings simply meant the right to validate the Hastings hegemony, for after nasty electoral reverses early in the century, the fifth earl had accorded the highest priority to controlling the electoral results. Notwithstanding a sometimes awkward relationship with the Corporation, Huntingdon established a claim on one of Leicester's seats. This was no small feat, since the Duchy of Lancaster, which had a powerful interest in the town, battened down on the other. Thus, in the seven elections from the 1610 to 1628, a short letter from Donnington Park gained admission to the Commons for the earl's brother, Sir George Hastings; his sister's brother-in-law, Sir John Stanhope; his cousin, Sir Henry Rich, later Earl of Holland; and his Deputy Lieutenant, Sir Richard Morison. Only once did this system fail; in 1624 the town was able to slip in a prominent citizen after the earl endorsed the Duchy candidate so enthusiastically that the Corporation rather disingenuously thought he was the Hastings candidate.[17]

While a record of having prised one seat in seven elections out of Huntingdon's hands verged on the pathetic, the Corporation had a better track record than the county voters did. Buckingham in 1621 and Shirley in 1628 had challenged the earl, and for their boldness, they confronted a phalanx of Hastings supporters, not only numerous but, more important, well trained; at drum commands they used staves to hold potential defectors in with the Hastings men. Not surprisingly, all of the other county Knights stood unopposed, thus easing a stream of relatives and clients into the Chapel of St Stephen with a minimum of fuss. For the ten Knights of the Shire returned in the 1620s, the requirements for office were quite brief; either their last name was Hastings, or they were senior members of the earl's militia mafia. The one accounts for the earl's brother, Sir George; his cousin, Sir Henry of the Abbey; and his son, Lord Hastings. The other explains his Deputy Lieutenants, Sir Thomas Hesilrige, Francis Staresmore and Sir Wolston Dixie; and the brother of a militia captain, Sir Edward Hartopp. In his analysis of Huntingdon's electoral influence, J. K. Gruenfelder failed to appreciate the importance of the militia elite in the earl's system; thus he interpreted Dixie's return in 1625 as a revolt against the earl. Even so he still pronounced the earl 'a remarkable example of the success an aristocratic patron could enjoy in early seventeenth century England'.[18] The belated correction of this error arguably alters his conclusion; Huntingdon's success in the 1620s could well make him *the* remarkable success story.

This background makes the earl's disposition of the seats early in 1640 olympian, but entirely routine. Confident that his eldest would be summoned to the House of Lords, Huntingdon pushed his second son, Henry Hastings, and his protégé, Sir Henry Skipwith, for the county seats, and what would convert his wishes into reality were a few letters like the one ordering the Mayor of Leicester to 'send Your Constables in there severall wards to the freeholders to signifie my desire to them that as for my sonne in the first place soe for Sir Henry in the second'. The question of the Corporation's two burgesses was even easier. Admittedly the Countess of Devonshire, a prominent resident of the town, pressed the Corporation to elect Thomas Coke, the former Secretary of State's son, but her suit Huntingdon passed over in contemptuous silence. For the Duchy's seat, the Chancellor lobbied for Simon Every, the Receiver General of the Duchy and a choice whom Huntingdon heartily endorsed. For his own, the earl asked the Corporation to delay its election so that he could slip in a relative or friend who had come to grief elsewhere. Confident of the results, not only had he no intention of moving from his town house in Covent Garden, but he ordered his son to forgo canvassing and to join him in the metropolis.[19]

Henry flatly refused, since 'it is unfitt for mee to be absent out of the Countrey at this presente'. His uncharacteristic defiance stemmed from a recent visit to Leicester, where he had detected unmistakable signs of disaster. There he heard 'whisperings or surmises' plainly 'intended to poyson the opinions and affections of any condition or sorte of the people in this Countrey, by which meanes to alienate their hearts from you and make your power and honor lese and others greater'. Even worse, he discovered Stamford and Sir Arthur Hesilrige feting a group of prominent gentlemen and JPs. It is hard now to tell which frightened Hastings more, those who 'have received favors from him [Huntingdon]' openly attacking Skipwith as 'a Courtier' who 'hath bin Sherriffe and collected Shipmoney' or the presence of erstwhile Huntingdon protégés like his Deputy Lieutenant, Sir Wolston Dixie. Worse news quickly followed; the Earl of Rutland had thrown his considerable interest in the Vale of Belvoir against the Huntingdon slate. Equally implacable was Sir Roger Smith of Edmondsthorpe. Although a JP, he had declined any involvement with the forced loan, and his refusal to pay Huntingdon's military assessments in 1639 had earned him a visit to the Council board. In fact, it soon became apparent that Stamford and Hesilrige 'have laboured allmost every man through out the whole country'. In short, since 'they had binne all over the Countrey and received promises', the Hastingses had no other choice than 'playing but an aftergame, our worke being to perswade men from what they have allready promiste'.[20]

Hastings measured well the magnitude of his task. Skipwith's chances he rated as nil; the only question was whether he might avoid sharing the old Deputy Lieutenant's humiliation. So extensive was the rot that Henry begged his father not to push his uncle, Sir George Hastings, for a seat in Leicester. Since the Hartopps and the Bales, then only weakly supporting the earl, had their eye on those places, the entry of another Hastings candidate would only drive them into the Grey–Hesilrige coalition. A far worse problem than 'Uncle George' were the three Council messengers who had unexpectedly shown up to arrest a number of chief constables. Hastings, with his hands full piecing together electoral alliances, had no patience for minuscule arrearages in militia assessments, which came 'not to halfe soe much as the Pursevants fees'. Yet this issue proved his ball and chain. For decades, as Henry reminded his father, the family's hegemony had been based on one guiding principle: 'his Maiesties service shalbe performed, your Honour encreaste, none punisht without iust meritt, and our selves free from Censure'. The messengers had just violated this arrangement, and because no one could believe that Huntingdon had not asked for their arrests, 'these and such like things will make us that are your inferiour officers ill thought off'. Needless to say, the constables, who were normally 'very usefull men' at elections, were now likely to be 'mischeevous'. All Henry could think to do was to have the militia treasurer pay the arrears. Until this matter was resolved, 'it was not in the braynes or power of your Lordships opposers to doe anythinge soe much to disadvantage the businesse now in hand, or loose you the hearts of your Countrey as this acte'.[21]

In the electoral history of early Stuart Leicestershire, nothing equals this *cri de coeur*. Equally unprecedented were the results of the poll. The old peer eventually bestirred himself, but not in time to offset the danger of the three messengers. Instead of Mr Hastings, the county returned Lord Grey of Ruthin, the Earl of Kent's heir, and Sir Arthur Hesilrige. Scarcely had Earl Henry digested this news before Leicester heaped on fresh insults. Ignoring his wishes, the Corporation had proceeded with their election. After hearing that they had returned the Duchy candidate, the earl may have been somewhat reassured that paternalism and deference had carried the day. Any comfort in this thought promptly vanished on reading the second name: Sir Roger Smith of Edmondsthorpe.[22] Lest Huntingdon fail to absorb the Corporation's defiance, the Mayor and burgesses repeated the insult. Smith, although delighted 'beyond my expression' with the unexpected election, nonetheless declined the honour. His decision placed the Corporation in an even more awkward situation; in their first vote, they could have justified themselves with the customary dodge about Huntingdon's letter arriving too late. Smith's demurral removed that option, for by the time of the second vote Hastings had lost to Grey and Hesilrige. Yet even in this circumstance, when confronted with the stark choice between the earl's son and the Countess of Devonshire's nominee, they did not hesitate in returning Thomas Coke.[23]

The voters' message was unmistakable. Although Huntingdon had earlier defied Buckingham and refused the forced loan, he had later embarked on one of the more spectacular examples of Renaissance political self-fashioning, and since his metamorphosis into a courtier regrettably coincided with the

1640 elections, any freeholder searching for those responsible for the excesses of the Personal Rule did not have far to look. Further politicising the election was Hesilrige's presence at the hustings. After a long political apprenticeship, he knew by heart the old complaints about the earl's administration, and after witnessing the fate of his father, Sir Henry Shirley, and Sir William Fawnt, he voiced them with emotion. In response, Huntingdon nominated two of his Deputy Lieutenants, one of whom his son and the other, a prominent Ship Money sheriff. The outward calm at these polls was not as disturbed as in neighbouring shires. No one followed the Lincolnshire practice and papered the county with doggerel urging the electors to 'Choose no ship money sheriff,' and at the hustings large crowds did not break out, as they did in Northamptonshire, into chants of 'Wee'le have noe Deputy-Lieutenants! take heed of Deputy-Lieutenants!'[24] Nevertheless the spectacle of the freeholders and the Corporation giving the earl's candidates a wide berth was equally sensational. Indeed, it was revolutionary in a county as tightly controlled as Leicestershire.

It is impossible to overestimate the force of these blows. At their most ambitious, all that either Buckingham or Shirley had ever wanted was one of the two county Knights. Yet in the Short Parliament elections, not only had the earl lost both of them, but his son had been rejected by the county once, and by the Corporation twice. Not only did the passage of time do nothing to soften the sting of these insults, but it soon became clear that these electoral results simply heralded further repudiations.

A SECOND CHANCE

Thanks to the electoral debacle, Huntingdon had to enter an important session without anyone in the Commons looking out for his family – other than Sir Arthur Hesilrige. Mercifully, Hesilrige had yet to find his voice, and even if he had, pressing national questions dominated the early debates to the almost complete exclusion of local matters. For his part the old peer ran true to his new courtly form. On 29 April, following the Commons' vigorous protest against the Lords' meddling with supply, Huntingdon was quick on his feet defending the Upper House: 'it is cleare our Privileges are brook'. That he was seconding Strafford and Arundel and countering Wharton and Saye indicates a good deal about his political stance.[25] He was unable to develop his thoughts, for Charles dissolved the session three weeks after the opening.

This decision is unlikely to have displeased Huntingdon. Although as late as 1634 his fervent prayers asked for a new Parliament, he was by 1640 too deeply implicated in controversial aspects of the Personal Rule to welcome a session. To be sure, the Short Parliament heard no specific complaint of either the earl or his Deputies, but there were more than enough general ones to have made him uneasy. Before the Commons had seriously begun business, Sir Francis Seymour denounced 'the abuses of the Sheriffs', whose high-handed manner of collecting Ship Money made him wonder if 'the Lawe of Villany were better to be in force'. Having glanced at Skipwith, Roberts and Whatton, the debates touched the Lord Lieutenant. Pym then labelled the knighthood scheme as a 'great vexation', unjustly laying 'greivous distresses' on the realm, and the depopulation compositions as a practice 'of dangerous consequences when Lawe is made a couller for private men'. Others expanded the criticism to include the Star Chamber. What had originally been a court 'for punishment onlie of such enormities and crimes as the common lawe could not reach into' had recently been transformed into 'a verie Court of Exchequer and revenue for the Kinge, by the Imposition of heavie and deepe fines which were soe insupportable that they tended to the utter ruine and subversion of mens estates and fortunes'. Yet overshadowing all of these in their sheer ubiquity were attacks on military assessments. Huntingdon's neighbours, the freeholders of Northamptonshire, petitioned the Commons against the array of 'undue impositions': 'armie monie, waggon monie, horse monie, conducte monie'. Moreover they were indignant that those who failed to meet the assessments found themselves 'molested distryned and impris-oned'.[26] Given that each passing day increased the volume and vehemence of such complaints, Huntingdon cannot have mourned over the dissolution.

In this instance, the polically expedient also proved financially disastrous. Since the Commons had refused to fund another Scottish campaign before the redress of domestic grievances, some councillors argued that the king should employ his prerogative rights to raise another army. Immediately after the dissolution, Strafford reasoned with Charles that since the members had 'refused, you are acquitted toward God and man'. Laud developed the logic further: having 'tryed all wayes and refused all wayes, by the lawe of God, you [Charles] should have substance and ought to have it'. Charles himself came around to the idea willingly enough, issuing a wave of orders initiating the Second Bishops' War.[27] These commands presented Huntingdon with a clear choice. Given the criticism which poured out of the Short Parliament and the recent electoral reverses, he might have reassessed his close alignment with the regime and responded in a desultory fashion. On the other hand, the parliamentary debacle may have strengthened Huntingdon's commitment to the regime. Given his track record, the earl not surprisingly seized the latter option with both hands.

Technically the Council did not mobilise the realm for a second campaign; that order had already been given. If the government's decision to issue the command in late March between the elections and the parliamentary opening guaranteed a restive session, the text of the order ensured a tumultous one. All previous levies had carefully excluded the militiamen, but in March 1640, the

Council reversed this policy, ordering the men to be taken 'out of the Trayned Bands'. To cushion the blow, the councillors called for the selection of the lesser sort, those who presented arms for others. Yet this consolation was dwarfed by the magnitude of Whitehall's demands. The 1639 impressment order had handily broken all previous records with its call for 230 men. This too fell with the Council's latest demand for 400 men, roughly a third of Huntingdon's newly expanded regiment. Equally unprecedented was the order to impress their weapons; while the state had always assumed the cost of arming the pressed men, the councillors now shifted that responsibilty onto the local ratepayers. Even the customary aggravations of coat and conduct money took on a more painful twist. The Council had previously maintained the polite fiction that the regime's share of the expenses would promptly be repaid out of the Exchequer. By 1640, however, such politesse vanished; instead the money should 'bee leavyed in that County as hath been usuall heretofore'.[28]

The timing of this decree, three weeks before the parliamentary opening, is indeed puzzling, for by seeking to demonstrate its determination to prosecute the Scottish war, the scale and tenor of the government's demands virtually ensured that this goal was lost amid the confusion and protests in the provinces, as Leicester's case illustrated. On 25 April, while Huntingdon was busy in Parliament, his Deputies ordered all militia-men to muster at Loughborough, where they would 'Impresse so many of them, as wee shall thinke fitt'. While unwilling to order 'anie acte to Infringe the antient privileges or Immunities of your Corporation', they relayed the sad news that the 'Statute exempts noe Corporation from haveing theire soldiers Imprest out oft'. The town did not see the matter in the same light, and instead of sending its men north, the Corporation dispatched a wave of protests. The recent election results made an emotional plea to Huntingdon for a reprieve, 'a favor which we have often obtained from your Lordship', a wasted effort. But the returns left the Corporation much better placed with Lord Newburgh, the Chancellor of the Duchy, and together with Leicester's Recorder, Thomas Chapman, Lord Newburgh tracked Huntingdon down in Westminster to lobby him on the Corporation's behalf. At first, the earl returned such 'an Indiffert answer' that it filled Chapman with fears that the earl would then 'complayne to the counsayle of you and get a messenger sent down'. To forestall this possibility, he persuaded Newburgh to press Huntingdon again, and this received an unambiguous answer. Yet even in this concession Chapman perceived considerable ill will toward the Corporation: if Newburgh had not intervened, Earl Henry, Chapman insisted, 'would one way or other have done you a displeasure or at least indeavoured it'.[29]

Any celebrations in the Town Hall were short-lived. The Corporation's influence with the Chancellor was directly linked with the session, and this dissolved with the Short Parliament on 5 May. Hence three weeks after Chapman's letter, the Deputy Lieutenants celebrated their own triumph in the grim bureaucratic struggle with the Corporation. Then, after coaxing the trained band to a muster, it promptly pressed twenty-six of its men.[30] As they readied the men for the march north, the members of the Corporation pondered the irony that their success in avoiding the initial impressment muster in April had simply earned them the privilege of belatedly making up the personnel shortage for the rest of the county and the honour of presenting 65 per cent of their trained band in a levy which called only for 32 per cent of the expanded regiment.

Whitehall's demands were equally insatiable for horses and carters, While it had required fifty horses and seventeen carters in the previous year, the figure rose to seventy and twenty-three respectively in 1640. Although the previous equine impressment had taken place in each of the hundreds, the earl abandoned this scheme in 1640 in favour of a single muster at Loughborough. Bureaucratic efficiency certainly endorsed the idea of a central county staging ground for the Tweed, but geography prevented many residents from applauding, especially if they did not live in north central Leicestershire. It drove even Richard Halford, a new Deputy Lieutenant, to beg the earl to reconsider. Since everyone involved had 'had soe manye Journeys thither alreadie about the Souldiers', Halford's neighbours in southern Leicestershire naturally objected to 'the tediousness' of another trip to Loughborough. His pleas ultimately fell on deaf ears, and so hundreds of owners began the now familiar journey, tiny Branston's contingent of six horses being led by widow Smith. Once there, they discovered that the Lord Lieutenant had another surprise for them. Rather than borrowing the horses at a prescribed *per diem* rate, the county treasurer purchased them. As the earl explained, 'the country would be better contented' with a compulsory purchase at £9 to £10 apiece than with another loan.[31] This innovation, while administratively inspired, was financially painful, requiring as it did another levy of almost £700, but in 1640, the ratepayers' comfort was the least of Huntingdon's concerns.

In early June his diligent labours had the county's band of 400 soldiers, seventy horses, and twenty-three carters fully equipped and ready to march. The exhausting mobilisation had not overwhelmed the earl's fondness for a special touch; hence he unilaterally added a knapsack to his men's kit. Extended wrestling with less biddable shires made the councillors regard Leicestershire's 'forwardness' as one of their few bright spots, and on 13 July 1640 they expressed their gratitude. Having stunned Charles with news of Huntingdon's 400 knapsacks, they were able to report that 'by his Maiesties expresse direction, wee doe give you harty thankes for the same'. Charles himself professsed that he 'hath therein bene confirmed in the impression, which he formerly had of your affection and Care of his Service'. The councillors themselves vowed that 'wee shalbe alwayes ready to putt his Maiesty in minde thereof whensoever the occasion may be offered for your advantage'.[32] For Huntingdon, the aggressive proponent of the knapsack, this letter was a belated triumph after the Council had declined to punish Shirley's denunciation of knapsacks as so much chicanery. Now, as he waited with his troops for the order to march, he could savour the councillors' 'harty thankes'.

In the event, they had to wait a long time. This already painful levy quickly became more excruciating as Whitehall dithered about the expedition's launch date. The mobilisation orders of late March required the contingent to be at York on precisely 20 May. When this proved too soon after the parliamentary dissolution, the Council shifted the date back to 1 June and ordered weekly drills for the troops. Yet even this relaxed timetable moved the Caroline military machine at too swift a pace, and on 23 May the councillors set a new date of 1 July. Four days' cool reflection made Whitehall realise that it needed more time; thus on 27 May, the Council rolled the date back to 15 August, almost four months after the initial date of the rendezvous. These recurrent delays and intermittent trainings produced not so much a taut unit as exasperated ratepayers. Against the Covenanters, Branston dispatched the indefatigable Mr Newton, but only at the cost of driving its annual rates up to £18 18s. 6d., almost all of which went on the Second Bishops' War. Waltham on the Wolds had a similar experience when Huntingdon's Deputies impressed two of its three trained men, and by the time they marched north, the annual rates had nearly doubled, skyrocketing to £41 17s. 4d. Leicester meanwhile enjoyed its customary advantage of central location and comparative independence. Nevertheless when its twenty-six men eventually set out for the Tweed, they left behind bills totalling £158 16s. 2d. and a Corporation thunderstruck by its largest military expenditure.[33]

Amid these truly sobering figures, the most modest cost per soldier was Leicester's £6, and on this basis, the expense of Leicestershire's 400 men *at the very least* came to £2,400, well in excess of three parliamentary subsidies. Furthermore Branston and Waltham, with averages easily double those of Leicester, only drive the total higher still. These figures serve as a cautionary tale against assuming that the local costs of raising an army under the early Stuarts were all roughly the same and all notional. Each of the levies for the Bishops' Wars were significantly larger in scale than its predecessors in the 1620s, and their burgeoning size enhanced the shock, coming as they did within a year of each other. While 670 men and 120 horses in 1639-40 were bad enough, what further inflated the bill was the government's dithering approach to the 1640 campaign, for by rolling back the rendezvous for nearly four months the Council drove the expense through the roof. So callous did Whitehall appear in 1640 that its senior officers appeared indifferent to the suffering which their orders were causing. In an eerie reprise of the Council's attitude after the 1626 dissolution, the councillors seemed intent on making the ratepayers underwrite the campaign, with or without Parliament.

Early September, as the earl and his men anxiously waited to march, Huntingdon had plenty of time to consider the campaign's likely effects on 'my crazie bodie', and the results gave him half a mind to plead 'indisposition of health' and to send Lord Hastings to shepherd the men north. Yet the only Lieutenant distressed with the cancellation of the regional musters in 1628 would not willingly pass up the belated opportunity to set his regiment against others. His devotion even led him to decline the Earl of Kingston's kind offer to break up the trip with a visit to his country house; 'I cannot leave my charge for the keeping of that numerous body in order.' Thus in his newly refitted coach, the erstwhile warlord led the regiment north, the men shouldering their knapsacks and the few remaining carts with gears carrying the regimental tent and the impressive saddle which the county had purchased for him over a decade earlier.[34]

Huntingdon's labours with this administrative mountain of paperwork, in the end, produced a particularly disappointing mouse, for the men arrived on time at York to find that the war had effectively ended with the battle of Newburn a few days earlier. The subsequent negotiations and debates at least afforded Huntingdon a good deal of free time in York where the sublime uneasily shared centre stage with the mundane and the ridiculous. The Scottish war had transformed York into another Westminster where throngs of noblemen, bureaucrats and soldiers gathered for the fateful confrontation. For Huntingdon, who had spent his youth there in the care of his illustrious great-uncle, the truce allowed him time to tour the city and to inspect the Minster and its monuments. Thanks to Fawnt, he did so in some style, having bespoke from a York tailor a scarlet coat with a crimson lining. But his most extraordinary blend of business and pleasure came on 6 October at the first meeting of the Council of Peers. Amid the confusion, a £2 tip to a royal servant allowed Huntingdon to indulge his curiosity, which a bumpy trip north had only piqued: he was able to sit in Charles's coach, carefully inspecting the fittings and testing the suspension.[35]

From this surreptitious inspection, he hurried to the crucial meeting. The earl had derived some satisfaction in discovering that the Covenanters bore no hard feelings towards the English peers, all of whom (excepting the hated Strafford) they regularly toasted. As Clarendon recalled, there was no one among the peerage 'to whom this kind of discourse was not grateful enough'. Yet neither such complimentary language nor the dismal results of the brief campaign could dampen Huntingdon's ardour. On 6 October, the peers debated a proposed Treaty of Ripon. The results of such an assembly, the Earl of Berkshire had earlier maintained, were predictable, since 'the Peeres will speak of nothing but a Parliament', and an overwhelming majority of them quickly proved him right, plumping for the truce and another session. One of the few intransigents was Huntingdon. In this distinguished gathering, the old Lord Lieutenant insisted 'not to give money' (to the Scots). Rather, if the counties would only redouble their efforts, 'the King's army may keep them where they are'. Above all else, he plumped for a hard line 'to let the Scots, being rebels, to know, that the Lords will not give them a penny'.[36] His isolated position is quite comprehensible. He had bullied the county into compliance, drawing his local standing down to perilously low levels, and all for nothing if Charles accepted the Anglo-Scottish agreement. The Treaty of Ripon's daily requirement of £850 for the Scottish army effectively forced Charles, willy-nilly, to confront another Parliament, and the bitter complaints of local abuses, which had filled the Short Parliament, left little doubt about where another Parliament would begin. Therefore, when Charles eventually bowed to the inevitable, accepting the treaty and summoning another Parliament, Huntingdon could only pack his new scarlet coat and ride back to face the repercussions of his actions.

Reflecting on recent incidents, Huntingdon had ample grounds for anxiety. Earlier in the summer, some troops passing through the east Midlands had rioted, attacking Melbourne Hall and slaughtering deer in Ashby Park. Such outrages, if random, could have been the accidents of war. Yet the care with which the mutinous soldiers directed their attention to the estates of a former Secretary of State and an active Lord Lieutenant suggested something much more ominous. Secretary Coke certainly thought so; he reported that the soldiers had been encouraged by malicious neighbours and by their own officers, who had made 'themselves interested in the differences of great men'. Nor was this an isolated episode of popular disdain for Huntingdon's faithful service; in Warwick, for instance, a man denounced the heavy exactions which the earl had laid on Leicestershire for coat and conduct money. Meanwhile Scottish propaganda had finally reached the shire, prompting secret groups of clergy and gentlemen to discuss the legality of the war, in which Leicestershire was so heavily involved. The strain was even apparent in Rutland, where the Deputies could not persuade the rump of the trained band to muster, so fearful were they that Huntingdon would order them 'to march towarde the Armye'.[37]

These unsettling reports all paled before another one involving a few horses. For almost two decades, Huntingdon and Stamford had co-operated in governing the county. Admittedly Stamford's role in the recent election had sorely strained their relationship, but the two men had yet to clash directly. This remarkable state of affairs ended in May amid mutual recriminations. Late in 1639, Stamford had taken six of the pressed horses, for which he promised to pay £4 each 'assoone as hee should see the Accompt for that businesse presented'. Since Stamford never received one, thanks to Huntingdon's aversion to public reckonings, the horses had remained at Bradgate Hall over the winter. Yet on 10 May, Stamford found himself before Charles and his councillors attempting to explain his action. After hearing him out, Charles minced no words, 'much disliking that any particular man should presume to take upon him to detaine (without the Leave of the Lord Lieutenant of the County) any Horses which were raised upon the generall charge of the County'. Following the king's lead, the Council ordered him to return the animals.[38] Since the king had not understood that the request for a full accounting was actually an indictment of Huntingdon's administration, the next day Stamford returned to the Council table to make this abundantly clear, formally charging an unknown person with defrauding the entire 1639 levy 'as well on behalfe of himselfe as of divers others his Tenants and Inhabitants of the County'. Such a grave accusation could not be ignored, but unfortunately for Stamford, the councillors named Huntingdon to head the investigation. Little wonder then that when the Lord Lieutenant summoned the local officers to examine the matter, Stamford turned up with no fewer than twenty warrants out of the Court of Chancery. Baffled about how to proceed, the earl promptly adjourned the hearing and never reconvened it.[39] Although unproductive, these charges served notice of the fact that Stamford was no longer willing to accept subordinate status.

These developments left Huntingdon with little hope of a better showing in the new elections. Rather than attempt the impossible, the earl simply seconded Lord Newburgh's efforts on behalf of Mr Every. Yet late in 1640 even that limited goal was too much for a majority of the Corporation. Newburgh and Every had ultimately failed to save the Corporation from Huntingdon's selections and levies, and if the memory of £158 in military charges had faded, Huntingdon revived it with an order for another £50, which arrived within days of his recommendation of Every. Their resentment could scarcely appear if Every and Coke were the only candidates. Mercifully for the Mayor and his brethren, Stamford eventually presented them with a clear choice; although seats elsewhere were readily available, none of them pleased his son, Lord Grey of Groby, as much as the notion of representing a town 'with whom he is like to bee a Neghbour'.[40]

Cleverly chosen, the plea of neighbourhood afforded the Corporation a moderately graceful excuse. In a letter to the earl, the Mayor insisted that he and a few graver burgesses dutifully backed Every only to discover 'neither your Lordships expectations nor our owne ... was any whitt answeared', their plea being 'overswaied with the greater parte of voices', which supported Grey and Coke. The result the Mayor begged Huntingdon not to interpret either 'as an acte of disrespecte to your Lordship, whome so many obligations binde' or as 'a Testimony of any backwardnes in us'. Unfortunately the Mayor undercut his own logic with another letter written on the same day, announcing the

Corporation's refusal to pay another £50 military levy; he and his brethren were still wrestling with the previous assessments, totalling over £150, 'which as yet wee knowe not how to raise by way of Tax'.[41] These two letters therefore made Huntingdon aware of the dire political costs of zealously supporting the Caroline regime.

Whether or not the events in England in 1640 were actually revolutionary, there plainly was a revolution of sorts in Leicestershire. There a majority of the county shook off Huntingdon's firm grasp, and this remarkable development was apparent at the county hustings as well as in the town. Huntingdon's willingness to stake his prestige on backing a candidate in Leicester quite significantly did not extend to the county seats where even he appreciated the futility of opposing Lord Grey of Ruthin and his old enemy, Sir Arthur Hesilrige. Admitting the inevitability of their election, however, did not make Huntingdon and his administrative elite accept it with any grace. Unable to hold his tongue after Sir Arthur's return, Richard Halford blurted out that 'they had chosen a man who had more Will than Wit and that it was to the disparagement of the County'. Lord Grey of Ruthin later dismissed Halford as 'no gentleman', someone who had 'kept hogs'. Yet notwithstanding his humble origins he had risen to be Sheriff, a Justice of the Peace and a Deputy Lieutenant. His memory of six decades of life in the county had left him with a very clear idea of which candidates would not embarrass the county; and Fawnt's young protégé was not among them.[42]

The electoral results were more than a grave offence to the family's honour. In the impending Parliament, likely to be the most momentous in a generation, the earl had the unnerving experience of having no one interested in the family except Stamford's son and Sir Arthur. Hence, 'his crazie body' notwithstanding, Huntingdon had to take his seat in the Lords, if only to limit the potential damage. As he rode south, he can only have reflected on how radically his notion of Parliament had changed. Throughout the 1620s, he had been careful not to allow his commitment to the war effort to override his support for parliamentary rights, and as late as 1634, his devotion to the institution had led him to pray for a new session, the best hope for the realm and himself. Yet, by November 1640, Parliament, long the embodiment of all his hopes, had assumed a more ominous aspect.

NOTES

1 'Mr Price his acquittance', 23 November 1637; 'Mr Northfolke his acquittance', 31 December 1638 and 25 March 1639, HAM 66/18–20; and 'Mr Clement Austen ... his bill', 10 November 1638; 'Mr Northfolke his acquittance', 6 April, 4 December 1639 and 6 March 1640; and 'Mr Fuller his acquittance', 1 June 1640, HAF 13/31 [Misc.], 14/7,12, 18 and 20; and PC to H, 10 April 1639, PC 2/50, fol. 120.

2   PC to H, 30 June and 18 November 1638, PC 2/49, pp. 154 and 268v–9; Charles to H, 19 December 1638 and 19 February 1639; HA Corr. 15/1348 and 1350. See also M. C. Fissel, *The Bishops' Wars* (Cambridge, 1994), pp. 10–18.

3   Leics. RO, DE 720/30, fols. 43v–45; Common Hall, 18 March and 10 July 1639, Leics. RO, BR II/18/21, fols. 496 and 519; List of defaulters, 29 December 1638; and H to Nicholas, 15 January 1639, SP 16/404/126 and 16/409/88.

4   H's charge, 8 January 1639, HAM 26/6.

5   H's charge, 8 January 1639, HAM 26/6; Leics. RO, DE 720/30, fols. 43v–45; and PC to H, 15 and 29 March 1639, PC 2/50, fols. 77–8 and 96–6v.

6   Leics. RO, DE 720/30, fols. 29v–51.

7   Roberts to Coke, 21 January 1639; and Whatton to Nicholas, 25 April 1639, SP 16/409/165 and 418/51. See also Whatton to Nicholas, 24 May 1639, and same to constables, 18 June 1639, SP 16/421/175 and 16/424/22; and Nichols, *History and Antiquities*, III, p. 912.

8   Vane's account, 7 September 1639, SP 16/428/40; and Ship Money writs, 9 November 1638, PC 2/49, p. 455–71.

9   Sharpe, *The Personal Rule*, pp. 799–803.

10 Charles to H, 26 January 1639, HA 15/1349; H to Windebanke, 14 February 1639, SP 16/412/125; same to Northumberland, [1639], HA 15/5549; and 'Mr Cave the cutler his bill', 2 April 1639, HAF 14/6. See also the responses of the other peers in SP 16/412; Fissel, *The Bishops' Wars*, pp. 152–62; and Cope, *The Life of a Public Man*, pp. 158–67.

11 Arundel to H, 20 June 1639; and PC to JPs and DLs, 25 August 1639, HA Corr. 15/6922 and 4271.

12 Charles's Letter Patent, 5 March 1640, HA Oversize 1/3; and W. Dugdale, 'Historicall and Geneologicall Collections', HA Misc. 13/78.

13 [William Dugdale's Notes], Bodleian Library, Carte 78, fol. 153; and PC to H, 18 February 1633, PRO PC2/42, fols. 456–60.

14 Windebacke to JPs, 4 July 1639; and JPs to Windebanke, 2 October 1639, SP 16/425/16 and 16/430/10; and Chamberlain's Accounts, Michaelmas 1639–40, Leics. RO, BR III/2/81, p. 180. For the earlier gifts, see BR III/2/81, pp. 43, 72, 102 and 144–5.

15 Stamford to Coke, 31 March 1639, BL Add. MS 64,918, fol. 81; Leics. lieutenancy commission, House of Lords RO, Main Papers, 27 December 1638; and PC order, 22 November 1639; and 10 May 1640, PRO PC2/51, p. 65; and 2/52, p. 478.

16 FEH to H, 30 December [1640], HA 16/4868.

17 Mayor to H, 16 January 1624; and same to Mayor, January 1624, Leics. RO, BR II/18/15, fols. 283 and 281. See also Gruenfelder, 'The Electoral Influence of the Earls of Huntingdon', pp. 22–4.

18 On the Hastings machine, see Beaumont's complaints on 7 February 1621, *CJ* I, pp. 511–12; and Gruenfelder, 'The Electoral Infuence', pp. 20–1.

19 H to Mayor, 20 January, and 8 and 13 February 1640; Countess of Devonshire to same, 20 January 1640; and Newburgh to same, 19 December 1639, Leics. RO, BR II/18/21, fols. 548–52.

20 FEH to H, 3 February 1640, HA Corr. 16/5558; and PC's order for his arrest, 10 April 1639, PC 2/50, fol. 119v.

21 FEH to H, 13 January 1640, HA Corr. 16/5557.

22 H to Leicester Corporation, 8 February 1640, HA Corr. 16/5551; and *The Catalogue of ... Knights*, London, 1640), TT, E 109(4). See also *The Short Parliament (1940) Diary of Sir Thomas Aston*, ed. by Judith Maltby (London, 1988), p. 48 n. 1.

23 Smith to Mayor, 27 March 1640; Common Hall order, [late March–early April 1640]; and Devonshire to Mayor, 7 April 1640, Leics. RO, BR II/18/21, fols. 578, 579 and 592.

24 Holmes, *Lincolnshire*, p. 138; and 'A Declaration shewing the Practices and Proceedings concerning the Elections of Knights', Bedfordshire RO, St John (Bletso) MSS, DDJ 1369. I am indebted to Richard Cust for the last reference.

25 *Proceedings of the Short Parliament*, ed. by W. Coates and Esther Cope (London, 1977), pp. 86–7.

26 *Ibid.*, pp. 143, 152, 212–13 and 275.

27 'Sir Henry Vanes notes', 5 May 1640, HA Parliament 3/25. For a further discussion of this document, see also Russell, *The Fall of the British Monarchies*, pp. 125–7.

28 PC to H, 26 March 1640, PRO PC2/51, pp. 392–400. See also Fissel, *Bellum Episcopale*, pp. 207–14.

29 DLs to Mayor *et al.*, 25 April 1640 [damaged], Leics. RO, Winstanley MSS, Second Deposit, DG5/897; Mayor to FEH, 27 April; same to H, 30 April; Newburgh to Mayor, 4 May; and Chapman to same, 6 May 1640, Leics. RO, BR II/18/21, fols. 594a and 594b, 596 and 599.

30 [DLs] to Mayor *et al.*, 25 May 1640, Leics. RO, Winstanley MSS, Second Deposit, DG5/905.

31 Halford to H, 26 June 1640, HA Corr. 16/4355; H to PC, 7 July 1640, SP 16/454/50; and Leics. RO, DE 720/30, fol. 48v.

32 H and FEH to PC, 24 June 1640, SP 16/458/4; and PC to H, 13 July 1640, PRO PC2/52, p. 629. See also Vane to Windebanke, 11 September 1640, *Hardwicke State Papers* (London, 1778), II, p. 175.

33 PC to H, 26 March, 3, 23 and 27 May 1640, PRO PC2/51, pp. 392–400; 2/52, pp. 470, 503–4 and 511; Leics. RO, DE 720/30, fol. 48–48v; DE 625/60, fols. 58–61v; and 'A Note of the Charge payd for the Souldyers', 1640, Leics. RO, [Miscellaneous Financial MSS] BR III/8/104.

34 H to Kingston, 3 September 1640, HA Corr. 16/1352.

35 2, 4 and 9 October, 'Yorke Jorney', HAF 14/24. On his childhood in York, see Cross, *The Puritan Earl*, pp. 54 and 60.

36 H to FEH, 1 October 1640, HA Corr. 16/5553; Clarendon, *History*, p. 63; PC minutes, 2 September 1640; and Borough's minutes of the Council of Peers, 6 and 9 October 1640, *Hardwicke SP*, II, pp. 168, 244 and 250. See also Russell, *The Fall of the British Monarchies*, p. 161.

37 Coke to Holland, May 1640, BL Add. MS 64921, fol. 99; Rossingham to Conway, 4 July 1640; [Reports of sedition], June 1640; Hill to [Lambe], 26 August 1640, SP 16/459/36, 458/110 and 461/73; and Rutland DLs to H, 5 September 1640, HA Corr. 16/10623.

38 Order, 10 May 1640, PRO PC2/52, p. 478. See also above, p. 260.

39 Order, 11 May 1640, PRO PC2/52, p. 480; and H and FEH to PC, 24 June 1640, SP 16/458/4.

40 Newburgh to Mayor, 29 September and 28 November 1640; Stamford to Mayor, 9 October 1640; and Countess of Devonshire to same, 17 October 1640, Leics. RO, BR II/18/22, fols. 2, 14, 8; and Angel to Coke, 29 September 1640, BL Add. MS 64,921, fol. 118.

41 Mayor to H, 28 November 1640, Leics. RO, BR II/18/22, fols. 14 and 16.

42 Rushworth, *Historical Collections*, III, p. 38; and *The Journal of Sir Simonds D'Ewes*, p. 95, n. 8. On Halford, see Nichols, II, pp. 870 and 874.

Chapter 13

For the king
and the Hastingses

In the aftermath of the elections, the tensions within the county community, so plainly evident at the hustings, apparently vanished. After vexing the ratepayers for months, heavy military charges disappeared almost entirely, and with these taxes went the harsh attitude towards the unco-operative; the grand jury early in 1641, for example, refused to indict four pressed men who had deserted on the march north.[1] Similarly the opening of the Long Parliament had effectively exorcised the fiscal demons which had long tormented the ratepayers. The removal of these grievances early in 1641, so it seemed, brought peace to Leicestershire. Yet the calm was deceptive; the rift within the county, far from miraculously healing itself, had simply moved to the metropolis, where the quarrel between Huntingdon and his opponents regularly disrupted Parliament. Months of wrangling in Westminster succeeded only in bringing the dispute to a rolling boil when less than two years later it spilled back into the county. Finally, in the summer of 1642, a spirited attempt in Leicester to raise a cheer 'for the King and the Hastings' produced a response which had not been heard in the county for decades. From this humiliation it was only a short step to Huntingdon's son raising a vengeful banner over the shire.

FAWNT'S REVENGE

Between the public ceremonies and private reunions, a festive air invariably surrounded any parliamentary opening. In November 1640, however, Huntingdon had little to celebrate as he watched his enemies parade into Westminster Hall. The presence of Stamford and his son, the new burgess from Leicester, was initially more galling than actively dangerous, because neither was much of a public speaker. Safe in this knowledge, Huntingdon quickly exacted vengeance, purging Stamford from the lieutenancy. Hesilrige on the other hand was a more troubling matter. Although Sir Arthur had spoken very little in the Short Parliament, this development was only a matter of time, given close friends like John Pym and Lord Brooke. The spectacle of Fawnt's legal destruction had spurred his interest in the Sayebrooke colony in Connecticut, where he toyed with settling. Only the Scottish crisis and a parliamentary summons saved him from an Atlantic voyage, thrusting instead the angry young man onto the national stage. Yet what doubtless most alarmed Huntingdon was neither Sir Arthur nor the Greys. Rather it was a more modest figure hanging around the edges of the commotion at Westminster – George Fawnt, Sir William's heir.[2] In the following months, these men were to repay Huntingdon for the concern he had earlier shown his critics.

The old peer did follow their retribution from a safe distance. With too much going on in Parliament simply to retire to Donnington Park, Huntingdon was almost invariably present whenever the House was called in 1641, and during Strafford's trial, he was one of the handful not to miss a day. Assiduous attendance regrettably did not necessarily translate into political importance; his colleagues tended to overlook the old man when forming politically sensitive committees, awarding him instead more routine assignments. Alongside him was his son Ferdinando, whom Charles early in the session summoned to the Lords.[3] Thus both men were in the Palace when Hesilrige opened the assault on their joint administration of the shire.

One of the more agreeable aspects of Sir Arthur was his willingness to remember his friends. All of his considerable enthusiasm for attacking Strafford and the episcopacy did not make him forgetful of Leicestershire. Indeed, he found alleged abuses of power in his native shire invaluable in focusing his colleagues' attention on larger issues. His first words in the new Parliament conveyed his outrage over Halford's disparaging comments, thus ensuring the aged Sheriff a stay in the Tower and public submission in Westminster and Leicester. While Charles soon eased the punishment by bestowing a barontcy on the old man, the incident had given fair warning of Hesilrige's new power, which made Huntingdon begin to stir uneasily in the Lords.[4] The earl was not directly involved in the old Sheriff's comments, but even before the Commons had finished with Halford, Hesilrige corrected this omission by reopening the Fawnt case.

On Sir William's death in 1639, his estate, having cleared the £2,000 obligation to the earl, was unsuccessfully struggling with its debt to the Crown. Therefore early in 1640, the Sheriff distrained Foston and other Fawnt lands. His action only intensified the heir's pleas for mercy, and later in 1640 with the timely assistance of Sir John Coke, Mr Fawnt persuaded the court to reduce his uncle's debt by £1,000.[5] Since he had had in mind a more substantial reduction, the harassed nephew saw a sympathetic court of appeal in the new Parliament. At first, Fawnt planned to lodge his petition with the Lords, but, perhaps nervous about gaining a sympathetic hearing from a host of Lieutenants and judges, he instead petitioned the Lower House, where Hesilrige was eager to bring his case forward. His decision paid an immediate dividend; the Commons promptly ordered the Sheriff to return the extended Fawnt estates to the heir pending a parliamentary investigation.[6]

In the following months, the Parliament men heard much more about the Fawnt case, which soon became a *cause célèbre* of those eager to abolish Star Chamber. Unfortunately for Huntingdon, Hesilrige had not done with him. In early December 1640, Sir Arthur launched a campaign to focus attention on 'the particular Grievances of Leicestershire, concerning military Charges'. Although the House referred the question to the committee considering Fawnt's petition, this committee 'to examine the Misdeanours of the L. Lieutenant and Deputy Lieutenants of the County of Leicester' quickly expanded its brief to consider how such officers everywhere dealt with 'assessing, levying, collecting and taking of Coat and Conduct-money and all other Levies of money'. Huntingdon could find some comfort in the other Lords Lieutenant being dragged into the limelight with him. But with Hesilrige and Lord Grey on this committee, the agenda retained a predictable bias; other complaints, the committee resolved, would be considered only 'after the Leicestershire Cause'.[7] Over the Christmas holidays, Huntingdon was joined in Westminster by his Deputy Lieutenants and militia captains, who had to defend themselves from Hesilrige's accusation that 'they have of spleene charged divers poore men with armes and after discharged them of the same for moneys'. Not content with their testimony, the House also requested information from other local officials, a request which the Corporation of Leicester was delighted to grant. While Huntingdon and his Deputies eventually escaped imprisonment or punishment, it was due less to their persuasiveness than to the committee's new brief; on 14 December the House ordered it 'to prepare a Bill for regulating of the actions of the Lords Lieutenant and Deputy Lieutenants'. Hence in less than a month, the committee appointed to consider the Fawnt petition set off in pursuit of a more ambitious goal, one which Fawnt and Shirley would have applauded.[8]

This wider assignment consumed the committee's attention for another year, but in the interim, the Fawnt case did not languish. When considering Star Chamber, any contemporary could have rattled off the sensational cases during the Personal Rule: the MPs in 1629, Alexander Leighton, John Lilburne, Bishop Williams, and especially Prynne, Burton and Bastwick. These cases, however, represented only a fraction of the more routine ones during the Personal Rule, and out of this mass only two emerged as examples of gross abuse of power. One concerned George Walker's indiscretion in the pulpit, and the other, Sir William Fawnt. Sir Arthur's presence on the committee considering Star Chamber helps account for the inclusion of his old friend's case, but another reason also drew the committee's attention.[9] While crippling fines, like those on Bastwick and Burton of £5,000 each, were part and parcel of the celebrated trials, they were less common in more mundane hearings; for example, after a brief imprisonment, Walker simply had to post a £1,000 bond for good behaviour. Fawnt on the other hand was assessed a crushing penalty of £7,000, which the court had generously reduced to £6,000. Therefore Fawnt's case illustrated that the practice of using enormous fines to ruin defendants was not confined to a few political trials, and his experience helps explain how the committee appointed to regulate Star Chamber came to recommend its abolition.

The persuasive power of this case partially accounts for the timing of the committee's final report on Sir William's trial. On 9 June 1641 the Parliament men sent up a Bill abolishing Star Chamber, when it promptly ran into difficulties. Joint conferences and amendments followed one after another and still the Bill languished in the Lords where Manchester, Huntingdon's cousin, led a spirited opposition. On 1 July, the committee on Star Chamber finally reported to the Commons that since 'the sentence against sir William Faunt ... was without ground of anything that appears either in answer or proof', it should be reversed. On the following day, the Bill belatedly emerged from the Lords, and Charles, in spite of considerable reservations, accepted the Bill on 5 July.[10] Until these public discussions, Fawnt's case was largely unknown outside of Leicestershire, and for precisely that reason, the details of Sir William's travail proved all the more useful with wavering voters.

In July 1641, Sir William Fawnt received belated vindication. In earlier weeks the Commons had formally reversed the judgements against John Bastwick, Henry Burton, John Prynne, Alexander Leighton and John Lilburne. On the 14th, Fawnt was added to that distinguished list. The entire House listened as a committee member read aloud first the 1626 letter to Sir Wolston Dixie and then the court's sentence. After some discussion, the House pronounced the verdict 'without any just ground' and resolved to petition the Lords to reverse the judgment and to restore the fine and Foston to George Fawnt. After such a public exposure the Fawnt case suddenly became a national news item worthy of detailed reportage in the newsbooks. Five days later, the House ordered the committee to prepare the matter for the Lords, only to have the Fawnt case abruptly disappear at this point. Perhaps because the affair directly touched a peer who would have been ruined by a reversal, some were willing to let the matter drop. Those who were not were distracted by more important business, and they had even less reason to revive the matter after 29 November 1641, when the court of Exchequer formally removed any further royal claims on the Fawnt estates.[11]

Although none of these proceedings mentioned a word about Huntingdon, the Lord Lieutenant can only have shuddered at Fawnt's rehabilitation; after

all, he had directed the prosecution, which the Commons had just pronounced illegal. Thus the earl witnessed the apotheosis of someone whom he
regarded as 'a man of perverse and factious disposition' into the pantheon of
sacred martyrs of the Stuart tyranny. This sudden glorification of Sir William
had further dire implications, since Fawnt's grave doubts about Huntingdon's
competence and integrity were now in the public record and in the
newsbooks. For someone who amid an otherwise dismal financial situation
had spent years burnishing a well developed sense of honour, this development was a profound embarrassment. Unfortunately for the earl, the pain
only became more intense.

A year after beginning its deliberations, the committee assigned to correct
the abuses of Lords Lieutenant had apparently gone to earth, baffled by the
problem. On 7 December 1641, Sir Arthur Hesilrige presented his own solution: a Militia Bill which granted near dictatorial power to three Lords General
nominated by Parliament. Luckily for the earl, the proposal produced a storm
of criticism, in which Sir John Culpepper, leader of the nascent royalists,
could not resist a splendid occasion for levity at Hesilrige's expense: 'hee
wondred' that the Knight for Leicestershire 'should bring in such a bill, having
soe often complained of the exorbitant power of the Deputie Lieftenants in his
cuntrie'.[12] In the end, although Hesilrige had considerable support among his
colleagues, Culpepper and his supporters scored enough points off Sir
Arthur's Militia Bill to block its further progress. Culpepper's success makes it
ironic indeed that the only person capable of ensuring the passage of a variant
of the Bill was Charles himself. By 4 January 1642, those around the king had
concluded that Hesilrige was 'an absurd, bold man', something Huntingdon
could have told them long ago. So obnoxious did Charles find Hesilrige that
he was willing to risk all in order to remove him and four other members from
the House, and with the attempt to arrest the Five Members, Hesilrige's
already impressive position in Leicestershire became impregnable. The
county immediately petitioned Parliament, denouncing this 'most horrid,
high and wicked attempt' against *their* Parliament man; as the petitioners
explained, 'wee conceive our selves exceedingly concerned in this'. Five
months later the local elite was still telling Charles of their support for 'the
honour and innocency of our worthy Knight'. Finally the eerie fashion in
which Huntingdon's old militia officer suddenly came to embody the nation's
hopes was not a phenomenon peculiar to the east Midlands. Later in 1642, a
divine messenger reportedly urged Charles to support the 'best of his Subjects';
that select list of a dozen men included Warwick, Essex, Pym – and Sir Arthur.[13]
Thus, in short order, Fawnt's old protégé leapt to the front rank of the nation.

Coming hard on the heels of Sir William's canonisation, the glorification of
Huntingdon's erstwhile horse captain was understandably hard for the old
earl to stomach. What was harder still was the Militia Bill, which Charles's

attempted arrest propelled through the Commons. Hence a month after the planned *coup de main*, the Parliament men began discussing their slate of Lords Lieutenant. The selection process for the 'placed and displaced' reveals an extraordinary level of politicisation; when a member argued for a peer who was 'an honest man', others retorted that 'this is no time to choose honest men'. In this volatile atmosphere, the Hastings defeat at the hustings assumed critical importance, for the county members had a great, indeed almost overwhelming, influence over the House's final decision. It is impossible to imagine any set of circumstances in which either Stamford's son or Hesilrige would have acquiesced to Huntingdon's nomination. Yet other members outside of the shire might have objected to the earl's callous dismissal. In the debate over Northamptonshire, for example, Lord Spencer overcame the objections of most county members and turned out the Earl of Peterborough, because 'he had so many friends in the house'. Here the Fawnt case and the host of Leicestershire complaints did their damage in repeatedly besmirching Huntingdon's reputation. In many contested counties, the winning side often was the one that could argue, as the supporters of Sir John Bankes did, 'he having deserved so well as he hath done of the public'.[14] Hesilrige's success in undermining any latent belief that Huntingdon deserved well verged on overkill; by December, Sir Arthur was well known as the man who 'soe often complained of the exorbitant power of the Deputie Lieftenants in his cuntrie'.

These factors help explain the decision about Leicestershire, which the Parliament men routinely awarded to Stamford. With equal calmness, they gave Rutland to the Earl of Exeter, the Countess of Stamford's first cousin. In the bland list of the new Lords Lieutenant, the Parliament men delivered Huntingdon a devastating blow. It is hardly coincidental that Huntingdon's first absence from the House came on 9 February 1642. Quite understandably, he was reluctant either to vote for a Bill stripping him of local office or to watch as his successor at the head of the Leicestershire regiment carried the Militia Bill to the king. While no evidence survives on Huntingdon's reaction, it cannot have been far from that of the Earl of Derby, the longtime Lord Lieutenant of Cheshire and Lancashire. 'To blast a man of his honor with putting forth of his place,' one Parliament man argued, '... I conceive not becoming the gravity of this house.' Pending formal charges against Derby, the member begged the House to retain him so that, if nothing else, 'the good old earl ... may go with honor to his grave'.[15] The House nonetheless appointed Lord Wharton, and Derby joined Huntingdon among the blasted who had to face the prospect of a dishonourable retirement.

A final indignity was in store; on 5 March the House of Lords ordered all Lords Lieutenant to turn in their old commissions. One day after the deadline of 21 March, the Earl of Huntingdon laid the commission of himself and his son on the table. A few days later, Lord Hastings, having established his credentials as a moderate Parliamentarian, received a consolation prize, being named Lord Lieutenant of Westmorland. Yet this did nothing to soothe the injured honour of 'the good old earl' and, if the truth be told, little enough to soothe that of the son. Nor did the pain quickly pass; when Parliament immediately published the names of the new Lieutenants, the gentlemen of Rutland, many of whom had long worked with Huntingdon, petitioned Parliament to express their delight with the new arrangement. Given this background, Huntingdon's last appearance in the Parliament not surprisingly appears to have been on 22 March when he turned in his commission. Less than two weeks later, the London carrier dropped off eleven trunks, four boxes, one hatcase and a bundle of bedding at Donnington Park. The earl's long sojourn at Westminster was over.[16]

THE LAST MUSTER

Earlier in 1641, a petition to the Commons explained that the county's 'backwardnesse' was entirely due to 'the remotenesse of their dwellings' from the centre of events at Westminster. By the spring of 1642, as if in answer to this complaint, the focal point of the nation suddenly shifted northward, making the once isolated county 'the Seat of our War'.[17] What attracted most attention was the regiment, over which Huntingdon had so long fussed, and the munitions which he had badgered the county into buying.

Between harrying his Deputies, reversing the Fawnt judgement and stripping Huntingdon of his lieutenancy, Parliament's brusque treatment should have signalled the earl's political eclipse. Yet ironically his disgrace only elevated his importance in a country slipping into civil war; until Stamford had the regiment under control, the officers and men naturally would look to their old commanders, a tendency which increasingly horrified Parliamentary supporters as they brooded over the military balance of power. Bellicose rhetoric, while increasingly common, could not erase the fact that both sides, as Conrad Russell has observed, were hobbled by 'the lack of any force of soldiers instantly available'. Poverty sharply limited any royal plunge into the international mercenary market, and the peerage could only raise a group of less than formidable retainers. Weapons themselves were even more of a crippling deficiency, and as both sides jostled for advantage, the control of arms stocks rapidly emerged as the paramount issue. Having set up his court at York, Charles initially hoped to receive ample arms shipments from the continent through Hull, only to find that Sir John Hotham's boldness thwarted such uncomplicated plans.[18] Frustrated at their own impotence and terrified at the prospect of their opponents' rearmament, both sides fastened their attention on the trained bands, especially on the more professional ones like Leicestershire's.

Following his withdrawal from Parliament in late March, Huntingdon rallied to the king at York, where he emerged as one of the earliest royalists. The grand declaration of the peers supporting the king on 13 June had Huntingdon fifth on the list, and of the peers to help Charles raise cavalry units, he was one of the first. Given his health, there was little likelihood of seeing him in arms, and as the harried Exchequer officials soon discovered, extracting the promised contribution was nearly impossible. Nevertheless he had declared his loyalty publicly and promptly, something many peers were still reluctant to do.[19]

Huntingdon's sons were equally emphatic, albeit sharply divided, in their alignment. A London merchant learned of this division after selling Lord Ferdinando and Henry Hastings almost £70 worth of cloth; although the brothers had agreed to settle the account jointly, the plan collapsed, the tailor noted mournfully, when Henry 'tooke up armes soone after and so never finished what he pretended'. Lord Hastings could scarcely carry the family colours for his father, since he remained at Westminster. The extent of his radicalism can be easily gauged by his response to the impeachment of Attorney General Herbert; while Hastings would not charge Herbert with treason or imprison him in the Tower, he was willing to discuss the possibility of fining him. Such lukewarm support, however, was enough to earn him the attention lavished on the peers who remained in the increasingly empty House of Lords. Much to his delight, Hastings found himself named to powerful committees like those on Ireland and on the army, and his commitment led him to stand beside Essex at Edgehill.[20] Hastings's most awkward task in 1642 consisted of sitting quietly while the House pronounced his younger brother first, 'a Public Enemy to the State', then a delinquent, and finally a 'Firebrand' guilty of high crimes and misdeameanours.[21] Parliament's wrath was well deserved; Lord Hastings's brother emerged as one of the king's earliest adherents, and his tenacious struggle to gain control of his father's old regiment became an obsession. Regrettably the opening rounds went to Stamford.

The news that the parliamentary Lieutenants 'have had but cold entertainment in most counties' and were 'wholly unregarded' in some delighted Secretary Nicholas. In Leicestershire, however, neither situation obtained. On 5 May 1642, after repeated prodding from the Commons, Stamford finally exercised his authority by ordering a muster at Leicester on 8 June. Since this routine administrative act was certain to be controversial, parliamentary worthies from Hesilrige and Grey to Dr Bastwicke came up to assist Stamford. Charles countered on 27 May with a proclamation ordering the trained bands to obey only a sheriff acting on a royal writ.[22] These contradictory commands set the stage for high drama on 4 June, market day in Leicester. Stamford and Henry Hastings both arrived at the Angel tavern at almost precisely the same time, one armed with the parliamentary Militia Ordinance and the other with a royal writ giving Hastings command of the regiment. Rather predictably, a brawl ensued between the rival commanders and their men. At this point the crowd intervened, but not to restore order. Rather, the mob drove Hastings away, denouncing him as a 'popish lord'. This outcome understandably overwhelmed Stamford. He had begun the day uncertain about the county's reaction, and when the crowds in the market place began crying 'a Stamford! a Stamford!' he broke down entirely, 'tears of joy standing in his eyes to see his Country's love and obedience'.[23]

This latest popular rejection of the Hastingses should not overshadow an equally important result of the fracas; it stopped Hastings from officially reading the proclamation, and this failure spared local officials from having to decide between Stamford and the earl's son. Whether formally announced or not, the proclamation was well known within the shire, and it figured prominently in attempts to persuade the militiamen to mutiny. Rev. Leveston used incantations of the document to halt the constable and trained men of Ibstock from attending the muster; Captain Wortley employed it to persuade his men that although Parliament went 'about to settle the antient laws of the kingdom', its supporters were only following 'their aspiring humors'; and Ensign Dudley similarly begged a soldier to consider that if he obeyed Stamford, 'his estate was lost and his life hazarded'. For their pains, which earned them a parliamentary summons, these three and several others had cast considerable doubt on the legality of Stamford's order. Isolated in far north-eastern Leicestershire, the constable of Stathern was so baffled that his solution to the administrative conundrum was for him to go to Leicester – without the trained men. Such fine compromises were too much for his counterpart in Waltham, who simply ignored Stamford's command.[24]

The success of Henry Hastings's subversion of Stamford's authority might well have been total if his father had not so thoroughly instilled obedience to a Lord Lieutenant's command; thus the muster order brought forth many trained men as well as numerous volunteers. In Leicester, for example, the Mayor and burgesses unanimously resolved to ignore Stamford's order – provided the proclamation formally reached the county by 7.00 a.m. on the 8th. Since it did not, they ordered the trained men to follow the new Lord Lieutenant's directives. Enough others followed their logic for Stamford to proclaim that 'the Countrey came in'. Since the results went 'farre beyond expectation', Stamford promptly ordered a series of company drills, which were even more heartening. Leicester set no more deadlines on its men's attendance; the Stathern constable turned up with his soldier; and Waltham's three men even made a belated appearance. These triumphs earned Stamford lavish praise as the 'very constant and vigilant' Lord Lieutenant who, 'notwithstanding hee was often opposed, yet did not desist, but did proceed in the performance of his trust'.[25]

Increasingly desperate, Mr Hastings struggled to find a legal mechanism to loosen Stamford's grip on the regiment, and the ideal solution soon appeared in a warrant, which had not been seen in the kingdom in almost a century. The most striking illustration of Charles's interest in Leicestershire was that he issued the first Commission of Array to Huntingdon and his son as well as no fewer than three proclamations and Charles's public declaration of Stamford as a traitor. Unfortunately the first attempt to deploy this administrative heavy artillery backfired. Anxious to disrupt Stamford's musters, Hastings and a small party hurriedly gathered the Sheriff and some Corporation officials to witness his formal declaration of this impressive Latin document. After stumbling through some of the text, he then launched into a halting translation, which eventually flummoxed him completely. At this point, the Town Clerk insisted on rereading the entire commission in Latin, whereupon Archdale Palmer, the Sheriff, arrested Hastings. In the ensuing brawl only the timely intervention of some burly butchers allowed the would-be local governor to flee from the county he planned to take over. Palmer's defiance led Charles to another extraordinary action, this time dismissing the wayward Sheriff and naming Henry Hastings in his place. Unfortunately this move had no better luck than the Commission of Array, as Henry's cousin soon discovered. Riding into Leicester with Lord Lovelace and Thomas Killigrew, Walter Hastings, the son of Sir Henry Hastings of Braunston, loudly vowed that 'he would eat up the lord Stamford', prompting one of his companions to beg him to 'leave one bit for me'. All jollity ended when Hastings concluded a rousing address to a crowd by calling for a cheer for 'the King and the Hastings, who have ever been true to the Crown'. The reply was crushing: 'We are all for the King and the Parliament.' Little wonder Walter Hastings and his friends left town, 'in an outragious and uncivill manner, swearing and cursing'.[26]

By the end of June, the military position was clear-cut. Many of the trained men and a sizeable number of volunteers were under Stamford's command, while most of their officers and senior NCOs had rallied to Henry Hastings, who had cobbled together an incongruous posse of coal miners and clerics, equipped with odds and ends from Ashby Castle's storeroom. The key to the situation was the militia's powder stocks, without which Stamford's preponderance of muskets was useless. Here Henry Hastings learned that his father had inadvertently complicated his task; in January, the earl had ordered the powder reserves, which had been distributed in six smaller caches, to be centralised again in Leicester, and Stamford already controlled the county magazine, transferring most of it to Bradgate and leaving the rest under guard at the Newark Tower. These tempting prizes tormented Charles and Hastings.[27] Neither a new sheriff nor commissioners of array being able to secure the magazine, Mr Hastings employed more dubious means ranging from shouting out 'malicious and most opproborious termes' against Stamford to a desperate midnight assault on the Newark Tower. In the end, these only earned a parliamentary impeachment for his efforts, fulsome praise for Stamford and Hesilrige, and a number of furious pregnant women who had miscarried during his nocturnal raid.[28]

By early July, the Corporation was so fed up with repeated skirmishing that it set a strong guard on all gates in order to keep out both Stamford and Hastings. Since its attempt at neutrality nonetheless left Parliament in control of the vital powder stocks, Hastings's inability to alter the local balance of power forced him to play his trump card – the king. If much of the trained band was blithely indifferent to royal warrants, then they would have the opportunity to repeat their contemptuous refusal to Charles's face. On 18 July, the king himself issued the command for the regiment to muster before him at Leicester four days later. As Secretary Nicholas explained, Charles went 'to settle well that county'.[29]

It began happily enough. A day before Charles's arrival, Hesilrige, Grey of Groby and Bastwicke mustered the regiment, and to their apprehensive men 'they gave out how glad they were of his majestys coming and they would stand to what they had done'. Their confidence eventually collapsing, 'all the whole rout of them ran away as though quicksilver had been in their heels'. Hesilrige proved 'too nimble' for the royalist pursuit, but Bastwicke was less fortunate, being dragged back for another bout of prison. Doubtless, the doctor's sharpest pain came from witnessing the king's rapturous welcome into Leicester. In stark contrast to Hull's response, the town readily opened its gates. The crowd, which one commentator estimated at 10,000 and another at 20,000, laboured to express 'their ioyes'; the mass of people, one writer noted, 'shouted as though their throats would burst asunder'. Charles graciously noted that while 'persons of as ill dispositions have been busie in it, and amongst you, as in any County in England', there were also 'very many worthier persons amongst you', who would certainly 'bring Horse, Men, Money and Hearts worthy such a Cause'. After such gracious words, various local gentlemen declared for the king and promised to field sixty horse, a number which the county itself agreed to match. Their enthusiastic response allowed the county to boast that its contributions were second only to Yorkshire, and given the rapid turn of events, 'the Roundheads are most horribly battered'.[30]

All of this skirted the central issue of the Newark Tower magazine and its guard of forty men, who vowed to blow up the supplies before surrendering them. Charles formally denied any designs on the magazine other than 'to preserve it for the County whose it is' from those who might employ it 'in a warlike manner'. Lest such lofty language fail to secure his ends, he ordered three cannons to be wheeled up to the Tower. The royal standard might well have been raised at Leicester rather than at Nottingham a month later if it had not been for the town's decidedly unsympathetic petition. It grieved over

Charles's 'long estrangement from and opposition to your highest and safest Councell of Parliament'; it protested at Henry Hastings's 'hostile manner to the great terrour of your Majesties peaceable subjects'; it requested the vindication of Sir Arthur Hesilrige, 'our worthy knight'; and it firmly asked that Stamford should retain control of 'our Magazine and Militia'. Predictably Charles was 'very much discontented'. At this point the grand jury proposed a compromise; the Newark magazine should again be distributed among the hundreds and all involved should vow never to reassemble it under pain of being labelled 'a disturber of the publick peace of this county'. Although Charles agreed, this arrangement was hardly satisfactory for his purposes. Not surprisingly, decades later Clarendon bitterly recalled that 'if the king were loved there as he ought to be, then parliament was more feared than he'.[31]

The disappointing results of the royal visit ensured that the fledgling royal army did not lack targets once hostilities began a month later. When Walter Hastings had attempted to raise a cry 'for the King and the Hastings', the Leicester crowd had responded 'for the King and the Parliament', and Charles himself had heard the same refrain. What might have been remotely acceptable in June became much more politically charged three months later; by that time, as one cavalier noted, 'wee know that language well enough'.[32] If the locals refused to turn over the militia magazines, the solution was simple enough, especially when Henry supplemented his flying squad of colliers and clerics with 400 light horse. Hitherto the actions over the summer had all illustrated John Rushworth's recollection that in Leicestershire there had been 'many Bickerings one with another'. The first sign of something seriously different came in mid-August when Stamford hurried along 500 foot and a horse troop on a forced march to Bradgate Hall. Early attempts at storming the mansion having failed, the royalists had ominously proclaimed that 'there was an Arrow comming that would bring all ... to obey Mr Hastings Commands'. The arrow was actually Prince Rupert and several hundred cavaliers, and it arrived at Bradgate before Stamford did.[33] Earlier Hastings had threatened to burn Bradgate down; once he actually had possession, he contented himself with sacking it, taking everything of the Greys, even 'the cloathes of his Chaplaine', and pulling down part of the house. Most important, Hastings at last had the bulk of the militia's munitions.[34] The remainder they gathered from Leicester, where Hastings's men were so thorough in their search for 'Armes and ammunition' that they left the citizens 'not so much as a Forke or staffe to defend themselves'. For good measure Rupert also extorted £500 and a feast out of the terrified Corporation.[35]

The rest of the arms and stock were in the hands of the militiamen themselves. To secure these, Hastings summoned his father's old regiment before him, and in response, many of the men 'were so bold as openly to say they were for the King and Parliament'. Hastings half expected such a reply, having already resolved that his 'Maxime is not to trust the trained band'. 'We will make the best use of them we can,' one of Hastings's men commented, 'and that is of their armes, which I may tell you we have need enough of.' After that, Sir Henry dismissed them. Those who eluded this seizure did not find parliamentary agents more scrupulous. A few months later, the committee in Leicester ordered all trained and private men to muster before them. The intent was obvious in the command that the troops should turn up with all their weapons and armour 'togeither with the proportion of such matche and powder and other Ammunition lately dispersed amongst you out of the Magazine'. Those who did were relieved of these items and dismissed.[36]

Roughly at the same time, the shire crossed a sombre threshold. As Hastings struggled to control the magazines, he ineluctably brought the county closer to the brink of open violence. By early July, his obsession made Sir John Coke the younger in neighbouring Derbyshire anxiously exclaim, 'I wish it come not to blood.' But since neither side would relent, the only solution for Coke was a sudden departure for London, 'desiring to be absent if any clashing' should break out 'betwixt the ordinance and commission of array'. In short order, Coke's apprehensions proved to be well founded. The subsequent death toll was low; the significance incalculably great. The first blood having been spilled, the polarisation of the county accelerated, dissolving it into royalist and parliamentary camps. A few weeks of this were enough for Anthony George, the constable of Branston, to pour out a heartfelt prayer into the parish account book. There at the end of a page of bills for morris dancers and muster masters, hayricks and horse levies, he begged:

> Turne us, o good God, and soe shall wee bee turned. Bee favorable to thy people, O good lord, bee favourable who turne to thee in weepinge, fastinge and prayinge for thou art a mercifull god full of compassion, long sufferinge and of great pitty; thou sparest when wee deserve punishment and in thy wrath thinkest uppon mercy, spare thy people, good Lord, spare them, and let not thine heritage bee brought to Confusion; heare us, O good lord, for thy mercy is great, and after the multitude of thy mercies, looke uppon us.[37]

Far better than any of the local clergymen and poets, George had composed the most moving elegy for the passing of the old society over which Huntingdon had long presided. The only irony concerned who had brought 'thine heritage ... to Confusion'.

When Sir Henry Hastings escalated the conflict to such a deadly height, he consciously crossed a significant intellectual threshold. For a century his family had fussed over the the inhabitants of Leicestershire, and his father's administrative motto proclaimed that 'the world shall see that I make every mans burden as light as may be so as I preserve the king's service'. Yet by late August 1642 Henry Hastings was willing to kill these same people. The explanation was personal as well as ideological. In 1640–42, Huntingdon and his son had to witness a general repudiation of their family's customary guardianship of the shire. The county's rejection of the Hastings candidates twice in 1640, the enthusiastic cheers for Stamford, the adulation lavished on Hesilrige, and the silence which greeted calls for a cheer 'for the king and the Hastings', all represented electric shocks, whose pain made it easier for a Hastings to preside over the brutalisation of Leicestershire. Indeed, this sense of outrage and rejection explains Henry Hasting's otherwise gnomic banner, which featured a fiery furnace and the motto *Quasi Ignis Conflatoris*; to others who had forgotten their duty to their monarch and to the Hastingses, he and his men, as the motto proclaimed, would be as hot as the fire of a furnace.

THY TOWERS, O ASHBY!

In June 1649 Lord Hastings, the heir of the sixth Earl of Huntingdon, suddenly died on the eve of his wedding, and this doleful development plunged the family into mourning. Yet as the lamentations continued and even intensified, they become less comprehensible, especially given the survival of several potential male heirs, not the least of whom was the earl's brother. Closer examination reveals the answer to the mystery: the family were bemoaning their own fate at the end of the Civil War as much as they were the ill-fated bridegroom. There was little metaphor in Charles Cotton's observation that 'His House is bury'd in his Funeral.'[38]

The outbreak of hostilities only further confused the situation in the county. Stamford's relief force in 1642 finally reached Leicestershire, vowing 'to cleere that County of the Blood-sucking Cavaleers, that doth so much oppresse the distressed Protestants'. Yet although the earl secured Leicester for Parliament, he could not flush Huntingdon's son out of Ashby Castle, the old Hastings stronghold. Consequently, unlike happier counties where an early skirmish decided their allegiance for the rest of the war, Leicestershire remained divided as rival armies moved through it with awful regularity. 'Poore Leicestershire!' a newsbook lamented in 1644, for no other county had been 'so tottered and torn as it hath been'. The situation only became worse in the following year when Leicester was captured twice and sacked once and when the deciding battle of the Civil War took place just over the Northamptonshire border. For four long years, the inhabitants of the county, Alan Everitt noted, 'were always in the front line of fighting', and the result, Simon Osborne has judged, was 'a particularly bitter popular experience of the war'.[39]

The division of loyalties was largely an extension of patterns already apparent in 1642. Although Henry Hastings served in the field army at Edgehill, his real talents lay in irregular warfare. He quickly blossomed into one of the premier regional commanders, first as 'Col. Hastings' at the head of a regiment of dragoons, then as Colonel General of the North Midlands Army, and finally as Lord Loughborough. Thus Huntingdon's son rocketed to national prominence, denounced by one side as the 'rob-carrier' just as fervently as the other praised his valiant defence of an exposed position. Under his care, Ashby Castle was among the last places to haul down the king's banner, surrendering only in March 1646.[40] Open resistance then gave way to conspiracy as Loughborough helped organise the Sealed Knot and the defence of Colchester in 1648. His obstinate devotion earned him a place of honour in the royalist pantheon, one poet setting him between Newcastle and Hopton. Such fame, unfortunately for his family, came at a high price. His involvement in the second Civil War brought a parliamentary garrison to Ashby Castle in May 1648. A few months later Ferdinando's wife was in Westminster when Parliament suddenly placed Ashby on a list of royalist strongholds to be demolished. She promptly mounted a furious lobbying campaign to reverse the decision and managed to persuade no less than Lord Saye himself. In the meantime, she begged her husband at Ashby, 'I beseech you stop the pulling down.' Her labours might well have been successful if the garrison commander had not been Lord Grey of Groby; still angry over the destruction of Bradgate, he embraced the order with considerable enthusiasm. Lord Hastings's death later in 1649 prompted John Joynes, the family chaplain, to exclaim, 'Our misery's compleat.' The heir's passing 'Thy Tow'rs (O Ashby) did prognosticate.' Since the stones and mortar understood 'There was no further use of them at all / Since he must fall,' then 'these Prophetick Buildings did perceive / And bowing to the ground, took leave'. After this debacle, Loughborough eked out a meagre existence, flitting in and out of exile and fending off his relatives' financial claims for embarrassingly small amounts of money.[41]

The demolition of Ashby led to an outraged petition for compensation from Loughborough's elder brother, but Parliament's cold response to a parliamentary peer of 1642 reveals the depth of the abyss into which he had fallen in six years. His problems had begun at Edgehill, where he literally cut too dashing a figure. The fact that he was the first person to arrive back at Westminster was awkward enough, but what made it worse was a confident report of Essex's crushing defeat. Even an abject apology to the Lord General for 'leaving the Army without first asking leave from your Lordshipp' could not save him from popular ridicule. Royalist poets did not have to search for something to rhyme with a line about Lord Wharton, 'the Saw-pitt did hide him'. A solution came quickly readily enough; 'whilst Hastings did out ride him'.[42] After this embarrassment, he withdrew to Donnington Park, which he attempted to establish as a neutral zone. This noble design foundered when parliamentary forces briefly carried the sixth earl off to Nottingham, prompting him to withdraw to his brother's protection at Ashby where, he later protested, 'he neither took arms, nor gave contributions, nor joined in their councils or commissions'. In an era when his contemporaries were winning distinction on the field of battle, poets anxious to celebrate his virtue could think of nothing more plausible than 'Ferdinand the meek'.[43]

Both sides, needless to say, had trouble accepting the idea of a royalist garrison protecting a moderate parliamentarian from Parliament. Nevertheless, their governing philosophy, Ferdinando's wife explained, was to cling to 'a middle course and is (yet) to fly extreames'. Such a cautious policy had much to recommend it. Ferdinando's service at Edgehill, however inglorious, allowed him to claim that he 'assisted in the wars in England'; his wife thoughtfully kept the parliamentary troops beseiging Ashby in beer; and Ferdinando ended the war with his parliamentary bona fides sufficently intact for him to accept his brother's surrender of Ashby. Unfortunately grave doubts about his commitment remained. Awkward enough was a steady procession of cattle, sheep and pigs from Loughborough's foraging expeditions, which regularly ended up on the countess's table. Worse still was Ferdinando's brief visit to the Oxford Parliament early in 1644. 'My Lords goeing to Oxford,' his wife predicted, 'I feare will proove of very greate danger to him and his estate,' and events proved that she had inherited her mother's powers of prophecy. Although he attended the session briefly and set his hand only to one document, that one could hardly be missed, since it was an open letter exhorting the Scots to withdraw from the English conflict.[44]

Had Ferdinando clung to 'the middle course', the family might have escaped without grievous damage. Unfortunately, since the oddities of his career made it increasingly hard to know where to place him, Parliament not only ignored his plea for compensation, but required him to compound for 'his severall crymes committed against the Parliament'. This fine, together with the loss of the Irish estate, reduced his income in 1646 to less than £900. Worse news soon followed for a family with debts of £13,000 when the aristocracy's customary privileges with creditors vanished with the House of Lords in 1648. Consequently Ferdinando's mourning over his son in 1649 was inconsolable, for the bride's father, a wealthy physican, had prepared for the privilege of vaulting his daughter into the aristocracy by 'Melting the Indies'. With the loss of this massive dowry came an even more chilling discovery; 'there is a bottom of borrowing', which Ferdinando soon struck, and the Fleet prison, where the councillors had confined Shirley and Fawnt, welcomed Huntingdon's son.[45] Only an Act of Parliament, placing the remnants of the Hastings property on the block, allowed him to return to Donnington Park where he could brood over 'the ruine of our family' and its 'despicable condition'. In the new political universe of the 1650s, lit by 'Democraticke Stars', the old 'World/ Is into her first, rude, dark Choas, hurl'd,' and with it went the Hastingses.[46]

The sudden eclipse of the 'House of Ashby' did not bring the family's enemies much happiness. The end of the first Civil War found Hesilrige, Stamford and Grey in the glow of parliamentary favour and in possession of generous pensions and cash gifts; indeed, such was the House's gratitude to Sir Arthur that in 1645, it rather improbably petitioned Charles to raise one of the Five Members to the peerage as Lord Hesilrige. Although the peerage eluded him, Sir Arthur ended the Civil War able to invest some £14,000 in land. Outward prosperity, however, masked more troubling problems. Early successes had brought Stamford and a large parliamentary army into the West Country, where Sir Ralph Hopton first shattered this force at Stratton. Stamford's reputation never recovered, and he ended the war frantically fore-stalling a formal investigation of his incompetence. Even more bitter was Stamford's increasingly rancorous private struggle with his son; while the earl became a Presbyterian whose monarchism strengthened daily, Lord Grey hardened into an equally rigid Independent with decidedly republican tendencies. He soon had the notoriety of being one of the few peers to support Pride's Purge and the only one to sign Charles's death warrant. Yet in spite of his zeal, Grey soon fell out with Cromwell and ended his life in the Protector's jails. On the Restoration, only Stamford's belated return to the royalist fold saved his son's corpse from exhumation with those of his fellow regicides.[47] Sir Arthur for his part had long since fallen out with his local allies; in 1645, he so irritated Stamford that the earl and two of his servants waylaid Hesilrige in a London street, and notwithstanding a parliamentary censure, Stamford re-peated the assault three years later. This bitter hostility doubtless helped persuade Sir Arthur to construct a new power base around Newcastle, far from Bradgate Hall. His departure, however, could not save him from falling out with the Lord Protector and his son. Charles II's accession brought him to the Tower of London, where Huntingdon's embittered old militia captain died in 1661.[48] Therefore both Stamford and Hesilrige were alive to witness the fifth earl's belated vindication in 1660 when the new monarch appointed Loughbough Lord Lieutenant of Leicestershire and the aged Sir Wolston Dixie as Sheriff.[49]

For anyone who knew these men before 1642, their individual trajectories through the Civil War cannot have been too surprising. More puzzling was the way in which the rest of the shire divided. When Rupert and Hastings attacked Bradgate in August 1642, an observer marvelled that 'the Gentry of these Counties do not draw after them such a number of commons as His Majesty presumed upon', and this pattern held true for the rest of the war. This unusual situation led some to lament that 'the generall Body is now out of frame, even from the head to the foot'.[50]

The sharp social cleavage became more pronounced with time. While the Earl of Stamford, Lord Grey and 'Lord' Hesilrige gave local parliamentarians considerable social cache, they were frequently absent. To fill the social void, there were precious few members of the old county elite to grace the parliamentary committee. The biggest catches were the Hartopps, Sir Edward and Sir Thomas, and Sir Roger Smith of Edmonthorpe, but these men were rarely, if ever, involved with the committee's work. In short order, 'all the committee ... went away one after another in displeasure', leaving effective government in the hands of a captain, the Mayor of Leicester and a lone gentleman. The rest had all slipped away, pleading ill health and advanced age, although the humbler members 'know well, but know no infirmities of bodie in them, such as may hinder them altogether for the service, divers of us being as aged and infirme as some of them'. In their place came those of 'Meaner rancke' like Peter Temple, a former apprentice turned linen draper. Such an unusual group of local governors prompted the county knight to protest that 'wee are now ... fallen under the Government of such, whose defects of numbers, acquaintance amongst us, and interests in the County, cannot afford us any probable hope of preservation'. In their defence, the committee men asked, 'Shall we be all blamed if the best qualitie will not act for the Parliament?' This phenomenon admittedly was common enough in other shires, but in Leicestershire it was so pronounced that later, in 1645, John Selden persuaded the Commons that the committee men were in fact 'a company of clowns'.[51]

Logically, the local gentry should have met these upstarts with a solid front, but here something peculiar happened. In 1642, a commentator observed that 'the Gentry of the Country are most of them for the King only, and were very active with Him'. By and large, this judgement is correct if it assumes a very loose definition of the word 'active'. Aside from the Greys and the Hesilriges, almost none of them wanted anything to do with the parliamentary war effort. But equally sparse were the number willing to take up arms in support of the king. While a significant parliamentary force controlling much of the shire naturally bridled the loyalist impulse in many gentlemen, Leicestershire nonetheless is striking for its paucity of active royalists. Some scholars have ascribed the phenomenon to widespread neutralism, but a careful examination of the active royalists provides a fuller explanation. Some came from recusant families which had little choice in the conflict; John Beaumont of Gracedieu raised an infantry regiment and served as Governor of Worcester before dying at the siege of Gloucester in 1644, while Walter Hastings, the son of Sir Henry Hastings of Braunston, earned a knighthood as well as a colonelcy in the same cause.[52] Yet aside from such Catholic gentlemen, the rest of the active royalists eerily overlapped with the fifth earl's militia elite.

In its final composition in 1641, Huntingdon's Deputies and veteran captains numbered old stalwarts like Sir John Skeffington, Sir Wolston Dixie and Sir Henry Skipwith as well as new additions like Sir John Pate, Sir John Bale, Sir Richard Halford, Sir Henry Hastings of Braunston, and Sir Thomas Hartopp. Aside from Hartopp, the rest actively served and suffered for the king. Sir

Wolston's son served as a colonel in Ireland and in the Welsh Marches. Bale offered up two of his, one serving in the north with Sir Marmaduke Langdale before returning as Loughborough's Lieutenant Colonel and the other dying in the defence of Ashby itself. Pate himself took the field, raising two regiments and, after a distinguished service as Colonel of Horse, arranged the surrender of Lichfield. Meanwhile his brother was a sergeant-major in the royal army. Their labours, quite logically, earned baronetcies for their families.[53] Their other colleagues in the militia were no less committed. Skeffington's son, Sir Richard, was another of Loughborough's lieutenant-colonels. Furthermore Charles's fateful decision in 1645 to plunge his field army into the east Midlands owed much to the insistence of Sir Henry Skipwith and Sir John Pate that the parliamentary defences of Leicester were quite weak. They paid for their devotion in coin as well as in blood. Parliamentary committees assessed compositions on Dixie, Halford, Hastings of Braunston, Pate, Skeffington and Skipwith which totalled almost £18,000, easily the bulk of the county's fines. The price that they paid for their royalism could be easily seen in the county. The fines led Hastings to sell off some of his manors in the old Forest of Leicester, and it forced the Bales and the Skipwiths to part with their family seats at Carlton Curlieu and Prestwold Hall. In fact Skipwith's sons found the prospect of living under parliamentary rule so unpleasant that they moved the family *en masse* to Virginia.[54]

The younger officers were no less devoted. After serving as foot captains under Huntingdon, Francis Rooe, Francis Wortley and William Roberts each blossomed in the Civil War; Roberts rose to be a captain, Rooe a lieutenant-colonel and Wortley headed his own regiment. In spite of their comparatively modest estates, their compositions collectively exceeded £3,000. Given the devotion of Huntingdon's militia cadre, it was entirely fitting that one of their number, Francis Wortley, should have had the honour of raising Charles's banner at Nottingham in 1642.[55]

The remarkable loyalty of the old earl's officers casts a new light on the widespread neutralism of the local gentlemen. Outside of their circle, active royalism was rare indeed. From Sir Erasmus de la Fountaine, the wealthy magistrate whose house the parliamentarians burned and whose purse they plundered, it is a swift descent to the likes of Abraham Wright, the High Constable of Sparkenhoe, and William Foster, a poor farmer whose fields where close to a royalist stronghold, with precious few gentlemen in between. Hence, the energetic labours of Huntingdon and his officers to raise a large royalist party ironically may have backfired. Given the heavy political baggage of Huntingdon and his protégés from the preceding quarter-century, many local gentleman may well have opted for careful neutrality when they found themselves unable to separate the king's cause from the earl. After all, the cry with which the early royalists sought to rally the shire was not 'for the King'; it was 'for the King and the Hastings'. The prospects of an uncertain future under Parliament may have looked better than having the Hastingses restore their old hegemony by wrapping themselves in the royal standard. The dearth of Leicestershire loyalists therefore may have owed much to the same logic that led a majority twice to reject Hastings candidates in 1640. The Hastingses' failure in turn left the family and their clients embittered by 1649. Lord Hastings's unexpected passing coming months after Charles's execution and the fall of Ashby Towers was just as well, Mr Bold argued, since the fertile ground of England had been transformed into

> A Soil, that nurses Briars, Weeds, and Rape:
> But Starves the Olive, Fig-tree and the Grape,
> Those Nobler Plants, and glory of the Wood,
> To all who know what's Soveraign, Sweet and Good.

In the new climate, 'Nobles here must be none, / Nor gen'rous Plants, whilst Brambles hold the Throne.'[56]

Huntingdon himself avoided these sombre developments. By February 1643, the growing parliamentary military presence made Donnington Park unsafe for 'this most loyal Earle'. 'For his greate safety', he packed up his feather bed and moved to Ashby, and once there, contemporaries had no doubt about his alignment. When Henry Ireton seized a group of horses at Donnington Park, he carefully distinguished between the earl's animals and those of Lord Hastings; the former he confiscated, the latter he released. By this point, the earl was in no condition to threaten anyone, as 'his old distemper the Lethergie to which hee had bin long inclined' finally overcame him late in 1643. Attended only by Loughborough's officers, his son buried him in the family chapel in Arthur Hildersham's old church.[57] Well before his departure from this world, he had already practically disappeared from the pages of history. His last sighting, however, was entirely in character, catching him alone in his chamber casting accounts. Since one of his steadier, albeit modest, sources of revenue came from the mills on the Trent, it is appropriate that the last words of a man who had once spoken so eloquently on behalf of Frederick of the Palatinate in 1620 and of the faltering Caroline regime in 1639 should be a notation on milling receipts: 'I have reade seene perused and examined this accompt.' Then he turned to ponder a longstanding bill from a scrivener. In balmier days, Mr Hough had written out twelve copies of Fawnt's first letter to Dixie, seven copies of Huntingdon's brief against Sir William, and five copies of his charge to the 1639 assize. For his pains, he claimed only £9 19s. 6d., but by the end of 1642 even this modest sum was more than Huntingdon could easily disburse. Therefore he set it back among the other unpaid bills.[58] Eventually Mr Hough had no other choice but to write it, and the Hastingses, off as another bad debt.

The anonymity surrounding the last year of a man whose thoughts and actions were otherwise well documented sets the stage for the final irony in his long career. In a modern analysis of the county's architecture, Nikolaus Pevsner found precious little out of the ordinary, except for the county's early modern funeral monuments, 'and here Leicestershire is a rich county'. In fact, its wealth permits a scholarly pilgrimage in honour of the major and minor figures of early Stuart Leicestershire. Both the Hesilriges, Sir Thomas and Sir Arthur, have massive tombs, honouring the father for having been 'trusted with the Places of Greatest Honor and Power in the county' and the son as 'a Lover of Liberty and Faithfull to his Country'. So too do many of Sir Thomas's colleagues among the Deputy Lieutenants. Skeffington's tomb celebrates his learning and remarkable skill in six languages, while that of Francis Staresmore commemorates his honours as Justice of the Peace, Deputy Lieutenant and Parliament man. Halford continued in death his bitter struggle in life against the 'profane axes, hammers all the dire / Engines of cursed heathenish deformation', and Pate celebrated his strenuous efforts on behalf of his sovereign. Nor can others in the earl's administrative elite be easily forgotten; indeed, oblivion is impossible when confronted with granite masses celebrating the virtues of Sir William Roberts, the Ship Money sheriff and militia captain, and reciting the merits of Sir John Bale, Huntingdon's quasi-literate protégé. Even at the lower end of the social scale, Sir Thomas Gerard, the JP whom Stamford found so offensive, has a handsome wall marker, as does Walter Rudinge, the long-serving county treasurer.[59]

These monumental riches make it only more astonishing that there is nothing above ground even noting the existence of the fifth earl, much less his precise grave. For long periods in his life, Huntingdon struggled to disassociate himself from Sir Henry Shirley and Sir William Fawnt. Thus it is perhaps fitting that he, like his adversaries, should rest in a unmarked grave.

NOTES

1 Kallendar of Prisoners, April 1641, Leics. RO, BR II/18/22, fol. 41.

2 H's appointments, 1641, HAM 58A/11; *The Winthrop Papers*, III, pp. 198–9; Cotton Mather, *Magnalia Christi Americana* (Cambridge, Mass., 1977) p. 164; and J. Coke to Sir J. Coke, 15 November 1640, BL Add. MS 64,921, fol. 128. See also M. F. Keeler, *The Long Parliament* (Philadelphia, 1954), p. 213; and Nichols, *History and Antiquities*, II, p. 743.

3 *LJ*, IV, pp. 269, 269, 271, 279, 337, 340, 345, 443, 452 and 467. See also John Timmis, *Thine is the Kingdom* (University, 1974), p. 194.

4 7 November and 2, 5 and 10 December 1640, *CJ*, II, pp. 21, 43, 45 and 48; Nichols, II, p. 874; and *Complete Baronetage* (Exeter, 1902), p. 150.

5 PRO E159/479, Star Chamber fines; T. Coke to J. Coke, 12 May 1640, BL Add. MS

64,921, fol. 94. See also the Court of Exchequer decree, 29 November 1641, quoted in Nichols, IV, p. 170.

6 'Articles', 6 November 1640; and J. Coke the younger to J. Coke, 15 November 1640, BL Add. MS 64,921, fols. 125v and 128. See also Nichols, IV, p. 170.

7 3, 14 and 15 December 140, *CJ*, II, pp. 44, 50 and 51; and *D'Ewes* (Notestein), pp. 102 and 145.

8 [J. Coke] to [Sir J. Coke], 16 December 1640, BL Add. MS 64,921, fol. 138v; Widdrington to Mayor, 14 January 1641, Leics. RO, BR II/18/22, fol. 21; and 14 December 1640, *CJ*, II, p. 50.

9 20 May 1641 and 3 December 1640, *CJ*, II, pp. 151 and 44.

10 1 July 1641, *CJ*, II, p. 195; and 2 July 1641, *LJ*, IV, p. 298. See also 28, 29 and 30 June, and 1 July 1641, *CJ*, II, pp. 191, 197, 193–5; Anthony Fletcher, *The Outbreak of the Civil War* (New York, 1981), pp. 73–4; and Russell, *The Fall of the British Monarchies*, pp. 354–5.

11 14 July 1641, *CJ*, II, p. 209; *The Diurnal Occurrences*, November 1640–41, TT E.523 (1), pp. 259–60; Court of Exchequer decree, quoted in Nichols, II, p. 170; and 19 July 1642, *CJ*, II, p. 216. For the earlier reversals, see 23 and 25 February, 12 and 24 March, 20 and 21 April, 4 May, *CJ*, II, pp. 90, 92, 102, 112, 123–4 and 134.

12 7 December 1641, *D'Ewes* (Coates), pp. 244–5.

13 Clarendon, *History*, p. 111; *Two Petitions of the County of Leicester* (London, 1642), TT E.135 (13), [A4]; *A Petition from the Towne and County of Leicester* (London, 29 July 1642), TT E.108 (20), p. 3; and *A Perfect Relation*, 29 September–11 October 1642, TT E.240 (39). p. 13.

14 11–12 February 1642, *Private Journals*, I, pp. 350-1, 346 and 356; and *Diurnall Occurrances*, 7–14 February 164Z, TT E.201 (16), [A4v].

15 10–11 February 1642, *Private Journals*, I, pp. 341, 343 and 351; 9 and 14 February 1642, *LJ*, IV, pp. 571 and 583. See also J. Richards, 'The Greys of Bradgate in the English Civil War', *TLAHS* LXII (1988), pp. 36–7.

16 5, 22, 26 and 29 March, *LJ*, IV, pp. 628, 663, 674 and 680–1; the Leicestershire commission, Main Papers, 27 December 1637, House of Lords RO; *A True and Exact List*, 12 February 1642, TT 669.f3 (44); and Thomas Taynes's Bill, 4 April 1642, HAF 15/9. See also six other London tradesmen's Bill, which all end in April; HAF 15/11–14 and 17–18.

17 *Two Petitions of the County of Leicester* (London, 1642), TT E.135 (13), [A3v].

18 Russell, *The Fall of the British Monarchies*, p. 456.

19 H to FEH, [December 1641], HA Corr. 16/5554; Nicholas to Roe, 22 June 1642, SP 16/491/30; *His Maiesties Declaration* (York, 1 July 1642), TT E.154 (45), [A2vl; *The Catalogue of the Names* (York [London], 22 June 1642), TT 669.f6 (41); and PC to H, 10 August 1642, HA Corr. 16/4277.

20 'Mr Chamberlins Bill', 26 November 1640, HAF 14/30; and 15 and 28 March and 22 September 1642, *LJ*, IV, pp. 645 and 677; and V, p. 367. See also 28 March, 2, 15 and 21 Aprii, 2 May, 6 June and 22 September 1642, *LJ*, IV, pp. 615, 629, 718–19; and V, pp. 8, 35, 106 and 367.

21 6 and 18 June, 1 and 8 July 1642, LJ, V, pp. 106, 145, 170 and 190. See also E. W.

Hensman, *Henry Hastings, Lord Loughborough and the Great Civil War* (1911); and Martyn Bennett, 'Henry Hastings and the Flying Army of Ashby de la Zouch', TLAHS LVI (1980–81), pp. 62–70.

22　Nicholas to Roe, 22 June 1642, SP 16/491/29; Stamford to Mayor, 5 May 1642, Leics. RO, BR II/18/22, fol. 154; 4 June 1642, *CJ*, II, p. 604; and 27 May 1642, *Stuart Royal Proclamations*, ed. by J. F. Larkin (Oxford, 1983), II, pp. 767–9.

23　*Horrible Newes from Leicester* (London, 9 June 1642) TT E.150 (9), [A4].

24　LJ, V, 132; 'Stathern', *AJ*, 141; Leics. RO, DE 625/60; and *A True Relation* (London, 5 July 1642), TT E154 (4), [sig.] A2.

25　Vote and Resolution, 6 June 1642, Leics. RO, BR II/18/22, fols. 155 and 170; 'Stathern', *AJ*, pp. 141; Leics. RO, DE 625/60, fol. 65v; and *The Earle of Stamfords Resolution* TT E154 (25), [sig.] A3.

26　Leicestershire Commission of Array, 11 June 1642, Rushworth, *Historical Collections*, IV, p. 655; 18 and 20 June and 4 July 1642, *Royal Stuart Proclamations*, II, pp. 770–5 and 777–84; Hastings's appointment as Sheriff, 25 June 1642, HA Extra Over-size 1/4; and *A True Relation of the Transaction*, pp. 4–5 and [8–9].

27　*A True Relation of the Transaction*, pp. 1–2; and Nicholas to H, 7 July 1642, HA Corr. 16/9677.

28　*A Perfect Diurnall*, 4–11 July 1642, TT E.202 (15), p. 1; and 'To the Kings most Excellent Maiestie ... by many women', 24 July 1642, printed in *Truths from Leicester and Nottingham* (London August 1642, TT 669.f6 (57). See also *The Impeachment and Charge of Mr Henry Hastings* (London, 22 July 1642), TT E.107 (39); *The Earle of Stamfords Resolution* (London, 1642), TT E.154 (25); and *Terrible Newes from Leicester, Warwick and Staffordshire* (London, 30 July 1642), TT E.108 (26).

29　Resolution, 2 July 1642, Leics. RO, BR II/18/22, fol. 172; Charles to H, 18 July 1642, HA Corr. 16/1357; Nicholas to Roe, 20 July 1642, SP 16/491/84; and *Perfect Diurnall*, 25 July–1 August 1642, TT E.202 (26), p. 24.

30　Tovey to Warner, 26 July 1642, SP 46/83/unfoliated, quoted in Norah Fuidge, 'Letters from a Seventeenth Century Rector of Lutterworth', *Leicestershire Historian* III (1983–84), p. 16; *His Maiesties Speech at Leicester* (York and London, 1642), TT 669.f5 (63); *Truths from Leicester and Nottingham* (London, 1 August 1642), TT 669.f6 (57); and *A Catalogue of the Moneys, Men and Horse* (London, 5 August 1642), TT 669.f6 (64). On the subscription, see Skeffington to H, 15 August 1642, HA Corr. 16/10,879.

31　*A Diurnall and Particular* [19]–26 July 1642, TT E.202 (21), pp. 7–8; *Declaration and Resolution of the Countie of Leicester* (London, 29 July 1642), TT E.108 (9); *A Petition from the Towne and County of Leicester* (London, 29 July 1642), TT E.108 (20); and Clarendon, *History*, p. 279.

32　*A Private Letter from an Eminent Cavalier* (London, 10 September 1642), TT E.116 (32), p. 6.

33　Rushworth, *Historical Collections*, III, p. 655; Charles's Commission, August 1642, HA Corr. 16/1358; *Perfect Diurnall*, 15–22 August 1642, TT E.293 (9); and *Terrible Newes from Leicester, etc.* ([London], 30 July 1642), TT E.108 (26).

34　'An Information from Leicester', *Remarkable Passages from Nottingham* (London, 1 September 1642) TT 669.f6 (75); and *Perfect Diurnall*, 29 August–5 5eptember 1642, TT E.239 (14), [Nv]. For the earlier threat, see *Perfect Diurnall*, 27 June–4 July 1642, TT E.202 (13).

35   A *True and Perfect Diurnall*, 29 August–6 September 1642, TT E.202 (43); Rupert to
     Mayor, 6 September; and Rupert's receipt, 9 September 1642, Leics. RO, BR III/8/168
     and 170; and BR III/2/82, fol. 63a.

36   A *Private Letter from an Eminent Cavalier* (London, 10 September 1642), TT E.116 (32),
     pp. 6–7; and *Perfect Diurnall*, 19–26 1642, TT E.240 (10) and E.240 (14); Leics. Commit-
     tee to Constables, 15 February 1643, HA Military 1/34.

37   J. Coke the younger to J. Coke, 5 July 1642, BL Add. MS 64,929, fol. 20; and 'Anthonie
     George his praier', Leics. RO, DE 720/30, fol. 52v. See also for example *An Exact and
     True Relation of a most cruell and horrid Murther* (London, 17 September 1642), TT E.117
     (20).

38   Nichols, III, p. 308; and *Lachrymae Musarum; the Tears of the Muses* (London, 1649), p.
     13. See also Eleanor Davies, *Sions Lamentation* (London, 1649).

39   A *Famous and Joyfull Victory* (London, 10 September [1642]), TT E 116 (30), [A4];
     Parliament Scout 15 August 1644, TT E7 (4); A. M. Everitt, *The Local Community and the
     Great Rebellion*, p. 11; and Simon Osborne, 'The War, the People, and the Absence of the
     Clubmen in the Midlands, 1642–1646', *Midland History* XIX (1994), p. 97.

40   HLL's commissions, 1 August 1642, HA Corr. 16/1358; and 22 November 1644, HA
     Military 1/32; Articles of surrender, 28 February 1646, Nichols, III, p. 608; and A *Dogs
     Elegy* (London, 1644), TT E3 (170), p. 8. See also Bennet, 'Henry Hastings and the Flying
     Army'; Hensman, *Loughborough*; and Roy Sherwood, *The Civil War in the Midlands*
     (London, 1992), pp. 63, 66, 110–13, 123 and 152.

41   29 August and 28 November 1648, CJ V, p. 689 and 692; and VI, p. 87; 28 July 1652,
     CPCC IV, pp. 3029–30; C. of H to H, [late 1648], HA Corr. 19/5745; and *Lachrymae
     Musarum*, pp. 28 and 31. See also David Underdown, *Royalist Conspiracy in England
     1649–1660* (New Haven, 1960), pp. 76–9, 88–90, 108–14 and 322–4; and John Joynes,
     A *Sermon Preached ... at the Baptizing of Theophilius (then Lord Hastings) now Earl of
     Huntingdon* (London, 1668).

42   'For demolishing Ashby Towers', 1648, HAP 19/7; FEH to Essex, 3 November 1642,
     HEH, HA Corr. 16/4865; and 'London farewell to the Parliament', HEH HM 165,228
     [Conway Poetical Miscellany], p. 67.

43   H's Petition, 4 November 1645, LJ IV, p. 675; and *Lachrymae Musarum*, p. 19. See also
     A. C. Woods, *Nottinghamshire in the Civil War* (Oxford, 1937), pp. 46–7.

44   LCH to HLL, 12 February [1644], HA Corr. 16/5740; 'A note of hogsheads ... to the
     garrison at Cole-orton, 2 December 1644, HAF 15/33; 27 March, 20 and 21 May 1643,
     'Daily expences of provision', HAF 15/30, unfoliated; House of Lords to Scottish Coun-
     cil, January 1644, Rushworth, *Historical Collections*, V, pp. 561–3; and H's petition, 2
     March 1653, CPCC II, p. 1043.

45   Leicester Committee to all Captains, 29 January 1646, HAP 19/5; C. of H to H, 4
     December [1649], HA Corr. 19/5743; 'Actions and Executions', 1649, HAF 16/35; and
     Dugdale, 'Historical and Geneologicall Collections', HA Misc. 13, fols. 85–6. On the
     'erasing of former privilege', see C. of H to H, 29 January [1649], HA Corr. 19/5742.

46   HLL to H, 2 April 1651, HA Corr. 19/5568; H's Act of Parliament, HAP 19/12; 18 and 31
     October, 1 and 9 November 1653, CJ VII, pp. 336, 342, 343 and 347; and *Lachrymae
     Musarum*, p. 29.

47   Richards, 'The Greys of Bradgate in the English Civil War', pp. 33–52; Nichols, II,

pp. 745–6; and Mary Coate, *Cornwall in the Great Rebellion* (Oxford, 1933), pp. 41–72.

48 28 June 1645, *CJ* IV, p. 188; Roger Howell, *Newcastle upon Tyne and the Puritan Revolution* (Oxford, 1967), pp. 181–4, 197–9, 202, 233–5, 266 and 346; and Hesilrige's petition to Charles II, 1660, Leics. RO, Hazlerigg MS, DG21/254.

49 HLL's Lieutenancy warrant, 15 January 1660, HA Oversize 1/6; and Nichols.

50 *A Private Letter from an Eminent Cavalier* (London, 10 September 1642), TT E.116 (32), p. 6; and *Terrible News from Leicester* (London, 30 July 1642), TT E.108 (26), [p. 3].

51 *An Examination Examined* (London 1645), TT E 303 (13), pp. 14–15; *A Speech Delivered ... 6 November* (London,1644), TT E.16 (19), p. 2; Lilly, *History of his Life and Times*, p. 48. See also James Innes, *An Examination of a Printed Pamphlet* (London, 1645), TT E.261 (3), p. 1; and Nichols, III, appendix, p. 41 n. 1.

52 Martyn Bennett, 'Leicestershire's Royalist Officers and the War Effort in the County, 1642–1646', *TLAHS* LIX (1984–85), pp. 44–51; David Fleming, 'Faction and Civil War in Leicestershire', *ibid.*, LVII (1981–82), pp. 26–36; P. R. Newman, *Royalist Officers in England and Wales* (New York, 1981), pp. 20 and 180; and Nichols, III, p. 661*; and IV, pp. 618–19.

53 Newman, *Royalist Officers*, pp. 15, 111 and 187; and Nichols, III, p. 283; IV, p. 596.

54 *CPCC*, pp. 835, 1191, 1760, 2016, 2032 and 2207; and Nichols, II, p. 540; III, pp. 367–8 and 612; and IV, pp. 618–19. See also James Horn, *Adapting to a New World* (Chapel Hill, 1994), pp. 58 and 180.

55 Newman, *Royalist Officers*, pp. 317, 423; *CPCC* 962–3, 1077, and 116–71; and Nichols, IV, pp. 544–7 and 1005.

56 *CCC*, 1236, 1651 and 3021–2; Nichols, II, pp. 231–2, and *Lachrymae Musarum*, p. 34.

57 Carrier's bill, 8 February 1643, HAF 15/22 (misc.); Ireton to LCH, 12 June [1643], HA Corr. 16/7009; and William Dugdale, 'Historicall and Geneologicall Collections', HA Genealogical 1/26 and Box 13, p. 79.

58 'William Goldings booke of Accompt', 1640–44; and Mr Hough his bill, 9 September 1642, HAF 14/33 and 15/22 [Miscellaneous bills].

59 Nikolaus Pevsner, *Leicestershire and Rutland* (London, 1989), p. 28; and Nichols, I, p. 317; III, pp. 253, 444 and 753; and IV, p. 547.

Conclusion

Whitehall and Leicestershire

'So sad have been the sufferings of that County, and Rutland, by the reason of the disharmony there', one commentator noted in 1644. 'Poore Leicestershire!' he continued, unable to imagine any other 'County so tottered and torn as it hath been'.[1] The bleak situation, as we have seen, only became worse, until by the end of the decade, the shire's 'disharmony' brought Ashby Towers and the Hastingses to the ground. Amid the wreckage of mid-century, we can now analyse the powerful forces that wasted Leicestershire.

During the mobilisations of the Bishops' Wars, the Earl of Newcastle arguably best captured the popular image of the early Stuart militia in his play *The Country Captaine*. It is hard to tell which is more amusing, the local gentleman whose recent appointment as a militia captain sweeps him away with vainglorious dreams or his servant whose profound ignorance leads him to assume that tactics are actually 'ticktack', a new kind of board game. The comic high point of the play arguably comes when the increasingly mystified captain surveys the books which the servant has purchased for his military education: 'The Buckler of Faith', a 'Booke of Mortifications' a 'Booke of Cannons' and a folio of Shakespeare. When the new captain protests that the last purchase contains only 'playes', the servant smoothly asks, 'Are not all your musterings in the Country soe, Sir?'[2]

This line would have garnered few laughs in Leicestershire, where bitter experience had taught contemporaries what came of underestimating the amount of money necessary to run a militia unit. From 1618 to 1630 the regiment mustered at least once a year, with the sole exception of 1621, and to underwrite this activity, Huntingdon levied assessments which totalled approximately £3,800. Including the coat and conduct money, the figure rises to £4,300, almost the equivalent of six parliamentary subsidies and well in excess of the county's contribution to the forced loan. To be sure, for much of the following decade the sums became much more manageable; from 1631 to 1635, Huntingdon asked for less than £800. Unfortunately for contemporaries, this idyllic world vanished when the Privy Council decided to shift much of the expense of the Bishops' Wars onto the local ratepayers. While it is now impossible to speak of the figures for 1639–40 with any precision, the frantic activity in rural parishes and in Leicester, together with the comparatively staggering amounts of money which the constables collected, suggests that the ratepayers then witnessed a quantum leap in local military assessments, well beyond the levels of the late 1620s. These amounts become even more impressive once it is appreciated that the local costs carried by villages which presented trained men and by gentlemen responsible for private men and the horse troop certainly doubled and probably tripled Huntingdon's assessments.

Granted that Huntingdon's zeal for the service was comparatively extreme; after all, no other Lord Lieutenant ever received the suggestion from the Council, as he had in 1633, to hold down militia assessments. Nevertheless, the costs of the Leicestershire militia were not all that extraordinary. In the late 1620s, the situation in East Anglia was equally tumultuous. The mobilisation of the Essex trained band for a few weeks in 1625 ran up a bill of some £5,000, and the Exchequer's inability to retire this debt poisoned further efforts at perfecting the local troops and caused the number of defaulters to soar. Suffolk meanwhile began Charles's reign protesting over having to retain a professional muster master and then quickly slid into bitter squabbles over local rates. Similar problems bedevilled the Norfolk Deputies, who found the intensity of the disputes over militia rates so frustrating that they resigned *en masse* in 1628. Nor were such difficulties only common to exposed coastal counties. In Cheshire, the same Council order of 10 July 1626, which caused so much turmoil in Leicestershire, prompted the Deputies to lay out £4,000. Likewise Lancashire's trained band of 650 foot and 150 horse produced military assessments from 1625 to 1640 of approximately £10,000. The fact of the matter was that local military charges, while often individually modest, had an inherent tendency to add up. Consequently the Parliament men in 1641 were not exaggerating when they protested in the Grand Remonstrance that military charges 'amount to little less than the ship-money'.[3]

Gentlemen from Leicestershire would have confirmed this fact as readily as others elsewhere, but their complaints would not have been exclusively financial. While some Lieutenants ignored their responsibilities, others, Fletcher noted, 'exploited their role skilfully in order to strengthen their local command and authority'. This assessment admirably described Huntingdon's motives, and it deserves more attention than it has received. From the late 1610s, Whitehall's increased demands allowed the earl to tighten his already formidable grip to the point where the shire effectively donned, just as the

Leicestershire pressed men did in 1625, his family livery. Leicestershire as a result evolved into a political system different from that in more familiar counties. Decades of practice allowed the Justices in counties like Sussex and Somerset, Suffolk and Norfolk to decide for themselves all matters from poor relief and justice to tax collection and the militia. Their comparative freedom from outside pressure moreover allowed them to internalise all of the customary dodges which excused them from uncongenial national service. In these shires, the physical and mental distance between magnates and their counties was so vast that it permitted the emergence, as MacColloch noted in Suffolk, of a county's 'self-confident ... identity', for the local community 'had no immediate superiors to challenge that identity'. In Leicestershire, matters were arranged wholly otherwise. Recently, to ease local history out of the problems of typicality, Ann Hughes has suggested thinking of individual county communities as 'a unique combination of various elements or components, the elements being present in all counties', and the components, which she proposed for greater scholarly attention, were largely 'geographical, economic and social'. While endorsing this notion, the present study suggests the addition of political factors and, in particular, the need for greater sensitivity to the possible variables in county administrations.[4]

Huntingdon may well not have been unique in his attitude to local government, and some of the more promising places to search for the remains of similar regimes are in Derbyshire and Nottinghamshire, and in Cheshire and Lancashire, where the Cavendishes and the Stanleys dominated the local scene with a thoroughness that Huntingdon could only have admired. Pending conclusive findings elsewhere, Leicestershire stands as a striking illustration of the wide range of variables in local political structures, of the breadth of which historians need to be more aware. The lieutenancy, it now appears, underwent a dramatic transformation at the Restoration. 'Rather than practising a politics of inclusion and compromise, as had been the goal before the civil wars, the lieutenancy,' Stater observed, 'became the enforcer of a system that rigidly excluded a large part of society from participation.'[5] Yet as Shirley, Fawnt and Hesilrige would have testified, enforcers among the Lieutenants existed well before 1642. Consequently contemporaries at mid-century may well have witnessed a shift towards a style of local government already present in early Stuart England, rather than an abrupt transformation from consensus to conflict.

Sharp differences were apparent not only between Lords Lieutenant but also within their individual careers. In a matter of months between 1625 and 1627, Huntingdon plunged from being the Council's model local governor to a political pariah, and his favoured position was regained only after a decade of loyal service. To comprehend these administrative rhythms, therefore, is to unravel many of the puzzles in the relationship between Whitehall and the provinces. Since wayward Lords Lieutenant, unlike obstinate JPs, were rarely dismissed from office, the councillors appear to have dealt with these nearly immovable local governors by carefully calibrating their hearing. Scholars have long had few illusions about the councillors' ability to follow developments in every county.[6] Sloth and inefficiency of course account for much of the answer; so too does the fact that the councillors were constantly revising a league table of local governors. Those at the top were more likely to receive prompt attention, while those relegated to the bottom were effectively banished to an administrative Siberia from which their most fervent complaints sounded faintly, if at all, in Whitehall.

A clearer appreciation of the financial burden of a trained band and of the possibilities of administrative aggrandisement which it presented underscores the need for a fundamental revision of our perceptions of the militia. Over three decades ago, Thomas Barnes brilliantly depicted the many times and ways in which Sir Robert Phelips and Lord Poulett used the Somerset militia to conduct their own vendetta throughout the 1630s. A decade later, Hassell Smith found a similar situation in late Elizabethan Norfolk, where Sir Arthur Heveningham and Sir Nicholas Bacon waged a bitter administrative struggle over the local militia. Since the Privy Council in the 1620s put at least as much pressure on the local units as in the 1590s and more than in the 1630s, it follows that there should have been similar problems in this decade. Yet the entire wave of controversy about the 'localist' thesis swept through the archives without uncovering anything other than periodic flashes of tension over the militia. In Leicestershire, however, with Shirley, Fawnt and Hesilrige, we have at last struck archival pay dirt, precisely where Barnes and Smith suggested it should have been. Writing in the mid-1980s, Penry Williams wondered aloud about the typicality of Smith's findings; given the absence of any supporting evidence, he could only conclude that 'Norfolk seems to have been exceptional.'[7] The discovery of another series of bitter militia disputes, and these far from the obvious pressure points along the coast, forces us to revisit the question of Norfolk's atypicality. This discovery suggests that what may be at issue is not so much the uniqueness of an odd county as the patchy nature of surviving evidence, which precludes uncovering similar controversies elsewhere. After all, the vital piece of evidence which brought together all of the stray bits of information about the Leicestershire regiment was the fifth earl's lieutenancy book, and that volume surfaced only a few years ago. Further research is, of course, necessary to exhaust the possibilities of remaining evidence, but what is already clear from these three early strikes, widely separated in time and place, is that scholars have hitherto underestimated the magnitude of the potential problems associated with the militia.

To correct this deficiency, we need to pay closer attention to these local military activities and to remember that Lindsay Boynton produced, not the definitive analysis, but rather, as he readily conceded, an admirable 'general study' of the militia. In a renewed emphasis on the early Stuart militia, the question of how much the unit cost is at least as vital as what it actually did, for after the repeal of the Marian statute in 1604, even the most notional militia levy could raise awkward constitutional questions. Equally important is the task of establishing how a county's military elite related, on one hand, to the local bench and, on the other, to the Privy Council. A decade ago, Andrew Coleby lamented the scholarly tendency to underestimate the importance of the late seventeenth-century Lords Lieutenant, a tendency which is even more pronounced among early Stuart historians; no less an authority than Lawrence Stone himself excluded the lieutenancy from the list of offices able to satisfy the aristocratic 'desire for employment, prestige and emoluments'.[8] This study, it is hoped, will encourage the rehabilitation both of these often ignored figures and of the units which they commanded; and the time is surely auspicious, given the recent publication of Victor Stater's pioneering survey of the seventeenth-century lieutenancy. Beyond simply being aware of these local governors, scholars would do well to attend to the occasions when their power and importance could mushroom just as dramatically as it could fade. A clearer appreciation of the administrative rhythms of a Lieutenant's standing with the local magistrates and with Whitehall will, in turn, afford us a sharper perspective on the larger, and even more vexed, question of the relationship between the early Stuart monarchs and the provinces.

With a more serious appreciation of the militia and the lieutenancy comes a fundamental reappraisal of the early Stuart state. Customary analyses of Whitehall's financial success have often focused almost exclusively on parliamentary subsidies and a few controversial prerogative taxes like the forced loan and Ship Money. The former netted the Exchequer roughly £10,000 between 1621 and 1629 from Leicestershire, while the two extraparliamentary levies brought in another £3,386 and £15,842.[9] This cumulative total of slightly more than £29,000 meant that, from 1614 to 1638, the Leicestershire ratepayers on average had to produce £1,160, or the equal of some one and a half parliamentary subsidies yearly. And if we stop our calculations in 1634, before Ship Money drives up the total, then the average plummets to £637. Since the early Stuart state apparently ground down on the shoulders of the local gentlemen with all the weight of a feather, the regime's finances understandably seem precarious indeed. (See Fig. 4.)

Tempting though this conclusion is, it necessarily casts a blind eye on a number of other payments into the Exchequer. Behind this wilful ignorance lies the belief that any other levies must have been more of a nuisance than a serious grievance. Yet as this study has repeatedly emphasised, the central tenet of provincial politics was that little things add up, and often quickly.

Figure 4   **Parliamentary subsidies, the forced loan and Ship Money, 1614–38**

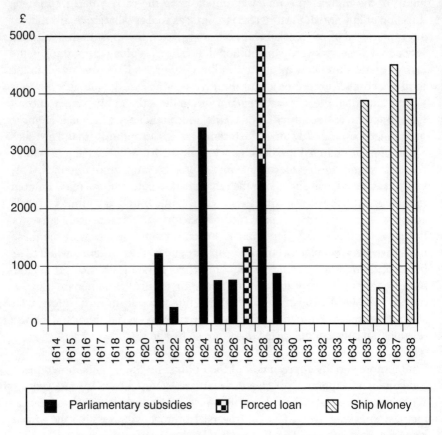

Sources: (the 1621 subsidies) PRO E401/1906 and 1907; (the 1624 subsidies) the discussion of estimating this yield, above, p. 38; (the 1625 subsidies) PRO E401/2441 and 2442; (the 1628 subsidies) PRO E401/2445–6; (the forced loan) PRO E401/2322, 2323, 2443 and E403/2804; and (Ship Money) SP 16/364/23, 16/400/113, 16/431/62 and 16/473/103.

Therefore while scholars can all too easily overlook the £541 from various Privy Seal campaigns in 1622–26, it is harder to miss the £2,320 which came from distraint of knighthood in 1630–32, and harder still to ignore the windfall profits of the Depopulation Commission of 1635–40, which produced another £8,861, almost as much as parliamentary subsidies in the 1620s. In short, to the total of some £29,000 from parliamentary and a few prominent non-parliamentary taxes must be added a further £12,000 which the county also paid into the Exchequer.

At this point, with subsidies and fifteenths of some £10,000 accounting for about a quarter of the total £41,000, the proportion between parliamentary and non-parliamentary taxes is roughly where we would expect it to be. But the total mounts higher still if we recall Michael Braddick's recent observation about the difficulty of calculating 'the costs of government' before the Civil War. 'The cost of some activities,' he noted, 'is concealed, for the simple reason that the money was raised and spent locally'; and since these collections do not 'appear in the national accounts', they are now hard, if not impossible, to recover. Properly speaking, purveyance cannot be reckoned a 'concealed' tax. Nevertheless it effectively was one, since the money was paid into the Lord Steward's office, not the Exchequer, and in any case, these records have almost totally disappeared. Although it is now impossible to be certain about actual payments, the regular letters from the Green Cloth officials reveal that they noticed any intermission in purveyance payments and that they were swift to exact their due.[10] Consequently it is safe to assume that the county made its annual payments of £983, which between 1614 and 1638 yielded slightly more than £24,500. We are on firmer ground with £1,578, which the county paid for a 1620 benevolence that went directly to Frederick and Elizabeth of the Palatinate. Finally, the militia rates in the same period came to over £6,000. After this, we enter Braddick's twilight zone where the precise figures are well concealed, for the tally of the militia regiment does not include either the 'local' costs of military levies or the expenses of the 500 private men, and it excludes the heavy burden of the Bishops' Wars. Nevertheless, even without uncertain categories, which were likely to have doubled, if not tripled, the militia levies, the regime still extracted an additional £32,000, which never passed through the Exchequer. Therefore, the county's grand total from 1618 to 1638 rises to some £73,000, of which only £29,000 came from parliamentary subsidies, the forced loan and Ship Money.

Meditation on the fact that Parliament provided only £10,000 of the £73,000, or less than 13 per cent of Whitehall's exaction, initially only further discredits the apparent importance of that institution.[11] Conversely, the central government had only very limited leeway over the expenditure of the 'concealed' taxes. The Exchequer could intercept neither the militia assessments nor the Palatine benevolence, and purveyance offered even less wriggle-room,

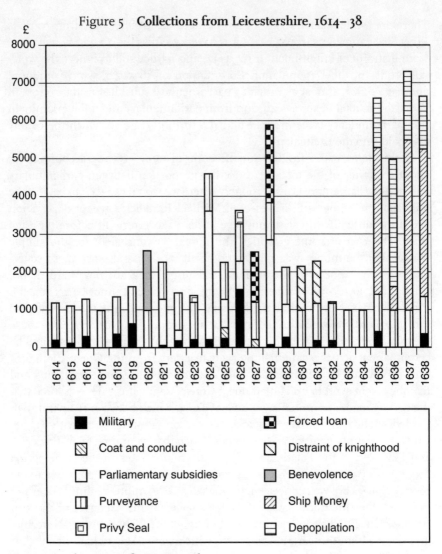

Figure 5   **Collections from Leicestershire, 1614– 38**

Legend:
- Military
- Coat and conduct
- Parliamentary subsidies
- Purveyance
- Privy Seal
- Forced loan
- Distraint of knighthood
- Benevolence
- Ship Money
- Depopulation

Sources: see those given for Figs. 2 and 3.

pending the court's rediscovery of the merits of fasting. Parliament thus accounted for about a quarter of the disposable income. Nevertheless the figure of 13 per cent remains exceedingly useful, if only to underscore the surprising size and vigour of the early Stuart regime's 'demense revenue'.

Since over 60 per cent of the resulting £73,000 which the local ratepayers produced from 1614 to 1638 came from these more obscure sources, it is time that scholars broadened their vision to include these categories. While Russell has maintained that national taxes barely touched the wealth of early Stuart England, he conceded that 'locally it may have been another story'. Leicestershire's experience in these years suggests that this judgement's conditional 'may' should be replaced with a more emphatic verb. Likewise these figures illustrate the considerable wisdom which O'Brien, Hunt and Braddick have displayed in delaying any definitive estimate of the regime's financial resources, pending a more thorough analysis of local rates.[12] The present study endorses the necessity of clarifying this grey area. Admittedly scholars have often been unnecessarily timid about Exchequer documents; they could scarcely find the Lord Steward's records of purveyance; and above all else, they have been all too willing to underestimate the contemporary importance of militia rates. After correcting these omissions, a more formidable picture of the state will emerge. [See Fig. 5.] The material does not support the conclusion that the demands of the early Stuart state represented a crushing burden. Any Exchequer officer would have argued that the realm could have coped with higher rates of taxation, and in short order, its inhabitants were soon forced to admit as much in the 1640s and '50s. Yet it is equally clear that the weight of the early Stuart state on provincial society was significantly heavier than scholars have assumed.

The county's weekly assessment in the 1640s, the basic unit of parliamentary taxation, routinely produced £9,750 a year, and additional levies periodically drove up the total, as they did in 1647, to some £15,000. These demands predictably raised the volume and intensity of complaints in a shire where 'many complaine the taxes ... have exceeded the Incombes of Rent'.[13] In their anguish, contemporaries could have found some comfort in the fact that the various levies of James I and particularly Charles I had prepared them for the brave new world of weekly assessments and the excise. In order to gauge the burden of the early Stuart state with more precision, it is useful to recall Colbert's adage about the art of taxation; it consists in plucking the largest number of feathers from the goose with the least amount of hissing. Ultimately, whether or not the contemporaries of Shirley and Fawnt were heavily taxed is irrelevant if they felt they were. Given the long period of minimal state intervention in the 1610s, Leicestershire in the subsequent two decades was understandably filled with the sound of honking, to say nothing of hissing. With the inclusion of these additional payments of some £44,000, a very different picture of the state's financial success emerges. Although the payments brought Leicestershire's annual average to slightly more than £2,900, easily the equivalent of four parliamentary subsidies, averages were quite deceptive in this period, as Fig. 4 reveals. Side by side with a half-dozen years when the state barely extracted £1,000 went an equal number of more disturbing ones when the totals edged somewhere between £2,500 and £3,500. All of these, however, paled before six years with amounts in excess of £4,500, three of which topped £6,000 and one, £7,000. These figures are particularly chilling, since they represented actual payments, not assessments, which were often substantially in arrears during the 1640s.

This background underscores the validity of Conrad Russell's observation about the regime's financial structure; it was indeed so ramshackle as to resemble 'a broken-down system, like a fifth-hand Mini', almost 'ready for the scrapheap'.[14] While his judgement is perspicacious, the figures from Leicestershire suggest that, notwithstanding high mileage, erratic maintenance, and sometimes alarming amounts of exhaust smoke, this venerable fiscal engine was still capable of producing relatively high r.p.m.s and a throaty snarl. Its performance was of course uneven and rarely satisfied its owner. Nevertheless, a heavy emphasis on the regime's inability to gather money necessarily tempts scholars to de-emphasise its triumphs, and it is folly to yield to the temptation, since the memory of those triumphs, not the failures, helped persuade contemporaries to take up arms.

In addition to revealing a sometimes startling financial vitality in a regime frequently described as moribund, the careful analysis of Fig. 5's peaks and troughs highlights the contours of the political topography of the early seventeenth century. While some of these fluctuations have received attention earlier, they all are worthy of general reconsideration here in order to appreciate the realm's trajectory in the quarter-century before the Civil War.

Thanks in large part to the Cadiz voyage late in 1625 and to the descent on Ré in 1627, England's involvement in the Thirty Years War naturally appears to have been a phenomenon of the late 1620s. Against this assumption, the first jump in payments from 1619 to 1621 stands as a vivid warning, for the reverberations of the 'cold war' in 1620–23, when English volunteers defended the Palatinate, were unmistakably felt in Leicestershire. In 1620–21, the shire contributed £3,000 directly to the war effort, and the continental conflict roused the militia from its slumbers and exacted another £1,500 in the five years after 1618. Therefore, the common scholarly decision to hurry past this early episode on the way to the main event at the end of the decade makes it easy to interpret later parliamentary criticism of the war effort as so much malingering. Some of it likely was, but the intellectual leap involved in applying this argument beyond a fairly limited audience inevitably stumbles over the stark fact that James I had squandered contributions which were as generous as they were substantial. Thanks to James I's erratic attitude to military intervention, the local ratepayers could have been forgiven if they perceived the war which Charles opened late in 1625 as the second attempt in the decade to move onto a war footing; and since their earlier contributions had vanished to no apparent end, they were understandably wary of a repeat performance.

Two of the earl's protégés in the Commons neatly illustrate this point. Near the end of the 1625 Oxford session, Sir Richard Weston pleaded for a second vote of supply, only to have one of Huntingdon's Deputy Lieutenants from Rutland thwart it. All Sir Guy Palmes did was to cite the old adage, *fidem qui perdit, perdere ultra nihil potest*, 'He who loses his good faith has nothing else to lose'. Uneasiness on the part of the long-serving Chancellor of the Exchequer quickly gave way to anger when Palmes recalled that grave financial problems on Henry VIII's accession ended with the summary execution of some prominent officers. His tart intervention understandably earned Palmes an unexpected stint as sheriff. The relationship between Lord Lieutenant and his bold Deputy, moreover, does not seem to have been entirely coincidental; in 1626, for example, Sir George Hastings, the family's Knight of the Shire, supported the return of another awkward sheriff, Sir Edward Coke, and when the lack of hard evidence threatened to stymie the duke's impeachment, the earl's brother supplied solid information against the favourite.[15] To be sure, Sir Guy and Sir George may have simply been eager to sabotage an expensive war. A more logical explanation, however, is that they were demonstrating the notion that, in politics, there is no fury like taxpayers who feel themselves scorned.

The second upward curve at the end of the decade, while more predictable, nonetheless remains baffling, thanks to the turmoil surrounding these exactions. The picture becomes clearer if we use the Leicestershire material to set the county's most successful son against a novel backdrop. One of Buckingham's greatest feats, Russell has maintained, was his smooth transition from King James to King Charles, but this triumph was in fact routine, thanks to the close emotional bond which Charles and Buckingham had forged in 1623-24. What was much more astonishing was Buckingham's *volte-face* in 1624 from a Spanish stalwart to an advocate of an international anti-Habsburg coalition. To establish himself in this new role, the favourite sacrificed a host of prominent hispanophiles, starting with his kinsman, the Earl of Middlesex, while surrounding himself with godly divines like Dr Preston. Such hefty investments could not guarantee the one thing which would have secured his new status as arch-hispanophobe – success. Over the winter of 1624–25, James proved almost uncontrollable, blocking the duke's interventionist plans and delaying a massive amphibious strike against Spain. Meanwhile a *coup d'état* at Fontainebleau and a Huguenot revolt in Brittany destroyed early hopes of a favourable Anglo-French league. Finally, comparatively easy success in the 1624 session led the duke to underestimate the difficulties of a new Parliament. Stunned by the subsequent criticism in 1625, he wagered almost all of his remaining prestige on a last, desperate throw of the dice at Cadiz. When he subsequently appeared to have forgotten the precise size of the bet, the Parliament men in 1626 thoughtfully prodded his memory.

Late in the 1626 session, the war effort – and the new king's reign – hung in the balance. The ill-starred favourite might have stepped back, shedding a number of offices, if not stepping down altogether. Instead, with Charles's energetic support, he vaulted higher still, becoming Chancellor of the University of Cambridge, and called his parliamentary critics' bluff by launching the forced loan campaign. In this ambitious campaign, Buckingham relied heavily on Arminian divines, who displayed their capacity for learning a new political tune; thus the clerics, who had earlier hymned the cause of peace and remained deaf to the continental Protestants, discovered an unexpected commitment to the war effort. Along with Montague and Laud came a host of Catholics: Rivers, Maynard, Cottington, Calvert – and Sir Henry Shirley. To this odd domestic coalition, which godly contemporaries regarded as political kryptonite, Buckingham clung until his death in 1628. Since the Arminians and the Catholics had supported the favourite in his earlier role as a pro-Spaniard, it naturally followed that many came to suspect that Buckingham was a closet Spanish agent, and the fact that 'all went wrong' in later military efforts confirmed the suspicion. Hence Buckingham went to his grave as the man who made certain that

> Thus is our land made weake, our treasure wasted,
> Our court corrupted, and our honour blasted,
> Our Lawes are broke, our iustice sold ...
> Our strength's decay'd, the flow're of all the land
> Have perish'd under Buckinghams command.[16]

In recent years, scholars have stressed the gross distortions involved in such beliefs and have instead begun to develop a more realistic picture of the duke. As a result, we can dismiss the idea of the duke as a Spanish stooge by examining his persistent efforts to mount a credible war effort. Similarly it is clear that the duke did not so much choose his controversial Arminian and Catholic supporters as the other way around; after the 1626 Parliament, they were practically alone in their ability to deal with the favourite without gagging.[17] Nevertheless the admirable drive to better understand Buckingham will have gained us nothing, if it prompts us to lose any sense of how so many contemporaries could have entertained such uncharitable thoughts. Here details of Huntingdon's extended struggle with Shirley are invaluable. While scholars have long understood the importance of the rise of the Arminians, they have remained more uncertain about the parallel Catholic revival.[18] The present study, it is hoped, has done something to remedy this deficiency. After following Shirley's persistent and at times outrageous attempts to dislodge the local Protestant elite, it is much easier to understand the bitter contemporary hostility to Shirley's ducal patron.

The graphic depiction of the county's financial progress across the next decade is equally suggestive, for it illustrates that, as far as the provincial ratepayer was concerned, the Personal Rule had two distinct segments. During this decade, England in Clarendon's famous assessment 'enjoyed the greatest calm, and the fullest measure of felicity, that any people in any age, for so long together, have been blessed with'. Since contemporaries judged 'the country rich, and which is more, fully enjoying the pleasure of its own wealth', they naturally 'thought it a time, wherein those two miserable adjuncts, which Nerva was deified for uniting, *imperium et libertas*, were as well reconciled as is possible'. Given this general happiness, Clarendon could only point to 'a strange absence of understanding in most, and a strange peevishness in the rest' to explain how they 'took pains to make, when we could not find, ourselves miserable'.[19]

Later scholars have often shared his bewilderment, but Leicestershire's financial relationship with Whitehall in these years clarifies some apparent contradictions. From 1629 to 1635, large indeed would have been the chorus of local residents eager to sing anthems in praise of imperium et libertas. They had apparently entered a rural idyll, but it was not one presided over by a powerful sovereign exploring the limits of the prerogative. Rather it was the blessed one of the middle years of James I's reign, for, aside from the knighthood scheme, the Exchequer officials had again apparently misplaced their maps of the Midlands. Even critics of prerogative finance could have endured this phase of the Personal Rule with equanimity, if not enthusiasm. Quite simply, in the early 1630s, as in the early 1610s, there was not much to endure. By the same token, this attitude was dependent on the Crown's continued inactivity; hence, once the central government's memory of the world north of Watford improved, so too a more hostile opinion rapidly hardened. Ship Money has long loomed large in the historiography, and with good reason, but, as Fig. 4 reveals, it was far from the end of the local community's worries; there were also troubling developments in Star Chamber. On one hand, the Roper case brought on substantial fines for depopulation, and on the other, the Fawnt case presented a chilling object lesson of what came of challenging militia levies. Fig. 5 therefore dissipates much of the mystery about many contemporaries' capacity to make themselves miserable in the late 1630s.

Huntingdon's misfortune was to have become too closely identified with the revenue enhancement schemes of the late 1630s. To be sure, the fifth earl rarely met with an order he was not eager to implement. Yet even he was not immune to paralyzing bouts of conscience, most notably over the forced loan. His immunity, however, increased with the death of his powerful local rival, the Duke of Buckingham, and with the steady deterioration of his own finances. Hence, Huntingdon's interests soon became almost inextricably linked with those of the Crown. A close alliance between a stubborn loan refuser and an equally stubborn monarch, which initially seems unlikely, becomes less surprising, once we recall that the strong authoritarian, albeit paternalist, nature of the king's edicts in the 1630s merely echoed the earl's pronounced tendencies in that direction. Since the king's business went so easily hand in hand with the earl's pleasure, the local community in 1642 was not confronted with the luxury of a simple, abstract decision between King or Parliament; in Leicestershire, residents had to choose either Parliament or the king *and* the Hastingses.

The intensity of this decision places us in the midst of what Russell has aptly called 'the traditional blood-sport of English historians, the hunt for the origins of the civil war'. Explanations inevitably mix religious and political factors in some proportion, and of late, scholars have tended to emphasise the former – 'the crucial issue' for John Morrill – while downplaying, although not dismissing, the latter. This study stands in counterpoint to this trend. This is not to deny the importance of religion, which plainly exercised a formidable impact on Leicestershire. On one hand, Sir John Lambe, Laud's zealous agent in Leicester, ensured that contemporaries were well acquainted with the arch-bishop's designs; and on the other, equally zealous puritans in Ashby de la Zouch kept local parliamentary commanders so well informed during the Civil War that Lord Loughborough protested 'there was not a Fart let' among the royalist garrison before it reached their ears. The fact remains, however, that historians are prisoners of their archives, and this shire's surviving evidence quite simply does not highlight bitter religious differences within the local elite. Kevin Sharpe rightly pointed out that Huntingdon cannot be considered a puritan; but it is equally true that a friendly letter to the archbishop does not make him an Arminian. Admittedly during a scuffle in Leicester in 1642, the earl's second son was dubbed 'popish', but, pending the discovery of further evidence of his Catholicism, this obscure incident arguably best illustrates the use of a stock epithet against royalists.[20] Therefore, in Leicestershire, thanks to the absence of sharp religious divides among the elite, we can more clearly see the importance of political factors, which are less visible elsewhere.

Ship Money, depopulation fines, knighthood compositions, the forced loan, purveyance, benevolences, coat and conduct money, militia rates and Star Chamber judgements, all contributed to the county's dissatisfaction. This constellation of grievances, however, was symptomatic of a certain governmental style, for the early Stuart regime's increasing taste for money and manpower had spawned the development of a powerful local governor, whose orders – as Sir William Fawnt discovered – only the rash defied. Therefore, as much as anxiety over the realm's religious orientation, what brought Hesilrige and Stamford to oppose Huntingdon at the hustings in 1640 and in the field in 1642 was the earl's grip over the shire, which the growth of the state in the preceding quarter-century had only tightened. This conclusion, while surprising to some modern historians, would have sounded thoroughly ordinary to contemporaries in Languedoc, who witnessed a similar process in which the local elites were busy 'feudalising' the new absolutist state. Likewise other English contemporaries may well have recognised Leicestershire's political situation if resident Lords Lieutenant presided over their counties.

To underscore the significance of these political factors is not to undercut the significance of religion; rather it is simply to note that the recent emphasis on religious issues may have left us less able to comprehend some baffling moments of crisis. Take, for example, the controversy over the Militia Ordinance, one of the last signposts, if not the last one, on the high road to Civil War. Anthony Fletcher and Conrad Russell have both offered thoughtful commentaries on its passage and implementation, but neither discusses the text of the Bill in any detail. Given their lack of interest, full marks go to John Morrill for stressing the vital importance of analyzing the ordinance itself. Regrettably the results of the investigation underwhelmed him. This document, which set the kingdom by the ears, 'merely names the men who were to control local defence forces throughout England', but the names, he suggested, may unlock the hidden meaning of this controversy. Since the list contained 'twice as many men whose family gained their titles before 1559 as there were in the group they replaced' and indeed since 'almost no men whose titles had been created since 1603 were appointed', he concluded that the Militia Ordinance was the centrepiece of 'an aristocratic coup', a 'reactive' one which sought to check Charles I by reviving the 'traditions of noble paternalism' and by restoring 'the ancient peerage to its dominant role around the Crown'.[21]

Such an ingenious reinterpretation would naturally compel ready acceptance, if only nagging mathematical problems could be resolved. Early in 1642, thirty-seven peers served as Lords Lieutenant, twenty-two of whom boasted a title created before 1559 and fifteen one created after that date.[22] The Militia Ordinance, in contrast, named thirty-six peers to the lieutenancy, of whom nineteen could date their family's nobility from before 1559 and seventeen after.[23] Dismay over this discovery is fortunately short-lived, for closer examination of the lists only generates new doubts about an 'aristocratic coup'. First, there is the small matter that the new Act named fourteen men to office, who owed their peerages to the early Stuarts; and while it is easy to overlook lords like Howard of Esrick and Carberry, the same feat is harder with earls like Clare, Holland, Leicester, Salisbury and Stamford.[24] Second, sixteen of the initial thirty-seven peers ended up on the second list. Calculations of a general success rate of over 40 per cent are disturbing enough, but worse is the fact that twelve of the twenty-two 'old' peers made it onto the parliamentary list. Given that the 'old' peers actually decreased from twenty-two to nineteen, and given that well over half of this distinguished group found their way onto the second list, this phenomenon does not seem to have been a dramatic change as much as yet another successful mutation of an indispensable elite.

In one sense, however, the shift in the lieutenancy's composition did assume revolutionary proportions. To a remarkable degree, nonentities were absent from the first list; the Earl of Carnarvon initially appears the most out of place until it is recalled that he was the son-in-law of the Earl of Pembroke, the Lord Steward. Yet on the second list, the recitation of the interlocking network of the 'old' Caroline families is regularly interrupted. Among the 'old' peers, Lord Dacre seems something out of a chivalric romance rather than mid-seventeenth century politics. The trickle of relatively obscure peers becomes a flood among the recent creations. Brooke, Carberry, Grey of Warke, Howard of Esrick and Robartes could never have vied for inclusion in the aristocratic Premier League, and while Clare, Holland and Stamford, as well as the two eldest sons, Lords Newnham and Kimbolton, stood a better chance, all of them were hobbled by titles which were less than twenty-five years old. In this regard, the Militia Ordinance did resemble a coup, but since it benefited the parvenu lightweights, not the grandee heavies, it is a little hard to see how the Militia Bill restored 'the ancient peerage to its dominant role'.

Bewilderment over the Militia Ordinance fortunately gives way to more confidence after analysing the power base which a sedulous Lord Lieutenant like Huntingdon had been able to develop. The 'traditions of noble paternalism' were in fact at the heart of the controversy, but for most Parliament-men, if they could not place this power in safe hands, they were intent on sabotaging it. The House allowed a few grandees, whose loyalties could be guaranteed, to retain their local offices; hence Northumberland, Pembroke, Warwick, Essex, Holland, and Salisbury continued in their lieutenancies. To supplement this handful, the Parliament men turned to peers like Lincoln, Saye, Wharton, Brooke, Kimbolton and Stamford, whose zeal offset their relative obscurity and inexperience. This shrewd policy, however, could only go so far before running aground on the increasingly apparent inclination of a majority of the Lords to side with the king. The solution to this predicament was the appointment of almost absurdly young Lords Lieutenant. Consequently, the Commons cheerfully sent a group of politically uncertain twenty-two year-olds like Lord Chandos to Gloucestershire, Lord Dacre to Herefordshire and Lord Spencer to Northamptonshire; their administrative inexperience was a positive advantage compared with allowing veteran local governors like Northampton, Bridgewater and Peterborough retain these potentially pivotal county militias. If they established Parliament's control over these units, so much the better; if not, then nothing was better than something for the king.

With the ordinance's list of names, the House eloquently spoke about the profound anxieties which the lieutenancy excited. Parliament's relentless campaign against Arminians, Morrill noted, contrasted sharply with the fate of 'those lords lieutenant who had vigorously supported unpopular royal policies, those who had exceeded their powers during the Bishops' wars'; early attacks on them notwithstanding, they proved 'exempt from investigation and penalty'.[25] Yet the Commons' approach to the veteran lieutenants doubtless did not seem generous to Berkshire, Derby, Devonshire, Lindsey, Manchester, Newcastle, Peterborough or of course Huntingdon himself. As the list of the new lieutenants testified, the Commons had forgotten neither about punishing them, nor about disrupting their potentially powerful militia units.

Previous scholarship on this controversy has largely focused on the constitutional issues behind this clash between king and Parliament. Historians could scarcely do otherwise after Boynton's study, which, Lois Schwoerer explained, revealed that 'the resentment and unco-operativeness of the gentry' had doomed Charles's fond plans for 'a strong efficient force'.[26] Yet if only a few of the militia units equalled the Leicestershire regiment, then the contemporary willingness literally to kill for control of them becomes more understandable. In short, by raising the low assessment of the early Stuart militia, and indeed of the state itself, we can see that underneath all the lofty principles was something quite real, something which contemporaries had regularly seen in the summer: with drums beating, a large group of generally well armed men went through complicated drill, while their commander with local worthies in attendance watched the proceedings from the comfort of a pavilion.

In the end, the tale of how a magnate consistently intruded himself between Whitehall and the local community cannot be used to justify a wholesale revolution in early modern historiography. But it can be deployed to illustrate the desperate need to delineate the exact dimensions and to gauge the precise character of the fledgling Stuart behemoth. Only then can we fully comprehend the subtle nuances in the mosaic of provincial society and politics, whose full range we are only beginning to perceive. Plainly religion played a major role in dividing the realm; so too did the rise of the state. After all, what finally pushed the realm into war was not Arminianism, but Parliament's insistence on separating Charles I and a group of local governors like Huntingdon from their prized county regiments. Again, this is not to undercut the contemporary importance of religion; it is simply to suggest that it is perhaps time to leaven the religious explanations of the Civil War, which have recently bulked so large in the historiography, with a greater appreciation of the role played by the transformation of the early Stuart regime.

Granted the early seventeenth-century state was not as formidable as its successors plainly were in extracting money, but it was rapidly expanding its reach in ways which contemporaries understandably found alarming. By appreciating their mounting anxiety, we can in turn appreciate the irony of the situation in 1642. From the perspective of Charles and his financial officers, the state had failed to meet their financial requirements, thus practically forcing Charles to raise his banner.[27] Yet for others like Hesilrige, it was the magnitude of the state's successes in previous years which also brought them into the field in arms.

NOTES

1 *Parliament Scout*, 15 August 1644, TT E.7 (4).

2 [Earl of Newcastle], *The Country Captaine* (London, 1649), pp. 5 and 25.

3 Fletcher, *Reform in the Provinces*, pp. 302–8; Carter, 'The Exact Militia in Lancashire', p. 100; and S. R. Gardiner, *The Constitutional Documents of the Puritan Revolution* (London, 1889), p. 144.

4 Fletcher, *Reform*, pp. 291–2; MacCulloch, *Suffolk and the Tudors*, p. 347; and Hughes, 'Local History and the Origins of the Civil War', pp. 231–2.

5 Stater, *Noble Government*, p. 187. See also Coward, *The Stanleys*.

6 Hirst, 'The Privy Council and the Problems of Enforcement'.

7 Williams, 'The Crown and the Counties', pp. 138–9.

8 Boynton, *Elizabethan Militia*, p. 3; Andrew Coleby, *Central Government and the Localities: Hampshire, 1649–1689* (Cambridge, 1987), p. 234; and Stone, *The Crisis of the Aristocracy*, p. 465.

9 The Ship Money total comes from SP 16/334/43, 16/373/16, 16/421/79, 16/428/40 and 16/465/36. I am most grateful to Dr Alison Gill for this information.

10 Braddick, *The Nerves of the State*, p. 22; and for the proportion, see pp. 12–13. For examples of the care with which the officers of the Green Cloth following the county's payments, see their letters to H, 15 May 1617, 4 July 1617, 14 February 1618, 4 May 1618, 25 July 1618, 22 February 1619, 11 March 1621, 1 October 1621, 25 January 1622, 6 January 1625 and 19 January 1635, HA 7/4126–9, 8/4130–2, 9/4133, 10/4134 and 15/4135.

11 Conrad Russell, 'Parliamentary History in Perspective', *History* LXI (1976), pp. 1–27.

12 Russell, *Causes*, p. 175; O'Brien and Hunt, 'The Rise of a Fiscal State in England', pp. 135–6; Braddick, *The Nerves of State*, p. 196; and *Parliamentary Taxation in Seventeenth Century England*, p. 3.

13 24 February 1643, and 23 June 1647, *Acts and Ordinances*, I, pp. 85–100 and 958–84; and William Lilly, *The Starry Messenger* (London, 1645), sig. [A4v].

14 Russell, *Causes*, p. 167.

15 *PP 1625*, pp. 444 and 451; and *PP 1626*, III, p. 131; and III, p. 41.

16 I.R., *The Spy* (Strasburgh, 1628), [sig. E4 and Fv].

17 For more realistic assessments of the duke, see Lockyer, *Buckingham*; Conrad Russell, *Parliaments and English Politics*; and Thomas Cogswell, 'Prelude to Ré: the Anglo-French Struggle over La Rochelle', *History* (1986).

18 N. Tyacke, *Anti-Calvinists* (Oxford, 1987); and Cust, *The Forced Loan*, pp. 196–201, 260–8 and 311–12.

19 Clarendon, *History*, pp. 30–1.

20 Russell, *Parliaments*, p. 4; John Morrill, 'The Religious Context of the English Civil War', *TRHS*, 5th series, XXXIV (1984); reprinted in *The Nature of the English Revolution*, p. 47; and William Lilly, *Mr William Lilly's Life and Times* (London, 1715), p. 5. On Huntingdon's Arminianism and Henry Hastings, see above, pp. 211–12 and 284.

21 John Morrill, 'The Nature of the English Revolution', *Nature of the English Revolution*, pp. 11–13; and 'Charles I and Tyranny', Religion, *Resistance and the Civil War*, ed. by W. Lamont (Washington, 1990); reprinted in *Nature of the English Revolution*, pp. 300–1 and n. 55. See also Russell, *The Fall of the British Monarchies*, pp. 464–84 and 505–13; and Fletcher, *Outbreak*, pp. 347–66 and 382–6.

22 For the 'old' peers, see Bedford, Chandos, Cleveland, Cumberland, Hertford, Lennox, Lindsey, Northumberland, North, Nottingham, Pagett, Peterborough, Southampton, and Warwick, as well as four father/son acts: Arundel and Maltravers, Derby and Strange, Huntingdon and Hastings, and Pembroke and Herbert. For the 'new' creations, see Berkshire, Bridgewater, Carlisle, Carnarvon, Devonshire, Dorset, Essex, Holland, Manchester, Maynard, Newcastle, Northampton, Suffolk, as well as one father/son act, Salisbury and Cranborne; J. C. Sainty, *Lieutenants of Counties, 1585–1642* (London, 1970), pp. 11–40. See also Stater, *Noble Government*, pp. 58–65.

23 For the 'old' peers, see Bedford, Bolingbroke, Chandos, Cumberland, Dacre, Herbert, Hertford, Lincoln, North, Northumberland, Nottingham, Paget, Pembroke, Rutland, Saye and Sele, Strange, Warwick, Wharton, and Willoughby of Parham; for the 'new', see Brooke, Carberry, Clare, Essex, Exeter, Grey of Warke, Holland, Howard of Esrick, Kimbolton, Leicester, Littleton, Newnham, Robartes, Salisbury, Spencer, Stamford and Suffolk; *LJ*, IV, pp. 587–9.

24 For the Lords Lieutenant whose earliest title dates from after James's accession, see Brooke, Carberry, Clare, Grey of Warke, Holland, Howard of Esrick, Kimbolton, Leicester, Littleton, Newnham, Robartes, Salisbury, Spencer and Stamford.

25 Morrill, 'The Religious Context of the Civil War', p. 52. For a similar analysis of the Ordinance, see Stater, *Noble Government*, pp. 61–2.

26 Lois Schwoerer, "The Fittest Subject for a King's Quarrel: an Essay on the Militia Controversy, 1641–1642', *JBS* XI (1971), p. 60.

27 Conrad Russell, 'Charles I's Financial Estimates for 1642', *BIHR* LVIII (1985), pp. 109–20. For a promising start to correcting this scholarly omission, see Braddick, *The Nerves of State*.

Select bibliography

MANUSCRIPT SOURCES

BADMINTON HOUSE

Gloucestershire Lieutenancy Book (504/M14/31/3)

BEDFORDSHIRE RECORD OFFICE

St John (Bletso) MSS

BODLEIAN LIBRARY

Carte MSS

Herrick MSS (Engl. Hist. C 476–83)

BRITISH LIBRARY

Buckingham's Accounts (Add. 12,588)

Devereux MSS (Add. 46,188–9)

Coke MSS (Add. 64,883–921)

Mead–Stuteville Letters (Harl. 390)

'The Lineal Descent of ... the Sherleys' (Harl. 4028)

'The Genealogicke History of the House of Shirleys' (Harl. 4928)

Carlisle MSS (Egerton 2597)

Trumbull MSS (uncatalogued)

CENTRE FOR KENTISH STUDIES (FORMERLY KENT ARCHIVE OFFICE)

Cranfield MSS (U269/1)

WILLIAM ANDREWS CLARK LIBRARY, LOS ANGELES

Robert Codrington, 'An Elegie' (C6715M1/E38)

FOLGER SHAKESPEARE LIBRARY

'Diverse Cases' (Xd 337)

Leicestershire Commonplace Book (V.a. 402)

William Sampson, 'Roomes his est ille Cicero' (V.a. 301)

HAMPSHIRE RECORD OFFICE

Southwick MSS (4M53)

Wriothesley MSS (5M53)

HARVARD LAW SCHOOL LIBRARY

Star Chamber Reports (LMS 1128)

HATFIELD HOUSE

Salisbury MSS

HENRY E. HUNTINGTON LIBRARY, SAN MARINO, CALIFORNIA

Hastings MSS

 Correspondence

 Personal

 Financial

 Genealogy

 Inventories

 Legal

 Manorial

 Military

 Miscellenous

 Religion

 School Exercises

Ellesmere MSS

Temple MSS

Huntington Manuscripts

 Book of Baronets (HM 3124)

 Conway Poetical Miscellany (HM 165)

HOUSE OF LORDS RECORD OFFICE

Main Papers

ISLE OF WIGHT RECORD OFFICE

Oglander MSS (OG)

LEICESTERSHIRE RECORD OFFICE

Corporation of Leicester Records

 Hall Book (BR II/1)

 Hall Book, Loose Papers Bound (BR II/18)

Charter Loose Papers (BR I/2)

Correspondence (BR II/5)

Chamberlains' Accounts (BR III/2)

Misc. (BR III/8)

Branston, Constables' Accounts (DE 720/30)

Ferrers MSS, First Deposit (26D53)

Hartopp MSS (8D39)

Hazlerigg MSS (DG 21)

Waltham on the Wolds, Constables' Accounts (DE 625/60)

Winstanley MSS, Second Deposit (DG5)

LONGLEAT HOUSE

Seymour MSS

LOSELEY PARK

More MSS

NATIONAL LIBRARY OF WALES

Wynn of Gwydir MSS (9061E)

PUBLIC RECORD OFFICE

State Papers Domestic, James I (SP 14)

State Papers Domestic, Charles I (SP 16)

State Papers, Misc. (SP 9 and 46)

Privy Council Register (PC 2)

Chancery

Chancery Masters' Exhibits (C115)

Liber Pacis, (C 66)

Crown Office Docquet Book (C 231/4)

Exchequer

Receipts (E 401)

Payments (E 403)

Exchequer Misc. (E 163)

'Booke of Certificates' (E 405/226)

'Books of Compositions for ... Knighthood' (E 407/35)

'Book of Receipts ... for Depopulation' (E 405/547)

Signet Office Docquet Books (SO3)

Lord Steward's Department (LS)

QUEEN'S COLLEGE, OXFORD

[T. Shirley], 'The Catholick Armorist'

SOMERSET RECORD OFFICE

Phelips MSS (DD/Ph)

TRINITY COLLEGE, CAMBRIDGE

Anonymous diary (MS o.7.3)

WARWICK COUNTY RECORD OFFICE

Feilding of Newnham Paddox MSS (CR 2017)

WILLIAM SALT LIBRARY, STAFFORD

Chetwynd MSS

CONTEMPORARY BOOKS AND TRACTS

Bancroft, Thomas. *Epigrammes and Epitaphs*. London, 1640.

Barnes, Thomas. *Vox Belli*. London, 1626.

Breton, Nicholas. *A Mother's Blessing*. London, 1621.

Buggs, Samuel. *Miles Mediterraneus*. London, 1622.

Burton, Henry. *The Baiting of the Popes Bull*. London, 1627.

Burton, William. *The Description of Leicester Shire*. London, 1622.

(Davies, Eleanor). *Woe to the House*. Amsterdam, 1633.

Davies, Eleanor. *Sions Lamentation*. London, 1649.

Davies, John. The Scrouge of Folly. London, 1611.

Fage, Mary. *Fame Roule*. London, 1637.

Hildersham, Arthur. *CVIII Lectures on the Fourth of John*. London, 1629.

— *CLII Lectures upon Psalme LI preached at Ashby*. London, 1635.

I.F. *A Sermon Preached at Ashby-de-la-Zouch*. London, 1635.

Innes, James. *An Examination of a Printed Pamphlet*. London, 1645.

John Joynes. *A Sermon Preached to ... Earl of Huntingdon*. London, 1668.

Lilly, William. *The History of his Life and Times*. London, 1715.

— *The Starry Messenger*. London, 1645.

Markham, Francis. *The Booke of Honour*. London, 1625.

Duke of Newcastle. *The Country Captaine*. London, 1649.

Parkes, William. *The Rose and the Lily*. London, 1639.

Pestell, Thomas. *Gods Visitation ... Preached at Leicester*. London, 1630.

(Scott, Thomas). *Vox Dei*. Utrecht, 1624.

Sampson, William. *Virtus Post Funera Vivit*. London, 1636.

Vaughan, Edward. *A Divine Discoverie of Death*. London, 1612.

Williams, John. *Great Britains Solomon*. London, 1625.

ANONYMOUS WORKS

A Catalogue of the Moneys, Men and Horse. London, 1642.

The Catalogue of ... Knights. London, 1640.

The Catalogue of the Names. York (London), 1642.

Declaration and Resolution of the Countie of Leicester. London, 1642.

A Dogs Elegy. London, 1644.

The Earle of Stamfords Resolution. London, 1642.

An Exact and True Relation of a most cruell and horrid Murther. London, 1642.

An Examination Examined. London, 1642)

A Famous and Joyfull Victory. London, (1642).

His Maiesties Declaration. York, 1642.

His Maiesties Speech at Leicester. York and London, 1642.

Horrible Newes from Leicester. London, 1642.

The Impeachment and Charge of Mr Henry Hastings. London, 1642.

Instructions for Musters and Arms. London, 1623.

Lachrymae Musarum. London, 1649.

A Petition from the Towne and County of Leicester. London, 1642.

A Private Letter from an Eminent Cavalier. London, 1642.

Remarkable Passages from Nottingham. London, 1642.

A Speech Delivered ... 6 November. London, 1644.

Terrible News from Leicester. London, 1642.

A True and Exact List. London, 1642.

A True Relation. London, 1642.

Truths from Leicester and Nottingham. London, 1642.

Two Petitions of the County of Leicester. London, 1642.

NEWSBOOKS

Diurnall Occurrences.

A Diurnall and Particular Parliament Scout.

A Perfect Diurnall.

A Perfect Relation.

A True and Perfect Diurnall.

LATER EDITIONS AND COMPILATIONS

'The Accounts of the Constables of ... Stathern, Leicestershire', *Archaeological Journal* LXIX (1912).

Acts of the Privy Council. Ed. by J. D. Dascent. London, 1890.

Calendar of Clarendon State Papers. Ed. by O. Ogle *et al.* Oxford, 1872.

Calendar of the Proceedings of the Committee for Compounding. London, 1889–93.

Calendar of State Papers Domestic. Ed. by M. A. E. Green *et al.* London, 1857.

Calendar of State Papers Venetian. Ed. by H. F. Brown *et al.* London, 1870.

Ceremonies of Charles I: the Note-books of Sir John Finet. Ed. by A. Loomie. New York, 1987.

'Chetwynd Papers', *Collections for a History of Staffordshire* (1941).

Claredon, Edward Hyde, Earl of. *The History of the Rebellion.* Ed. by W. Macray. Oxford, 1888.

Complete Baronetage. Ed. by G. Cockayne. Exeter, 1902.

Complete Peerage. Ed. by G. Cockayne. London, 1910.

Davenant, William. *The Shorter Poems and Songs.* Ed. by A. M. Gibbs. Oxford, 1972.

D'Ewes, Simonds. *The Journals of Sir Simonds D'Ewes.* Ed. by W. Notestein. New Haven, 1923

D'Ewes, Simonds. *The Journals of Sir Simonds D'Ewes.* Ed. by W. H. Coates. New Haven, 1942.

Donne, John. *The Complete English Poems.* Ed. by A. J. Smith. London, 1983.

The Earl of Hertford's Lieutenancy Papers, 1603–1610. Ed. by W. P. D. Murphy. Devizes, 1969.

Gerard, John. *The Autobiography of an Elizabethan.* Trans. by P. Caraman. London, 1951.

Hardwicke, Philip Yorke, Earl of. *Hardwicke State Papers.* London, 1778.

Select bibliography

Historical Manuscripts Commission Reports.

   Salisbury MSS

   Dudley and De l'Isle MSS

   Portland MSS

   Cowper MSS

The Journals of the House of Commons. London, 1742.

The Journals of the House of Lords. London, 1767

Laud, William. *The Works of ... William Laud*. Oxford, 1854.

The Letters of Sir Francis Hastings. Ed. by Claire Cross. Frome, 1969.

Letters of John Holles. Ed. by P. R. Seddon. Nottingham, 1975–86.

'Letters from a seventeenth-century Rector of Lutterworth', *Leicestershire Historian* III (1983–4).

Market Harborough Parish Records. Ed. by J. E. Stocks. Oxford, 1926.

Markham, Gervase. 'The Muster Master'. Ed. by Charles L. Hamilton. *Camden Miscellany* XXVI (1975).

Mather, Cotton. *Magnalia Christi Americana*. Ed. by K. B. Murdock. Cambridge, Mass., 1977.

The Montagu Musters Book. Ed. by Joan Wake. Northampton, 1626.

Nichols, John. *History of Leicestershire*. London, 1795–1815.

Northamptonshire Lieutenancy Papers. Ed. by Jeremy Goring *et al*. Northampton, 1975.

Notes on the Debates in the House of Lords. Ed. by S. R. Gardiner. London, 1870.

The Poems of Sir John Beaumont. Ed. by A. B. Grosart. N.p., 1869.

The Poems of John Marston. Ed. by A. Davenport. Liverpool, 1961.

The Poems of Thomas Pestell. Ed. by Hannah Buchan. Oxford, 1940.

The Private Correspondence of Jane Lady Cornwallis. Ed. by Lord Braybrooke. London, 1842.

The Private Journals of the Long Parliament. Ed. by W. H. Coates. New Haven, 1982–92.

Proceedings in Parliament, 1610. Ed. by E. R. Foster. New Haven, 1966.

Proceedings in Parliament, 1614. Ed. Maija Jansson. Philadelphia, 1988.

Proceedings in Parliament, 1625. Ed. by Maija Jansson *et al*. New Haven, 1987.

Proceedings in Parliament, 1628. Ed. by R. C. Johnson *et al*. New Haven, 1977–83.

Proceedings of the Short Parliament. Ed. by W. Coates and E. Cope. London, 1977.

The Progresses ... of James I. Ed. by John Nichols. London, 1828.

Records of the Borough of Leicester. Ed. by Mary Bateson *et al*. London, 1899–1923.

Royal Stuart Proclamations. Ed. by J. F. Larkin. Oxford, 1983.

Rushworth, John. *Historical Collections*. London, 1682.

Selected Cases on Defamation to 1600. Ed. by R. H. Helmholz. London, 1985.

The Short Parliament (1640) Diary of Sir Thomas Aston. Ed. by Judith Maltby. London, 1988.

A Transcript of the Register of Stationers' Company. Ed. by E. Arber. London, 1874–94.

Winwood, Sir Ralph. *Memorials of Affairs of State*. London, 1725.

Winthrop Papers. Boston, Mass., 1929–1943.

Index

Alford, Edward 111
Amsterdam 74
Anglesea, Christopher Villiers, Earl 87
Ann, Queen 25
Armada 42, 136
Arminianism 132, 142, 211–12, 248, 312, 314, 317
Array, Commission of 285
Arundel, Thomas Howard, Earl 62, 90, 102, 171, 197, 212, 237–8, 258, 264
Ashby, George 232–4
Ashby Castle 24, 30, 88, 213, 285, 289–90, 295–6
Ashby de la Zouch 34, 35, 74, 90, 119, 151, 240, 270, 314
Ashby Magna 260
Ashton, Robert 9
Astley, Col. Jacob 256
Astlyn, Thomas 121–2, 125, 138, 170

Bacon, Sir Francis 89
Bacon, Sir Nicholas 304
Bainbridge, John 232
Bale, Sir John the elder 81–2, 88, 91, 95
Bale, Sir John the younger 232, 235, 293–4, 296
Bancroft, Thomas 26
Bankes, Sir John 281
Barker, Gilbert 163–4
Barnes, Thomas 40
Barnes, Thomas Garden 5, 60–2, 180, 215, 247–8, 304
Barnestre, Sir Robert 198
Barrington, Sir Thomas 157
Bastwicke, John 221, 278–9, 283, 286
Bath 157
Beaumont, John of Gracedieu 293
Beaumont, Sir Henry 79–82, 89–90

Beaumont, Sir John 66–7, 98, 165–6
Beaumont, Sir Thomas 17, 79, 89
Beaumont, Sir Thomas of Stoughton 80–2
Bedford, Lucy Russell, Countess 23–5, 99, 212
Beik, William 8–9
Belgrave, Sir George 78–9, 82
Belvoir Castle 86, 98
Bent, William 195
Berkeley, Henry Berkeley, Lord 99, 102
Berkeley, Sir Maurice 36
Berkshire, Thomas Howard, Earl 317
Berwick, Pacification of 258
Billers, William 235
Billesdon 87
Bishops' Wars 255–8, 265–72, 301–2, 307
Blaby 120
Bolingbroke, Oliver Saint John, Earl 144, 155, 157
Bowden, John 120–1, 138, 149, 191
Boyton, Lindsay 60, 130, 180, 304, 317
Braddick, Michael 4, 307, 309
Bradgate 78, 90, 260, 221, 287, 290, 292
Braithwaite, Richard 191
Bramston, Sir John 237
Branston 111, 178, 181, 191, 214–15, 231, 256–7, 267, 268, 288
Braunston 80, 287
Breedon 100–1, 163, 173
Brett, Arthur 87
Brewer, John 4
Bridgewater, John Egerton, Earl 23, 155, 197, 208, 212, 316
Bromley, Judge 41
Brooke, Robert Greville, Lord 193, 277

Index

Henri IV 14
Henrietta Maria 213
Henry, Prince 14, 24, 25, 101
Henry VII 99
Henry VIII 78, 100, 311
Heralds, College of 90
Herbert, Sir Edward 283, 286
Hereford 196, 198
Herne, John 223–30, 236–8
Herrick, Robert 30
Hertford 195–6
Hertford, William Seymour, Earl 99
Hesilrige, Sir Arthur 93–4, 131, 174, 188,
    192–5, 197–200, 213–17, 221–2,
    233, 257, 266, 262–4, 272, 276–9,
    280–1, 283, 286–9, 292–3, 296,
    303–4, 318
Hesilrige, Bertine 94, 192–3
Hesilrige, Dorothy 217, 221
Hesilrige, Sir Thomas 43, 83, 93–4, 113,
    117, 141, 162, 192–4, 226, 261,
    296
Heveningham, Sir Arthur 304
Hicks, Sir Baptist 143
High Commission 169
Hildesham, Arthur 27, 119, 190, 295
Hinckley 120, 121
Hobart, Sir Miles 209–10, 213
Holland, Henry Rich, Earl 261, 315–16
Holles, Denzil 209
Holmes, Clive 7, 130, 178
Holt, William 223–30, 236–8
Hopton, Sir Ralph 290, 292
Hotham, Sir John 282
Howard of Esrick, Edward Howard, Lord
    315–16
Hughes, Ann 7, 60, 303
Hull 282, 287
Hutton, Sir Richard 237–8
Hunt, Philip 4, 309
Huntingdon, Dorothy Hastings, Coun-
    tess 69
Huntingdon, Elizabeth Hastings,
    Countess 23, 71, 90–1, 203–12, 241
Huntingdon, Ferdinando Hastings, Earl
    28, 167, 169, 190, 203–5, 230,

260–3, 269, 277–83, 290–1
Huntingdon, Francis Hastings, Earl 78
Huntingdon, Henry Hastings, fifth Earl
    decline and death 294–5
    and the Duke of Buckingham 86–92,
        165–72, 180–4, 311–12
    family background 21–30
    and Sir Arthur Hesilrige 192–200,
        276–82
    and Sir Henry Shirley 97–104, 137–
        84, 195–200
    and Sir William Fawnt 92–7, 140–2,
        192–200, 221–9, 236–41, 245–51
Huntingdon, Henry Hastings, third Earl
    29, 70–2, 77–8, 92, 207, 259
Huntingdon, Lucy Hastings, Countess
    74, 203–5, 290–1
Huntington Library 2, 28
Hurst, John 193

Ibstock 284
impressment 15, 39–42, 149–54, 256–8,
    266–9
Ipswich 198
Ireland 50
Ive, William 37, 139

Jackson, John 192, 197
Jacombe, Richard 214, 17
James I 13–14, 17–18, 25, 35, 37, 39, 52,
    60, 68–9, 71, 75, 79, 89, 90, 113,
    162, 213, 309
Jermyn, Sir Thomas 237
Jonson, Ben 66
Joynes, John 290
Julich 16

Kent, Henry Grey, Earl 155, 157, 235
Killigrew, Thomas 285
Kimbolton, Edward Montagu, Lord 316
Kingston, Henry Pierrepont Earl 237,
    269
Kirby Muxloe 70, 207
Kirke, Elkington 233
knapsacks 121–2, 169–70
Knight, Bryan 169